BRITAIN AND THE CONFLICT IN THE MIDDLE EAST, 1964–1967

BRITAIN AND THE CONFLICT IN THE MIDDLE EAST, 1964–1967

THE COMING OF THE SIX-DAY WAR

Moshe Gat

PRAEGER

Westport, Connecticut
London

Library of Congress Cataloging-in-Publication Data

Gat, Moshe
    Britain and the conflict in the Middle East, 1964–1967 : the coming of the Six-Day
  War / Moshe Gat.
     p. cm.
   Includes bibliographical references and index.
   ISBN 0–275–97514–2 (alk. paper)
    1. Middle East—Relations—Great Britain. 2. Great Britain—Relations—Middle
  East. 3. Arab-Israeli conflict—1948–1967. I. Title.
DS63.2.G7 G38 2003
956.04—dc21   2002068608

British Library Cataloguing in Publication Data is available.

Library of Congress Catalog Card Number: 2002068608
ISBN: 0-275-97514-2

First published in 2003

Praeger Publishers, 88 Post Road West, Westport, CT 06881
An imprint of Greenwood Publishing Group, Inc.
www.praeger.com

Printed in the United States of America

∞™

The paper used in this book complies with the
Permanent Paper Standard issued by the National
Information Standards Organization (Z39.48-1984).

10 9 8 7 6 5 4 3 2 1

In Memory of Prof. Avrom Saltman,
Teacher and Colleague

Contents

Acknowledgments

Many helped me in conducting this research. I owe a depth of gratitude to the late Professor Avrom Saltman, teacher and colleague in the Department of History, who accompanied the writing of the book step by step, from beginning to end. This book is dedicated to his memory.

Many thanks are owed to the staff of the Public Record Office in London, the National Archives in College Park in Washington, the Israeli State Archives in Jerusalem and the British Library of the London School of Oriental and African Studies.

I owe thanks as well to the Faculty of Jewish Studies; the Faculty of Social Sciences; the Department of Political Studies; to Mr. Yitzhak Kerner, Head of the Jewish Studies Faculty Administration, and to Ms. Yael Gafni, Head of the Social Sciences Faculty Administration, without whose assistance this book could not have been published.

Many thanks also to the secretarial staff of the Department of Political Studies, who greatly helped to bring this book to its completion.

Introduction

The end of the Second World War marked the beginning of a new war: the Cold War. The Soviet Union, the pariah of the 1920s and 1930s, having emerged from the Second World War stronger and more powerful than ever, had, together with the United States, become one of the world's two new superpowers. In Europe, the Soviet Union had first liberated and then subjected most of Eastern and Central Europe to its power. Soon it sought to extend its influence outside Europe, mostly at the expense of the West, especially of the British Empire, which still governed vast tracts of land in Asia and Africa. A new era had begun, and the Soviet Union and the United States, as well as its Western allies, bared their teeth at one another while vying for power and influence.

The West was determined to check Soviet and communist expansion. The question was how to stop the Soviet Union from overrunning and dominating the world. The answer was provided by the heavily ideologically slanted Containment Theory, which emerged as the foundation and driving force behind the West's, and, above all, American Cold War policy. Among other things, Containment Theory emphasized the need for regional alliances to block the Soviet Union's progress. Accordingly, in April 1949, the North Atlantic Alliance Treaty was created. The treaty was a defensive alliance. Its eleven members, with the single exception of Italy, were to be found on both sides of the Atlantic. Three more countries, West Germany, Turkey and Greece, were to join the alliance at a later date. Article 9 of the treaty called for the setting up of a military and political organization, which eventually became known as the North Atlantic Treaty Organization (NATO). Its task was to actively deter and, if necessary, repel Soviet aggression. Similar alliances were concluded in both Asia and the Middle East. In September 1954, Australia, New Zealand, the Philippines, Pakistan, France, Britain and the United States signed the Southeast Asia Treaty Organization and established SEATO, the Asian equivalent of NATO. In 1955, Pakistan, Turkey, Iraq and Britain concluded the Baghdad Pact. In 1958, however, Iraq withdrew from the alliance, which became known as the Central Alliance; its military-political organization was named the Central Treaty Organization (CENTO).

Until 1949, Cold War and superpower rivalry had centered on Europe. By 1950, once Europe had been divided and the iron curtain was firmly in place, the Cold War began spreading to other parts of the globe. First came the Far East, and though the Korean (1950–1953) and Vietnam (1954–1972) wars both had distinctly local roots, they were equally manifestations of Cold War rivalry. The Middle East was next in line. Here the process began in 1955, with the signing of the Czechoslovakian-Egyptian arms deal, which marked the beginning, in earnest, of Soviet penetration of the region. In October 1956, the Suez Crisis presented the Soviet Union with the opportunity to further extend its influence in the Middle East. The Soviet Union made full use of this and other opportunities to make huge inroads in the Arab world, a process that reached its peak in June 1967.

Great Britain played a key role in defending Western interests against the Soviet threat, especially in the Middle East. A senior member of both NATO and CENTO, Britain also had a longstanding and personal interest in the area. It still owned vast tracts of territories in the Persian Gulf, and had air, land and naval bases scattered throughout the region. However, by the mid-1950s, Britain did not have the military capability or economic wherewithal to govern, or even maintain, a significant military presence in the Middle East. Its problems were made much worse by the onset of the decolonization process. Britain, unfortunately, was at its weakest precisely at a time when Third World nationalism began to rear its head, with local, indigenous nations struggling to rid themselves of their imperial masters. This process, which began in earnest after the Second World War, took off following the Suez crisis, especially in the Middle East. In these circumstances, Britain had no alternative but to modify its Middle East policy. It decided to quit its Middle East dependencies and pare down its military forces in the region to a bare minimum. It was not an easy decision to make or execute. Some problems were, no doubt, psychological, others material. One problem, for example, was how to ensure that its withdrawal did not undermine Western or British interests in the region. Another no less serious problem, related to the growing Soviet threat, was how Britain would maintain enough force and influence in the region to guarantee that the Soviet Union wouldn't fill any possible vacuum created by its retreat from the Middle East.

Britain decided that the best way to ensure that both its and Western interests emerged unscathed from its retreat from the Middle East was to withdraw slowly and with careful deliberation. At the same time, Britain would also seek to establish friendly and mutually beneficial relations with the new political forces and governments that would eventually take its place. This, in a nutshell, was Britain's Middle East policy after Suez. It depended, among other things, on maintaining a relatively stable and peaceful Middle East. Accordingly, from 1956 onward, Britain devoted itself single-mindedly to the arduous task of preserving the Middle East's precarious stability. Naturally, the last thing Britain wanted was a war between Israel and its Arab neighbors. A war would threaten and undermine its interests in the region. It would also bring to a dramatic end the tenuous stability that was so essential to the successful completion of its withdrawal from the Middle East. Finally, war would, or so Britain assumed, have the unhappy result of accelerating and consolidating the process of Soviet penetration of the Middle East.

It was Britain's desire and need to preserve stability and to avoid the war that lay at the bottom of Harold Macmillan's statement to the House of Commons in May 1963. Echoing a statement made by President John F. Kennedy only a few days earlier, Macmillan underlined the vital need to preserve the status quo in the Middle East and the no less critical duty to deter any form of aggression. Britain's obsession with stability also explains its readiness to supply Israel with weapons. Britain assumed that unless Israel was sufficiently powerful to deter its Arab neighbors, war would inevitably ensue.

By the end of 1963, Israel had finally finished building the National Water Carrier, a highly ambitious project, which had taken five years and a lot of money to complete. Israel considered the water carrier vital to its future economic and demographic development. For example, it was only thanks to the pipeline that Israel, at long last, was able to convey much needed water from Lake Tiberias in the north to the water-hungry Negev Desert in the south. The Arab states saw things quite differently. They considered the project no less a dangerous a threat to them than that which had been posed by the establishment of the state of Israel in 1948. What was at stake, they claimed, was the very existence of the Arab nation. To their mind, the National Water Carrier was patently both a product and reflection of Israel's aggressive, expansionist ambitions. Whether the Arabs truly believed the plan was a genuine and immediate threat to their interests or whether their objections were rooted in their longtime ambition to destroy Israel, is a moot point. The net result was same: they sought to disrupt, cripple and, if possible, wreck the Israeli water project.

The water dispute kindled and inflamed the Arab-Israeli conflict. It also undermined the fragile stability that the West, and Britain in particular, had struggled to maintain. Finally, it inaugurated a dangerous pattern of increasingly aggressive response and counterresponse, which greatly aggravated the conflict between Israel and the Arab states. This being so, there is little doubt that the dynamics produced by water dispute were partially responsible for the outbreak of the Six-Day War.

Unlike the West, the Soviet Union was delighted with this turn of events. It regarded regional tension as an excellent way to advance its interests. A continuously simmering Arab-Israeli conflict would allow the Soviet Union to successfully pursue its expansionist policies, thus benefiting it greatly. Accordingly, between 1964 and 1967 the Soviet policy in the Middle East could be described as one of promoting tension to a point just short of explosion. Soviet policy certainly did nothing to ease the conflict. In practical terms this meant that the Soviet Union gave the Arab states total and unconditional military, economic and diplomatic support and did nothing to curb their more dangerously aggressive actions. Accordingly, the outbreak of the Six-Day War was unquestionably due, in no small part, to the Soviet Union's out-and-out endorsement of the Arab states' policies, especially during the tension filled days of May 1967.

The turbulent history of the Middle East, between 1963 and June 1967 can be divided into two periods. The first lasted from the end of 1963 to mid-1965. It was during this time that the water dispute reached its zenith. The Arab states were busy trying to put into effect their counterdiversion scheme, intended to deny Israel its full and equitable share of the River Jordan's water. Israel, in turn, regarded the scheme as a genuine threat to its existence and endeavored to stop the Arab states from executing their plans. It began, deliberately and systematically, to destroy the Arab engineering and technical equipment, knowing that this action risked war. But it was a calculated risk, and one that ultimately paid off. Israel's aggressive and uncompromising policy eventually persuaded Lebanon and Syria to postpone indefinitely the execution of the counterdiversion scheme, and the water conflict ended in mid-1965.

The second period lasted from mid-1965 to June 1967. This time Syrian-inspired Palestinian guerrilla activities held center stage. Palestinian operations had, in fact, begun well before mid-1965, but once the water dispute faded from view, Palestinian activities burgeoned, and, for a time, became the outstanding feature of the Arab-Israeli conflict. The Palestine Liberation Organization operated out of Lebanon, Syria and, above all, Jordan. Its activities accelerated the dynamics of action and counteraction, which had been established by the water dispute, and, thus, further exacerbated the tempestuous situation in the Middle East. In response to this surge of Palestinian operations, Israel adopted a policy known as "Reprisals." It retaliated and hit back at those countries known to harbor, aid and abet Palestinian organizations. Palestinian activities and Israel's reprisals pushed the region further along the downward spiral of aggression and counteraggression, which culminated in the denouement of June 5, 1967.

This work focuses on British policy during this particularly stormy moment in Middle East history. By 1963, Britain was no longer the dominant power in the region and was in the process of withdrawing, albeit gradually, from the Middle East. Yet, unlike its fellow Western powers, Britain's interests in the region remained many and varied. Nor were they all of the sentimental kind. Britain had extensive oil and trading interests in the region. What is more, Britain's economy and financial well-being depended, or so it believed, to a large extent on safeguarding these interests. So whatever happened, on one point, Britain was clear: British interests demanded a stable Middle East. Accordingly, from 1956 onward, it strove to maintain the rather shaky stability that had been established after the Suez Campaign.

In 1964, this frail stability faltered with the eruption of the water dispute. Throughout the dispute and in the hope of preserving its interests, Britain adopted, as it did in almost all subsequent crises, a policy of rigid neutrality. Wishing to avoid being identified with either Israeli or Arab interests, Britain religiously refused to support either side to the conflict. All British governments,

Conservative and Labour alike, assumed that by adopting an impartial, nonpartisan stand, they would be able to limit the damage to British interests if and when an armed conflict between Israel and its Arab neighbors erupted. Accordingly, between 1963 until almost the very end of the period under discussion, Britain resolved to maintain a low profile. It was a policy that often forced it to perform, as Britain was the first to admit, the most complex, certainly impressive political and diplomatic contortions.

Britain also hoped that by keeping a low profile and observing a neutral stance it would finally free itself of the wretched heritage of Suez. This, however, proved little more than wishful thinking and certainly had little chance of success. In the early 1960s, Arab memories of Suez were still as fresh and as powerful as ever. The Arab states, and Egypt especially, instinctively interpreted Britain's neutrality as an expression of Britain's pro-Israeli and anti-Arab policy. Nor is this very surprising. They deemed Britain to have played a key role, if not the key role, in the establishment of the state of Israel, which was, to their mind, the original sin. Britain had also been one of the principle conspirators in the Suez Campaign and plot to overthrow Gamal Abdel Nasser's regime. Yet, far from repentant, this selfsame Britain was still supplying Israel with weapons to be used against the Arab countries. Given Britain's past history in the Middle East, in the early 1960s the Arabs would have regarded anything less than outright, unequivocal and public support of their cause as pro-Israeli.

After Nasser announced on May 23, 1967 that he was closing the Straits of Tiran to Israeli shipping, Britain changed its strategy, abandoned its low profile and adopted a more active and directly engaged policy. With the region rushing headlong toward armed confrontation, it struggled tirelessly to prevent war from breaking out. To this end, it promoted the idea of an international naval task force, which was, if necessary, to reopen the Straits by force. The Arabs regarded Britain's efforts less as a return to the days of Suez and more as the logical extension of Britain's anti-Arab policy, which, they believed, it had never abandoned. To their mind, Britain, as Nasser had once claimed, had manifestly failed to learn the lessons of Suez. Whether it did or not, one thing is certain: in 1967, Britain, despite its indefatigable, sometimes desperate efforts, failed to escape the destructive consequences of war in the Middle East.

1

Britain and the Middle East
Between Stability and Tension

BRITISH STRATEGY AFTER SUEZ

The Suez Campaign marked the end of Britain's days as one of the world's greatest, if not the greatest, colonial powers. After the crisis, and owing to its less than happy consequences, Britain was forced to abandon any illusions it might have had and admit that the process of decolonization was not only inevitable, but also on the ascent. True, Britain did not lose or surrender its Middle East possessions in the immediate aftermath of the Suez fiasco. Nevertheless, it knew that it was only a question of time before it would be forced to quit the region. This being the case, Britain assumed that it would be far better for it to withdraw from the region gradually and soberly than to abandon it abruptly and in haste. A controlled and prudent evacuation would safeguard Britain's as well as Western interests in the region, or so Britain thought.[1]

What then were these interests? First and foremost, it was to prevent the Soviet Union from realizing its expansionist ambitions in the Middle East. For centuries, Russia had periodically sought to extend its influence in the Middle East. It had done so first in its former guise of the Russian Empire, and from 1945 onward, as the Soviet Union, it redoubled its efforts to penetrate the region. NATO and CENTO were charged with containing the Soviet Union and blocking its expansion westward toward Western Europe and southward toward the Persian Gulf and the Middle East. As a member of both alliances, Britain played a crucial role in checking Soviet ambitions, particularly in the Middle East. Britain maintained a large military presence in the Gulf area and with forces in Bahrain, Aden and the Trucial Coast, as well as with bases scattered throughout the region, it was well placed to curb Soviet expansion.

Britain considered it essential to counter and contain the Soviet Union. Should the Soviet Union succeed and penetrate the Middle East, the effect on British and Western interests would be disastrous. The West's reputation and prestige would be gravely, perhaps irreversibly, undermined. The Soviet Union's opportunities to expand in the Middle East would multiply and in Africa and Asia as well, where, owing to the its success in the Middle East, the Soviet Union's scope for intimidation and duress would greatly increase. The newly emerging governments would experience a crisis of confidence in the West's ability and power to offer them sufficient protection, thereby succumbing to the power of the Soviet Union.

Britain was particularly anxious to prevent the Soviet Union from becoming the dominant power in the Middle East. The reason: oil. Britain feared that were the Soviet Union to achieve its ambitions, Britain would lose its control over the vast and vitally important oil resources of the Persian Gulf. Outside of the United States, the Middle East was the second largest oil-producing region in the world. At the time, it commanded 60 percent of the world's known oil resources. In the beginning of the 1960s, it produced 300 million tons of crude oil, of which 150 million tons alone went to Europe. Of these, 40 million went to Britain. In practical terms, it meant that four-fifths of Britain's crude oil imports and two-thirds of its total oil imports—including oil products—came, directly and indirectly, from the Middle East. The numbers were much the same for the rest of Western Europe.

Plainly, Britain and Western Europe, as a whole, were heavily dependent on Middle East oil. Britain, of course, realized that in the future the relative amount of oil Europe imported from the Middle East would decrease slightly and new, oil-rich areas, especially in North Africa, would assume greater importance. Nevertheless, the Middle East would remain Western Europe's principal source of oil. In fact, in absolute terms, there might even be an increase in the amount of oil Europe imported from the Middle East.[2] Not surprisingly, therefore, given the Europe's dependency on Middle East oil, Britain sought to guarantee the supply of Middle East oil to Britain and its fellow Western European countries.[3]

Admittedly, there were alternatives to Gulf oil, for example, the Western Hemisphere. At the time, it was the only known oil-producing region that offered a viable alternative to the Middle East as Europe's main source of oil. The question was how viable? Joint American-British studies revealed that the Western Hemisphere, even together with other oil producers such as North Africa, could, at best, furnish Western Europe with only 70 percent of its normal oil consumption levels. In addition, it would take at least six months before it could begin to supply even this much. The oil would also cost a great deal more than Gulf oil. The obvious conclusion was that to replace the Middle East as Europe's principal oil supplier, would not only take much too long, years possibly, but would also prove to be a very expensive business indeed. All this would have an adverse effect on Britain and Western Europe's economy, where growth depended on a steady increase in the supply of energy. After Suez, energy meant oil, and until the late 1950s, it was assumed that this highly satisfactory trend of more oil, more economic growth would continue, uninterrupted, well into the future.[4] By the early 1960s, things appeared a lot less certain.

In considering its oil interests in the Middle East, Britain also had to take into account the British oil companies that operated in the region. These companies made a vital contribution to its economy, especially its balance of payments. It was thanks to the petroleum companies that the cost of Britain's oil imports was, in balance of payment terms, considerably less than their absolute market value. In 1962, for example, Britain imported 550 million pounds sterling worth of oil for its own consumption, at a net expenditure of 150 million pounds sterling on the foreign exchange. This was a huge saving and for the next few years this pattern happily continued.[5] Should British Petroleum, Shell and other British oil companies be forced to terminate their activities in the Middle East, the effect on Britain's balance of payments would be catastrophic. Indeed, a loss of several hundred million pounds sterling per annum was projected. Barred from operating in the Middle East, the oil companies' expenses would skyrocket. The cost of transporting, refining and distributing oil would increase, while alternative supplies of crude oil were likely to prove much more expensive. Thus, several million pounds sterling was probably a conservative estimate, and the damage to Britain's balance of payment was likely to be far greater still.

Trade was also an important consideration. With money to spend, the oil-rich countries of the Middle East had become rapidly expanding and highly profitable markets for British exports. By the 1960s, British exports to the region had reached the several hundred million pounds sterling mark. With oil production on the rise and the Gulf states' bank accounts swelling, Britain eagerly anticipated a long and lucrative trade relationship with the region. Several hundred million pounds, it hoped, was just the beginning.[6]

The Foreign Office summed up the connection between Britain's oil interests and British policy. Britain had an interest in

[the] smooth production and transportation of the oil [sic], in the profitability of the operation of British companies, which have a large share in most of the main fields, and in the maintenance of satisfactory economic conditions for the operation of the oil companies and for the sales of oil consumer countries including our own.[7]

In the Middle East, Britain had the dual task of checking Soviet expansion and securing the conditions for the regular and steady exploration, production and transportation of oil. Its military bases, which were scattered throughout the Gulf region, played a key role in fulfilling these goals. The Foreign Office contended that the steady supply of oil to the West, as well as international and regional peace and stability, were dependent on Britain's regional defense arrangements. Britain's military presence was a crucial factor in maintaining the Middle East's physical security.[8] No less important, it underpinned and boosted the confidence and resolve of the region's pro-Western oil-rich countries, such as Iran, and enabled them to brave and withstand Soviet threats and pressure. These British interests were at one with those of the United States.

Two countries threatened Britain's position and interests in the area. One, the Soviet Union, has already been mentioned. The other was Egypt, led by General Gamal Abdel Nasser. One of the Egyptian president's overriding ambitions was to eject Britain from the Middle East once and for all. Nor would Nasser be satisfied by the mere evacuation of Britain's bases in the Gulf. He wanted to expel the British, complete with bag and baggage, from the region. Nasser was convinced that that of all the powers bent on exploiting the Arab nations, Britain was the worst. Moreover, as it still ruled vast tracts of land in the region, Britain was well placed to achieve its selfish, imperialist goals. Nasser also believed Britain to be a personal and bitter enemy of his regime. He interpreted the Suez Campaign, in 1956, as an (albeit clumsy) attempt to overthrow him. Moreover, he was certain that having failed once, Britain, undaunted, was nevertheless still intent upon getting rid of him. It was this goal, he claimed, rather egoistically, that underlay Britain's Middle East policy. In sum, Nasser considered Britain's continued presence in the Middle East as a threat in every sense of the word. It threatened his position in Egypt and his standing in the Arab world. It also made a mockery of and threatened his regional policies, which waved the flag of Arab nationalism and socialism and sought to liberate the Arab people from the yoke of Western imperialism.

Were Nasser in need of further proof of, to his mind, Britain's poisonous and uncompromising anti-Egyptian and anti-Arab policies, all he had to do was point to the support Britain gave the reactionary monarchies of Saudi Arabia and Jordan and, above all, to its close relationship with Israel. And so he did. The state of Israel, Nasser maintained, had come into being largely owing to Britain's iniquitous policies. In the 1960s, in order to compound its sins, Britain began also to supply Israel with weapons.[9] As for Britain's backing of the reactionary Arab regimes, Nasser regarded this as the natural outgrowth of its traditional imperialist policy, which sought to exploit the Arab nations for the benefit of Western interests.

Nasser believed that Jordan, Saudi Arabia and other conservative Arab states were little more than willing surrogates for British power and interests. Accordingly, he embarked on a vicious campaign of hate designed to undermine and eventually destroy their regimes. In 1958, a revolution in Iraq brought down the Iraqi monarchy. In September 1962, a similar revolution, though less successful, took place in Yemen. Nasser hailed both events as heralding the end the reactionary Arab regimes and the inevitable victory of the "progressive" Arab states. These revolutions, he crowed, also marked the beginning of the end of British influence in the area.[10]

If Nasser saw Britain as a threat to his regime and policies, the British government regarded the Egyptian president and his aggressively nationalist policies as no less of a threat. Britain was acutely aware of Nasser's ambition and efforts to rid the Middle East of its military, economic and political presence. It believed that this was part and parcel of Nasser's overwhelming desire to gain personal control over the Middle East. Yet, having failed to oust him from power in 1956, Britain realized that this option was now closed to it. It no longer had the ability or the power to carry off such an ambitious project. Were it to try again the result would be the same: dismal failure.[11]

Moreover, Britain had no desire to quarrel openly with Nasser. Given the currently divided and factitious character of the Arab world, to explicitly oppose the

Egyptian president might simply boomerang on Britain and undermine its interests. Public opposition to Nasser and Arab Nationalism would serve merely to unite the Arab states behind the Egyptian president, making it doubly difficult to preserve British interests. It would certainly persuade Nasser, should he need persuading, that Britain was his irrevocable and bitter enemy, thus adding to the already existing tension between the two countries.[12]

Overt British opposition to Nasser and Arab socialism would also make it much more difficult for the conservative Arab states to garner the public support they needed to preserve their regimes. It would turn Nasser, who was already a charismatic figure, adored by the Arab masses, into a martyr. Britain believed the best way to preserve these friendly regimes and undermine Nasser's poisonous influence was not to oppose Nasser, but to encourage and help the conservative Arab regimes modernize and develop their countries economically, socially and perhaps even politically.

Nor could Britain ignore the fact that even though the Egyptian president was bitterly opposed to its presence in the region at this point in time, he was content to limit himself to forceful, if malevolent, anti-British propaganda. Nasser was, at present, far too busy building up Egypt's military strength and economic power and extending Egypt's influence throughout the Arab world to do anything more. Certainly Britain had no intention of provoking him into taking more concrete, anti-British action. Britain, rightly or wrongly, assumed that Nasser, rather than initiating action, tended to respond to the actions of others. If Nasser was currently, for whatever reason, not devoting all his time and effort to undermining Britain's position and interests in the Middle East, he was certain to do so once Britain took an active and public stand against him. Such action would remove such restraints as existed upon Nasser. He would unleash his full fury on Britain and do his damnedest to wreck havoc on British interests.

Though a dangerous foe, Nasser was not, Britain thought, all bad. In the early 1960s, for example, both Britain and Egypt discovered, to their surprise, that they had several interests in common. In 1961, both wished to defend Kuwait against an Iraqi invasion. This explains, in part, why in 1961 the two former enemies decided to reestablish the diplomatic relations that were severed following the Suez Campaign.

Nasser's promotion of Arab nationalism could also, under certain conditions, serve Western interests. Britain thought that Arab nationalism, like other forms of nationalism, could act as a powerful antidote to the poisonous, insidious influence of communism. Nasser's glorification of Arab nationalism had engendered a hard core of radical national feeling in the Arab world, weakening the attractions of communism. Even so-called progressive Arab states, such as Iraq and Egypt, regarded communism, at least its domestic variety, as a threat to their regimes and fiercely suppressed it.[13] Britain had no doubt that whatever happened Nasser would continue to crush Egypt's home-grown communists. On the other hand, were Britain to openly oppose Egypt in the Middle East, Nasser might be tempted into greater cooperation with the Soviet Union. Conversely, were Britain, when possible, to cooperate with Nasser, Nasser might reward it by adopting a neutralist, nonaligned policy.

In any case, regardless of the pros and cons of the matter, Britain knew that without American cooperation, British opposition to the Egyptian president would be largely ineffective. Nor did American cooperation to this end appear forthcoming. Although the United States firmly supported the conservative regimes of Saudi Arabia and Jordan, it also sought to establish good relations with the Nasser, offering him, for example, much needed financial aid.[14] In view of the above, the inescapable conclusion was that the most sensible policy Britain could adopt was to stay out of all inter-Arab disputes, to "keep out of Middle East quarrels ... not taking sides for or against Nasser ... trying to work on as friendly terms as possible with all Middle East governments, whether republican or monarchies, and avoiding all ideological commitment."[15]

The Soviet Union was a much more dangerous adversary than Nasser's Egypt. Ever since the end of the Second World War, the Soviet Union had endeavored to expand southward and increase its influence in the Persian Gulf and Middle East. As early as 1945–1946, in the course of the Italian peace treaty negotiations, it had demanded a portion of the former Italian colonies, specifically Cyranaica in Libya on the Egyptian border. It based its claim for Cyranaica on its right to receive just compensation for Italy's part in the German campaign against the Soviet Union. Britain rejected the Soviet demand out of hand.[16] To allow the Soviet Union even the smallest foothold in the Mediterranean would, it thought, be the start of a process that would only end once the Soviet Union had totally undermined Britain's position and ultimately expelled it from the region.

Britain was convinced that the Soviet Union was intent upon sapping British influence in the Middle East. It was why the Soviet Union had supported the establishment of a Jewish state in Palestine in 1948–1949.[17] It was not love for Israel, which had prompted the Soviets to endorse the state of Israel, but its Cold War ambitions, which demanded that it support those states opposed to Western presence in the area. Sadly, for the Soviet Union, Israel proved too close and too dependent on the West to serve its purposes. Accordingly, it soon switched its support to the region's nonaligned Arab countries. In time, as East-West polarization deepened, the Soviet Union began to exploit the Arab-Israeli conflict to increase its influence in the Middle East.

The Kremlin believed that the Arab-Israeli conflict offered it an excellent opportunity to establish and cement closer economic, military and diplomatic ties with the Arab world and thus to increase Soviet influence in the region. It began to sell arms to the Arab states, first to Syria and then, in what subsequently became known as the Czech arms deal, to Egypt. Indeed, the 1955 Czech arms deal marked the beginning, in earnest, of growing Soviet influence in the Middle East. In 1956, at the height of the Suez Crisis, the Soviet Union offered Egypt its political and diplomatic support. It also stepped in when the United States reneged on its promise to finance the Aswan Dam.[18] By the start of the 1960s,

Egypt was receiving liberal and ever mounting Soviet economic aid. Furthermore, the Soviet Union also began to supply Egypt with copious amounts of weapons and to increase, generally, the level of its military aid. Although Egypt was the principal beneficiary of Soviet largess, Iraq and Syria also enjoyed a close and profitable relationship with the Soviet Union.[19]

With the Soviet Union busy wooing the Arab states, the Middle East was slowly, but inexorably, being drawn into the Cold War. By the early 1960s, it had become an integral part of the war. The Middle East and Africa, like Europe and Asia before them, had become the object of superpower rivalry, with the East and West each vying for more power and more influence. In the context of the Cold War, Britain, rightly, assumed that the Soviet Union would exploit and seek to benefit from any conflict in the region. Accordingly, Britain realized that there was absolutely no chance of reaching any kind of an agreement with the Soviet Union over the Middle East. The Soviet Union did not share Britain's interest in maintaining a peaceful and stabile Middle East. On the contrary, ferment, tension, and instability suited it well. Britain was well aware that the Arab-Israeli conflict had helped the Soviet Union establish its influence in the area by giving it the opportunity to supply the Arabs with weapons and offer them with political support. It was a policy, which had proved highly successful in the past, and there was no earthly reason, Britain assumed, why the Soviet Union should suddenly agree to abandon it. To its mind, the Soviet Union clearly had no incentive to either restrict the sale of arms to the Arab states or curb its activities in the region in any other way. Quite the opposite. Of course, if the West and, above all, Britain were to agree, of their own free will, to significantly reduce their influence and restrict their freedom of action in the area, the Soviet Union might consider moderating its own policies. But even then, Britain suspected, it would, probably offer no more than a symbolic quid pro quo.[20]

In an inherently turbulent, even explosive Middle East, Britain thought its interests would be best served by seeking to maintain something resembling stability. The exploitation and distribution of Middle Eastern oil—which was, after all, one of Britain's principal interests in the region—demanded stability. Nor was it just the oil-producing countries that required stability. Countries such as Lebanon, Jordan, Syria and Egypt, through which the oil passed on its way to Europe, also needed a stable system. In addition, trade between Britain and the region's rich oil-producing countries depended on maintaining the region's stability. Stability also offered the best hope of curbing Soviet influence, as well as that of the local Arab communist parties. Finally, stability held the best chance of preventing the currently quiescent Arab-Israeli conflict from erupting into a general war. War would, of course, provide the Soviet Union with further opportunities to extend its hold in the Middle East, not the least because it might serve to divide the Western powers. Britain was under no illusion that it, or indeed anyone else, was capable of effecting absolute stability in the volatile Middle East. But, it would do its damnedest to secure a minimum of stability. Britain's military presence in the Middle East was designed, inter alia, to achieve this end.[21]

Britain was very much aware that, regardless of its efforts, war between Israel and its Arab neighbors could erupt at any moment and at the smallest provocation. The Arab states considered the establishment of the state of Israel to be one of the most heinous crimes in the history of the world. They had never hidden their intention to go to war and wipe the Jewish state off the face of the earth.[22] Nasser, for example, constantly argued that speeches and declarations, however belligerent, were not enough to eradicate Israel. War was the only solution. But Nasser also reminded his listeners that war demanded careful planning and preparation. The humiliating defeat of 1948 was, he claimed, the result of inadequate and sloppy preparations on the part of the Arab states. Accordingly, before going to war against Israel for the third and, hopefully, final time, the Arab nations, Nasser exhorted, must modernize their armies and secure ample quantities of sophisticated weapons. They must also establish Arab unity and, above all, coordinate their armies, as well as their military strategy, and tactics. Only then, he contended, would the Arab states have sufficient military power to embark upon war and prevent any outside interfering busybodies from thwarting their plans. Only then could the Arab nation roundly and finally defeat Israel and wipe out the painful memory of 1948. War, the Egyptian president concluded, was inevitable, but it must not take place until all Arab preparations were in place.[23]

Nasser's list of the preconditions necessary to wage the final war of annihilation against Israel explains why there was no Arab initiative to start a war with Israel in the early 1960s. Quarrels and divisions within the Arab world, lack of military coordination between the Arab states and Egypt's own entanglement in the civil war in Yemen combined to rule out the possibility of war, at least in the near future.[24] But even had the Arab states been tempted to go to war with Israel, the latter's military strength was sufficient to dissuade them from embarking upon such a reckless, foolhardy enterprise.[25]

Whether it realized it or not, Israel was, in military terms, the region's most powerful country. Britain considered Israel's military power as a key factor in helping to preserve peace and stability in the Middle East. Simply put, Israel's military might acted as a powerful deterrent. It convinced the Arab states that it would be foolish and foolhardy to wage war against the Jewish state. Helping Israel maintain its relative military strength was therefore imperative, if one wished to maintain the region's stability. It was why Britain agreed to sell Israel arms, including tanks, submarines, and other military equipment. Britain's ambassador to Israel explained:

We do not give the Israelis arms because they are pro-Western or because we admire their achievement. We give them arms because our interests in the Middle East are to keep the place quiet and to prevent war. Anything, which makes war in the Middle East more likely, is against the interests of the Western powers.[26]

Harold Macmillan, Britain's prime minister, believed that by supplying Israel with arms and sustaining its military capability, Britain was helping to preserve and consolidate the region's stability.[27] Or, to put it more bluntly, it was one way of ensuring that war would not erupt.

The Israeli government did not share Britain's assumption that war would not break out in the near future. In the early 1960s, Israel sincerely doubted, or was perhaps unaware of, its relative military strength, a form of cognitive blindness, that would reassert itself on the eve of the Six-Day War.[28] The Soviet Union's growing influence in the Middle East also worried Israel as did Egypt's ever-growing haul of modern Soviet weapon systems and technology. That Egypt, with the help of German scientists, was busy developing its own rocket program, was also a cause for concern. Nor was Israel happy with the fact that Egypt was the beneficiary of large-scale financial aid from the United States and other Western countries. It was convinced that this aid enabled Egypt to buy Soviet arms, which it would eventually use against Israel.[29]

The Israeli government had no doubt that Egypt was bent on war. When Nasser announced the prospective union of Syria, Egypt and Iraq in April 1963, Israel was certain that war was simply a matter of time. These three, ostensibly progressive, Arab states shared one overriding ambition: to destroy the Jewish state. They hoped that political union and above all military unity would allow them to finally rid the Middle East of this Zionist interloper and its Western Imperialist patrons.[30] Thankfully, the prospective union did not materialize, but the Israeli government was sufficiently alarmed to beseech the Western powers, not once but several times, to guarantee its security and territorial integrity. It wanted them to promise that they would consider an attack on Israel as tantamount to an attack on the West itself. Only such a commitment could, the Israeli government believed, secure Israel's continued existence, without it first collapsing under the weight of a monstrous defense budget.[31]

Britain and the United States took the opposite view. In their opinion, to offer Israel an explicit and public guarantee would only harm Israel's interests. It would convince the Arab states that the West identified wholly with Israel. Accordingly, it would encourage them to weaken, if not completely severe, their ties with the Western powers. None of this was in the West's or Israel's interest. On the contrary, it was, as the two Anglo-Saxon powers pointed out, in the best interest of both the West and Israel that the West maintain its influence and standing in the Arab world. Only by holding a meaningful dialogue with the Arab states would the West be able to preserve regional stability. In addition, the Western powers would be able to, discretely and diplomatically and without rocking the boat, convey their commitment to Israel's existence and security. On the other hand, a guarantee, or any other kind of open commitment, would produce nothing but trouble. It would, among other things, present the Soviet Union with the opportunity of offering the Arabs a similar commitment. It would allow it to proclaim itself the champion of the Arab cause and further increase its iniquitous influence in the region at the West's expense.

A guarantee would also, though it is doubtful whether the British raised this point with the Israelis, boost Israel's self-confidence. As a result, Israel might be less inclined to compromise on the manifold issues on the Arab-Israeli conflict's agenda, such as, for example, the refugee problem. In sum, an open guarantee to Israel would act as a destabilizing not stabilizing factor.[32] This does not mean that Britain was unaware or insensitive to Israel's fears, however unjustified these might be in view of its military strength. It was also worried lest Israel's anxiety in face of the Arab world's military potential might encourage it to act hastily, and, for instance, intervene in Jordan, while, at the same time, taking the opportunity to conquer the West Bank.[33] A guarantee, however, was out of the question. The question was what was the alternative?

Like Britain, the United States, too, was preoccupied by the question of Israel's security. Like Britain, it was not prepared to grant Israel an explicit public guarantee. Yet the Americans did want to alleviate Israeli fears. They also wanted to make abundantly clear that the United States was, in general, committed to maintaining a stable Middle East. The United States shared Britain's view of the Middle East as one of the world's key geostrategic areas. It agreed with Britain that the unimpeded supply of oil from the Middle East to Europe was essential and depended on regional stability. Accordingly, on May 8, 1963, President John F. Kennedy made the following formal and momentous declaration: the United States, Kennedy declared, adamantly opposed the use of force; it rejected even the threat to use force. The United States, he continued, endorsed and upheld the security of both Israel and its Arab neighbors. He warned that "in the event of aggression or preparation for aggression, whether direct or indirect, we would support the appropriate measures in the United Nations, adopt courses of action of our own to prevent or put a stop to such aggression." Finally, Kennedy stated, the United States had a keen interest in the Middle East's economic, social and political development. It would thus seek to curb the regional arms race, which robbed the Middle East of precious resources while failing to bring the regions' nations any kind of security.[34]

Macmillan approved and seconded the president's statement. To his mind it was a comprehensive, categorical and practical expression of Britain's own policy of maintaining peace and stability in the Middle East. A few day later, Macmillan, echoing the president, told the House of Commons that "Her Majesty's government are deeply interested in peace and stability in this area and are opposed to the use of force or the threat of force there as elsewhere in the world."[35] In his statement Macmillan had deliberately used the word force rather than war. War, Britain assumed, was not on the cards, at least not in the foreseeable future. Acts of aggression, however, were. Britain was far from oblivious to the dynamics of the Arab-Israeli conflict, and it believed that the border incidents between Israel and its neighbors were the main threat to the stability in the Middle East. These incidents, which had become increasingly frequent since the Suez Campaign, might, Britain feared, escalate and eventually lead directly to war.

Britain had good cause to be worried. It was about this time that Israel, in response to persistent Syrian provocation, launched a series of retaliatory operations.[36] Britain did all it could to ensure that these incidents did not escalate into war. However, lacking confidence in its ability to influence the Arab states, Britain exercised most of its persuasive skills on Israel. It was imperative,

Britain's representatives told Israel, to prevent minor incidents from spiraling out of control. They pointed out that because in these kind of incidents, prestige played as great a role as security; the result was that further, more vicious fighting ensued. This, unfortunately, was exactly the effect of Israel's reprisals. Furthermore, the border incidents, the British explained, not only threaten the region's stability, but also gave the Soviet Union the opportunity to fish in troubled water. Israel would be best advised, they suggested, to abandon the policy of retaliation and look to the United Nations and its peacekeeping machinery to resolve its disputes with its neighbors.[37] Macmillan wrote personally to Levi Eshkol, Israel's prime minister, and advised him that "the principle hope for peace in the area must be in building up the Rule of Law based in the principles and institutions of the United Nations."[38] In supporting the United Nations's precepts, he continued, Israel would be making its own vital contribution to the preservation of peace in the Middle East.

Owing to its desire to preserve peace and stability in the Middle East, Britain could not afford to offer public or explicit support to either side of the Arab-Israeli conflict. Indeed, Britain, on the whole, sought to distance itself, as much as possible, from the conflict and certainly took no initiative to resolve it. But its desire for stability was not the only reason why Britain adopted a neutral position. Britain was intensely aware that its precarious position in the Arab world, coupled with its extensive interests in the region, made it the most vulnerable power in the Middle East.[39] It was convinced, and not without cause, that any overt identification or expression of sympathy with the Israel cause would severely, if not irredeemably, damage its interests. Thus, Britain refused to condemn, for example, the Arab trade embargo on Israel.[40]

None of this, as noted, prevented Britain, in the cause of regional stability, from secretly supplying Israel with weapons. Britain also, and for much the same reasons, offered military and economic aid to King Hussein of Jordan. Britain believed that a stable, conservative Jordan would help prevent an Arab-Israeli conflagration. At the same time, Britain also labored to improve its relations with the more radical Arab countries such as Iraq, Syria and Egypt, which would, it hoped, not only safeguard Britain's oil and Cold War interests, but also allow it to bring its influence to bear should a crisis erupt.[41]

Not that a crisis appeared likely. After the Suez Campaign, the region had settled down to enjoy a period of relative calm. Moreover, there were various indications that the 1960s would be a far quieter decade than the turbulent mid-1950s and even the comparatively tranquil late 1950s. War, it seemed, had receded into the distant future. Not surprisingly, the British government felt that it could afford to be cautiously optimistic about the future.

THE MIDDLE EAST: SIGNS OF CALM

During the Sinai Campaign, Israeli forces, within a space of only a few days, conquered the entire Sinai Peninsula and Gaza Strip. Not that Israel had much time to enjoy its new conquests, as it came, almost immediately, under heavy American pressure to evacuate its forces from the area. David Ben Gurion, Israel's then prime minister, refused, however, even to consider withdrawing from Sinai unless Israel were first guaranteed free passage through the Straits of Tiran and a peaceful Egyptian-Israeli border. In early 1957, the United States yielded. It was willing to acknowledge Israel's security needs and even came to an arrangement with the Israeli government to that effect.[42] Further, it assured Israel that the United States regarded the Gulf of Aqaba and the Straits of Tiran as international territorial waters and that no country had the right to deny ships sailing innocently free passage through the Gulf of Aqaba or the Straits of Tiran. The United States had, in effect, promised that the Gulf of Aqaba and the Straits, international waterways both, would remain open to Israeli shipping. The United States did more than that. It also undertook to join other countries and procure the general recognition of this principle. Finally, should international action, whether carried out in the framework of the United Nations or any other international coalition, fail to secure the opening of the Straits, the United States admitted Israel's right to defend itself against any violation of the principle of free passage. Britain fully endorsed the American stand, as did France, and quite emphatically at that.[43]

It was no secret that the United States had committed itself to upholding the principle of free navigation through the Straits. Israeli Foreign Minister Golda Meir mentioned the American pledge when speaking to the United Nations Assembly.[44] Ben Gurion, when explaining to his countrymen why Israel had agreed to withdraw from the Sinai Peninsula, reassured them that Israel would still be able promise its ships free and unimpeded passage through international waterways and seas. "Israel," he boomed, from the Knesset podium, "will regard ... any interference by force with the passage of Israeli ships, which were using their right of free navigation in good faith ... as an attack. It will use all means necessary to guarantee its ships freedom of passage."[45]

The United Nations, too, contributed toward meeting Israeli security requirements. In February 1957, the General Assembly decided to send an Emergency Force (UNEF) to the region. The force, to be stationed along the Straits of Tiran and in the Gaza Strip, was charged with the twin tasks of ensuring that Egypt observed the principle of free passage through the Straits and preventing terrorist infiltration of Israel. Egypt submitted, albeit reluctantly, to the United Nations's resolution. Privately, however, Nasser rejected the principle of free passage through the Straits and regarded the decision to station troops on Egyptian territory as a monstrous insult. He summed up the decision as one that rewarded Israeli and Imperialist aggression. Nasser knew that, at present, he had little choice other than to submit to UNEF's presence, but he was resolved to overturn this obscene act of aggression once Egypt had acquired sufficient power to do so. The day would come, Nasser vowed, when he would expel the UNEF from Egypt and cease to observe the principle of free navigation through the Straits.[46] Until then he would carefully bide his time.

After Suez, calm reigned along the Egyptian-Israeli border. This owed little to Egypt's desire to preserve the peace or willingness to obey the United Nations's decisions. It owed much, as noted, to Nasser's sense that he had no choice but to accede to the United Nations's resolution. Nor can one ignore the fact that the presence of the UNEF on Egyptian territory made a powerful impression, practical and no less significantly psychological, on Israel and especially Egypt. Its presence encouraged or rather forced both countries to adopt a more restrained and moderate policy.[47] Above all, however, the Egyptian-Israeli peaceful border was the product of Egypt's fear of Israel's reaction to any hint of Egyptian aggression.

Israel's stunning display of military prowess during the Sinai Campaign and its overwhelming victory were sufficient to deter Egypt from closing the Straits to Israeli shipping. Israel left Egypt with no doubt as to how it would react were Egypt to violate the principal of free passage through the Straits. Time and again, Israeli officials warned that if Egypt dared close the Straits to Israeli ships, Israel would not hesitate to reopen them by force.[48] Nasser, who still believed that a war of annihilation was the only solution to the Arab-Israeli conflict, strictly adhered to the strategy of no war until total victory, that is, the destruction of Israel, could be assured. Thus, he had no wish to provoke an untimely war with Israel. Accordingly, for the time being at least, Israeli ships were free to sail through the Straits.

After Suez, Israel's borders with Jordan and Lebanon were also relatively trouble free. Not so the Syrian border. The July 1949 cease-fire agreement between Syria and Israel had, among other things, established a demilitarized zone between the two countries. The zone extended between the cease-fire line and the boundary of mandatory Palestine, the recognized international boundary. It lay west of the international boundary, in an area conquered by the Syrian Army during the 1948 war.[49] The cease-fire accords did not determine who had sovereign power over the zone. That was a matter for the final peace settlement. However, the accords did posit that "pending [the] final territorial settlement between the Parties the armed forces of both sides will be totally excluded, and ... no activities of military or paramilitary forces will be permitted."[50] Finally, the accords ruled that, without prejudice to the final peace settlement, routine civilian life was to be slowly resumed in the zone.[51]

Both Syria and Israel had very different interpretations of the phrase "the restoration of routine civilian life." Israel believed it meant that it was free to develop the zone, build settlements, farm the land and so on. Syria, on the other hand, insisted that it meant upholding the status quo in the disputed zone. It argued that until the question of sovereignty was resolved in the final peace settlement, things should remain as they are and the whole area temporarily ceded to the United Nations's control.[52] Not that Syria showed any sign of wanting to reach a peace agreement. It did not shrink from changing the status quo and, for example, seized the east bank of Lake Tiberias and started to pump water from the lake. This was despite the fact that according to the cease-fire agreement the lake, including an area of 10 meters along its eastern shore, was under Israeli sovereignty.

Unlike Syria, Israel was not prepared to leave the status of the demilitarized zone hanging in the air until the conclusion of a peace agreement, especially as none appeared forthcoming. Accordingly, it set out to settle the issue of sovereignty unilaterally, on its own terms. It sought to establish Israeli sovereignty de facto by initiating various development projects and farming the land in the demilitarized zone.[53] Syria, naturally, refused to take this lying down, and the result was frequent exchanges of fire between Syria and Israel. The chief of the United Nations Truce Supervision Organization (UNTSO), Swedish General Karl Van Horn, generally sided with Syria in these incidents. General Van Horn thought that Syria's response constituted a legitimate act of defense against what he considered were acts of aggression by the Israelis within the demilitarized zone.

The border incidents were not provoked solely by Israel's decision to go ahead and resettle the demilitarized zone. There were occasions when the Syrian government would orchestrate border incidents to serve its own internal needs.[54] At other times, the Syrians would exploit the UN commander's sympathetic attitude, that is, to fire upon Israeli army patrols in Israeli territory. Instigating border incidents also became an integral part of Syrian policy during the water dispute. As though the Arab-Israeli conflict weren't complex enough, after Suez the troublesome question of water rights reared its head, adding to an already difficult situation. In 1958, the Israeli government had decided to embark upon an ambitious project to channel much needed water from Lake Tiberias in the north to the Negev Desert in the south.[55] Seeking to thwart the Israeli plans, Syria escalated the border incidents, in the hope that by doing so it would force the other Arab states and, above all, Egypt, to take action against Israel. Its plan failed, as Nasser, faithful to his strategy, refused to be drawn into an untimely conflict with Israel.

On one occasion, however, Syria almost succeeded in bringing Israel and Egypt to the brink of war. In early February 1960, after a series of Syrian provocations, Israel finally lost patience and attacked the village of Tawfik, which sheltered at the foot of the Golan Heights. Syria had expected a much harsher response and had even considered the possibility of an Israeli invasion. Egypt, too, was worried, and in order to deter Israel from carrying out its ostensible plan to invade Syria, Egypt sent three divisions into the Sinai Peninsula. It was purely a deterrent measure, and Nasser had no intention of initiating any kind of military action against Israel. Unsure of Nasser's motives and with little cause to trust him, Israel then secretly mobilized its reserve and armored forces. But, like Nasser, Israel had no desire for war. Ben Gurion, using the Western Powers as intermediaries, made it clear to Nasser that Israel had no plans to attack Syria. He even allowed Egypt to withdraw its forces from the Sinai desert without losing face, remaining silent when Nasser announced smugly that his forces had fulfilled their task and successfully deterred an Israeli attack.[56]

Other than this mini-crisis, the Syrian-Israeli border clashes between 1956 and 1964 were all relatively minor and isolated affairs. As Arthur Lourie, Israel's ambassador to London, told Britain's foreign minister, R.A. Butler, "other than a few aggressive incidents, mostly along the Syrian border, the country's [Israel's] borders were reasonably peaceful."[57]

Even if the Arab states, and, above all, Egypt, were prepared to go to war with Israel, recent events in the Arab world and the international arena served to ensure that the region would remain, for the present, peaceful. One such event was John Kennedy's assumption of the presidency in January 1961. In marked contrast to his predecessor, President Eisenhower, Kennedy did not believe that nonalignment and Third World neutralism were necessarily or simply a guise for Soviet power and interests. Neutralism, Kennedy held, could in fact be turned against the Soviet Union and used to contain Soviet expansion. Nor did Kennedy deem Arab Nationalism as fundamentally or conclusively anti-Western and communist inspired, which certainly was the view of his British allies.[58]

Accordingly, the Kennedy administration thought it possible to steer Egypt, the foremost Arab nation, in the direction of West and Western interests. The key to achieving this was American economic strength, and Kennedy assumed that by offering Egypt economic aid and helping to develop its economy, the United States would be able to maintain and develop a positive relationship with Egypt. The United States would, as a result, be able to exercise a calming influence over the Egyptian president and his currently hostile policies. For example, it might be able to moderate Egypt's hostile policies toward the West. By extending economic aid to Egypt and consolidating the latter's economic ties with the West, the United States would also be able to prevent Egypt from becoming too dependent on the Soviet Union. This, in turn, would allow the United States to secure Egyptian neutrality in the Cold War conflict. All this was for the ultimate cause of a stable Middle East.[59]

Within days of entering office, Kennedy began to put his strategy into operation. He increased American economic aid to Egypt on a multiyearly basis. He expressed a willingness to help resolve the Palestinian refugee problem, suggesting that they either return home or receive compensation for their lost property.[60] His strategy, at least initially, appeared to be successful. In October 1962, Egypt and the United States signed an economic agreement, which provided Egypt with American economic aid for the next three years. Egypt, in return, assured American officials that it had no intention of attacking Israel or rather that Egypt would not be the first to shoot. The United States regarded these assurances as a sure sign that Nasser was willing to put the Israeli-Arab conflict on hold and adopt a far more constructive approach toward the Arab-Israeli conflict.[61]

The United States had ample cause to be satisfied with the results of its new policy. American aid did have a positive effect on Egypt's relations with the West. It also influenced, to a degree, Nasser's current policies on the Arab-Israeli conflict. But although it is true that Nasser was, at present, on his best behavior, what the Americans ignored, or perhaps didn't know, was Nasser's overall strategy had remained the same: He would wait and bide his time until Egypt was strong enough to defeat Israel. Perhaps the United States should have suspected something, as Nasser, himself, had told it, on several occasions, that he would never forgo Egyptian interests in lieu of economic aid and good relations with the United States. That, he emphasized, was too high a price to pay. He would continue to work toward a progressive Arab world, or, in other words, seek to engineer the destruction of the Arab conservative regimes.[62] Indeed, within weeks of signing the aid agreement Nasser was busy supporting the rebel forces, which had deposed the newly crowned king of Yemen.

In September 1962, a group of radical pro-Nasser officers in Yemen, led by Colonel Abdulla al-Sallal, overthrew the conservative regime of King al-Imam Badr and proclaimed the establishment of the Arab Republic of Yemen.[63] Yemen was immediately swept into the maelstrom of civil war. Al-Imam Badr, deposed only one week after ascending the throne, escaped to the hills and began to wage war on the new regime. He was able to do so thanks to the support, in arms and money, he received from his fellow conservative monarchs, King Feisal Ibn Saud of Saudi Arabia and King Hussein of Jordan.[64]

Nasser, naturally, took the side of the revolutionaries. A friendly, pro-Nasser regime in Yemen, subject to Egyptian influence, might, he hoped, become the spearhead of a revolutionary wave, which would sweep through the Arab world and wipe out the reactionary regimes of Saudi Arabia, Jordan and the Persian Gulf's Oil Emirates. The destruction of the conservative regimes had the additional attraction of bringing to an end Britain's influence in the region. In order to ensure the revolutionary regime's survival and the realization of his plans, Nasser decided to send an expeditionary force to Yemen to aid the rebels. Initially, the Egyptian force numbered several thousand soldiers, but as the war progressed, Nasser was forced to send more and more men and equipment to Yemen. Yet, years passed and victory was still nowhere in sight. Yemen proved to be a quagmire, drawing and tying down an enormous number of Egyptian soldiers. By May 1967, there were 70,000 Egyptian soldiers fighting in Yemen.[65] The war also claimed numerous Egyptian casualties and drained the Egyptian Treasury to the tune of 50 million pounds sterling a year.[66]

The civil war in Yemen, with Saudi Arabia and Jordan supporting King al-Imam Badr and Nasser the rebels, deepened the divisions in the already split and factious Arab world. The traditional Arab conservative regimes, such as Jordan and Saudi Arabia, had long been immersed in bitter conflict with the "progressive" states of Egypt, Syria and Iraq. The civil war in Yemen was merely one more, albeit brutal, expression of this ongoing and fierce conflict. Nasser, in particular, as the self-appointed standard bearer of the "progressive" Arab states, promoted the cause of revolution everywhere. In Algeria, for instance, he supported the National Liberation Front (FLN) in their fight for independence against France.

Nasser saw himself not only as the champion of progress and socialism, but also of Arab unity and solidarity. Unfortunately these two goals were clearly at odds. His fellow Arab leader King Hussein, for example, was forced to spend much of his time suppressing Syrian- and Egyptian-inspired conspiracies and subversive activities. Nor were relations much better between the "progressive" states. The union of Egypt and Syria lasted a mere three years, from 1958 to 1961, before collapsing in ignominy, amidst much mutual recrimination. A second attempt to form a union between Egypt, Syria and Iraq, in April 1963, never even got off the ground. Instead, Egypt embarked upon a campaign of hate and vilification against Syria's Ba'ath regime, whereas Syria, in response, mercilessly persecuted Nasser's Syrian supporters. Relations between the Arab states, on the periphery of the Arab-Israeli conflict, were equally tense. Border disputes between Algeria and Morocco had, on several occasions, led to armed clashes. In addition, Algeria, angry at Tunisia's recognition of Mauritania, was barely talking to its fellow North African country. In fact, of the thirteen members of the Arab League, only three, Kuwait, Libya and Sudan, enjoyed good relations with all the rest. By the summer of 1963, internal Arab disputes and quarrels had reached peak level.[67]

The conservative Arab regimes were not the only ones vexed by Egypt's intervention in Yemen. Britain, too, was upset and worried. All set to withdraw from its bases in the Middle East, Britain had hoped first to ensure the presence and durability of friendly, moderate regimes in the South Arabian Federation and Aden. The revolution in Yemen threatened to spoil its plans. Britain, with some justification, suspected Nasser of engineering the revolution, with the aim of sparking similar revolutions throughout the Arabian Peninsula and precipitating the collapse of the conservative regimes bordering Yemen. Accordingly, it, too, like the Saudis and Jordanians, began to secretly supply the Yemenite monarchist faction with arms.[68]

Israel, by contrast, was quite happy with Nasser's involvement in Yemen. As the Egyptian army was sucked ever deeper into the morass of the Yemen civil war, it began to view the Egyptian intervention as a stabilizing factor in the Middle East, at least as far as the Arab-Israeli conflict was concerned. The civil war in Yemen, like all inter-Arab conflicts, had pushed the Arab-Israeli conflict to the bottom of Egypt's agenda. It explained, in part, why Nasser refused to be drawn into a war against Israel despite the fact that the situation along the Israeli-Syrian border was daily becoming increasingly ugly. In sum, Israel assumed that the deeper Egypt sunk into the Yemen quagmire the smaller the chances for war.[69] In the autumn of 1963, Abba Eban, Israel's deputy prime minister, when speaking to Britain's ambassador to Israel, noted that "the Middle East situation looked a great deal less dangerous ... [as] Nasser's involvement in Yemen had a useful hampering effect on UAR (Egypt) ambition."[70] It was a view Britain would eventually come to share.

Only a few months earlier, in the summer of 1963, Israel itself had experienced a momentous political event. In June 1963, Ben Gurion, Israel's long serving, all-powerful prime minister, had finally resigned. Ben Gurion had been a towering figure in Israeli politics. Often aggressive, he completely dominated Israeli politics. Externally, Ben Gurion was a hawk. He was relentless in his battle against the Arab states and utterly contemptuous of the United Nations. Levi Eshkol, Ben Gurion's successor, was his almost complete opposite. Mild mannered, Eshkol was considered both a moderate and conciliatory in temperament. A man of compromise, Eshkol's appointment marked the beginning of a new era in Israel and in the Middle East in general.

In substance, there was no difference between Eshkol and Ben Gurion's foreign and defense policies. But the style was very different. This was apparent almost from the beginning. When introducing his government to the Knesset, Eshkol seized the opportunity to make an appeal to the Arab states and especially to the Egyptian president. He was, he said, ready, at all times, to meet and converse with any Arab leader willing to do so. Furthermore, he was certain that once seated around the negotiating table the Arabs and Israelis would discover that the many problems that afflicted their relations could be resolved. The desire for peace, Eshkol stressed, underlay and guided Israel's policy. Moreover, once peace was in place, it would be possible to tackle the real problems of the region: poverty, hunger, disease and ignorance.[71] Israel and the Arab states would be able to work together for the benefit of the region. It was a call Eshkol would repeat many times in the future. No wonder Britain believed it had cause to be, albeit cautiously, optimistic.

Eshkol genuinely believed that there was a chance for a new beginning in the Middle East. The prospective union of Egypt, Syria and Iraq was currently off the agenda. Indeed, division and dissension, rather than unity, distinguished the Arab world. Globally, too, things looked promising. The high-pitched drama of the 1962 Cuban missile crisis was succeeded by the "minidetente" and the general relaxation of superpower tension. The United States and the Soviet Union began to discuss arms limitation and, in the summer of 1963, signed an agreement banning above-ground nuclear testing, the first agreement of its kind and a turning point in Cold War nuclear rivalry. President Kennedy talked of peace as "the necessary rational end of rational men."[72] Eshkol hoped that Middle East, too, would benefit from the minidetente. The thaw in superpower relations, he believed, offered a real chance to resolve the Arab-Israeli conflict. With summit meetings and high-level discussions galore, there was an opportunity to place the conflict on the agenda of every single superpower meeting that took place, in the hope that somehow a solution to the conflict would finally emerge.[73]

Eshkol did more than just proclaim Israel's peaceful intentions. He embarked upon a diplomatic campaign designed to prove to the West that Israel genuinely sought peace. Of all the problems of the Arab-Israeli conflict that of the Palestinian refugees was perhaps the most tragic, complex and intractable. During the 1948 war, numerous Palestinians had either abandoned their homes or been expelled by Israeli forces. So far, all the efforts to resolve the refugee problem had met with little success. By the early 1960s, there were about 750,000 Palestinian refugees scattered throughout the region. The vast majority lived in Jordan, but there were also numerous refugees in Egypt, Syria and Lebanon. Most of the refugees were housed in temporary, poverty-stricken camps close to the border with Israel.

The Israeli government had always been willing to discuss and resolve the refugee problem. But Israel rejected the proposition that the refugee problem could be treated in isolation from the Arab-Israeli conflict as a whole. It insisted that any solution to the problem must be formulated in the context of direct negotiations between Israel and the Arab states; these negotiations would eventually lead to an overall peace settlement. As far as Israel was concerned, until peace was firmly established, to allow the refugees to return to their homes was tantamount to installing a fifth column in Israel. Nor was it willing to accept an externally imposed solution to the refugee problem. Hence, its rejection of the General Assembly's resolution from 1963, which gave the refugees a choice between returning home or receiving compensation for their lost property.[74]

Under Eshkol, Israel softened its stance on the refugee problem. It abandoned its insistence on an overall political settlement and was willing to discuss a solution to the refugee problem with any Arab country that sheltered Palestinian refugees. To its mind, the most likely candidates for such negotiations were Jordan and Lebanon. Israel was even prepared to allow a third party, say the United States, a role in the discussions. Israel also told the United States and Britain that it would agree the return of a substantial number of refugees—100,000 to 1500,000 was the number mentioned by the Israeli ambassador—on the condition that the remainder were settled elsewhere. Israel made one final gesture. It announced that it would consider paying compensation to those refugees unable to return home, though only if it were to receive international aid to this end and if the value of the abandoned or confiscated Jewish property in the Arab states was deducted from the overall sum. On this basis, Israel had little doubt that the refugee problem could, at long last, be brought to a satisfactory close.[75]

The fact that Israel was prepared to make a constructive effort to solve the refugee problem did not guarantee a similar readiness on the part of the Arab states. Indeed, Britain doubted whether any Arab state would be courageous enough to embark upon direct negotiations with Israel. It certainly was not surprised when there was no immediate response to the Israeli initiative. Lebanon and Jordan—Israel's prime candidates for negotiations—were fearful of the consequences of sitting around the negotiating table with Israel. King Hussein was convinced that independent negotiations with Israel would result in his personal, and most likely the Hashemite regime's, demise. Likewise, the Lebanese government was certain that such negotiations Israel would engender a dangerous internal upheaval in Lebanon.[76] Still, Arab silence notwithstanding, Britain viewed the Israeli initiative as a promising sign that might, in time, set in motion the process of Arab-Israeli negotiation.

The Israeli initiative on the refugee issue was not an isolated gesture, but part of the Eshkol government's new, moderate policy. This policy received its most persuasive expression in Israel's newfound restraint in light of Syria's continued provocations. Under Eshkol, the Israel exhibited a remarkable degree of self-restraint and refrained from taking retaliatory action. For instance, on August 19, 1963, two Israeli soldiers were killed and one wounded as a result of a Syrian ambush in Israeli territory. The following day, Syrian soldiers fired upon Israeli observation points, settlements and farmers working in the fields.[77] Yet, rather than retaliate, as Ben Gurion surely would have done, Eshkol's government decided, instead, to lodge an official complaint with the Security Council.

Israel expected the Security Council to condemn Syria's flagrant aggression. A decision condemning Syria, Golda Meir told the British ambassador, would encourage the Israeli government to respect and trust the United Nations. It might also deter Syria from further acts of aggression. But, she warned, should the Security Council refuse to condemn Syria, Israel would be left with no choice but to take the military measures necessary to protect its citizens and their property.

Britain, on the whole, was pleased with this new turn in Israeli policy. Appealing to the United Nations was precisely the policy it had been counseling Israel for so long. It judged Israel's decision to turn to the Security Council as signaling a significant change in Israel's policy. It was definitely evidence of Eshkol's more conciliatory approach, certainly as compared to Ben Gurion, whom Britain regarded as "an eye for an eye" man. In the Security Council, keeping in mind Meir's warning, the British together with the Americans hoped to push through a proposal that expressed regret at the acts of military aggression and suggested conducting a survey of the disputed zones.[78] The Soviet Union promptly vetoed even this relatively innocuous proposal. Aware of just how frustrating Israel found the Soviet veto, Britain tried to persuade it not to give up hope on the United Nations. Appealing to the United Nations, they advised, might still serve Israeli interests, as regional stability depended in no small part on strengthening that organization's observation and supervision mechanisms.[79]

Eshkol's goal of maintaining, inasmuch as possible, a peaceful Middle East also had an effect on Israel's nuclear policy. In the mid-1950s, Israel had launched a full-blown nuclear program. Both Britain and the United States were troubled by the fact that Israel appeared to be bent on becoming an independent nuclear power. Britain warned Israel that by introducing nuclear weapons into the region it was playing with fire. Its decision to develop nuclear capacity was an extraordinarily dangerous one, which might well boomerang. Although Israel,

Britain elaborated, might be the first to acquire such weapons, it would certainly not be the last, and a highly explosive Middle East, complete with nuclear weapons, was a nightmare not to be contemplated. Thus, Britain concluded, nuclear weapons, far from vouchsafing Israel's security, would make it more vulnerable still. Consequently, it urged, every effort should be made to exclude nuclear weapons from the Middle East.[80]

Eshkol, conciliatory as always, sought to set Britain and U.S. minds at rest. He promised that once Israel had completed the construction of its nuclear plants, it would allow scientists from friendly countries to come and inspect the plants. It would even permit, to begin with, American scientists to visit the nuclear plant in Dimona before it went critical.[81] Did Eshkol's concessions reveal a readiness, on Israel's part, to eventually expose its activities in the Dimona plant to public scrutiny? Perhaps. It is, however, equally possible that this gesture was no more than a tactical step aimed at allowing Israel to continue its work in the plant unhindered. Whatever the case, Eshkol's concessions were regarded and depicted as part of Israel's new, moderate attitude toward the Arab-Israeli conflict. It confirmed Abba Eban's statement that "Israel will adopt a new approach towards the Arab states, replacing the one pursued in the days of Ben Gurion."[82]

In the summer of 1963, with stability apparently on the cards, the British government remained relatively hopeful of the future. The 70,000 Egyptian soldiers bogged down in Yemen, Israel's military strength, President Kennedy and Prime Minister Macmillan's May declarations and Eshkol's moderation, which, admittedly, had as yet received no practical expression, all pointed to the fact that stability would continue to reign in the Middle East. If the region was not exactly moving in the direction of peace, neither was it marching toward war. Below the surface, however, things were a lot less promising. Ever since the end of the Suez War, both the Arabs and Israelis had been assiduously preparing for the next war, a war that the Arabs, at least, believed was inevitable. Each side sought to augment its military strength as much as possible. The result was an unrestrained and uninhibited arms race between Israel and its Arab neighbors.

Rising Self-Confidence: The Arab-Israeli Arms Race

The one thing that marred the relative calm in the Middle East in the years after Suez was the Arab-Israeli arms race. The end of the Suez campaign marked a turning point in the Arab-Israeli arms race. An intensive, ever-expanding arms race began that even the states supplying the region with weapons arms could do nothing to stop. A vicious circle was established, which no one appeared able to break. The arms race, with each side bent upon enlarging its military arsenal to the utmost, produced so much tension and anxiety, that, in this context, the years between 1956–1967 became known the "Troubled Decade."[83]

On May 25, 1950, the United States, Britain and France, whose influence in the Middle East was at the time paramount, issued a joint declaration. They recognized the Arab states and Israel's right to maintain their armed forces at a level that allowed them to maintain their internal security and act in legitimate self-defense, as well as enable them to play their part in defending the region. "All applications for arms or war material for these countries," the three powers pronounced, "will be considered in the light of these principles" and these principles alone. The declaration concluded by recording and reaffirming "the three governments … opposition to the development of an arms race between the Arab states and Israel."[84]

Implicit in the three-power declaration was a determination to circumscribe the number of arms entering the Middle East. The three powers were clearly unwilling to feed the burgeoning arms race. Unfortunately, with the conclusion of the 1955 Czech arms deal, the Western powers arms policy, and with it their good intentions, collapsed. Following the Czech arms deal, the Soviet Union, who of course was not a party to the declaration, began to deliver massive amounts of weapons to Egypt. At the same time, Israel and France formed an informal alliance, as a result of which France began to furnish Israel with copious quantities of tanks and planes, and soon emerged as Israel's principal arms supplier. France was soon joined by Britain who began equipping Israel with tanks and other military equipment.

Despite Egypt's ignominious defeat in the Suez War, the Arab states, and above all Egypt, were still as determined as ever to destroy the state of Israel. But, Nasser, fearful of Israel's military might and adhering to his strategy of preparing very carefully for the final showdown with Israel, sought first to gain a strategic advance or, at the very least, balance, with Israel. He began to stockpile huge quantities of Soviet-made weapons. Only, thus, would Egypt avoid repeating the humiliating defeat of 1948 and crush Israel. Moreover, Egypt's involvement in civil war in Yemen had, as Nasser knew, depleted its weapons reserves, because a considerable amount of its military equipment had been either lost or rendered useless. If Egypt wanted to keep on fighting in Yemen and, at the same time, prepare for the final campaign against Israel, it must acquire the largest possible arms reserve.[85]

The Soviet Union was more than happy to supply Egypt with all the arms and military equipment it wanted. It considered arms deals, in general, as a useful way to extend its influence in the Arab world. But an arms deal with Egypt had two extra attractions. First, Egypt was a key, if not the key, Arab state. Second, Egypt could provide the Soviet Union's naval squadrons with a much desired port in the Mediterranean. Ever since 1960, the Soviet Union had been desperately searching for a Mediterranean port. Its fellow communist countries, Albania and Yugoslavia, had both refused to allow the Soviet Union to use their ports as a home base for its Mediterranean squadrons. Egypt proved the only country willing to open its ports to the Soviet navy.[86]

From the beginning of the 1960s onward, Egypt and the Soviet Union signed several arms deals and the Soviet Union began supplying Egypt with more and better quality arms. Soon, the Egyptian air force was able to replace its obsolescent British planes with modern Soviet MIG fighter jets. As a result, if in 1956, on the eve of the Suez Campaign, the only Soviet aircraft in Egypt's possession were the relatively time-worn MIG-15 and Ilyushin-28, by 1957 it was the proud owner of several MIG-17s. Three years later, it received the MIG-19, and in May 1962, the MIG-21, which stood at the very cutting edge of Soviet aerospace technology. By the end of 1964, Egypt owned approximately fifty MIG-21s. In addition to fighter jets, the Soviet Union also supplied Egypt with medium-range bombers, including the Tupolev-16 and the short range bomber, the Ilyushin-28. In June 1963, the Soviet Union and Egypt concluded their largest arms deal to date. Considered the most important arms deal concluded before the Six-Day War, it was, according to one estimate, a $500 million deal.[87] The Soviet Union began to equip Egypt with SA2 ground to air missiles to defend Egypt's airbases and other strategic sites. Finally Egypt received the advanced T-54B tank, a model employed by the Soviet army. After 1963, Soviet arms deliveries to Egypt continued at an accelerated pace. In 1965, the two countries concluded a $300 million deal, which further augmented Egypt's air and naval power. By June 1967, Egypt possessed close to 1,200 tanks and 500 aircraft, including over 120 MIG-21s. Nor was Egypt the only one to enjoy Soviet largess. Syria acquired Soviet weapons, as did Iraq, though the latter also bought arms from the United States. Jordan, by contrast, got most of its military equipment from Britain and the United States.[88]

The generous Soviet arms deals, and above all the fact that it now owned a large number of state-of-the-art fighter jets, all helped raise Egyptian self-confidence to new heights. Nasser was often heard boasting that Egypt's Soviet-made aircraft were more than a match for anything Israel possessed. Furthermore, the Egyptian president assumed that in the future Israel would not enjoy the benefit of British and French air cover, as it did during the Suez campaign, and this, too, boosted Egyptian self-confidence. It was Nasser's growing self-confidence that precipitated, to a degree, the events that led to the 1967 war.[89] But Egypt was not the only country whose self-confidence rose in those years. Israel, too, enjoyed a growing sense of self-assurance, which, as will be seen, affected its policies in the period prior to the Six-Day War.

With the Arab leaders making bellicose and belligerent noises, war, Israel realized, was merely a question of time. Accordingly, it regarded the acquisition of more and better weapons to be a matter of survival. Nor did it lag behind Egypt. After Suez, Israel began tirelessly to expand its weapons arsenal. It is worth noting that Israel, like Nasser, assumed that in the future it would not have the benefit of French or British air cover. In fact, it doubted whether it would enjoy, should war break out, the active military support, as opposed to diplomatic or financial backing, of any of the Western powers. In military terms, Israel realized it had no one to depend on but itself. It was therefore vital to enhance Israel's air power to the point were it could itself defend the country's airspace and ensure a speedy victory once war erupted. When formulating its strategic plans, Israel had to take two things into account: (1) the large number of enemies ranged against it, and (2) the fact that the Israeli economy could not withstand a long war. Consequently, regardless of who started the war, Israel's strategy was predicated on a swift and decisive victory.[90]

A powerful, well-equipped air force was a vital component of Israeli strategic planning. However, the success of Israel's wartime strategy was equally dependent on the possession of a wide variety of modern weapons, including tanks, armored vehicles, a sophisticated navy and so on. To this end, it sought to gain the patronage of Western states, other than France, to help it counter the current trends of arms acquisition in the Arab world. So far, both before and immediately after the Suez Campaign, France had been Israel's sole source of offensive weapons. Between 1961–1962, Israel and France signed several arms deals, and France supplied Israel with Mirage jets. The acquisition of the Mirage, a dual-purpose aircraft, used for both bombing missions and intercepting enemy aircraft, significantly raised the standard and level of technological sophistication enjoyed by the Israeli air force.

France and Israel both benefited from the relationship; Israel was perhaps the most obvious of the two. By the opening of the Six-Day War, Israel had seventy-two Mirage fighter jets.[91] Furthermore, in 1957, the two concluded an agreement whereby France would supply Israel with a nuclear plant. On the French side, the sale of arms to Israel was regarded as vital to French economic growth. It was not just that the arm deals brought in money, but that Israel was one of the few countries to actively use French aircraft, for example, during the Suez Campaign. That it purchased sophisticated French jets like the Mirage was considered excellent promotion for the French aerospace industry, which was, at the time, coming under strong British and American competition.[92]

But was French military aid enough? The Arab states, after all, had a superpower behind them, and France could not possibly hope to match the massive flow of sophisticated Soviet weapons pouring into to Egypt, Syria and Iraq. Moreover, the Soviet Union supplied its Arab clients with weapons on generous terms of credit, something France could ill-afford. Nor did the Soviet Union limit itself to selling arms to the Arabs. As part of its strategy of extending Soviet influence in the region, it provided the Arab states with economic aid and, no less important, diplomatic support. Should war erupt the Soviet Union would stand firmly by the Arab side. It was manifest that France could not hope act as a counterweight to Soviet power.[93] This was, however, on the assumption that it was willing to try.

Although Israel may have been reasonably certain that the supply of French weapons would continue in the years after the Suez campaign, it was far less confident that it would receive French support, if and when war erupted. In May 1958, Charles de Gaulle became president of France and proceeded to revolutionize French foreign policy, not the least in the Middle East. Acutely aware that the Suez Affair and the Algerian war had gravely undermined French influence within the Arab world, de Gaulle was determined to recover and rehabilitate France's position in the region. This meant that France would have to tone down, if not end, its close relationship with Israel. De Gaulle's presidency thus marked the beginning of the end of the tacit alliance between Israel and France. Israel was very much aware of these new trends in French foreign policy, which became even more conspicuous once the Algerian war ended in 1962.[94] Accordingly, it began to seek alternative arms suppliers or rather to try and vary its sources of weapons supply. As Prime Minister Eshkol rightly noted, it would be foolish to put all one's eggs in one basket.[95]

The power best placed to fulfill Israel's arms requirements and counterbalance the military, diplomatic and economic support the Soviet Union offered the Arab states was, of course, the United States. The arms race was a hugely expensive business and placed a colossal economic burden on Israel, not the least because it required massive quantities of diverse state-of-the-art weapons to offset the Arab nations' Soviet-manufactured weapons. The United States could easily supply Israel with a wide variety of modern, up-to-date military equipment, and, no less important, do so on relatively easy terms. It could also provide Israel the economic and financial assistance it needed to surmount the financial burden imposed by the arms race. Finally, it could offer diplomatic support, so that Israel would not find itself standing alone against a hostile Arab world backed by the power of the Soviet Union. All this, as Israel well knew, would prove crucial in time of war.[96] Hence, it was hardly surprising that after Suez, Israel devoted itself, almost single-mindedly, to establishing and cementing a special relationship with the United States. This had become Israel's principal, overriding foreign policy goal.[97]

Only months after the Suez Campaign, Ben Gurion began to vigorously woo the Americans. His initial aim was to persuade the United States to change its policy on supplying arms to Israel. Eventually, he hoped to inveigle it into generally cooperating more closely and fully with Israel. In October 1957, Ben Gurion proposed that Israel become an emergency base for American operations in the region and announced that to this end he was willing to develop and expand Israel's seaports and airfields. All he asked for in return was an American commitment to come to Israel's aid if either Syria or Egypt attacked it. The United States, having no desire to become intimately involved in the Arab-Israeli conflict, politely declined Ben Gurion's kind offer.[98]

Nor was Ben Gurion any more successful in his efforts to secure American weapons. The United States suspected that if it were to agree to supply Israel with weapons, the Arab states would immediately turn to the Soviet Union and ask for more and better weapons. The result would be an ever-spiraling and destabilizing arms race. The United States also feared that American intervention, of any kind, on Israel's side might lead to a dangerous polarization of the Middle East. Were a situation to develop whereby the United States furnished Israel with arms and the Soviet Union supplied arms to Egypt, friction, if not open conflict, between the two superpowers was bound to ensue. Accordingly, the United States stuck to the 1950 declaration not to supply arms to any of the rival sides in the Middle East. The most they were willing to do was to turn a blind eye to the sale of French arms, and from 1960 onward, British arms to Israel.

Under President Kennedy, American policy toward Israel underwent a fundamental change. January 1961 marked the beginning of a new era in American-Israeli relations.[99] It was symbolized by U.S. readiness to supply Israel with Hawk ground-to-surface missiles. In agreeing to the sale, the United States had deliberately abandoned the 1950 declaration, at least in spirit. The Israelis were jubilant. They had finally managed to close a high-level weapons deal with the Americans, something they had failed to do since 1948. Admittedly, Hawk missiles were categorized as defensive weapons, but the Israeli government believed that the deal established an important precedent for the future. The deal, as it rightly believed, signified a reversal of the American policy on supplying Israel with arms and military equipment.[100]

Kennedy also promised Israel that the United States would come to its assistance were it to fall victim to an Arab attack. In a meeting with Golda Meir, at the end of 1962, Kennedy affirmed that "the United States has a special relationship with Israel in the Middle East really comparable only to that which it has with Britain.... It is quite clear that in case of invasion, the United States would come to the support of Israel. We have the capacity and it is growing."[101] This was unprecedented. Until now, no American president had been willing to guarantee Israel's 1949 borders. Nor was this a careless slip of the tongue, as American officials reiterated Kennedy's pledge, both publicly and privately. They made a special point of underlining the presence of the Sixth Fleet in the Mediterranean, which would enable the United States to help Israel at all times.[102] All this was music to Israel's ears.

What had provoked this sudden change of heart? There was, of course, President's Kennedy natural sympathy with Israel. Internal politics and the desire to secure the Jewish vote also, no doubt, played their part. In addition, the American administration was increasingly troubled by the Soviet Union's rapid penetration of the Middle East. It was especially worried about the Soviet Union's growing ties with Egypt, not the least as its own relationship with Egypt was becoming increasingly shaky. Indeed, by 1962, tension between the United States and Egypt had reached new heights.

The Americans considered the increase of Soviet influence and the rise in Egyptian-American tension as constituting two sides of the same coin. Owing to the massive injection of Soviet arms, Egypt had become the spearhead of Soviet expansion in the Middle East—an expansion that took place largely at the expense of the West. In addition, Egypt's acquisition of massive quantities of Soviet weapons created a regional arms imbalance, with Israel the loser. Nor was the United States happy with Egypt's involvement in Yemen and efforts to subvert and depose other conservative Arab regimes.[103] What the United States found particularly galling was that although Egypt enjoyed American, as well as Soviet, economic aid, this seemed to have little or no effect on Nasser's subversive policies. In sum, Egypt was clearly a threat to American and Western interests in the Middle East. The Americans believed Israel was ideally placed to check Soviet and Egyptian ambitions and deter the latter from embarking upon a war. In other words, by helping Israel, the United States would be serving American and Western interests.

It is likely that it was the U.S. fear that Israel was on the verge of producing an atomic bomb that in the final count persuaded it to establish a special relationship with Israel.[104] One of the principal issues on Kennedy's foreign policy agenda was nuclear nonproliferation. Kennedy regarded the promotion of nonproliferation as a strong moral duty. It was also one of the U.S. principal national interests. Accordingly, Kennedy personally devoted much of his time and effort to the cause of nuclear nonproliferation.

Within days of assuming office, Kennedy began to press Israel to open its nuclear plant in Dimona for inspection. Despite bringing his own weight to bear on the issue, Kennedy's appeals met with little success. In 1960, the United States had discovered, to its horror, that Israel had finished work on the plant. To its mind, the Kennedy administration now faced the dreadful possibility that Israel might manufacture a bomb and use it to adopt a tougher policy toward the Arabs.[105] No less worrying was the question of how Nasser would react. Nasser had declared, on countless occasions, that Egypt would regard Israel's acquisition of a bomb as just cause for war. At best, the Americans thought, Egypt would, as Nasser had warned, take preemptive action against the plant—which he considered to be the center of Israeli aggression—before it could be turned against Egypt.[106] At worst, war would erupt. No wonder the Americans were alarmed.

Israel exploited the administration's fears in order to procure even closer American-Israeli relations. It assumed, correctly, that the United States would be more than willing to meet Israel's security needs, in the hope of that Israel, in return, would not develop nuclear weapons. Indeed, the sudden eagerness of the United States to supply Israel with sophisticated weapon systems was largely driven by its desire to put a stop to the manufacture of Israeli nuclear weapons. Israel also hoped that, by the same token, the United States would grant it a long coveted public guarantee. When in April 1963 the agreement announcing a union between Egypt, Syria and Iraq became public, Israel promptly renewed its request for an American guarantee.[107] Its hopes were quickly dashed as the United States, who still regarded a guarantee as inimical to Israeli and Western interests, refused its suit. The question of arms supply, however, was another matter altogether, and there was no longer any doubt that the United States would furnish and continue to furnish Israel with weapons.

At the end of 1963, an Israeli mission, headed by Deputy Chief of Staff Yitzhak Rabin, arrived in the United States to hold talks with American National Security Adviser Robert Komer. Most of their time was spent discussing the danger of Egypt developing, with the help of German scientists, ground-to-ground missile systems. Also on the agenda was Israel's military shopping list. Among other things, Israel asked for modern American tanks, which it needed to replace the Israeli Defence Force's (IDF) antiquated Sherman and British tanks and thus enable it to counter Egypt's fleet of advanced Soviet manufactured tanks.[108] Israel's request was granted, though not immediately. It took another change of president before the United States would consider selling Israel offensive weapons.

On November 22, 1963, President Kennedy was assassinated in Dallas, Texas. He was succeeded by Lyndon Baines Johnson, and under President Johnson, American arms policy underwent a further modification. The Johnson administration was willing to equip Israel with offensive as well as defensive weapons. Accordingly, by the end of 1964, the United States was supplying Israel with modern tanks. In 1966, following another arms deal, Israel acquired advanced American aircraft. Having first agreed to sell Israel missiles, then tanks and finally aircraft, the United States was well along the way to becoming Israel's chief weapons supplier.

It is worth noting, that despite U.S. generous arms policy and its, albeit shadowy, commitment to Israel's existence, Israel, nevertheless, managed to preserve its nuclear option. In other words, Israel had its cake and ate it. With no explicit American guarantee, Israel refused to give the United States extensive inspection powers over its nuclear industry. It refused to grant the Americans free and full access to the Dimona plant. At the same time, aware of the U.S. commitment to the principle of nonproliferation, and not wishing to unduly irritate it, Israel took several measures to appease the Americans and allay their fears. It announced that the plant in Dimona was intended for peaceful use only. Occasionally, it would permit American inspectors into the plant. It was even willing to sign an agreement banning nuclear testing in the Middle East. Finally, it assured the United States that Israel would not be the first to introduce nuclear weapons into the Middle East.[109]

With the American arms market finally open to it, Israel had plenty of room to maneuver and considerable flexibility as far as the acquisition of weapons was concerned. Unlike Egypt, who was almost wholly dependent on the Soviet Union for arms, Israel, from 1960 onward, could look to all three Western Powers to supply its needs. France stood by its commitment to furnish Israel with Mirage fighter jets; Britain equipped Israel with submarines, tanks and a myriad of military and naval equipment; while in 1962, the United States began providing Israel with Hawk missiles, then tanks and finally aircraft.

Britain was troubled by the ever-growing number of arms streaming into the Middle East. It had little doubt that the arms race, with both sides acquiring tremendous military power, would eventually shatter the stability it held so dear. To its mind, the prime culprit, responsible for the arms race, was the Soviet Union. Not that Britain entirely absolved its American ally from its share in creating this dangerous and increasingly intractable problem. The U.S. decision to sell Israel Hawk missiles had, it thought, greatly accelerated the arms race. "It is a pity," remarked Lord Home, Britain's foreign secretary, that "they risk stirring up the Middle East just as it seemed comparatively quiet."[110] But was it possible to check, let alone reduce the massive amount of arms now pouring into the Middle East?

The United States was certainly willing to explore ways of bringing the arms race to end.[111] But it was extremely doubtful, Britain thought, that the Soviet Union would follow suit. The Soviet Union, bent on expansion, would use any and all means to expel the West from its Middle East strongholds. Supplying the

Arab states with weapons, at low prices and on long-term credit, had proved a very effective way to increase and consolidate Soviet influence in the region. By furnishing Egypt and the Arab states with weapons, by providing them with diplomatic support, the Soviets quadrupled their influence in the Arab world and undermined Western interests to boot. There was plainly no reason for them to abandon this highly profitable policy.

Britain was also mindful of the effect of the Sino-Soviet conflict on Soviet policy. Intense competition with the Chinese over the leadership of the communist world had forced the Soviets to adopt a much more aggressive and uncompromising anti-imperialist policy. The Soviet Union knew that if it showed even the slightest sign that it was considering the possibility of discussing the reduction of arms to the Middle East, the Chinese would be quick to pounce and accuse them of conspiring with the West at the expense of the developing countries.

Yet, even if, by some chance, the Soviet Union were to agree to discuss the arms race, the price it would demand would be far too high. Britain took it for granted that the Soviets would be willing to discuss the arms race only at the expense of Western interests—only if, for example, the West would negotiate and make concessions over its bases in the Middle East and the activities of CENTO alliance. Finally, the British thought that an approach to the Soviet Union would prove counterproductive not simply because it would probably be rejected, but because the Soviet Union would almost certainly inform the Arabs of the West's desire to limit the supply of arms to the region, with the explicit intention of creating further bad blood between the two.[112]

The arms race appeared to be here to stay, with the Middle East countries feverishly hoarding more and more modern weapons. Since the end of the Suez War, Israel and the Arab states had acquired huge quantities of high-grade weapons and military equipment. Israel was determined to secure sufficient military power to deter the Arab states and bring a war, should one erupt, to a speedy and decisive end. Egypt sought first to establish a military balance with Israel, and eventually to acquire enough military force to allow it to launch a successful war against Israel. A vicious circle was formed, in which the acquisition of modern weapons by one side ensured that the other would not only do the same, but also strive to outdo its rival.[113] In the meantime, the Soviet Union was loath to abandon its chief means to garner influence in the Arab world: the supply of weapons and more weapons. The Western powers, and above all the United States, were equally loath to let Israel's military potential fall behind that of the Arab states. All this generated an ever-spiraling arms race from which there was, apparently, no escape.

There is little doubt the copious amounts and huge variety of weapons, plus the diplomatic support which Israel and the Arab states received from their respective patrons, increased their sense of security and self-confidence. Nevertheless, the arms race apart, the Middle East, as a whole, remained during these years relatively quiescent. Then, in late 1963, the water dispute burst onto the stage, shattering the region's fragile stability.

THE WATER DISPUTE

The water dispute between Israel and the Arab states centered on the question of who could exploit the waters of the Jordan River and to what extent. The Jordan River is fed by three rivers: the Hasbani, in Lebanon; the Banias, in Syria and the Dan, which runs through both Syria and Israel. The Jordan River itself runs the length of Israel's eastern boundary, forming the 16-mile long border between Israel and Jordan. In the north, it passes through the demilitarized zone and flows into Lake Tiberias. From there, it proceeds southward, where it is joined by two more rivers, the Yarmuk, which originates in Syria, and the Al Zarqa River in Jordan. At this point, it crosses over into Jordan and flows into the Dead Sea.

After the 1948 War, the Reconciliation Commission, charged in 1949 with resolving the various questions that divided Israel and the Arab states, as well as tackling the region's economic problems, devoted some of its time to considering how best to exploit the Jordan River. To this end, the Commission set up a Survey Commission. Its dual task was to suggest how to improve the local economies and to come up with a plan for the equitable apportionment of the region's water resources. Both these issues were closely connected, and it was thought that once resolved the huge number of the refugees, currently dependent on the United Nations welfare and relief organization, would be able to settle permanently in their camps. The Survey Commission failed in both tasks. It proved unable to devise a large-scale regional development program or to formulate a rudimentary water distribution system. The reason? The local governments, without exception, refused to cooperate with the Commission or with each other on these issues.[114]

Both before and after the establishment of the state in 1948, Israel had had plans to utilize the Jordan River for irrigation purposes.[115] It soon began to explore ways to exploit the Jordan River independently. In 1952, it set up a government corporation under the name: "Water Planning for Israel." The corporation began to draw up a master plan for the development of Israel's water economy, including a project designed to channel the waters of the Jordan River southward to the Negev Desert. The plan was considered imperative to Israel's future development as without water the Negev would stagnate and perhaps even perish. On the other hand, water, as Ben Gurion proclaimed, would allow the desert to flourish, its land could be farmed, settlements could be established, immigrants absorbed and industry developed. Without water, not only would the Negev languish, but also Israel would be forced to reduce immigration and possibly even restrict the natural expansion of its indigenous population.

The Water Planning for Israel corporation also suggested that Israel dig a canal north of Lake Tiberias, which would run parallel to the Jordan River. This would allow Israel to channel water to the lake and, at the same time, to exploit the difference in the water levels between the canal and Lake Tiberias to generate cheap electric power. In September 1953, with its plans in place, Israel started to construct the National Water Carrier. It began work at a point north of Lake Tiberias in Gisr Banat Yaacub, which lay bang in the center of the demilitarized zone.[116]

Not that Israel thought this a problem. As far as it was concerned, the demilitarized zone was sovereign Israeli territory. Moreover, as the project was of a purely civilian nature, designed to serve Israel's economic needs, it no way contravened the cease-fire accords. Syria took a very different view of things. No sooner had Israel began work on the project, than Syria lodged a complaint with General Benike, the Danish chief of the United Nations Truce Supervision Organization, to the effect that Israel was violating the cease-fire agreements. Moreover, Syria claimed, by diverting the waters of the Jordan River southward, Israel would reduce the amount of water in the River and increase the salt levels of what little water remained. Israel was also, Syria accused, infringing on the rights of the Arabs who owned land in the demilitarized zone and preventing those Syrians living along the banks of the river from irrigating their land. Finally, Syria charged that the project was the first step toward an Israeli military takeover of the zone, and Syria demanded that all work on Israeli project cease immediately. There is little doubt that its long list of list of specific objections apart, Syrian opposition to the project stemmed chiefly from its, and the Arab world's, desire to thwart any measure designed to develop and strengthen the state of Israel.

General Benike sided with the Syrians. He believed that, regardless of the question of the water project itself, the mere presence of Israel in the demilitarized zone would give it an unfair strategic advantage over Syria. Benike ordered Israel to stop, at once, all work on the National Water Carrier. Israel refused, and Syria, furious, turned to the Security Council, lodging an official complaint against Israel on October 16, 1963.[117]

The United States backed General Benike, less because it was persuaded by his arguments, and more because it was afraid that the Israeli diversion project and a subsequent clash between Israel and Syria would threaten its own plan for apportioning the waters of the Jordan River. John Foster Dulles, the American secretary of state, warned Israel that the U.S. government would delay the forthcoming $50 million grant Israel was supposed to receive until Israel obeyed General Benike's orders and called off the project. It was a powerful and persuasive threat. In straitened economic circumstances, Israel, which had just adopted an austerity policy, badly needed the $50 million, as without the money its economy would seriously falter, if not break down.[118] Ben Gurion was forced to back down and announce that work in the demilitarization zone would cease, at least until the Security Council reached a decision.

In the Security Council, the United States, Britain and France tabled a moderate, and to their mind, balanced proposal to resolve the dispute. The chief of the United Nations Truce Supervision Organization was to be given the authority to explore all possible solutions to the dispute and mediate between the rival sides. He was also to be empowered to take all measures necessary to enforce a just compromise, which served the interests of all parties. The Soviet Union promptly vetoed the proposal. This was the first time that the Soviet Union had exercised its right of veto in connection to the Middle East.[119] The Soviet veto, together with Dulles's threat to postpone the American grant, put an end to Israel's plans to begin the diversion of the Jordan River at Gisr Banat Yaacub. For the time being, Israel's water plans were put on hold.

The United States, unhappy at the Soviet veto, was not content to leave matters as they stood. It was simply too dangerous to leave the question of who could and to what extent exploit the Jordan River, and, therefore, consequential regional development hanging in the air. In addition, the United States hoped itself to promote regional and individual economic projects, which would help stabilize the Middle East and establish closer ties between it and the West. These projects would also, it hoped, reduce the tension between Israel and the Arab states and perhaps even resolve the Arab-Israeli conflict.[120] Furthermore, the Americans believed that an equitable water distribution scheme would help resolve the increasingly dismal refugee problem. For the past five years, the Palestinian refugees had been living in abject poverty in temporary refugee camps. They subsisted mainly on United Nations's handouts, most of which came from the United States. Congress, unhappy at the financial burden posed by the refugees, had long been demanding that a solution be found to the problem. In 1953, the Eisenhower administration bent to congressional pressure and appointed businessman Erik Johnston as special ambassador for water to the Middle East. Johnston's task was to devise a plan for the fair distribution of the Jordan River's waters and lay the groundwork for regional development projects.

Between 1953–1955, Johnston visited the Middle East four times. He talked to all the countries involved in the dispute and listened closely to their concerns. Having done that, he went home and taking into account Israel's relationship with its neighbors, the amount of agricultural land owned by each of the riparian states and the total amount of water available, came up with the Johnston Plan. According to the Plan, Israel would receive over 38 percent of the river's water. The remainder would be apportioned among the Arab states, with Jordan receiving the largest share.[121] His plan, equitable and fair, would also, Johnston hoped, engender some limited cooperation between Israel and its Arab neighbors.

The Israeli Cabinet examined Johnston's proposals, and concluding that they met Israel's water needs, approved the plan in July 1955. Nasser did not endorse the plan, but neither did he reject it out of hand. The Egyptian president had met Johnston, in the course of the latter's visits to the region and discussed with him the problem of water distribution, and, unlike Syria, he adopted and promoted a moderate view on the subject. Specifically, Nasser thought that the Johnston proposals could help the Arab states in their conflict with Israel and resolve the Palestinian refugee problem. The Arab League's Technical Committee, which had been set up as a result of the Johnston Mission, accepted the plan provisionally, but asked for more time to examine its political aspects. In October

1955, the Arab League rejected the plan. It did so purely on political grounds, in the belief that sanctioning the plan was tantamount to recognizing the state of Israel and renouncing the Palestinians' right to return to home.[122]

With tension in the region increasing, any hope the United States might have had of discussing the water issue on the basis of the Johnston proposals quickly evaporated. The Israeli raid on the Gaza Strip, in February 1955, the 1955 Czech arms deal and the general escalation along the borders in 1956, all combined to scotch the Johnston Plan. Moreover, having rejected the Johnston Plan, the Arab states continued to object to any unilateral Israeli plan to divert the Jordan River. They made their position on the subject clear to the United Nations's secretary general, Dag Hammerskjold, when he visited the Middle East in May-April 1956.[123]

The Johnston Plan did not, however, disappear without a trace. Despite being rejected by the Arab states, the plan, in practice, did provide the basis for the apportionment of the Jordan River's water between Israel and Jordan. The two countries tacitly agreed that neither would take more water from the river than had been allotted them by the Johnston Plan. For the next several years, both abided by this unspoken agreement. The Johnston Plan also formed the basis of U.S. water policy in the forthcoming years. The United States promised that any country, which acted in accordance with the Johnston Plan and limited itself to the quotas determined by the Johnston Plan, would receive American support and aid. Jordan and Israel were the first to benefit from this and to receive help from the United States in carrying out their respective water projects.[124]

After Suez, Israel and Jordan had each embarked upon ambitious water development schemes. In August 1958, Jordan, with American assistance, began to build the Ghore Canal. The canal would channel water from the Yarmuk and, running alongside the eastern bank of the Jordan River, allow Jordan to irrigate about 30,000 acres of land. Israel, inspired or perhaps provoked by the Jordanian project, renewed its plans to divert the Jordan River southward. In truth, Israel would probably have embarked on this project regardless of the Jordanian scheme. It urgently needed the water to build new settlements, to absorb future immigration and to redistribute its current population throughout the country in a more rational manner.

When authorizing the plan, Ben Gurion took into account the new U.S. policy on water. He knew that if Israel wanted American financial backing, its water project must conform to the Johnston Plan. Furthermore, he was aware, based on past experience, that the United States would oppose any project that utilized any portion of the river that ran through the demilitarized zone. With these two points in mind, the Israeli government decided, despite the expense involved, to relocate the diversion project from Gisr Banat Yaacub to a point south of Lake Tiberias, which was under undisputed Israeli sovereignty. It also promised to stay within the bounds of the Johnston Plan's water quotas. As a result, in 1959, Israel was the happy recipient of $50 million to help it fund its new water diversion project.[125]

American backing for the Israeli water project was both welcome and necessary, though Ben Gurion would, nevertheless, still have liked to reach an agreement on the distribution of water with Israel's Arab neighbors. But, with "Arab co-operation clearly not forthcoming," Ben Gurion acknowledged that Israel had no choice but "to do its part, taking only the more or less agreed upon quota of water." Moshe Dayan, Israel's former chief of staff, was less diplomatic. In an electioneering meeting, he warned that "if the Arabs will not co-operate in solving the problem of the Jordan waters, we will do what we did in the Straits of Eilat and take the water by force." In short, Israel was resolved to divert and exploit the Jordan River with or without Arab consent.[126]

In 1959, word that the Israelis were busy laying down pipes to channel water from the Jordan River to the Negev Desert began to slowly filter through. The Arab response to this news was a mixture of rage, confusion and bewilderment, compounded by misinformation and misrepresentation. They were certain, for instance, that Israel was already on the verge of completing the National Water Carrier, and had actually begun the process of pumping water from the demilitarized zone. Israel, they were quick to accuse, was acting contrary both to the cease-fire agreements and the 1953 Security Council resolution.[127] They denounced the Israeli diversion as an act of overt aggression. It was also, they lamented, a calamity equal to the Jewish conquest of Arab Palestine in 1948.[128] The diversion would deny Jordan the water it required for its survival. It would enable Israel to absorb a vast number of Jewish immigrants—4 million was the number mentioned—enhancing Israel's military, demographic and economic power. As a result, Israel would be tempted to make further conquests at Arab expense. All in all the diversion scheme posed a serious threat to Arab security. There were also, the Arab states maintained, humanitarian considerations. Increased Jewish immigration, they argued, would diminish any chance the Palestinian refugees had of returning home, for the simple reason that their lands would be used to build settlements for the newly arrived immigrants.

The Arabs pronounced the National Water Carrier an unequivocal and mistakable threat to the Arab nation. No country, they asserted, Israel included, has the right to unilaterally divert the Jordan River in a manner that might cause serious harm to its neighbors. Nor did Israel have the legal right to carry out a project that would permanently change the layout of the land allocated to the Palestinian State in the November 1947 partition plan.[129] In view of the above, the Arab states concluded, they had every right to defend themselves against this act of palpable aggression. To terminate the Israeli diversion, even by force, was, they insisted, no more than an act of legitimate self-defense. The Arab states would, they warned, take immediate steps, both individually and collectively, to thwart the Israeli plans and exploit the Jordan River for their own, and Palestinian, benefit.[130]

Unfortunately for them, none of the Arab states had a plan, military or otherwise, that they could put into action, once Israel actually began to divert the Jordan River. In truth, they were too busy quarreling among themselves to devote much time to Israel's diversion project, or tackle it in any constructive manner. The upshot was that, paradoxically, the water issue soon became another source of inter-Arab strife. The Arabs states accused each other of vacillation and impotence in face of the Israeli threat, with Jordan and Lebanon leading this chorus of mutual recrimination.[131] As both countries enjoyed close ties with the West and were, as a result, often the victims of vicious attacks from the more radical Arab states, it is very likely that their violent reaction was an attempt to preempt any charges of weakness and laxity on their part.

Jordan, outraged, damned the Israeli project. King Hussein underlined the concrete dangers arising from Israel's effort to divert the river's water to the Negev. He enjoined the Arab states to examine the issue very carefully and adopt a common policy in response. Lebanon, breathing fire and brimstone, went even further. It suggested that the Arab states sabotage the Israeli project by diverting the Jordan River at its source. It even began raising money to fund such a scheme.[132] The idea of diverting the Jordan River's headwaters was not a new one. Rashid Karami, the Lebanese prime minister, had mentioned the possibility, once before, during his talks with Eric Johnston in 1955.

By adopting an overtly aggressive stance, Jordan and Lebanon sought to enhance their standing within the Arab world. They also hoped to avoid being pilloried by the radical Arab states, for being willing, ostensibly, to accept the Israeli project and even reach an agreement with Israel over the distribution of water. As it happens, however, Hussein, for all his ranting and raving, was interested precisely in such an agreement. In 1959, during a conversation with Harold Macmillan in London, Hussein agreed that the only viable solution to the problem of the Jordan River was an agreement between all interested parties. He then added that, to his mind, the Johnston proposals offered a fair and equitable solution to the dispute.[133]

Belligerent and resolute declarations were all very well, but the Arab states had to decide what concrete steps to take in response to the Israeli diversion project. Once they realized that they had jumped the gun, that Israel was not working in the demilitarized zone and that the National Water Carrier would be completed only toward the end of 1963 or beginning of 1964, they settled down to devise a plan of action. They considered two courses of action: a military response and a counterdiversion scheme to divert the Jordan River at its source.

The Arab League immediately reactivated the Technical Committee, established in 1954 during the Johnston talks. In November 1960, the Committee, having examined the various aspects of the water problem, presented its recommendations. It advised the Arab states to begin to divert the Jordan River's headwaters, at once. It also made some practical suggestions to this end, including building a dam on the Hasbani River and digging a canal to channel the water thus accumulated to the Litani River. It further proposed to divert the Banias River southward in order to irrigate the land that lay between it and the Yarmuk River. It suggested that Jordan erect a reservoir to collect the water of the Yarmuk and complete the Ghore Canal project as soon as possible.[134]

The Arab states' chiefs of staff considered the military aspects of the affair. They recommended strengthening the Arab armies, so as to enable them to take common action against Israel. They also advised the Arab states to set up, forthwith, a Unified Arab Military Command, which would have authority over all the Arab states's armies.[135] The League Council, composed of the Arab states's defense ministers, foreign ministers and chiefs of staff, endorsed both the Technical Committee and the chiefs of staff's recommendations. It went even further and put forward a military plan of its own designed to prevent Israel from diverting the Jordan River by force.[136]

Impressive as they were, these recommendations were not put into effect. Other than making some very loud and very aggressive noises the Arab states did little or nothing to frustrate Israel's water program. Even Syria, who of all the Arab states was the most insistent that the Israeli project must be stopped, and at all costs, did nothing. Syria believed Israel was intent on plundering Arab water and must be prevented from doing so even if this meant recourse to arms. Any other course of action, it asserted, was self-deceiving. Yet, without Egypt, not even Syria, let alone any other Arab state, dared risk a military confrontation with Israel, and Egypt, true to its strategy, would fight only if victory were assured, which at this stage it most assuredly was not. The most Nasser was willing to promise was that if Israel began to divert the Jordan River in the demilitarized zone, Egypt would take the appropriate military measures. Nasser was not quite shirking his responsibilities, as he assumed that in order to complete the National Water Carrier, Israel would eventually have to begin work in the demilitarized zone.[137] This would take a few years, and by then Egypt and its fellow Arab states would be ready for the final showdown.

The disintegration of the Egyptian-Syrian Union in September 1961 deepened the divisions in the Arab world. With the Arab states quarreling among themselves, the League had no choice but to put the water dispute, like so many other issues on its agenda, on hold.[138] Once more the dispute became the subject of some very bitter Arab infighting. Syria, in particular, exploited the water dispute to attack Egypt. It accused Nasser of being weak and timid, impotent in the face of Israeli aggression. Nasser gave as good as he got, blaming Syria for the disintegration of the Arab Union. This, he fulminated, had encouraged Israel to continue its plans to divert the Jordan River. It was, Nasser charged, all Syria's fault.

Although the Israeli government did not disregard or dismiss the Inter-Arab conferences and decisions, it was not particularly worried about them. If the Arab states condemned its diversion plan as an act of aggression similar to that of 1948, Israel regarded the project as a matter of life and death. It pronounced the Jordan River's waters as vital to its existence as blood was to man's—a comparison it would repeat many times in the future.[139] Israel had no doubt that the Arab states' aggressive and hostile response to the project and their determination to thwart it was part of their declared strategy to destroy the state of Israel. Conversely, Israel left no one in doubt whatsoever as to how it would respond should the Arab states attempt to divert the Jordan River at its source or disrupt work being carried out the National Water Carrier. Faced with a flagrant attack on one of Israel's fundamental means of survival, the IDF would not hesitate to use all the means at its disposal to put an end to such malevolent, villainous activity.[140]

Israel also objected to any kind of United Nations intervention, and was unhappy when the secretary general tried to intercede in the affair. Israel was convinced that any discussion of the water dispute in the United Nations would inevitably turn into a general debate of the Arab-Israeli conflict as a whole, including the refugee problem. As a result, nothing would be achieved, other than to delay the construction of the National Water Carrier. This was totally unacceptable, as Israel considered it imperative to complete the project as scheduled at the end of 1963. In any case, Israel deemed the water project as an internal Israeli affair, beyond the UN jurisdiction. It was willing to furnish the United Nations with details of the project, but that was as far as it would go.[141]

The Israeli decision to begin the divergence at a point south of the demilitarized zone, together with its public commitment to observe the Johnston Plan quotas, paid off. It brought Israel, American and, to a lesser extent, British support. In the opinion of the United States, the National Water Carrier project, like the Jordanian Ghore Canal project, would help develop the Middle East. It certainly did not regard the Israeli diversion as detrimental to any of Israel's neighbors. Moreover, in its view, as long as Israel remained within the quotas it had been allotted by the Johnston Plan, it was free to make any use of the water it liked, including diverting it southward to the Negev. American support took the form of helping fund the Israeli project. At the same time, the United States began to canvass the Arab capitals in an effort to persuade the Arab states to reach an agreement on the Jordan River on the basis of the Johnston Plan, and thus prevent the situation in the region from deteriorating any further.[142]

Privately, Britain, too, approved of the Israeli project. But what concerned it above all was how and to what degree the water dispute would effect the region's stability. It rightly assumed that Israel was resolved to divert the waters of the Jordan River. In urgent need of water both to develop the Negev and absorb immigration, Israel would not agree to abandon the project under any circumstances. This was worrying. On the other hand, to give the Israeli government its due, it did take several constructive steps in an effort to prevent the project becoming another source of serious Arab-Israeli friction. It had moved the diversion site southward, despite the expense involved and despite having to abandon its plan to generate cheap electric power. It remained faithful, albeit tacitly, to the Johnston Plan. Most important, It had repeatedly expressed its readiness to discuss the water issue with the Arab states and reach an understanding, even agreement over the allocation of the Jordan River's water.[143]

In contrast to Israel's efforts to accommodate the interests of all concerned, the Arab states, refusing even to discuss the Israeli water project, rejected it out of hand. Furthermore, in Britain's opinion, their objections to the Israeli project lacked all foundation. Israel was not in breach of the cease-fire accords, nor was it acting in defiance of the Security Council's decision of October 1953. Israel could absorb any number of new immigrants within its present borders and had no plans to expand further. Nor was Israel in breach of international law or infringing upon the rights of others. As Britain pointed out, there were no universally accepted principles of international law governing the apportionment of river water between riparian states. In the absence of such principles, the best way to apportion such water was by international agreement. In that no such agreement existed over the Jordan River, and the Arab states consistently refused to negotiate such agreement, the claim that Israel was in breach of international law, was, to say the least, fallacious.

Britain did concede the Arab states one point: The Israeli diversion might effect saliency levels of the river, south of Lake Tiberias. However, it was much too early to assess if and to what degree the saliency levels would rise. Nor was saliency an insurmountable problem. On the contrary, it was one that should it emerge, could be easily resolved.[144]

Britain was quick to realize that for all their belligerent talk and apparently feverish activity—inter-Arab talks, chiefs of staff consultations, League meetings, the meetings of the League's Defence Council and Technical Committee meetings—in practice, the Arab states were doing nothing. Furthermore, their proposal to divert the Jordan River, at its source, was wholly impracticable. Owing to the nature of the local terrain, it was, technically, an incredibly complicated project. To carry it out would prove both difficult and prohibitively expensive, while the amount of water diverted in the end would be minuscule. Then there was the question of Israel's response to the scheme, which would probably be pretty severe and so serve to inhibit the Arab states from carrying out their plans.[145]

All things considered, Britain did not think that the water dispute conflict would undermine the region's stability. It would certainly not provoke a general conflagration. However, as the date for the completion of the Israeli National Water Carrier drew closer, Arab objections became louder and more violent. Syria, for example, demanded vigorous and immediate action against Israel. It insisted that effective steps be taken at once to terminate the water project, a project that threatened the national interests of all the Arab states. Nasser was bid to make good on his promise to institute military measures against Israel. Nasser, however, reluctant to take any kind of step that might spiral into war before the time was ripe, opted for a very different course of action.

NOTES

1. Jackson, *Britain's Triumph and Decline*, p. 136; Gorst, *Suez Crisis*, pp. xi, 151; Darwin, *Britain and Decolonisation*, pp. 223, 227, 280–286.

2. FO 371/170165, Minute by Hood, March 16, 1963; CAB 148/3, Note by Secretaries, October 31, 1963.

3. FO/371/170165, Minute by Hood, March 6, 1963.

4. FO 371/170165, Minute by FO, March 11, 1963; CAB 148/3, Note by Secretaries, October 31, 1963.

5. FO 371/175552, Minute by Crawford, April 13, 1963.

6. CAB 129/120, Memorandum by the FO, March 24, 1965; FO 371/163972, Minute by Stevens, March 26, 1962.

7. FO 371/175552, Minute by Crawford, April 13, 1964; FO 371/163972, Minute by Stevens, March 26, 1962.

8. FO 371/170165, Memorandum by FO, March 15, 1963; Parliamentary Debates, 5th series, vol. 707, cols. 1337–1338, March 3, 1965.

9. El Hussini, *Soviet-Egyptian Relations*, p. 111; Hurewitz, *Middle East Politics*, p. 138.

10. Burns, *Economic Aid*, p. 135; FO 371/170165, Memorandum by the FO, March 15, 1963.

11. FO 371/175550, Minute by Crawford, April 13, 1964.

12. FO 371/170165, Minute by Crawford, February 26, 1963.

13. Gazit, *President Kennedy's Policy*, p.12; Kaufman, *Arab Middle East*, p. 33; see also, Shimoni, *Arab States*, pp. 405, 525.

14. Spiegal, *Arab Israeli Conflict*, p. 101; Burns, ISA, Hez/2/748, Evron to Foreign Minister's Bureau, March 4, 1965.

15. FO 371/170165, Minute by Crawford, February 26, 1963.

16. Gat, *Britain and Italy*, pp. 117–123, 132–139.

17. Smolansky, "Soviet Role," pp. 66–71.

18. Golan, "Soviet Union," p. 285; Sadat, *Search of Identity*, pp. 142–143.

19. Vatikiotis, "Soviet Union," pp. 124–126; Yodfat, *Soviet Union*, p. 40.

20. FO 371/170531, Brief Talking Points, December 3, 1963; FO 371/ Minute by Stevens, March 26, 1962; Abadi, *Britain's Withdrawal*, p. 198.

21. FO 371164, Minute by Crawford, February 26, 1963; FO 371/163971, FO to Damascus, January 31, 1962.

22. ISA Hez/19/4327, Herzog to Israel's representatives, December 31, 1963; Harkabi, "Arab-Israeli Conflict," p. 13.

23. Ibid., p. 22; Yaniv, "Brutal Dialogue," p. 367; Mutawi, *Jordan in the War*, p. 72.

24. *FRUS*, "Near East, 1962–1963," p. 706; FO 371/170154, Minute by Hiller, July 23, 1963; Sela, *Unity within Conflict*, p. 26.

25. FO 371/170527, Minute by Figg, July 18, 1963 and Minute by Morris, November 22, 1963; Nadelman, "Setting the Stage," p. 435.

26. FO 371/150857, Tel Aviv to FO, October 25, 1960.

27. PREM 11/4933, de Zulueto to Prime Minister, November 21, 1961; FO371/170538, Macmillan to Eshkol, August 13, 1963.

28. The military was not a party to these fears. See FO 371/170569, Tel Aviv to FO, July 17, 1963; Ezer Weitzman, Chief of the Israeli Airforce, 1958–1966, Television Debates, June 10, 1997.

29. FO 371/170536, Washington to FO, June 19, 1963 and Tel Aviv to FO, June 21, 1963; FO 371/170531, Exchange of views with the Israeli Ambassador, July 22, 1963; ISA, Hez/4/3395, London, to Foreign Minister's Bureau, December 31, 1963; Gazit, *President Kennedy's Policy*, pp. 20–21; Glassman, *Arms for the Arabs*, pp. 24–25.

30. FO 371/170163, Minute by Crawford, May 16, 1963; El Hussini, *Soviet Egyptian Relations*, p. 112.

31. FO 371/170152, Minute by Morris, October 9, 1963; FO 371/170531, Record of Conversation, October 2, 1963; *FRUS*, "Near East, 1962–1963," pp. 773–775; NA, RG59/3728, Memorandum of Conversation, July 18, 1963.

32. *FRUS*, "Near East, 1962–1963," pp. 276–283, 659–660, 706, 777–778; FO 371/170527, FO to Washington, August 22, 1963; FO 371/170537, Minute by Morris, July 31, 1963; NA, RG59/3728, Ball to Tel Aviv, October 2, 1963; Peres, *David's Sling*, p. 76.

33. FO 371/170154, Minute by Scrivener, April 24, 1963; FO 371/170536, Washington to FO and FO to Tel Aviv, June 19, 1963.

34. FO 371/170164, Washington to FO, May 1963; *Jerusalem Post*, May 9, 1963.

35. FO 371/170520, Tel Aviv to FO, October 11, 1963; FO 371/170527, Minute by Figg, July 18, 1963; Parliamentary Debates, 5th series, vol. 667, May 15, 1963.

36. FO 371/170155, FO to Washington, August 20, 1963; FO 371/170156, Tel Aviv to FO, August 21, 1963 and Amman to FO, August 22, 1963.

37. FO 371/170053, Brief Talking Points, December 3, 1963; FO 371/170537, FO to Tel Aviv, July 22, 1963; Parliamentary Debates, 5th series, vol. 709, cols. 975–1978, April 1, 1965; Wilson, *Chariot of Israel*, p. 334.

The United Nations sent two organizations to the region: the United Nations Truce Supervision Organization (UNTSO) and the Mixed Armistice Commission. UNTSO was established in April 1949 after the 1948 war, at the initiative of the United Nations Security Council. Its task was to superintend the cease-fire accords between Israel and its Arab neighbors. The Mixed Armistice Commission was formed soon after to help UNTSO carry out its duties. The United Nations mediator Ralph Bunche described UNTSO's mission as one of ensuring the fulfillment of the 1949 cease-fire agreements until such time as the two sides either agreed to modify the cease-fire agreements or reached a final peace settlement. Neff, "Israel-Syria," pp. 27–29; Higgins, "The June War," pp. 253–255.

38. PREM 11/4358, Macmillan to Eshkol, August 13, 1963.

39. FO 371/170520, Tel Aviv to FO, September 22, 1963.

40. FO 371/170157, Tel Aviv to FO, June 29, 1963; ISA, Hz/4/3395, London, to Foreign Minister's Bureau, December 31, 1963.

41. FO 371/170527, Minute by Figg, July 18, 1963; FO 371/175552, Minute by Crawford, April 13, 1963.

42. Safran, *Israel*, p. 335.

43. FO 371/150586, Minute by Beith, January 4, 1960; *FRUS*, "Arab-Israeli Dispute, 1957," pp. 282–283; Johnson, *Vantage Point*, pp. 291, 293; Parker, *Politics of Miscalculation*, p. 53; Wilson, *Chariot of Israel*, p. 329.

44. Moore, *Arab-Israeli Conflict*, pp. 1023–1027; Seguev, *Red Sheet*, p. 51.

45. Knesset Debates, vol. 22, March 4, 1957.

46. Parker, *Politics of Miscalculation*, pp. 49, 72; Higgins, "June War," pp. 260–263; Green, *Taking Sides*, p. 196; see also PREM13/1617, New York to FO, May 17, 1967.

47. Khouri, "Policy of Retaliation," p. 435.

48. Yaniv, *Politics and Strategy*, pp. 156–157; Safran, *Israel*, p. 332; Peres, "Dimension of Time," p. 3.

49. The size of the demilitarized area was 65 square kms. It was divided into three zones: the smallest zone of 4 square kms was in the north; the central zone was approximately 28 square kms; the largest zone, located in the southern part of the demilitarized area, was 33 square kms. The cease-fire agreements stipulated that neither side could station armed forces in the three demilitarized zones. For convenience sake, the demilitarized area is referred to throughout the text as the demilitarized zone, unless one of the three subzones is specifically mentioned. See Shalev, *Shadow of Conflict*, p. 79.

50. See the Israeli-Syrian Cease-Fire Agreement, 20, 1949, article 5; Shalev, *Shadow of Conflict*, pp. 349–355.

51. Shalev, *Shadow of Conflict*, pp. 349–355.

52. Ibid., pp. 126–127; Harkabi, "Armistice Agreements," p. 2.

53. Yaniv, "Brutal Dialogue," p. 368.

54. FO 371/170156, Amman to FO, August 22, 1963 and Damascus to FO, August 21, 1963; FO 371/170155, FO to Washington, August 20, 1963; ISA, Hez/5/3395, Rafael to Lourie, May 27, 1962.

55. Nimrod, *Waters of Contradiction*, p. 87; Khouri, "Jordan River," pp. 41–42; Lowi, *Water and Power*, p. 118.

56. Yaniv, "Brutal Dialogue," pp. 368–369; Ma'oz, *Syria and Israel*, p. 73; FO371/151207, New York to FO, February 25, 1960 and Cairo to FO, 22–23 1960; ISA, Hez/3/3296, Herman to Foreign Ministry, February 23, 1960.

57. ISA, Hez/4/3395, London to Jerusalem, August 31, 1963; Khouri, "Policy of Retaliation," p. 435.

58. Burns, *Economic Aid*, p. 122; Kaufman, *Arab Middle East*, p. 132.

59. FO 371/170531, Record of Conversation, October 12, 1963; FO 371/175552, Minute by Crawford, April 13, 1963; Nadelman, "Setting the Stage," pp. 442–443; Spiegel, *Arab-Israeli Conflict*, p. 101.

60. Spiegel, *Arab-Israeli Conflict*, pp. 110–111; Gazit, *President Kennedy's Policy*, pp. 17–19.

61. Little, "Choosing Sides," pp. 150, 153; Gazit, *President Kennedy's Policy*, pp. 20–21.

62. Burns, *Economic Aid*, p. 134; Spiegel, *Arab-Israeli Conflict*, p. 101.

63. Beeri, *Officer Class*, p. 157; Vered, *Coup and War*, pp. 11–27.

64. Kaufman, *Arab Middle East*, pp. 34–35; Hurewitz, *Middle East Politics*, p. 257.

65. Burns, *Economic Aid*, pp. 134–135; Vered, *Coup and War*, p. 250.

66. El Hussini, *Soviet-Egyptian Relations*, p. 122.

67. Ibid., p. 112; Kerr, *Arab Cold War*, p. 127; Sela, *Unity within Conflict*, p. 26.

68. FO 371/170165, Minute by Crawford, February 26, 1963; Little "Choosing Sides," p. 153; Gazit, *President Kennedy's Policy*, pp. 23–24.

69. Haber, *War Will Break Out*, pp. 54, 95; Greenberg, *Defense Budgets and Military Power*, p. 128.

70. FO 371/170520, Tel Aviv to FO, October 11, 1963.

71. FO 371/170517, Tel Aviv to FO, June 21 and July 11, 1963; FO 170518, Tel Aviv to FO, October 29 and November 8, 1963; *Ma'ariv*, July 11, 1963; *Ha'aretz*, 1 September 1963; *Knesset Debates*, 38, October 21, 1963.

72. LaFeber, *America, Russia*, pp. 228–229.

73. FO 371/170537, Tel Aviv to FO, August 8, 1963.

74. Holborn, "Palestinian Arab Refugees," pp. 669–670; *Knesset Debates*, 38, December 2, 1963; *Ha'aretz*, December 3–4, 1963.

75. FO 317/150520, Tel Aviv to FO, October 11, 1963; FO 371/170527, Minute by Figg, July 18, 1963; *FRUS*, "Near East, 1962–1963," p. 661.

76. FO 371/170520, Tel Aviv to FO, October 11, 1963 and FO to Tel Aviv, November 13, 1963.

77. FO 371/170155, Jerusalem to FO, August 21, 1963; FO 371/170156, FO to Washington, August 20, 1963.

78. FO 371/170156, FO to Tel Aviv, August 27, 1963; FO 371/170157, Minute by Morris, August 27, 1963 ; Bhutani, *Israel-Soviet Cold War*, p. 98.

79. FO 371/170531, Brief, Brief by Morris, September 25, 1963 and Brief Talking Points, December 3, 1963.

80. FO 371/170520, Tel Aviv to FO, November 19, 1963; FO 371/170154, Minute by Hiller, July 23, 1963.

81. FO 371/170517, Tel Aviv to FO, June 28, 1963. In May 1963, in a meeting with President Kennedy, Ben Gurion promised that the nuclear plant in Dimona was to be used solely for research and peaceful purposes. See Gazit, *President Kennedy's Policy*, p. 39.

82. Seguev, *Israel*, p. 17. On December 18, 1963, Levi Eshkol announced that the compulsory military service in Israel would be shortened from thirty to twenty-six months. The reason behind this decision was chiefly financial. However, the Israeli assessment that there was little or no chance of war erupting in the near future no doubt played a part in the government's decision. See Greenberg, "Military Service," pp. 67–68.

83. Yaniv, *Politics and Strategy*, pp. 142–143; Hurewitz, *Middle East Politics*, pp. 468, 437.

84. Moore, *Arab-Israeli Conflict*, vol. 3, p. 86.

85. Glassman, *Arms for the Arabs*, p. 25; El Hussini, *Soviet Egyptian Relations*, p. 141.

86. Yodfat, *Soviet Union*, pp. 44–45.

87. Glassman, *Arms for the Arabs*, pp. 24–25; Burns, *Economic Aid*, p. 141.

88. Kaufman, *Arab Middle East*, p. 48; Glassman, *Arms for the Arabs*, pp. 25–26.

89. Mangold, *Superpower Intervention*, p. 117; Glassman, *Arms for the Arabs*, pp. 25–26.

90. Yaniv, *Politics and Strategy*, p. 143.

91. Greenberg, *Defence Budgets*, pp. 175–176; Gee, *Mirage*, p. 101.

92. Bar-Siman-Tov, *Israel*, p. 86; Crosbie, *Tacit Alliance*, p. 185; Weizmann, *On Eagles' Wings*, p. 196.

93. Bar-Siman-Tov, *Israel*, pp. 85–86.

94. Gee, *Mirage*, pp. 103–109; Crosbie, *Tacit Alliance*, pp. 54–55; Yaniv, *Continuity and Change*, p. 2.

95. Haber, *War Will Break Out*, p. 56; Crosbie, *Tacit Alliance*, p. 185; Bar-On, "Rise and Fall," pp. 67–68.

96. NA, RG/2356, Memorandum of Conversation, February 25, 1964 and Tel Aviv to SD, April 8, 1964; NA, RG/2346, Memorandum of Conversation, March 4, 1964.

97. Yaniv, *Politics and Strategy*, p. 162; Rabin, *Service Notes*, pp. 125–126; FO371/170527, Minute by Morris and Washington to FO, November 22, 1962; *FRUS*, "Near East, 1962–1963," pp. 773–775, 777–778.

98. Gazit, *President Kennedy's Policy*, pp. 32–33; Mangold, *Superpower Intervention*, p. 144; Alteras, *Eisenhower*, pp. 313–314.

99. Nadelman, "Setting the Stage," p. 435; Schoenbaum, *United States*, p. 131.

100. Gazit, *President Kennedy*, p. 131; Nadelman, "Setting the Stage," p. 439.

101. *FRUS*, "Near East, 1962–1963," pp. 276–283; Cohen, "American Interests," p. 281; Aronson, *Nuclear Weapons*, pp. 272–273.

102. *FRUS*, "Near East, 1962–1963," pp. 781–783.

103. Heikal, *Cairo Documents*, pp. 200–201; Bar-Siman-Tov, *Israel*, p. 88; Little, "Choosing Sides," pp. 153–154.

104. Yaniv, *Politics and Strategy*, p. 171.

105. Cohen, "Battle over Dimona," pp. 100, 118; Cohen, *Israel and the Bomb*, pp. 99–102, 111–112, 158–161; Shalom, "Low Profile," p. 137.

106. Shalom, "Low Profile," p. 138; Cohen, "Cairo, Dimona," p. 192.

107. Nadelman, "Setting the Stage," pp. 141–142. Ben Gurion had raised the question of a U.S. guarantee to Israel, apparently in an attempt to divert the Americans' attention from what was going on in the Dimona plant. See Shalom, "Low Profile," p. 140; Cohen, "Battle over Dimona," p. 121.

108. FO 371/170/170527, Washington to FO and Minute by Morris, November 22, 1963; *FRUS*, "Near East, 1962–1963," pp. 777–778.

109. FO 371/170537, Tel Aviv to FO, August 8, 1963; Cohen, "Battle over Dimona," pp. 111, 115, 120; Little, "Choosing Sides," p. 154.

110. Prem 11/4933, Minute by Home, August 29, 1962.

111. FO 371/170154, Minute by Hiller, July 23, 1963.

112. FO 371/180660, Permanent Under-Secretary's Steering Committee, February, 17, 1965; FO 371/180646, Anglo-French Discussion, July 12, 1965.

113. Yaniv, *Politics and Strategy*, pp. 142–142; Glassman, *Arms for the Arabs*, p. 34; FO 371/170569, Brief by Colonel Yariv, October 31, 1963.

114. Khouri, "Jordan River," p. 35. In December 1949, the United Nations established the Palestine Conciliation Commission; its task was to promote peace between Israel and its Arab neighbors. See Shimoni, *Arab States*, p. 250.

115. Rabinovich, "Conflict over Jordan," p. 863.

116. Saliba, *Jordan River Dispute*, p. 74; Shapland, *Rivers of Discord*, p. 14; Nimrod, *Water of Contradiction*, p. 25.

117. FO 371/175579 Guidance no. 25, January 13, 1964; Shemesh, "Arab Struggle over Water," pp. 110–111; Rabinovich, "Conflict over Jordan," p. 864.

118. Bar-Siman-Tov, "Limits of Economic Sanctions," pp. 426–427; Bar-Siman-Tov, "Power of Economic Sanctions," pp. 46–47.

119. Kelee, *Struggle for Water*, p. 39; Shemesh, "Arab Struggle over Water," p. 11; Shalev, *Shadow of Conflict*, pp. 272–273.

120. Cooly, "War over the Water," p. 11; Khouri, "Jordan River," p. 36; Rabinovich, "Conflict over the Jordan," p. 864.

121. According to the Johnston Plan, Lebanon was to receive 35 cubic meters of water; Jordan, 720 cubic meters; Syria, 132 cubic meters and Israel, approximately 490 cubic meters. See *FRUS*, "Near East, 1962–1963," pp. 770–772; FO 371/151253, Washington to FO, June 15, 1960; FO 371/175574, Guidence no. 25, January 13, 1964; ISA, Her/8/3689, Kollek to Herzog, July 6, 1955; Hillel, *Rivers of Eden*, p. 161; Shapland, *Rivers of Discord*, p. 15; Mustafa, "Arab-Israeli Conflict," pp. 124–136.

122. *FRUS*, "Near East, 1962–1962," p. 764; Lowi, *Water and Power*, pp. 108–110; Nimrod, *Waters of Contradiction*, p. 66.

123. Golan, "Conflict over the Jordan," p. 855.

124. Lowi, *Water and Power*, p. 105; Hillel, *Rivers of Eden*, p. 161; Ma'oz and Inbar, "Conflict over the Waters," p. 50; Nimrod, *Waters of Contradiction*, p. 82.

125. FO 371/142383, Tel Aviv to FO, February 20, 1959 and Washington to FO, December 24, 1959; ISA, Hez/5/3395, London to Jerusalem, April 21, 1962; Oron, *Middle East*, p. 206.

126. *Ha'aretz*, June 9, October 18–19, 1959; Nimrod, "Conflict over the Jordan," p. 5.

127. Shemesh, "Arab Struggle over Water," p. 116.

128. FO 371/164364, Damascus to FO, May 27, 1962; ISA, Hez/5/3395, Lourie to Rafael, February 21, 1962.

129. FO 371/164364, Damascus to FO, February 21,1962; FO 371/164365, FO to Damascus, February 28, 1962; FO 371/151253, Example of Recent UAR Broadcasts, December 2 and 6, 1959; Khouri, "Jordan River," p. 43 and *Arab Israeli*, p. 226; Lowi, *Water and Power*, p. 119.

130. Oron, *Middle East Record*, p. 208; Khouri, "Jordan River," p. 43; Gilbo'a, *Six Years*, p. 25.

131. *LaMerhav,* February 10, 1959.

132. FO 371/151253, Minute by FO, January 25, 1960; FO 371/151245, Beirut to FO, January 16, 1960; *The Times,* January 16, 1960.

133. FO 371/151253, Record of Conversation, December 11, 1959; and Amman to FO, January 4, 1960; Sharett, *Making Policy,* pp. 1208–1210; Rabinovich, "Conflict over the Jordan," p. 866.

134. Lowi, *Water and Power,* p. 119; Nimrod, "Conflict over the Jordan," p. 9.

135. Oron, *Middle East Record,* p. 209; Lowi, *Water and Power,* p. 121.

136. Ma'oz, *Syria and Israel,* pp. 74–75; Nimrod, "Conflict over the Jordan," pp. 9–10; Sela, *Unity within Conflict,* p. 27.

137. Nimrod, *Waters of Contradiction,* pp. 90–91; Ma'oz, *Syria and Israel,* p. 74.

138. Shemesh, "Arab Struggle over Water," p. 127.

139. FO 371/142383, Tel Aviv to FO, May 11, 1959; Lowi, *Water and Power,* pp. 136–144.

140. FO 371/151255, Tel Aviv to FO, May 24, 1962; FO 371 164365, Tel Aviv to FO, February 27, 1962; *Ha'aretz,* January 1960, p. 21.

141. FO 371/151255, Tel Aviv to FO, May 24, 1960.

142. FO 371/142383, Ormsby-Gore to Prime Minister, May 19, 1959; and Minute by Beith, May 14, 1959; FO 371/151253, Minute by Tesh, January 15, 1960; FO 371/164365, Minute by Smart, February 27, 1962; FO 371 164368, Washington to FO, September 12, 1962.

143. FO 371/142382, Minute by Beith, May 14, 1959; FO 371/164365, FO to Damascus, February 28, 1962.

144. FO 371/151254, FO to Washington, February 3, 1960; FO 371/164365, FO to Damascus, February 28, 1962.

145. FO 317/151253, Minute by Tesh, January 15, 1960; FO 371/164365, Minute by Hiller, February 26, 1962.

2

Britain in the Middle
The Arab-Israeli Water Dispute Escalates

THE ARAB WORLD RESPONDS

By the end of 1963, Israel was busy working on the final stages of the National Water Carrier. As a result, after four years of little more than vain and fruitless discussions, the Arab states suddenly became much more active and businesslike. This burst of belligerent activism owed much to the dissension and strife that characterized the Arab world at the time, including, most particularly, the ambiguous love-hate relationship between Egypt and Syria and the conflict between these two "progressive" regimes and the conservative Arab states.

Of all the Arab states, Syria's response to the news that Israel was on the verge of completing its diversion project was the most extreme. The Syrian Ba'ath regime threatened to go to war to liquidate the project, even if it would have to do so alone. Salah al Bitar, Syria's prime minister, recapitulated all the dangers to the Arab nation arising from the Israeli diversion. He reminded his fellow Arabs that once Israel began to channel water to the Negev, it would, in all likelihood, double its population from 2.5 to 5 million. Then, stronger and more aggressive than ever, Israel would seek to expand at the expense of the Arab states. Only a violent and uncompromising campaign, al Bitar insisted, could stop Israel from realizing its evil dream of a greater Israel.[1] There was, however, an additional, ulterior motive behind Syria's advocacy of this aggressive, warlike policy. The Ba'ath regime hoped to exploit the water dispute to promote its own radical ideology. It believed that forceful action against the Israeli diversion might engender a revolutionary situation in the Middle East, setting the stage for a general revolution throughout the Arab world.[2]

Fearing that Syria would make good its threats, the Arab League decided to convene the League's Defence Council. First, however, it was thought advisable to hold a preliminary meeting of the Chiefs of Staff Committee. The Committee met between December 7 and 11, 1963, and while it was sitting, Egypt announced that it had no intention, at present, of embarking upon a military campaign against Israel.[3] This announcement possibly influenced on the chiefs of staff's decision to reject al Bitar's demand that the Arab states declare war on

Israel the moment it began to divert the Jordan River. The decision was unanimous. All favored it, including the Syrian chief of staff, Yusuf Shakour, who confessed to his colleagues that, in truth, Syria was incapable of any kind of military action. He further admitted that Syria could not even risk diverting the waters of the Banias River, which ran through in its own territory, as it knew that Israel would probably, as a result, attack it, and Syria would be powerless to respond.[4] The meeting, like many of its predecessors, ended with no practical plan for action.

The chiefs of staff did, however, make several recommendations. These were almost identical to those submitted at the onset of the dispute in the beginning of the 1960's and included a proposal to establish a Unified Arab Military Command or special military headquarters and to set up a special organization to execute the counterdiversion scheme. In addition, the committee suggested that the Arab states begin an extensive propaganda campaign, which would underline the grave damage the Israeli diversion would cause Arab interests. Disappointed at the outcome of the chiefs of staff meeting, Syria began a bitter propaganda campaign of its own against Egypt. Syria fulminated that Egypt was guilty of reneging on its commitment to go to war the moment Israel began to divert the Jordan River. It was thanks to Egypt's desertion of the Arab cause, Syria accused, that Israel felt itself free to pursue its aggressive policies. The fact that Egypt was shunning a military campaign had betrayed the interests of the Arab world.[5]

In point of fact, Egypt had no quarrel with Syria's estimate of the dangers accruing from the Israeli diversion. It, too, believed that once the National Water Carrier was put into operation, Israel, having acquired sufficient military strength and economic power, would be tempted to expand further at Arab expense. The Egyptian newspapers belabored this point, warning that the development of the Negev was only the first stage of an Israeli plan to conquer the entire Sinai Peninsula.[6] Nevertheless, Egypt was not willing to risk a military confrontation with Israel—not when it had thousands of soldiers bogged down in Yemen fighting in what increasingly appeared to be a futile war that was draining the Egyptian economy as well. What is more, Egypt was certain that if the Arab states were to declare war on Israel, the Americans and British would be sure to intervene on Israel's side. Worse, the United States would probably reduce, if not terminate, its much needed financial aid to Egypt.

Furious at the Syrian onslaught, Egypt went on the offensive. It attacked Syria, Saudi Arabia and Jordan, accusing them all of wanting to embroil Egypt in a senseless war. The weekly newspaper *Ruz al Yusuf* weighed in and, full of contempt, castigated "the propaganda trumpeted by these powers. They demand that Egypt crush Israel,""... but in truth all they want is to entangle Egypt in a war, after which they would stab it in the back and abandon it to its fate.... Egypt, however, would not fall into this, murderous trap. It knows when to and how to destroy the state of Israel."[7] An impressive counterattack, it was nevertheless a confession that Egypt, just as Syria claimed, could not fulfill its commitments.

In a speech given at Port Said, on September 23, 1963, Nasser sought to clarify Egypt's position. He declared that Egypt was ready to stand by it obligations, but only when the time was ripe. He explained that the water dispute could not be treated in isolation from the problem of Palestine as a whole. And, he emphasized, "noisy, belligerent, irresponsible and ultimately empty statements would no more solve the problem of Palestine today then [*sic*] they did in 1948. We cannot allow another 1948, which is why we refuse to dissemble. What we admit privately to ourselves and know to be true, we shall also acknowledge publicly. If we can fight we shall say so. If we cannot fight we shall say so and postpone the campaign." Nasser concluded on a positive, upbeat note that Egypt would "fulfil its commitments to the very end."[8]

Unwilling to see Egypt reviled and belittled as too weak and too cowardly to confront Israel, Nasser called upon the Arab states to rise above their various differences and disagreements and get together to decide jointly what steps should be taken to counter the Israeli diversion. To this end, he invited the heads of the Arab states to a summit conference in Cairo. Nasser announced he was personally willing to sit around the conference table and discuss the matter with the kings of Saudi Arabia and Jordan. By convoking a summit conference, Nasser sought not only to diffuse the Arab attack on Egypt, but also to impose Egypt's (i.e., his) strategy upon the Arab leaders. He would use the summit conference to prove to them that without Egypt's participation war was out of the question.

All the Arab states, without exception, accepted the Egyptian president's invitation. Those who had been victims of Egyptian censure and attacks interpreted the invitation and the summit as an endorsement of their regimes and, in a sense, they were right. If not quite an endorsement, Nasser's decision to convene a summit conference did mark the bankruptcy of his "Unity of Purpose" doctrine. Until then, Egypt had waged an uncompromising war against Jordan and Saudi Arabia, seeking to destroy their conservative, traditional Arab regimes. Now Nasser was prepared to meet with the kings of these two countries—men he had repeatedly abused and vilified for their links with the Western imperialist powers. It was, however one looks at it, an admission of failure.

The Cairo Summit Conference opened on January 13, 1964. It lasted four days, until January 17. The summit conference was, without doubt, one of the more momentous events in the history of the Arab world. All thirteen members of the Arab League took part, including Algeria, Morocco, Syria, Lebanon, Kuwait and Yemen. Nasser devoted most of his time to clearing the air and reducing the inter-Arab rivalry. Other than that, he concentrated upon making it abundantly clear that there could be no military solution to the water dispute. He stressed that the water dispute could not be treated in isolation from the Arab-Israeli conflict. The dispute, Nasser emphasized, was only one of a series of problems that would be resolved once the Jewish State was destroyed. As the Egyptian newspaper *Al Gumhuriya* put it, there must first be a comprehensive and conclusive solution to the Palestine problem as a whole.

War, however, was not, Nasser admonished, a matter to be approached lightly. It demanded careful preparation. There were several preconditions that must be fulfilled before the Arab states could wage war on Israel. First and foremost was Arab unity. Second, the Arab armies must be strengthened to the point where they were bigger, stronger and better than the Israeli army. Third, Israel must be isolated. None of these preconditions, Nasser pointed out, were in place, and so the Arab states must challenge the Israel water diversion by other means. Nasser himself favored the idea of a Unified Arab Military Command, as recommended by Arab Defence Committee in June 1961. The Unified Arab Military Command, he believed, would help prevent Israel from carrying out its plan to divert the Jordan River to the Negev.[9] In addition, Nasser resurrected the idea of the counterdiversion scheme first discussed in the 1950's and early 1960s.

Nasser proved extremely persuasive. The summit rejected Syria's demand for immediate military action against Israel, a demand that, as noted, was at odds with the views of the Syrian army. It also dismissed Syria's proposals to close the Suez Canal and impose an oil embargo.[10] Instead, it accepted Nasser's claim that the Arab states were, at present, incapable of launching a military offensive against Israel. Nasser's proposals also formed the basis of the summit conference's decisions.

Of all the Cairo Summit Conference's decisions, the most important one was its decision to establish three new organizations:

1. An Authority for the Exploitation of the Jordan River and its Headwaters. The authority was to draw up plans to divert the Jordan River at its source. By diverting the river's headwaters, which ran through Lebanon, Syria and Jordan, the Arab states would prevent Israel from exploiting the Jordan River for its own ends.
2. A Unified Arab Military Command. The command was to work out how to develop the military potential of the Arab states. It was to consider how to strengthen the Arab armies, improve their fighting abilities and, above all, create a unified and coordinated Arab front, based upon agreed and uniform battle orders. The command was also to draft, and eventually execute, military plans in preparation for the forthcoming war. The plans were to detail each Arab state's zone of operations, as well as its specific role in war.
3. A Palestinian organization, later known the Palestine Liberation Organization (PLO). The idea was to give the Palestinians the opportunity to take an active part in the struggle to liberate their homeland. It would also be a propaganda coup, presenting the world with the reasons for and motives behind Arab action against Israel.[11]

In addition, the conference decided to revive the Arab League's Technical Committee, which was charged with working out the technical details of the counterdiversion scheme.

The Cairo Summit Conference's endorsement of Nasser's views was evidence of his extraordinary ability to manipulate the Arab states. By accepting that no military steps could be taken against Israel, the Arab states, in effect, gave the stamp of approval to the Egyptian president's refusal to go to war. Thus, the summit conference underlined and underpinned Nasser's status as the unrivaled leader of the Arab world.

Nasser could add one more achievement to his list of summit accomplishments. He managed to get the Egyptian chief of staff, General Ali Ali Amer, appointed head of the Unified Command. This gave Egypt full control of the command, which had now become a tool of Egyptian strategy. Egypt could, as a result, prevent a military confrontation before time was ripe. By overseeing and controlling the Arab states's military preparations, Egypt could stop what it believed to be an untimely eruption of war.[12]

The Cairo Summit Conference marked a new chapter in the history of the Arab-Israeli conflict, and as such was to have far-reaching consequences. The heads of the Arab states's decision to meet and discuss the water dispute personally, rather than leave it to the devices of the Arab League and its various committees, was a sure sign that the water dispute had become a much more serious affair. Admittedly, the summit conference had declared that, as of yet, the Arab states were incapable, be it individually or jointly, of destroying the state of Israel or even of frustrating its development. Nonetheless, its decisions, though in essence no different than the League's decisions, were of much greater import. The reason was that this time it was heads of the Arabs states themselves who made the decisions, which, naturally, gave them extra added value. As a result, from 1964 onward, the water dispute headed the list of problems that plagued Arab-Israeli relations. It would, over the next couple of years, hold center stage, and have an incisive impact on regional relations. The summit conference's decisions and their subsequent consequences were to form the basis of the Arab-Israeli conflict in the future and establish the parameters of Arab-Israeli relations in the days to come.

Several of the more minor decisions also made it clear that the dispute had moved up in importance. For example, the decision was made to convene another summit conference in September when the heads of the Arab states would meet, in Alexandria, to assess the progress made in carrying out the decisions from January's summit conference. Furthermore, this time the Arab states took action to realize their decisions. The question of funding, for example, was addressed. Their experts calculated that the counterdiversion scheme would take at least eighteen months to complete, at the cost of 6.5 million pounds sterling. A further 15 million pounds sterling would be needed to set up the United Arab Command. It was agreed that the oil-rich countries, would contribute most of these funds, with Kuwait and Saudi Arabia topping the list.[13]

Nor was the counterdiversion scheme itself neglected. The League's Technical Committee met soon after the summit conference ended and started to draw up a detailed counterdiversion plan. It marked down the sites from which it would be best to divert the Jordan River's headwaters and estimated the amount of water that could be diverted. At the same time, the Unified Arab Command began to audit the condition of the Arab states's armies, their strength and organization. Finally, in order to garner and mobilize international support, should hostilities erupt, the Arab foreign ministers embarked on a tour of the world's capitals, highlighting the damage, which would be wrought by the Israeli diversion.

Of all the Western powers, Britain's position on the water dispute was the most vague and equivocal. Not surprisingly, the Arabs and Israelis both courted Britain, each hoping to win it over to its side. Britain recognized that the summit conference meeting marked the beginning of the end of the stability it had worked so hard to preserve. The Foreign Office went further, believing that the summit conference opened a new chapter in history of the Middle East. Although it was true that no new or immediate steps had been taken to obstruct the operation of the Israeli National Water Carrier, to the Foreign Office's thinking the summit conference foreshadowed the start of a long period of tension in the region, which would be characterized, in the main, by a rising number of border incidents.[14]

Israel's reaction to the Arab Summit Conference was mixed. On the upside, the summit conference revealed that the Arabs were clearly unable to challenge Israel on the battlefield. They were not even capable of launching a large-scale military operation to thwart the operation of the National Water Carrier. This verified both Israel's military intelligence and the Western powers's assessment of Arab strength.[15] The summit conference also nipped in the bud Syria's demand for immediate military action. Moreover, it made it clear to Syria, that were it to take wide-scale military action against Israel, on its own initiative, it would be left to face Israel's wrath alone.

The downside was that the Cairo Summit Conference signaled the onset of Arab political and military coordination and collaboration, a process that would, Israel feared, ultimately end in an Arab-Israeli military confrontation. Israel's anxiety was justified, as this was, after all, Nasser's strategy. After the summit conference, Shimon Peres, Israel's deputy defense minister, emphasized that Israel "should not make light of the Summit. There is every reason to be afraid that the Arabs who, as a result of the Summit, would begin to augment their weapons arsenals and accelerate their military preparations. None of this would help reduce the tension on the Middle East."[16]

Despite its concern for the future, Israel did not abandon the National Water Carrier project. As Prime Minister Eshkol stated time and again, water was Israel's lifeblood. It was Israel's future. If Israel failed to complete the project, it would be unable to channel water from Lake Tiberias to the Negev. This, in turn, meant that it would be unable to absorb new immigrants in any significant number and Jewish immigration to Israel would have to come to a stop. Nor would it be able to redistribute rationally its current population throughout the country. Industrial development, too, would grind to a halt. In short, Israel simply could not afford to cancel the project. As far as Israel was concerned, the National Water Carrier was a matter of life or death.

Only a few days after the Cairo Summit Conference, Eshkol, in order to underline the above point, announced "that Israel will continue to pump water from Lake Tiberias, within the limits established by the Johnston Plan. It will oppose any unilateral and illegal steps the Arabs might take and itself take action to preserve its vital rights ... the land of the Middle East should be irrigated with water, not blood and provocative action. The region craves economic development, not bloodthirsty war-mongering."[17] Though relatively moderate in tone, like most of Eshkol's statements, the prime minister was careful to leave no one in any doubt regarding the vital role the National Water Carrier played in Israel's future. Golda Meir, Israel's foreign minister, was much more blunt. She denounced the Arab attempt to pillage the Jordan River's water as an act of aggression equal to the seizure by force of Israeli territory. It was an act of blatant vandalism that threatened the very existence of the state of Israel, and Israel, she warned ominously, would view of all such activity very, very seriously.[18]

Neither Eshkol nor Meir nor any of the other Israelis, who made similar resolute statements, sought to exacerbate an already tense situation. A military confrontation was not on Israel's agenda. This explains why, as a rule, Israel kept a low profile on everything connected to the National Water Carrier. By any standard the Carrier was a mammoth project to undertake, particularly for a state as tiny as Israel, which had only 2 million citizens. It was an incredible challenge, technically, financially and logistically. Yet, when Israel had finally completed this massive project at the end of 1963, and on schedule, it deliberately shrouded the event in silence. There were no public celebrations and little or no fanfare; it was as though nothing particularly noteworthy or extraordinary had happened.[19] In addition, the Israeli government also took every opportunity to propose that Israel and the Arab states sit down and try to resolve all the problems of the area, including the water dispute. True, Israel was probably banking on the Arabs refusing even to acknowledge its proposal and in line with Nasser's strategy, they would continue to concentrate on their preparations for a military confrontation with Israel and the eventual destruction of the Jewish State.

Israel believed that one way to prevent the Arab states from taking action, military or otherwise, was to mobilize international support in favor of the Israeli diversion. Luckily, it already had the support of the United States. The United States, still devoted to the Johnston Plan, adhered to its policy of supporting and providing economic aid to any country whose policies, like those of Israel, were in line with the plan. It fiercely opposed any aggressive action designed to prevent countries, again like Israel, from observing the principles laid down by the Johnston Plan or receiving their allotted quota of water. Accordingly, Israel's plans to exploit the Jordan River already had the benefit of American aid and cooperation. The two countries worked closely together on numerous questions relating to the Israeli diversion. They discussed issues such as the Jordan River's saliency levels, how to channel water to Jordan and the establishment of international inspection mechanisms to oversee the way the water was exploited.[20]

Unfortunately France, with whom Israel had enjoyed close and profitable relations, both before and after Suez, was a different case. Ever since de Gaulle's assumption of the presidency in May 1958, France had been intent upon cooling down its relations with Israel and restoring France's position and influence within the Arab world. In the case of the water dispute, de Gaulle, while agreeing that all the region's states had the right to exploit the Jordan River, did not think that the Johnston Plan offered the sole equitable solution to the affair and was, therefore, nonnegotiable. As far as France was concerned, no solution to the water dispute had been found, which was acceptable to all sides. To its mind, the question of how to allocate the water of the Jordan River was still open to negotiation.[21]

That left Britain, the only Western power, which, so far, had kept its own council and failed to declare in favor of either the Arabs or Israelis. Israel devoted most of its time and effort to wooing and winning over Britain in the hope that it would eventually decide to support its position. Israel initiated numerous meetings with the representatives of the British Embassy in Tel Aviv and the number of Israeli officials visiting London markedly increased. All this was in order to persuade Britain that it must take Israel's side in the water dispute.

In the course of this diplomatic blitz, Israel's representatives emphasized that Israel, like Jordan, was strictly abiding by the Johnston Plan. Consequently, Israel was, again like Jordan, the recipient of American support and aid. Moreover, they pointed out, Israel had, of its own volition, taken steps to prevent the water dispute from escalating into an all-out confrontation. It had, for instance, moved the diversion site to a location outside the demilitarized zone and had done so despite the high costs involved, despite the fact that this made the project much more complex technically and despite losing the opportunity to manufacture cheap electrical power. They also stressed that the Arab leaders knew that National Water Carrier did not threaten the neighboring Arab countries' water supply. Hence, they concluded, it was obvious that the Arab plan to counterdivert the Jordan River was designed solely to undermine the state of Israel. It was all part of the Arab plan to destroy the Jewish State.

Israel's representatives explained that their government regarded the counterdiversion scheme as constituting a grave threat to Israel's future survival and would certainly not stand quietly by and do nothing if the Arab states carried out their plans. It would take all the military steps necessary to put an end to the wretched plan to divert the river's headwaters. Moreover, if the Arab states attempted to bombard and destroy Israel's water pumping equipment, Israel would respond with an air offensive. This last threat was a deliberate attempt to impress upon the British the seriousness of the Israel's intentions. Not since the 1950s had Israel, fearing to exacerbate the conflict even further, dared to employ its air force in any of its retaliation operations. The threat to launch an air strike was intended to signal to the British government that Israel would not hesitate to drag the whole region into the abyss of war should anything be done to damage its water project.

The Israeli government was firmly opposed to raising the water dispute in the United Nations. It had already one bitter experience of United Nations's intervention back in 1953, which had, it believed, established an unfortunate precedent. It explained to the British that with the likelihood of a Soviet veto any discussion in the Security Council would produce nothing but a new deadlock. In the meantime, however, much valuable time would be lost. The National Water Carrier was scheduled to start operating in May 1964, and Israel could not afford even the slightest delay.[22]

What then were the alternatives to the United Nations' intervention? Israel offered several. Ideally, it suggested, the best way to deter the Arab states from carrying out their plans was for Britain to grant Israel a guarantee. This was not the first time, of course, that Israel had raised the notion of a British guarantee of its security. It had already mentioned the possibility a number of times during the second half of 1963. Not that it was under any illusion that Britain or the United States, for that matter, had changed their views on the question. Both powers still believed that to guarantee Israel's security would undermine, if not bring to end, Western influence in the Arab world. Conversely, a guarantee would pave the way for further Soviet expansion in the Middle East. Accordingly, Britain, once again, refused Israel's request for a formal guarantee. It told Israel, as it had done many times before, that it believed that President Kennedy's and Prime Minister Macmillan's 1963 speeches were sufficient to deter the Arabs and preserve the peace and, thus, formed a kind of guarantee in themselves.

With an official guarantee out of the question, the next best thing, in Israel's opinion, was for Britain to publicly endorse the American stand on the water dispute. Since the end of the Cairo Summit, the Israeli government had been pressing Britain to declare that it supported Israel's position on the water dispute. An unequivocal declaration of British support might, Israel argued, deter the Arabs from using force or appealing to the United Nations. It would also, Israel pointed out, in an obvious bid to tempt the British into giving their support, ensure peace and stability. As a clear sign that the West stood as one behind Israel, it would give the Egyptian president the chance to abandon, without loss of face, the spurious and dangerous position he had adopted at the Cairo Summit Conference. In short, were Britain to adopt a policy on the water dispute akin to that of the United States, it would prevent the Arab world from catapulting the Middle East into war. If, however, Britain was reluctant to explicitly endorse the Israeli position, then Israel requested that it at least make an effort on the diplomatic front, in the Middle East and elsewhere, to deter the Arabs from taking aggressive action.[23]

Israel was not the only one busy wooing the British. The Arab states, too, sought to persuade the British of the justice of their cause. They labored to convince Britain that the counterdiversion scheme was a fair and legitimate response to the Israeli diversion. Their efforts, in this respect, were part of a general diplomatic campaign, or more accurately a tactical maneuver, designed to weaken Western, and especially French, opposition to the Arab plans. Occasionally they would let slip that there were, in fact, bigger issues behind the water dispute. Al Kyni, Egypt's representative to the United Nations, informed the British Foreign Office that Britain would be making a very big mistake if it thought for one moment that "there was any question of the Arabs reconciling themselves in the foreseeable future to the existence of Israel." Britain, he continued, should abandon any illusions it might have that the Arabs and Israelis could together live in peaceful coexistence.[24]

Plainly, it was the fundamental question of Israel's existence that, in truth, stood at the back of the water dispute. The counterdiversion scheme was merely the first stage of the Arab states' plan to destroy the state of Israel. It was an interim measure designed to prevent Israel from augmenting its power at Arab expense as, or so the Arab states believed, it was bound to do once the National Water Carrier project began to function. The Arab representatives emphasized, time and again, that by channeling water to its southern regions, Israel would be able to markedly increase its population, particularly along the Israeli-Egyptian border. Worse, thanks to its now considerably larger population, Israel would become much more powerful, economically and militarily, and would turn its newly acquired power against the Arab nation. Israel's scheme to exploit the Jordan River and divert it southward would also, they claimed, prevent a just solution to the Palestinian refugee problem. Owing to large-scale Jewish immigration, the Palestinians would no longer be able to return to their homes. Nor with the Jews using up all the water, would it be possible to settle them elsewhere. Thus, the Israeli water project, they concluded, was one more crime, in Israel's catalog of crimes, against the Palestinian people.

The Arab states emphasized that just as in 1948 Israel had attacked Arab land, it was now assaulting their territorial water rights. Moreover, it was, they claimed, acting in flagrant contravention of international law. The Arabs maintained that according to international law, common water resources could only be exploited with the agreement of all riparian states. If one country acts in breach of the law, its neighbors had no choice but to protect their rights. In this case, the Arab states would have the full right to divert the Hasbani and Banias rivers, which run through Arab territory, and exploit them for their own needs.[25]

The Arabs also drew Britain's attention to the fact that the Israeli diversion scheme might seriously mar the quality of the water Jordan drew from the river.[26] The diversion would raise the saliency levels of the Lower Jordan River, which ran south of Lake Tiberias, to a point where the river could not be used for agriculture and irrigation purposes. This would have an adverse effect Jordan's economy, as well as its population, a large number of whom were, incidentally, Palestinian refugees. In sum, the Arabs concluded, if the Israelis were operating within the parameters established by the Johnston Plan, then clearly the plan gave Israel complete control over the Jordan River and its headwaters. As the Egyptian foreign secretary stated, this was completely unacceptable. Consequently, as far as the Arab states were concerned the Johnston Plan was a dead letter.[27]

The Arab representatives left Britain, in no doubt as to the Arab states's intentions: They were resolved to carry out the counterdiversion scheme and thwart Israel's plans to exploit the Jordan River. Both during and after the Cairo Summit Conference, the Arab states voiced threats against the Israeli project, as well as against any country that dared to support it. After the summit conference, they began to put those threats into action, and they took several steps to foil the Israeli project. They also raised the possibility of oil sanctions against countries that supported Israel. Nasser had suggested, even before the Cairo Summit Conference, that the oil-producing countries should reduce the supply of oil to those countries that sided with Israel. The Syrians went even further and considered the possibility of sabotaging the West's oil installations or pipelines in response to the diversion of the Jordan waters.[28]

However, reducing the supply of oil to the West or sabotaging Western oil installations were not, at least at this stage, practical propositions. The oil-producing states needed the income generated by the oil trade. More significantly, oil revenue was to fund both the counterdiversion project and the United Arab Command. Nevertheless, the mere thought that the Arab states had raised the idea of oil sanctions sent shudders down Whitehall's spine. As its economy depended largely on oil, Britain could not afford to ignore the possibility that the Arab states might make good their threat. Admittedly, the oil-producing countries preferred not to use oil as a weapon, but as Foreign Office officials noted, given the violent and bitter feelings raised by the water dispute, there was no guarantee that the oil weapon would not be employed in the future.[29]

Meanwhile, as the date of the activation of the National Water Carrier drew nearer, Arabs threats became louder and more alarming. The Arab League avowed that the moment Israel began to divert the Jordan River southward, the Arab states would respond by force. True to its image as the most radical Arab state, Syria declared that it would never assent to the activation of the National Water Carrier, and despite the fact that the Arab states had rejected its demand for an immediate war and the risk of inviting Western imperialist intervention, it would attack the Israeli diversion installations.[30]

In light of past experience, it would have been reasonable to assume that these threats, like similar Arab threats in past, would remain little more than empty words. However, it seemed that this time the Arab states meant business. As Britain could see, the Arab states had been very busy. They had set up a Technical Executive Committee, composed of representatives of the Arab states, which was to supervise the counterdiversion scheme. Egypt sent a group of irrigation experts to Jordan, soon after the Cairo Summit Conference ended, to examine the possibility of joining the Banias River to the Yarmuk and to estimate how much water could be obtained by diverting the Banias and Hasbani rivers. In the meantime, Syria and Lebanon took some tentative steps toward diverting the Banias.

Arab military preparations were also in full swing. The Egyptian general, Ali Ali Amer, commander of the United Arab Command, visited Jordan, Syria and Lebanon to see for himself what progress had been made in setting up the command. Tunisia announced, and it was one of the first Arab states to do so, that it would attach a number of its senior officers to the United Arab Command. The

Arab states also established a committee entitled "The Committee of the Personal Representatives of the Heads of the Arab States," which was a kind of watchdog committee, charged with ascertaining whether, and to what extent, the Cairo Summit Conference's decisions were being carried out. All the Arab states, particularly the oil-producing states, were ordered to start providing the funds needed to finance these operations.[31] Britain realized that the Middle East was plainly moving toward a new tension filled era.

Israel and the Arab states took a completely antithetical view of the water dispute. The Arab states believed that the Israeli diversion would greatly increase Israel's military and economic power. They considered the diversion an act of aggression against the Arab nation. In essence, however, their opposition to the Israeli water plan stemmed from their refusal to accept the existence of the state of Israel per se. The Israeli position was almost a mirror image of the Arab stance. Israel feared that unless it diverted the Jordan River, Jewish immigration, the raison d'être and lifeblood of the Jewish state, would dwindle down to an insignificant trickle and Israel's industrial development would grind a halt. Not unreasonably, it regarded the Arab states's policy and measures, whose objective was to prevent Israel from exploiting the water, as part of the Arab strategy to destroy Israel. Indulging in mutual recriminations and employing a combination of threats and warnings, neither side left any doubt as to its future intentions. There would be no compromise—certainly not on the Arab side. The water dispute, the Egyptian president announced, could not be resolved peacefully. War with Israel was inevitable.[32]

It was in these dismal circumstances, with both sides competing for its favors, that Britain had to decide what to do. Until now Britain had tried to prevent a developing situation that might lead to an Arab-Israeli military confrontation. It did so chiefly, though not solely, because it feared that such a conflict would harm Britain's economy and further weaken its already limited political influence in the Arab world. Now, thanks to the water dispute, a military collision appeared increasingly likely. Whatever course Britain eventually decided to adopt, it would have to take into account British and Western interests in the Middle East. These included ensuring that the West would still be able to import oil, freely and at reasonable prices, from the region; that the British oil companies could continue to operate unhindered, as well as checking Soviet penetration of the region and preventing the Cold War and superpower competition from spilling over and engulfing the Middle East.

BRITAIN: KEEPING A LOW PROFILE

Britain's reaction to the Cairo Summit Conference was, like Israel's, mixed. It was thankful that the summit conference had ended without a decision to embark upon a large-scale military action against Israel, which might have provoked a general conflagration in the Middle East, hurt Britain's regional interests and accelerated Soviet penetration. On the other hand, the summit conference did not rule out, nor could it, the prospect of limited, or, for that matter, extensive border incidents between Israel and the Arab states. Syria, certainly, made it abundantly clear that it would not sit tight and do nothing while Israel implemented its water program.

Luckily, so far, nothing had happened other, of course, than the fact that Britain found itself the unhappy object of an intensive diplomatic offensive, with Israel and the Arab states each pressing it to declare itself. Unlike the United States, whose policy on the Jordan River was a matter of public knowledge, Britain had yet to make known its view on the affair. This was on the assumption, of course, that it even had one. Apparently it didn't, which explains why the British Foreign Office decided to carry out a detailed and thorough examination of the water dispute. Specifically, the Foreign Office sought to ascertain if, and to what extent, the Israeli diversion undermined the interests of its Arab neighbors. In other words, was there any truth to the Arab claims?

First on the agenda were the legal aspects of the case. Here the key question was whether the Israeli diversion was in keeping with or in contravention of international law. The Arab states argued that Israel, by pumping water from the Jordan River without the agreement of its neighbors, was in breach of international law. The question was referred to the Foreign Office's legal adviser, who affirmed that in cases where there was a dispute over the use of international river waters, the riparian states should solve the dispute themselves by negotiation and agreement. This was the best solution, which was also in accordance with international law. However, he continued, "It does not lie in the mouth of one party to a river dispute to refuse to negotiate on the problem and then deny to the other party the right to make use of the water." This was exactly what the Arab states were doing. Moreover, according to the Foreign Office's legal adviser, in the absence of an agreement a country may take unilateral steps to exploit the river's waters on the condition that its actions to not infringe upon the rights of the downstream riparian users.[33] This was precisely what Israel was doing. In sum, in legal terms, the Arab opposition to the Israeli National Water Carrier clearly did not hold water.

But what of the Arab claim that the Israeli project undermined their interests? What worried the Arab states, above all, was the link between the Israeli diversion and Jewish immigration. Their principal objection to the National Water Carrier was that it would allow Israel to absorb a large number of new immigrants, and so more than double its current population, which currently stood at 2 million. With 5 million citizens at its disposal, Israel would become more powerful than ever and pose an even a greater threat to its Arab neighbors.

John Beith, Britain's ambassador to Israel, was charged with investigating the effect of Israeli diversion on Jewish immigration to Israel. Having thoroughly examined the issue, Beith's conclusion was that diversion's effect on Jewish immigration would be negligible, if that. Beith pointed out that the Jewish communities of the United States, South America, Australia, France and Britain were, for the most part, quite content to stay where they were and had no great desire to immigrate to Israel, at least not in any significant numbers. Even in South Africa, most Jews preferred to stay put, in the hope that one day the doctrine of the white man's supremacy would win out. The Jews of the Soviet Union, on the other hand, who might very well want to immigrate to Israel, were not allowed to do so. This left North Africa, Romania and Hungary as the only sources of substantial Jewish immigration. But Jewish immigration from the two East European countries depended on the goodwill of the Rumanian and Hungarian governments, and this did not, at the moment, appear forthcoming whereas the Jews of Algeria and Morocco, given the choice, preferred to emigrate to France and Australia. In these circumstances, Beith estimated that the best Israel could hope for was the arrival of 50,000 new immigrants per annum. This meant that by 1970 the sum total of Jewish immigrants to Israel would be no more than 250,000. Were the Soviet Union to permit its Jews to emigrate, then another 500,000, according to American estimates, might be added to this number. When calculating Israel's future population, the ambassador also took into account Israel's natural population growth, which stood at around 22 percent and would thus add another 450,000 to the total sum of Israeli citizens. Accordingly, by the beginning of 1970, Israel's population would reach the 3 million mark, or, more optimistically, if one included Soviet immigration, 3.5 million.[34] This fell far short of the 5 million Israeli citizens the Arab states predicted.

The Foreign Office also examined the Israeli's diversion's effect on the development of the Negev. The Arab states claimed that a flourishing Negev, which enjoyed an abundance of water, would seriously harm their interests and, above all, deprive the Palestinians of their rights once and for all. The Foreign Office turned once more to Ambassador Beith, who assured it that in this case, too, the Arab states had little to fear. He noted that over the past few years Israel's "coastal aquifers have been strongly over-pumped in the knowledge and expectation that they could be allowed [sic] to be recharged, because the water from Lake Tiberias could be used in their place once the Jordan scheme had come into operation."[35] This meant, the ambassador explained, that the water pumped from the Jordan River would be exploited primarily for industrial and urban use. It would also be used to boost Israel's central region's depleted water tables. Accordingly, only a small part of the water that remained would be used to irrigate the Negev.

John Beith's assessment of the effect of the water diversion matched, to a remarkable degree, that of the Israeli government. In fact, in some cases, for example, future immigration, the ambassador's forecasts were far more optimistic than those of the Israeli government. The latter had calculated that by 1970, Israel's population would increase by 650,000, at most, with immigration and natural population growth contributing about an equal share. Diverting water to Israel's southern region might add an additional 25,000 to this number, but no more. Finally, according to Israeli projections, any large-scale settlement in the south would center on the town of Be'er Sheva and the area north of the town.

All this led the Foreign Office to conclude that Arab states's claims regarding extensive Jewish settlement in the Negev and, in particular, along the Egyptian border, were completely unfounded. For one thing it was extremely doubtful whether within the next couple of years new land in the Negev would be irrigated in any significant proportion.[36]

In light of the above, the British Foreign Office's final judgment was that the Arab states's opposition to the Israeli National Water Carrier project was completely unjustified. Their claims did not hold water and were, the Foreign Office suspected, no more than a transparent bid to sabotage the ongoing development of the state of Israel. What the Arab states really objected to, the Foreign Office thought, was the fact of Israel's existence. Both before and after the 1949 ceasefire agreements, the Arab states had stubbornly refused to recognize Israel. Determined to destroy the Jewish State, they considered even the most roundabout and oblique recognition of Israel as beyond the pale. Accordingly, what the Arab states really feared was that the Israeli diversion would increase Israel's power, making it very difficult, if not impossible, for them to carry out their plan to destroy it. It was hardly surprising, therefore, the Foreign Office concluded, that the Arab states refused to discuss, whether on the basis of the Johnston Plan, which they regarded as a dead letter, or on the basis of any other proposal, the allocation of the River Jordan's water.[37]

By contrast, Israel was perfectly willing to negotiate with the Arab states an agreement for the distribution of water, and was at pains to stress this at every possible opportunity. Moreover, while Israel did not deny that it had taken unilateral steps to procure water, it emphasized that the only reason it was doing so was because the Arab states rejected the Johnston Plan and refused to the discuss the issue any further. Finally, seeking to quash any suspicion of greediness or deleterious intentions on its part, the Israeli government promised to keep within the limits of the water quota it had been allocated by Johnston Plan. It would even agree to the institution of some form of international supervision over the water it pumped from Lake Tiberias. On the whole, Britain thought that the Israeli attitude was eminently fair. As long as it observed the water quotas established by the special ambassador for water, Israel, Britain adjudged, had the full right to exploit the water of the Jordan River, an opinion that was at one with the Israeli and American views on the water dispute.[38]

Israeli-British relations did not center exclusively on the water dispute. Israel's continued existence had long been a key, crucial element of Britain's strategy to maintain stability in the Middle East. Throughout the dispute, Britain constantly reminded Israel that it was totally committed to preserving Israel's security and existence. It frequently referred to Macmillan's May 1963 statement, as well as President Kennedy's statement a week earlier, regarding the need to preserve peace and stability in the Middle East, and reminding Israel that should it fall victim to aggression it could reply upon American aid.

Britain did more than offer Israel verbal reassurances, it also supplied it with weapons. A sufficiently large arms arsenal would, Britain believed, allow Israel to deter the Arab states, so that they would not be tempted to launch a war against it. In other words, it would promote regional stability. Britain, however, rejected the notion of furnishing Israel with an unlimited amount of weapons. In part, it was because Britain feared provoking the wrath of the Arabs, and in part, it was because Britain did not want to contribute to a situation whereby Israel, having acquired copious amounts of weapons, became excessively powerful and was thus tempted to resolve the Arab-Israeli conflict by force rather than negotiation. What Britain sought to do was to maintain a balance of arms in the Middle East skewed, but only to a point, in Israel's favor. Its policy was to supply Israel with arms, but only after Egypt had received comparable weapons.[39]

Although Britain considered Israel to be, fundamentally, a factor in favor of stability, it did worry about the effect Israel's nuclear policy might have on regional stability. It was concerned that the Israeli government, intent upon developing a nuclear bomb, would destabilize the region. It found little comfort in the fact that the Americans were monitoring Israel's nuclear program and had even visited the Israeli nuclear plant in Dimona. Britain assumed that Israel, having deliberately adopted an opaque nuclear policy, was by no means revealing, even to the Americans, especially to the Americans, all the relevant information and data on its nuclear program. According to Britain's information, for example, whatever Israel might say, the nuclear plant in Dimona was clearly not intended for peaceful use.[40]

The British government was sadly aware that its own ability to influence, let alone pressure, Israel was, at best, limited. The most it could do was warn Israel of the dangers inherent in developing nuclear weapons, something it had been doing, with little apparent effect, since 1960. Nevertheless, Britain persevered. It advised Israel that by acquiring nuclear powers, it would catapult the regional arms race onto another, infinitely more dangerous plane. This, in turn, would have a grave, destructive effect on the situation in the Middle East.[41] Yet, persuasive though this argument might be, Britain knew that when it came to actually stopping Israel producing nuclear weapons or at least redirecting its nuclear capacity toward peaceful purposes, it had no choice but to rely on the United States to do the job. Not that Britain had much confidence in the Americans, whom, it thought, were doing far too little to prevent the manufacture of an Israeli bomb.

As worrying as Israel nuclear policy might be, the water dispute, which could erupt into a full-scale conflagration at any moment, was nonetheless of more immediate concern. Britain had to decide, and soon, what position it was going to take on the dispute. Should it adopt the same policy as the Americans? Should it endorse the Johnston Plan and stand by Israel, whose policy, after all, Britain considered fair and equitable? Or should it, in the hope of safeguarding British interests, avoid any kind of public action or statement, which could be interpreted as siding with one side or the other? In other words, should Britain keep a low profile?

It was not an easy choice to make. The Foreign Office itself was divided on the issue, and most of its officials found it very difficult to choose between these two unpropitious alternatives. This was not true of John Beith, Britain's ambassador to Israel, who, of all the members of the Foreign Office, had the most clear-cut and decisive views on both the Arab-Israeli conflict and the water dispute. Beith argued that it was far too dangerous for Britain to adopt an ambiguous, equivocal policy on the water dispute, as such a policy left much too much to chance. He believed that Britain must face up to the admittedly disagreeable duty of telling the Arab states that Israel, like it or not, was a fact of life and here to stay. It must also warn them that the West would, if necessary, take action to stop any act of aggression, across the existing borders, regardless of who initiated it.[42] Beith was, in effect, advising Britain to act in accordance with President Kennedy and Prime Minister Macmillan's May 1963 statements proscribing the use of force. More than that, Beith's views were, in fact, at one with Israel's request that Britain publicly endorse its right to exploit the Jordan River.

Willie Morris, head of the Foreign Office's Eastern Department, took a more moderate view. Unlike the ambassador, Morris assumed that Britain must avoid, if possible, an overt declaration in favor of one side or the other in the Arab-Israeli conflict. This did not mean, however, that Britain was simply to bury its head in the sand and ignore the rising tension in the Middle East. Britain, Morris stressed, had a multitude of interests in the Arab world, all of which, he admitted, were very vulnerable, but it was precisely because of this that Britain must take action. The current burst of activity among the Arab states, he explained, had started a process that might end in an explosion between Israel and its neighbors, and a conflagration would further, and seriously, undermine Britain's regional interests. Britain must, therefore, Morris concluded, strive to preserve peace and stability in the Middle East. It must, especially, try to dissuade the Arab states from following their current dangerous course. With no political solution in sight, Morris proposed using the Johnston Plan as the basis for some kind of settlement. True, the Arab states had rejected the plan for political reasons, but, Morris pointed out, their technical experts had accepted the plan, which gave some cause for hope that an agreement might be reached in the future.

Britain's policy, Morris concluded, should be as follows: It should endorse the Johnston Plan and declare that "a government which draws no more water that the share allotted to it and otherwise respects the interests of other users is not acting unreasonably."[43] In addition, Britain should exercise such influence as it had among the Arab states and seek to persuade them that Israel, by drawing water within the limits established by the Johnston Plan, was acting reasonably. Even to convince them to accept that much, tactically, would be, Morris thought, quite an achievement. In addition, Britain should warn the Arabs that they could not expect to receive any international support if they attempted to thwart the Israeli diversion by force.[44]

Morris's suggested course of action had one very important advantage. It was in line with the American request that Britain do more to prevent the Arabs from taking violent action in response to the Israeli diversion. In essence, the two powers took the same view of the water dispute. They both believed that those governments that observed the Johnston Plan quotas and respected the rights of the other riparian states were acting legally and fairly. Moreover, Britain and the United States also, in general, cooperated with one another in the Middle East. The United States often apprised Britain of its activities among the Arab states and consulted with it on various issues connected to the Arab-Israeli conflict. In the case of the water dispute, the United States had asked its British ally to make a greater effort to help resolve the problem, and it was unthinkable that Britain should refuse the American request. It was equally inconceivable, in light of the recent events, that Britain should stand aside and assume the role of a disinterested spectator.[45]

The heads of the Foreign Office took a different view. Stewart Crawford, the assistant undersecretary, believed that when formulating British policy the paramount consideration should be British interests. These, he thought, were much too important to risk either by supporting Israel, however equitable its position, or by acting jointly with the United States, regardless of how attractive or important American goodwill might be. Most of Britain's interests were oil related, and must, Stewart insisted, be protected. Europe and Britain must be able to continue to import oil from the Middle East and at reasonable prices; the British oil companies must be allowed to keep on operating in the Middle East and thus contribute to Britain's balance of payments and economy. It was particularly important to prevent any hostile country, such as Iraq, from gaining control of the oil reservoirs of a friendly Arab country, for example, Kuwait, and using the latter's oil to blackmail the West.

In considering what course Britain should adopt, Stewart also took note of Britain's military presence in the Persian Gulf. British forces, he observed, played a vital role in preventing Soviet expansion in the Middle East. Furthermore, British rule in Aden and the Federation of South Arabia depended on the continued presence of these forces.[46] The radical Arab states had for some time challenged and attacked Britain's military presence in the region. Egypt, in particular, intent upon eradicating Western imperialism, was waging a vicious campaign of hate against Britain. Seeking to expel Britain from the region, the Egyptian government gave aid and support to local rebel forces, and it was largely thanks to its efforts that the internal political situation in both Aden and the Federation of South Arabia had seriously deteriorated. Given the precarious situation in the Gulf, Britain was very much afraid that an Anglo-Arab confrontation would soon erupt, endangering Britain's position in the region

Clearly, Britain, who had a much greater presence and many more interests in the region, was in a far more vulnerable position than its ally, the United States. "We are," the British Foreign Office noted, "far more exposed than the Americans ... we have relatively more at stake and ... were already dangerously near to a confrontation with the Arab states."[47] Moreover, thanks to its overwhelming political, military and economic power, the United States was even less threatened by Arab troublemaking. Accordingly, it could afford to become more involved in the Arab-Israeli conflict, whether by offering Israel extensive economic aid or supplying arms.

Plainly Britain's best option, in the circumstances, was to maintain a low profile. It should do so even at the risk of the Arab states interpreting this course of action as a sign that Britain agreed with the American view of the dispute. Not that the risk was too great, because in practice keeping a low profile meant that, in this instance, Britain would not publicly endorse the Johnston Plan. Britain was well aware that to sanction the Johnston Plan was tantamount to waving a red rag in front of the Arab Bull. The Arab states would naturally assume that the endorsement was Britain's indirect way of siding with Israel. The Foreign Office emphasized that Britain, in general, must be very careful not to express any opinion the Arab states might conceivably interpret as hostile to them or supportive of Israel. This was not an easy thing to do in view of the fact that, in essence, Britain believed that in the case of the water dispute Israel had right on its side. A Foreign Office directive spelled out how its representatives should meet any request to clarify Britain's position on the water dispute. They should explain, in the following innocuous, noncommittal terms, that

Britain is not directly concerned in this problem. She is, nevertheless, closely interested in the preservation of the peace and stability of the area, and in the development of its economic resources for the benefit of all the peoples living there. The water of the Jordan basin is a major economic resource. It is understandable that the riparian states should wish to develop their share of the waters, but naturally with due regard for the interest of the other riparian states.[48]

Britain's decision to maintain a low profile and its refusal to support either side might very well safeguard British interests, but it could not stop the dynamics of the dispute sparked by the Cairo Summit Conference. True, the summit conference had rejected Syria's demand for immediate military action against Israel, but the summit conference and subsequent Arab activity had made it equally clear that the Arab states were determined to thwart Israel's plan to exploit the Jordan River, which they believed to be inimical to their interests.

At least there was, much to Britain's relief, no danger of a conflagration erupting in near future. First, there was Egypt's involvement in the Yemen civil war. The assumption was that as long as Egypt was bogged down in Yemen, there was little chance of the Arabs embarking upon a war against Israel. Second, such military measures as had been pursued in the months following the summit conference were few and, so far, mostly inconsequential. For example, the process of establishing the Unified Arab Military Command was moving at snail's pace, if it was moving at all. One sticking point was that almost none of the Arab states were willing to accept the presence of foreign Arab troops on their territory. Even Syria would, at best, agree only to small token Egyptian force, and even that was not certain.[49] Trefor Ellis Evans, Britain's ambassador to Damascus, doubted whether the Arabs were capable of creating and running a proper command structure. Even if it were finally set up, the Unified Arab Command, he commented, "would be more like a confederation of tribes under a titular leader."[50]

Third, although there were various plans to counterdivert the Jordan River and to exploit its headwaters on paper, as of yet, nothing had been done to put them into effect. None of the Arab states wanted to start work on a counterdiversion project without being sure that they were protected from an Israeli military response. In other words, unless the necessary military measures were in place, that is, the United Military Command, the counterdiversion scheme was likely to remain a pipe dream. Both Jordan and Lebanon made it perfectly clear to their fellow Arab states, and above all to Egypt, that they wouldn't dream of beginning to divert the Jordan River's headwaters without being sure that they were absolutely safe from Israeli military action. What is more, Jordan, though it participated in the Cairo Summit Conference and was a party to its decisions, was, as noted, secretly cooperating with Israel. The two countries agreed, albeit tacitly, that the Johnston Plan offered a sound basis for the allocation of the River Jordan's waters.[51]

An all-out military confrontation was not, at least not at the moment, on the cards. But Britain had little doubt that the water dispute would soon give rise to mounting tension, especially along the Israeli-Syrian border. Britain assumed, rightly, that Syria, in an attempt to destroy Israel's pumping installations, would repeatedly initiate shooting incidents. Israel would probably respond in kind, though, Britain thought, it would be very careful not spark a wide-scale military conflagration, since this was contrary to Israeli policy.[52] Here Britain erred, and it did so because it grossly underestimated Israel's determination to exploit the Jordan River, at whatever cost. As a result, Britain's assessment of Israel's reaction to the Arab counterdiversion scheme was totally wrong. However, its prognosis that the border incidents between Syria and Israel might escalate, and eventually contribute to, general conflagration proved bang on the nose.

Britain anxiously sought to prevent the border incidents, which it believed contained the seeds of a future war, from escalating. To this end, it tried to convince Israel to exercise a measure of self-restraint in face of Syria's repeated acts of provocation, not to embark upon any large-scale reprisals or to adopt a policy of massive retaliation.[53] At the same time, it endeavored to strengthen the United Nations Truce Supervision Organization's authority. First, UNTSO could ensure that Israel and Syria cooperated and observed the cease-fire agreement. Second, it could deal more effectively with any violations of the cease-fire agreement. Yet, if the border incidents nevertheless continued, then Britain thought the whole issue should be turned over to the Security Council, before the situation escalated any further. But the Security Council discussions should be limited to the question of the border incidents, and be based solely on the United Nations's observers' reports. There should be no general discussion of the Arab-Israeli conflict and its manifold, complex problems, including the water dispute.[54]

Like Israel, which, albeit for different reasons, was categorically opposed to raising the water dispute in the United Nations, Britain, too, did not think that the United Nations could resolve the water problem. Moreover, not only would any discussion in the Security Council prove futile, but, worse, it might also force Britain to take a clear and unambiguous stand on the water dispute. In other words, it might force Britain to abandon its low profile. Britain, as noted, had concluded that the Arab position on the dispute was totally unjustified and had no intention of supporting it publicly. Conversely, it did think that the Johnston Plan was an equitable and fair settlement and acknowledged that Israel was operating within the plan's parameters. Consequently, if Britain wished to maintain a low profile, any discussion of the water dispute in the United Nations, or anywhere else for that matter, would be awkward, to say the least. The best Britain could do, in the circumstances, was to support Israel, indirectly, and state that the River Jordan's waters are an important economic resource that all countries had the right to use if they didn't infringe upon the rights of their neighbors.[55] Anything more would be interpreted as overt support for Israel and provoke an immediate and an unrestrained Arab attack, verbal and even physical, on Britain and British interests, especially by its arch-nemesis Egypt.

With the United Nations out of the picture, Britain, if it wanted to stop the border incidents from spiraling out of control, would have to appeal itself to parties to the dispute. It would have to exercise its persuasive skills on the Arab states and try to convince them to accept the Johnston Plan. This course of action had the advantage of reinforcing, albeit in a limited manner, the American efforts to do the same. This did not mean, however, that Britain had any intention of abandoning its low profile. When speaking to the Arabs, Britain's representatives were very careful to avoid taking sides in the dispute. Instead, in an attempt to appeal to the Arab states' reason, they underlined the dangers inherent in the Arabs' continued opposition to any plan for the just distribution of water between all the region's states, Israel included. Yet, as long as the Arab states refused to recognize the state of Israel, any British appeal, to reason or otherwise, was bound to fail.

In order to ensure that the Arab states realized that British policy was both impartial and disinterested, the Foreign Office told its representatives to the Middle East to stress that Britain was neither a party to the water dispute nor did it wish to become involved in the dispute. Its sole desire was "to maintain the role of an impartial observer, listening to the arguments put forward by both sides, and comment as little as possible."[56] They were to make clear that Britain welcomed the Cairo Summit Conference's decision not to use force in order to realize their goals. But they should make it equally clear that in Britain's opinion the Arab states would benefit far more if they were to concentrate on the constructive development of their economic and natural resources, such as water, for example. As for the Jordan River, it was Britain's view that the rights and interests of all sides should be respected and Israel as a riparian state had a legitimate right to its share of the river's waters. The bottom line, as Britain's representatives were to stress, was that it was in the Arab states, and especially Jordan's, interest that Israel adhere to the Johnston Plan's water quotas. In the

absence of an agreement, Israel, free of international supervision or legal restraints, would be able to pump as much water as it liked from Lake Tiberias.[57]

Of all the Arab states, Jordan was perhaps the most open to persuasion. In
part, this was because Britain still enjoyed a significant measure of influence in
the Jordanian court. In part, it was because Jordan, no less Israel, needed the Jordan River to survive. Jordan also needed Western and international financial and
technical assistance if it was to develop its own water resources, and this, it knew,
was unlikely to be forthcoming if it adopted a contrary position on the water
dispute. In view of all this, and as Jordan was already subjected to massive American pressure, it was thought improbable that it would comply with the Cairo
Summit Conference's decisions. But just to make sure, Britain intimated to King
Hussein that by implementing the summit conference's decisions, Jordan would
reduce its chances of receiving international aid to develop its own water resources. No international organization, Britain advised, would want to become
embroiled in the Arab-Israeli dispute by providing aid to a project designed to
prevent Israel from exploiting its water resources.[58]

Britain was under no illusions that it would manage to persuade the Arab
states to moderate their stance and accept the Johnston Plan. But the aim of the
British diplomatic campaign was not limited to singing the praises of the Johnston Plan. Britain also sought to impress upon the Arabs, admittedly in a roundabout way, two things they already suspected: first that they did not have
Britain's support in this affair; and second that Britain's position on the allocation of water was the same as that of the United States.[59]

By maintaining a low profile, Britain hoped to prevent the water dispute from
escalating into a general conflagration. In addition, this policy was designed to stop
the Arabs from assuming that the West, as a whole, was committed to Israel and,
as a result, from seeking Soviet support. Britain was determined to check any further Soviet penetration of the Middle East, which would threaten the West's own
position in the region and possibly impede the import of Gulf oil. Britain took it
for granted that any escalation of the Arab-Israeli conflict worked to the Soviet
Union's advantage. The water dispute, in particular, offered the Soviet Union a
wonderful opportunity to curry favor with the Arab states by giving them its unqualified support. The result would be an increase in the superpower tension, and
the Middle East, like Europe and the Far East before it, would be completely and
finally absorbed into the Cold War. Unfortunately, the British nightmare of a Middle East polarized between the East and West, a development that had the potential of dragging the whole region into open conflict, was soon to be realized.

The United States shared many of its British ally's anxieties. It, too, was afraid
that the water dispute might trigger a conflagration in the Middle East. The
United States was also worried that the Soviet Union would exploit any dispute
between Israel and its neighbors to make further inroads in the region. Nor did
the Americans think that the fact that the Arab states had decided to convene a
summit conference in Cairo augured well for the future. Consequently, both before and after the Cairo Summit Conference, the United States warned the Arab

states against embarking upon a war against Israel. It further insisted that there was no alternative to the principles laid down by the Johnston Plan. It hammered these points home again and again. Yet, ironically, it was precisely this American diplomatic onslaught, which sought to defuse the water dispute and block any further Soviet advance in the Middle East, that pushed the Arab states straight into the arms of the Soviet Union and allowed the latter to become more closely involved in the affairs of the Middle East.

A few days before the opening of the Cairo Summit Conference, the U.S. ambassadors to Cairo, Amman and Beirut were instructed to advise the heads of the Arab states of the administration's views on the water dispute. The ambassadors were told to emphasize that the United States was satisfied that Israel, both as a member of the United Nations and a riparian state, had the right to exploit the water of the Jordan River, on the condition that it did not violate the rights of the other riparian states. They were also to underline that the United States still regarded the Johnston Plan, which had never been formally rejected by either side, as the basis for the present and future apportionment of the River Jordan's waters. Further, they were to point out that Jordan and Israel, both of whom were tacitly abiding by the Johnston Plan, had received American support and aid in developing their water resources. In this context, the ambassadors were to emphasize that the United States supported the Israeli diversion subject to two conditions. First, the project was to come under some form of American supervision. Second, the United States was to have full and free access to all information concerning the diversion. Both conditions were being fulfilled, and the United States would, naturally, continue to closely supervise the project. However, the Arab states could, if they so desired, themselves monitor the amount of water Israel extracted from Lake Tiberias.

The ambassadors were also instructed to ally Arab fears over the possibility of increased Jewish immigration. They were to advise their hosts that the United States did not believe that the number of Jewish immigrants over the next decade would exceed the 200,000 to 250,000 mark, or 500,000, if the Soviet Union allowed its Jews to emigrate. Finally, the ambassadors were to stress that in view of the above, war or acts of sabotage, which in this case meant counterdiverting the Jordan River's headwaters, were, in the opinion of the United States, neither an appropriate nor a valid response to the water dispute. World opinion would not countenance such action, and it would, certainly, provoke much concern among those states interested in preserving the region's stability.[60]

In order to leave no one, and, above all, the Arab states, in any doubt as to the American position, Dean Rusk, the American secretary of state, reaffirmed U.S. commitment to Israel's safety and security, and its obligation to uphold Israel's ability to counter any form of counteraggression.[61] The fullest and most pointed exposition of American policy and resolve was offered only days after the Cairo Summit Conference by Alexis Johnson, the deputy undersecretary of state for political affairs. The United States, Johnson stated, had three goals: to maintain the independence of all the states in the Middle East, to preserve stability in the

region and to promote its economic development. These goals could only be realized through some kind of an accommodation between Israel and its neighbors. Johnson added that the United States regarded the ability of Europe to
import oil at reasonable prices from the Middle East to be a matter of the utmost importance. The European economy, he explained, is dependent on oil, and
a strong European economy is vital to the Free World's struggle to check the expansion of hostile forces. In the Middle East, the United States was chiefly concerned with preventing the increase of an inimical Russian influence. Finally,
Johnson underlined that although it was U.S. policy to refrain from taking sides
in the various disputes in the Middle East, this did not mean that it

> would stand idly by if aggression is committed.... In the event of direct or indirect ag-
> gression we would support appropriate course of action in the United Nations or on our
> own to prevent or to put a stop to such aggression. Any victim of a would-be aggressor
> can count on our support.[62]

The United States did more than adopt a new and tough stance toward the
Arab states; it also began to draw closer to Israel. As far as the water dispute was
concerned, it collaborated with Israel to the point where the two countries
worked out and coordinated the public relations aspect of the affair. In addition,
the United States promised Israel that as long as it observed the Johnston Plan
quotas, the United States would respond personally to any act of aggression that
might damage its water program.[63] It was an unprecedented and far-reaching
American commitment.

This new, and to their mind, pro-Israeli turn in U.S. policy worried and infuriated the Arab states. They believed that ever since President Johnson had
entered office in November 1963, American policy had assumed a blatantly pro-
Israel complexion. While Kennedy had, at least outwardly, sought to preserve a
neutral, impartial stance, Johnson, a self-declared pro-Zionist, championed Israeli interests and worked incessantly to strengthen U.S. ties with Israel. It worth
noting, that although in essence there was little difference between Kennedy's
May 1963 declaration and the speech by Alexis Johnson, undersecretary of state
for political affairs, in Arab opinion the latter encapsulated the Johnson administration's pro-Israeli stance on the Arab-Israeli conflict. They believed the speech
was an accurate reflection of U.S. surrender and submission to the Zionist state.

The Arabs were not entirely wrong in their assessment of President Johnson's
policy. A deeply religious man, Lyndon B. Johnson was indeed sympathetic to
the Zionist cause. His support for Israel no doubt stemmed, in part, from his
strongly held religious beliefs. There were also political considerations at play,
and in an election year no presidential candidate could afford to ignore the elec-
toral clout of America's Jewish community. Finally, Johnson honestly believed
that only a strong Israel could deter Egypt and prevent it from escalating the
Arab-Israeli conflict.[64]

Johnson did not limit his support of Israel solely to the water dispute. On
February 6, 1964, speaking at a gala dinner in New York, given in honor of the

Weizmann Institute, Johnson observed that the United States believed that the best and most sensible way to prevent war is simply that each country allow its neighbors to live in peace and prosperity. He then announced that the United States was willing to help Israel desalinate its water supply by means of nuclear technology. This was a revolutionary offer, and it is quite possible, even likely, that the only reason Johnson suggested it was that he hoped to enable the United States to better supervise Israel's nuclear program, that is, prevent the manufacture of Israeli nuclear weapons.[65] As far as the Arab world was concerned, however, Johnson's proposal was a flagrant and deliberate anti-Arab gesture. The Egyptian government, furious at this change in American policy, gave vent to its feelings, commenting that the United States appeared to believe that it was God's representative on earth.[66]

As the ties between the United States and Israel grew, U.S. relations with Egypt went from bad to worse. The United States was convinced that Egypt was able to sustain its intervention in the Yemen civil war largely thanks to American economic aid. Accordingly, Congress began demanding that the administration terminate American aid to Egypt and force Nasser to retreat from Yemen. Yet, even though the Johnson administration did threaten to end all economic aid to Egypt, to its disappointment, if not to its surprise, this did not produce a change in Egypt's policy in Yemen. What it did do was convince Nasser, once and for all, that the United States stood solidly behind Israel.

So, Nasser thought, did Britain. Despite having mustered all its diplomatic skills in an effort to maintain a low profile and despite having consistently insisted that it was not a party to the conflict, the Arab states remained firmly convinced that Britain supported the Israeli cause. How else were they to explain the fact that in the beginning of 1964 the British government agreed to sell Israel two more submarines. To their mind, it was a statement made by the leader of the British Opposition, soon-to-be Prime Minister Harold Wilson that reflected and revealed the true measure of British policy. No government of his, Wilson had declared, could be or would remain indifferent to any threat to peace in Israel.[67] The Arabs believed Israel enjoyed the practical and diplomatic support not only of the two Anglo-Saxon powers, but also of the entire West, which contrived to supply it with a myriad of high-quality weapons. This was true even of France, who, although it did not support Israel's aggressive ambitions and was in the process of cooling off its relations with Israel, still furnished it with weapons and approved of the principle that the water of the Jordan River should be allocated between all riparian states.

Nasser believed, not unreasonably, that the West's military bases in Libya, Cyprus and the Persian Gulf posed a direct threat to Egypt and the Arab world as a whole. He was very much afraid that in an Arab-Israeli military confrontation, the West would use these bases to come to Israel's aid. He was certain that Britain's forces in the Middle East were collaborating with Israel and helping it pursue its anti-Arab policy. Hence, Nasser violently and publicly denounced these bases which, he fulminated, were a grave danger to the safety and well-being of the Arab nations.[68]

Egypt, which regarded itself not only as the preeminent Arab nation but also as holding the key to victory over Israel, believed that it had a duty to ensure both its own and Arab security, and that to this end it must strengthen the Egyptian and Arab military forces. In order to fulfill its responsibilities and achieve these goals, Nasser turned to the Soviet Union for help. The Soviet Union, which had long sought to extend its power and influence in the Middle East, was more than willing to lend a hand. Closer relations with Egypt, the largest and most influential Arab state, would go far to help it achieve its ambitions. Egypt had other attractions as well: it controlled the Suez Canal and had excellent port facilities to which the Soviet Union had repeatedly tried to gain access.[69] All things considered, the water dispute was, as far as the Soviet Union was concerned, a gift from heaven. The Soviet Union knew that it was sure to win over the Arab world and Egypt, in particular, simply by giving them massive and unqualified support on this subject. The water dispute was a golden opportunity to increase the Soviet Union's influence and involvement in the Middle East and thus carve itself a position in the region equal to that of the United States and the West.

All this does much to explain the fierce propaganda campaign the Soviet Union now launched against Israel and the West. The Soviet Union condemned Israel's diversion of the Jordan River as an act of flagrant provocation. It was, the Soviet Union accused, an act of aggression directed against the Arab nation, as a whole but especially against Jordan, Lebanon and Syria, through whose territory the Jordan River's headwaters ran. As Soviet leader Nikita Khrushchev reproached, one could not ignore the fact that Israel was little more than a pawn in the hands of the imperialist powers.[70] This was an accusation the Soviet Union would repeat many times over the forthcoming years until, in fact, the outbreak of the Six-Day War. The diversion, Khrushchev, charged, was both a reflection and product of the imperialist powers' expansionist ambitions at the expense of the Arab states.

In May 1964, Khrushchev arrived in Egypt to take part in the celebrations marking the completion of the first stage of the construction of Aswan Dam. The Soviet Union had helped finance the dam, and the project was widely regarded as a symbol of Egyptian-Soviet relations. Khrushchev's visit signaled the start of a new, even more intimate phase of this relationship. Over the past few months, the Soviet Union had repeatedly reaffirmed its unwavering opposition to Israeli diversion, which, it declared, plainly infringed upon the Arab states' rights. It restated its support for the elimination of foreign bases from the region. Finally, it agreed to extend not only more military aid to Egypt, but also economic aid as well, offering Egypt a substantial $277,000 loan.[71]

Having lost faith in the West, the Arab states and especially Egypt turned to the Soviet Union for aid and succor, and the Soviet Union proved a very generous patron indeed. It granted Egypt liberal economic aid, offered Egypt unlimited diplomatic backing and furnished it with a plentiful supply of new weapons. Israel was naturally worried by the growing ties between Egypt and the Soviet Union. Increasingly nervous, it pressed the Western powers and, above all, the

United States, to help it maintain a balance of arms with the Arab world. All three Western powers, committed as they were to preserving a stable Middle East, by sustaining Israel's military power and ability to deter the Arab states, met Israel's appeals. Israel's supply Western weapons continued unabated.

This was all to the good, but the Israeli government wanted more. Eshkol coveted American patronage similar to the kind it granted to those countries that stood at the forefront of battle to help contain the Soviet Union's expansion.[72] In June 1964, Eshkol arrived in Washington. The first state visit of an Israeli prime minister to the United States, Eshkol's visit symbolized the deepening ties between the two countries. It was also, and perhaps, above all, a testament to Israel's success in obtaining an American commitment to supply it with offensive arms, as well additional economic aid. In the course of Eshkol's visit, President Johnson reaffirmed that the United States was wholly committed to preserving the territorial integrity and political independence of all the states in the Middle East. Johnson also underlined that the United States was sternly opposed to aggression. The United States utterly rejected, Johnson told Eshkol, the use of force or even the threat to use force against any state.[73]

Both Khrushchev's visit to Egypt and Eshkol's visit to the United States were a mark of the superpowers' growing involvement in the Middle East conflict. The same was true of the massive amounts of sophisticated weapons that were now pouring into the Middle East. It was this latter point that particularly worried Britain. Britain was certain that the huge quantities of arms that were streaming into the Middle East would increase the tension in the region and raise the self-confidence of the rival sides to new and dangerous heights. In an already volatile region this was a sure-fire recipe for a future conflagration. Accordingly, it began to explore the possibility of reaching an agreement with its fellow powers to limit the supply of arms to the Middle East.

Unhappily, Britain was soon forced to conclude that no such an agreement was possible. Any proposal to reduce the supply of arms was sure to spark off a furious Arab reaction. The Arab states would view it as an attempt to infringe upon their sovereignty. They would also regard it as Western pandering to Israel, not the least because the proposal to curb the arm supply was first voiced by Israel. Furthermore, as long as British forces and bases remained in the region, the Arab states would never agree to a plan to limit their supply of weapons. Consequently, anyone, and Britain above all, who even raised the possibility was bound to become the object of Arab ire. Then, of course, there was the Soviet Union. Britain recognized that the Soviet Union's policy of supplying arms to the Arab states was designed to maintain and extend Soviet influence in the region. It was, therefore, highly unlikely that the Soviets would agree to any measure that might impede the successful pursuit of both this policy and its objective.[74]

Britain's nightmare of a Middle East polarized between East and West was rapidly becoming a reality. Although Britain did not think that the Soviet Union wanted to provoke a conflagration between Israel and the Arab states, it did seek to encourage regional tension without igniting an explosion. The Foreign Office described Soviet policy as one of keeping the pot boiling without letting it boil over.[75] In Britain's opinion this was a high-risk policy, not the least because the pot might very well boil over. In seeking to maintain regional tension, which manifested itself in recurrent border incidents, the Soviet Union might ultimately push the region into war.

This was the state of affairs when, during the first week of June 1964, Israel finally activated the National Water Carrier and began to channel water from Lake Tiberias to the South. As a result, and as Britain feared, events swiftly took a turn for the worse.

NOVEMBER 13, 1964: THE CONFLICT ACQUIRES A NEW DIMENSION

The Arab states' steadfast and unified opposition to the Israeli diversion, as displayed at the Cairo Summit Conference, had, so far, received very little practical expression. Inter-Arab activity was limited, on the one hand to an extensive public relations campaign, and, on the other, to studying various issues connected to the execution of the counterdiversion scheme. Thus, the Arab foreign ministers had embarked on a tour of the world capitals, explaining the Arab position on the water dispute. The Arab counterdiversion scheme, they asserted, was a legitimate response to Israel's water program. It sole object was to prevent Israel from robbing the Arab states of the water that was rightfully theirs. Meanwhile, "The Authority for the Exploitation of the River Jordan and Its Headwaters" was initiated, in cooperation with a number of Yugoslav companies, to examine various counterdiversion plans.

Nor did much happen on the military front. The Unified Arab Command, which had finally been established, was busy assessing the quality of the Arab states' armies, exploring ways to increase their strength, considering ways to coordinate between the armies and examining various military strategies and tactics. One thing the Arab states did do was to begin to gather funds to finance these various military endeavors and the counterdiversion scheme.[76]

In truth, at this point in time, the Arabs states invested far more time and effort in internecine quarrels and disputes than in trying to block the Israeli water project. The civil war in Yemen, pitting the conservative and radical Arab states against each other, was still raging with no end in sight. Syria and Egypt were embroiled in a bitter conflict, sparked by collapse of the Union in August 1961. Ironically, the response to the Israeli diversion became another source of inter-Arab dispute. Lebanon stubbornly refused to divert the Jordan River's headwaters, until it was guaranteed sufficient protection against any possible Israeli reprisals. Although loudly protesting against Israeli aggression, Jordan was secretly adhering to the Johnston Plan and cooperating with the United States.[77] Syria tried, in vain, to convince the other Arab states that the sole solution to the water dispute was, as Nasser insisted, war and the destruction of Israel. But the Arab states turned a deaf ear to its demand for an all-out war of annihilation, leaving Syria alone and isolated.

While the Arab states were busy indulging in noisy propaganda and bitter infighting, Israel finally activated the National Water Carrier. It had tested the apparatus in the beginning of May, and, one month later, on June 5, exactly three years before outbreak of the Six-Day War, the National Water Carrier began to systematically channel water from Lake Tiberias to the Negev. Despite being Israel's largest development project to date, the launching of the National Water Carrier was accompanied by very little publicity. Careful not to trigger a furious Arab reaction, the Israeli government kept all official public celebrations to a minimum.

Celebrated or not, it was a splendid achievement, which had, like Israel's other development enterprises, certainly impressed Britain. Admiration apart, Britain was very much aware that the event was bound to produce a swift, violent and active inter-Arab response. And it was right. The Arab states reacted immediately, though, thankfully, they still limited themselves simply to condemning the Israeli diversion. They accused the Jews of stealing the water of the Jordan River. They denounced the Israeli diversion as an attack on the Arab nation's territorial waters. The Israeli diversion was, they railed, proof, if proof were needed, of Israel's expansionist ambitions, of its policy to rob and plunder the region, in total disregard of the Arabs's rights.[78]

The second Arab Summit Conference, which was take place in September in Alexandria, suddenly assumed immense significance. Originally the summit conference was to have assessed how much progress had been made in realizing the Cairo Summit Conference's decisions. Now, owing to the activation of the Israeli National Water Carrier, it seemed likely that the Arab states would use the summit conference to prove to the world that they would neither accept nor bow to Israeli aggression. They would probably decide at the summit conference what practical measures they should take in response to Israel's aggression. Syria, the most extreme of the Arab states, had embarked upon an aggressively active policy even before the September summit conference, possibly in the hope of forcing its fellow Arab states into a military confrontation with Israel.[79] It initiated a series of border incidents, with the result that, from July 1964 onward, shooting incidents between Syria and Israel became a daily occurrence.

The last thing Nasser wanted was to be dragged into an untimely war on Syria's heels. Although agreeing with Syria that the only solution to the water dispute and Arab-Israeli conflict was war, Nasser remained faithful to his strategy and refused to contemplate the idea of war before Egypt was able to wage one successfully, that is, able to destroy Israel. Accordingly, the Egyptian president sought to thwart Syria's attempt to bludgeon the Arab world into war by deliberately provoking Israel and escalating the conflict. The Alexandria Summit Conference provided him with the ideal opportunity to foil Syria's plans.[80]

At the summit conference, which met between September 5–11, Syria accused the Arab states of being so absorbed by the problem of the diversion of the Jordan River that they had lost sight of the big picture. The water dispute, Syria emphasized, was merely one facet, albeit an important facet, of the Palestinian problem as a whole. And, Syria reiterated, the Palestinian problem must be solved and solved soon. By 1970, Israel would possess an army of 1 million well-equipped soldiers. Worse, possessing atomic weapons, it would be able to repel any Arab attack, whether carried out by a single state or several. Therefore, Syria urged that Egypt's defensive policy should be abandoned and that the Arab states should go on the offensive immediately.[81]

In response, Nasser launched a minioffensive of his own against Syria. He acknowledged that the decision to go to war was not solely Egypt's, but one that had to be taken by all the Arab states. Yet, even if his fellow Arab leaders were inclined toward war, Nasser thought there were a few things that should be taken into account before the final decision was made. First and foremost, the Arab states were not yet ready or able to launch a successful war of annihilation. Nor, Nasser remarked, with a sly dig at Syria, could Syria escape responsibility for this unhappy state of affairs. In making his case, Nasser enlisted the help of General Amer, his chief of staff and now commander in chief of the United Arab Command. General Amer told the summit conference attendees that there were two military conditions that had to be met before the Arab states could wage the decisive battle against Israel. First, the confrontation states, Jordan, Syria and Lebanon, must allow the commander in chief of the United Arab Command to station foreign Arab troops on their territory at his discretion. Second, the Arab armies must coordinate their military strategy and tactics, establish a uniform military organization and standardize their weapon systems. These twin conditions were also necessary to protect the Arab counterdiversion scheme from Israeli aggression.

Neither condition was easy to fulfill. Lebanon and Jordan were both loath to allow foreign Arab troops inside their countries. Lebanon was worried lest these troops undermine the delicate balance between its Christian, Moslem and Druze communities. At the summit conference, Lebanon's representatives managed to smoothly avoid the issue by pointing out that only the Lebanese parliament had the authority to sanction such a step and until then their own hands were tied. Jordan thought that to allow foreign forces into Jordan was tantamount to letting a Trojan Horse to enter, which might provoke internal unrest and, on the other hand, initiate an Israeli attack. In addition, as both countries bought most of their weapons from the West they were equally opposed to the proposal to standardize the Arab countries' arms arsenal, at least on Egyptian terms. Egypt, not surprisingly, had demanded that the standardization be based on Soviet-made weapons.[82]

Syria, too, proved a problem. It had no objection to the proposal to standardize the Arab armies' weapons, as, like Egypt, it too received most of its arms from the East. However, it utterly refused to station foreign troops on its territory. Its refusal stemmed less from any practical reasons and more from Syria's desire to spike the guns of the Egyptian president and his accursed defensive strategy. The upshot was that the summit conference attendees had no choice but to bow to the three frontline states' refusal to host foreign troops on their soil. Nasser, curiously enough, was not, as the Syrians would have been chagrined to learn, particularly disappointed with this result. On the contrary, it served his interests well. It allowed him to push through a decision stating that foreign Arab troops only could be stationed on Arab territory with the sanction of the host country and only in time of war. Yet, regardless of who won this skirmish between Nasser and Syria, one thing was clear: as far as checking Israeli aggression, the Arab states were still treading water, if not actually regressing.

The summit conference did make a number of decisions concerning the counterdiversion scheme. It decided that Jordan would build a dam on the lower Yarmuk, next to the village of Mukheiba. The dam, with an estimated capacity of 200 mcm (million cubic meters) of water, would prevent Israel from exploiting the Yarmuk's waters. Syria was charged with diverting the Banias River. This demanded that the Syrians execute a rather complicated engineering project that involved digging a 73-km-long canal, and 4.5-km-long tunnel, linking the Banias to the Yarmuk and diverting about 100 mcm of water per annum. Ironically, Lebanon, regardless of the fact that it was still reluctant to embark upon any diversion scheme whatsoever, was assigned three diversion projects. It was to dig a 4-km-long canal between the Hasbani and Litani rivers, which could divert about 40 to 60 mcm of water per annum. It was to build two water diversion installations along the Central Hasbani, which were to channel flood and rain water into the Banias by means of a canal. This would divert an additional 30 cubic meters each year. Finally, Lebanon was ordered to construct a water pumping station alongside the Wazzani Spring, which ran into the Hasbani. This would allow Lebanon to exploit a further 90 mcm of water a year for irrigation purposes. The three Lebanese projects together would divert a great deal more water from the Hasbani than originally prescribed by the Johnston Plan.

The Alexandria Summit Conference decided that the Arab states were to start immediately to carry out the technical groundwork necessary to exploit the Jordan River's headwaters. It was estimated that the counterdiversion plan would take two years to complete and cost 16.5 million pounds sterling.[83] According to Arab calculations, once in place the counterdiversion would prevent 200 mcm of water from reaching the Jordan River, thus making a significant dent in Israel's future water supply and depriving it of about a third of the water it planned to channel through the National Water Carrier. Moreover, with less water coming in from the Banias and Hasbani rivers, the saliency levels of Lake Tiberias were likely to rise significantly. In short, the counterdiversion would cause serious damage to, indeed, wreck, Israel's development projects.[84]

In its closing statement, the summit conference attempted to present the Arab counterdiversion scheme in a positive light. The project was described as a legitimate and necessary response to Israeli aggression. The whole scheme was portrayed as no more than a legitimate act of self-defense. On a slightly contradictory note, the counterdiversion was also represented as a plan for wide-scale irrigation, and not an anti-Israeli measure at all.[85] Finally, the statement carefully underlined the Arab states' scrupulous observation of rules of international law.

The summit conference devoted some of its time to discussing the military measures that would be needed, if Israel responded aggressively, as it probably would, to the counterdiversion scheme. It was decided to push on with the buildup of special Iraqi, Syrian and Saudi Arabian forces, which were to be mobilized if the three countries carrying out the counterdiversion were to fall victim to an Israeli attack or were even threatened by the possibility of an attack. The remainder of the Arab states promised to keep their armed forces on stand by and be ready at all times to meet and repel an Israeli offensive. The summit conference also endorsed the establishment of the Palestine Liberation Army. As the military arm of the PLO, its task was to help liberate Palestine from the Zionist imperialist enemy. Finally, it decided to accelerate with the establishment of a joint Arab military force, and to rearm and reequip the Arab armies so that they would be ready for the decisive campaign against Israel when it came. The summit conference allocated 150 million pounds sterling to these projects, which, it was estimated, would take ten years to complete. On the diplomatic front, it was decided that, henceforth, the Arabs states would determine their relations with other countries in light of the position these adopted on the Palestinian question and other issues, which were of concern to the Arab world.[86]

The Alexandria Summit Conference's decisions were evidence that the Arab states were as determined as ever to prevent Israel from exploiting the Jordan River. In fact, given the detail with which the counterdiversion scheme was discussed at the summit conference, they appeared to be more committed to this goal than ever. If Israel was set upon diverting the Jordan River, the Arab states were no less resolved to pursue their counterdiversion plans to the end. Yet, in view of past experience there was every reason to believe, and hope, that the Alexandria Summit Conference's decisions would share the fate of their predecessors and that practically speaking nothing much would happen.

Certainly the Israeli government's reaction to the summit conference was much the same as its response to the Cairo Summit Conference. Israel highlighted the fact that Israel depended on the Jordan River and its water. Eshkol drew the analogy between blood and water. Water, he declared, was Israel's lifeblood, and it simply could not exist without it. It was, he pronounced, a life or death issue, and he warned that Israel would ensure that nothing impeded the flow of water from Lake Tiberias southward.[87] The government reiterated Eshkol's January 20 statement to the Knesset, which he had made in the wake of the Cairo Summit Conference. It announced that the Israeli government was resolved to continue pumping water from Lake Tiberias. It would observe the quotas established by the Johnston Plan. It would oppose any unilateral and illegal steps the Arab states might take in this respect and would take strong action against any attempt to interfere with its vital rights.[88]

This routine, almost automatic response pointed to a measure of Israeli self-confidence, even complacency. Israel was, evidently, not very worried by the Alexandria Summit Conference and its decisions. It assumed that the Arab states would continue to deluge it in a flood of invective and approbation, but little more. Nor was this assumption unfounded. According to Israeli intelligence, Nasser would not dare risk military action against Israel, as long as his forces were embroiled in the Yemen civil war.[89] In addition, it was clear that Lebanon, having declared, time and again, that without sufficient protection from Israeli reprisals it would not divert the Hasbani, would not start work on the counter-diversion scheme. Nor did such protection appear likely in the near future. One reason was that both Jordan and Lebanon refused to allow foreign Arab troops on their territory for fear of provoking internal instability. Furthermore, Jordan, on its part, stood by its promise to the United States to adhere to the Johnston Plan. The dam it was building alongside the Yarmuk was not a threat, as it conformed to the principles laid down by the Johnston Plan. The only loose cannon as far as Israel could see was Syria. By now, the shooting incidents between Israel and Syria had become an everyday affair. Thankfully, however, Syria, unpredictable, fanatical and dangerous though it might be, had found itself isolated in both the Cairo and Alexandria Summit Conferences.

Nevertheless, Israel thought it wise to take two precautionary measures, which would impress upon the Arab states, and, above all, Syria, its determination to secure its water rights, as well as other rights contested by the Arab world. First, it decided, shortly after the Alexandria Summit Conference, to resume farming the land in the disputed demilitarized zone. Second, the government decided to accelerate the construction of an army patrol track along Israel's northern border, known quite simply as the Patrol Track. Israel would exploit both the Patrol Track and the farming of the disputed zones to provoke border incidents with Syria. These, in turn, would, as they were intended to, offer Israel a useful opportunity to sabotage Syrian diversion equipment, which Syria, anxious to start diverting the Banias as soon as possible, had recently brought to its designated diversion site.

Until now, in order not to exacerbate the border incidents with Syria and endanger the work carried out on the National Water Carrier, Israel had studiously refrained from farming the land in the disputed zone. Now that the National Water Carrier was complete and fully functional, Israel felt itself free to start farming the land again. Much the same was true of the Patrol Track. Israel had begun building the track in late 1961, primarily in order to stop Syria from gaining control of the River Dan's underground rivulets. The Syrians objected to this, claiming that both the underground rivulets and part of the Patrol Track ran through sovereign Syrian territory.[90] The result, typically, was a series of shooting incidents between the two countries. In order to prevent the situation from escalating further and threatening its National Water Carrier, Israel stopped constructing the Patrol Track. Once the National Water Carrier was up and running, it resumed work on the track.

Britain regarded Israel's statements, which largely reiterated those made nine months earlier after the Cairo Summit Conference, its actions and its obvious self-confidence as a sign that the water dispute, rather than escalating was, in fact, abating. Also encouraging was the fact that Arab unity and resolve appeared to be on the wane. But perhaps the most important and promising result of the Alexandria Summit Conference was that the Arab leaders had endorsed Nasser's view that the Arab states were not yet ready to embark upon a war with Israel. The summit conference had, for the present, rejected any military initiative against Israel. The only decision of any significance to emerge from the summit conference was, Britain thought, its decision to push forward the counterdiversion scheme. But then again this was something the Arab states had been talking about for ages, and so far had done little to implement.

Nor did the Alexandria Summit provide the cement necessary to unite the deeply divided and factitious Arab world. The Cairo Summit Conference had been followed by a short period of Arab euphoria, which owed much to the sheer delight and excitement that such a gathering had taken place at all. This sense of elation soon evaporated, by the time of the Alexandria Summit Conference had convened, nine months later, discord rather than unity was the order of the day. The summit conference, itself, was characterized by tension, mutual antagonism and renewed friction. The British Foreign Office observed, with a degree of satisfaction, that there was some evidence to support the thesis that "the second Arab Summit Conference could prove to be the beginning of a breakdown in cooperation rather than a movement towards unity of action."[91] At the summit conference, it pointed out that the Arab leaders clearly recognized and acknowledged that each Arab country had its own separate identity, problems, interests and outlook.[92] This was one reason why General Amer found it impossible to persuade any of the Arab states to abide by the decision to standardize their weapon systems, or, in the case of the confrontation states, agree to the deployment of foreign forces on their soil. As a result, the Foreign Office noted, quite happily, the Unified Arab Command was still little more than a confederation of tribes.

As for the counterdiversion scheme, here, too, there seemed to be, as far as Britain could see, little cause for alarm. Although the summit conference had decided to put the various schemes into operation, forthwith, in practice, nothing much was happening, certainly nothing that might provoke an Israeli military response. Lebanon and Jordan, two of the three countries charged with carrying out the counterdiversion scheme, were extremely reluctant to do so. True, there was the Mukheiba Dam, but that project complied with the standards set by the Johnston Plan: The dam was being built south of Lake Tiberias and would in no way impair Israel's own exploitation of the Jordan River. In fact, Britain suspected, the Mukheiba Dam was more of a face-saving device than a practical measure to exploit the Jordan River.[93]

Lebanon, on its part, stuck to its refusal to start work on the counterdiversion project. It told Britain that it was very much concerned lest a scheme, which was apparently designed to pour fresh water into the sea, would turn world opinion against it. Perhaps. But what Lebanon really dreaded was Israel's reaction to the Arab counterdiversion. At Alexandria, Lebanon's representatives emphasized time and again that there was absolutely no way it would begin work on the counterdiversion without sufficient protection. This, as far as Britain was concerned, was all to the good, and the Foreign Office instructed Sir Derek Riches, its ambassador to Lebanon, to play on Lebanon's fears and weaken its resolve even further. "You need not," the ambassador was told, "officially strive to quieten any fears … about what the Israelis might do to a spite diversion."[94]

That left Syria, and Syria, as Britain knew, was definitely a problem. At both summit conferences, Syria had urged a tough, militant position. It had also been the first to start work on the counterdiversion scheme. Nevertheless, given that the Syrian project was immensely complicated technically and very expensive to boot, Britain presumed that Syria's efforts were little more than a not very impressive show of strength. Owing to soil porosity and other obstacles, its task of digging a 73-km-long canal plus a 4.5-km-long tunnel was, in Britain's estimation, only marginally feasible.[95]

But what about Israel? How would Israel react to the Arab counterdiversion scheme? On the assumption that the Arab scheme posed no real threat to its water economy, Britain believed that Israel would not do anything that might further exacerbate the situation. John Beith in Tel Aviv reinforced this judgment and reassured his colleagues in London that Israel's current government, despite the presence of the hard-line Golda Meir, was much more reasonable than any of Ben Gurion's governments. "The Israeli Government as at present constituted," he maintained, "would think very hard before taking retaliatory action against Arab projects to divert the Jordan headwater."[96]

The Foreign Office sighed with relief and noted with satisfaction that the Middle East and Britain, both, had apparently safely passed the hurdle posed by the Israeli National Water Carrier.[97] Admittedly, the water dispute remained on the agenda and might yet spark a conflagration. But, on the whole, the chances of that happening seemed remote. On the contrary, after the Alexandria Summit Conference, there was every reason to hope for the return of the stable climate, which had characterized the Middle East from the end of the Suez Campaign to the opening of the Cairo Summit Conference.

It soon became obvious that any such hopes were completely unfounded. Where Britain erred was in underestimating Israel's resolve to prevent any interference with the Jordan River's headwaters. Israel viewed any counterdiversion project, regardless of its stated objective, as a threat to its water economy. John Beith's assessment of the moderate character of Eshkol's government didn't help either, as it merely reinforced the prevailing view in the Foreign Office that Israel would act with restraint and think very carefully before taking strong measures. Israel knew that a disproportionate response to the counterdiversion scheme might escalate the Arab-Israeli conflict, possibly to the point of an open confrontation, and this was something, the Foreign Office assumed, that

Israel wanted to avoid. Finally, though Britain took it for granted that the border incidents would continue and the Syrians and Israelis will continue to exchange fire, it also presumed that these incidents would remain fairly low-key affairs, which the United Nations Observation Force could easily handle.

The Alexandria Summit Conference's decision to accelerate the execution of the counterdiversion scheme had two immediate results. First, Syria began to put into effect the plan to divert the Banias. Second, Israel was resolved to stop, at any price, the efforts to carry out the counterdiversion scheme. Accordingly, the situation along the Israeli-Syrian border soon deteriorated. Syria had been ready to start executing the counterdiversion scheme at a moment's notice. Even before the Alexandria Summit Conference had convened, it had begun to draft engineering plans and survey the land earmarked for the counterdiversion. In the beginning of November, having introduced engineering equipment to the site, it began to prepare the land and dig a canal, north and south of the Banias streams.[98] No sooner had Syria begun to work on the scheme, than Israel promptly destroyed its engineering equipment. Tired of the rising number of border incidents and shooting initiated by the Syrians, Israel saw this action also as way of settling its account with the Syrian government. Israel, at least initially, had no intention to strike a severe blow at the Syrians; it did assume, however, that at some point such a blow would become inevitable.[99]

On November 3, Israel began to deliberately provoke Syria. It resumed work on the Patrol Track and dispatched army patrols down the Track to ensure that Israel remain in full control of the entire route. Concurrently, it began to farm the demilitarized zone.[100] Syria was furious. Claiming sovereignty over part of the Patrol Track and opposed to Israel farming the disputed demilitarized zones, it reacted violently. It did not, however, quite follow the Israeli script. It stepped up the shooting incidents, but it also began to shell civilian settlements along the border. In defense of its actions, the Syrian government claimed, with some justice, that Israel had introduced heavy weapons into several of these settlements and used them against Syria. This was true to a point, except that Israel had only done so after Syria had done precisely the same thing on its side of the border.

On November 13, after a series of heavy artillery bombardments, Israel launched a massive air strike against Syria. The Israeli air force, which had been on standby for some time, was now ordered to silence the Syrian guns. The air strike took Syria, used to Israeli restraint over the border incidents, by complete surprise. But, as Ezer Weizman, the head of the Israeli Air Force, noted with pleasure: "We have waited for a long time to teach them [the Syrians] a lesson about the provocations."[101] And so Israel did. Using napalm, among other things, Israel completely wrecked the Syrian diversion equipment and in general caused havoc to Syrian ground targets.

Israel's decision to launch an air strike against Syria was no doubt a revolutionary one. The last time Israel had employed aircraft in a retaliatory strike was in 1951, during the Al Hamah incident, which took place south of Lake Tiberias and was, moreover, a limited operation that did not cause any damage. Since then, Israel had deliberately abstained from using its air force during border clashes with its neighbors. Ben Gurion, Israel's prime minister at the time, believed that to do so would lead to an escalation of the conflict and probably war.[102]

Ben Gurion was right, at least in part. The air strike against Syrian ground targets did mark a serious escalation of the conflict, and not only between Syria and Israel. Following the November 13 incident, the Arab states declared that an attack against Syria was tantamount to an attack against all the Arab states. They now began to talk of concentrating their forces in order to repeal Israeli aggression. However, as usual, there was an enormous gulf between the Arab states' words and actions. None of them, for example, proposed taking any active military measures in response to the Israeli air strike. It was evidence of the United Arab Command's impotence. It was also proof that Egypt was, as yet, unwilling to ignite an armed conflict over the water dispute.

The Israeli air strike was unprecedented, both in terms of the large number of aircraft and bombs Israel employed and the fact that it penetrated deep into Syrian territory. The Israeli government, hoping to preempt international censure, such as it had suffered following the 1951 air strike, emphasized that this time the strike was in response to Syrian shelling of Israeli civilian settlements, which was true. Nevertheless, the operation signaled to world opinion and the Arab states alike, as indeed it was intended to do, that Israel was determined to use all the means at its disposal to put an end to the counterdiversion scheme and deter the Syrians. The air strike was also a measure of Israel's growing self-confidence. Its leaders were convinced that, at this point in time, none of the Arab states, individually or collectively, posed a military threat to it. In particular because Israel enjoyed almost total American support on the water issue and some very concrete American sympathy as far as its security needs were concerned.

The November 13 air strike was a turning point in Israel's tense relations with its Arab neighbors. Its revolutionary decision to employ its air force would greatly effect subsequent developments in the region. Nor was the operation to be an on-off affair. There would be, as Eshkol knew, no turning back and Israel would continue to use its air force to retaliate against the Syrians. Thus, the operation heralded Israel's adoption of an even more relentless policy against Syria. Nor would Syria, on its part, submit quietly to this new, more aggressive Israeli policy.[103] In sum, the air strike introduced a new and much more dangerous dimension to the Middle East conflict.

Britain was not really surprised by Israel's decision to launch an air strike against Syria. It had been expecting something of the sort since the beginning of 1964 once the water dispute had clearly escalated.[104] Based on the reports of its representatives in Tel Aviv and Damascus, the Foreign Office concluded that, soon after the Alexandria Summit Conference, Israel had deliberately embarked upon a series of provocative steps designed to goad the Syrians into opening fire on it. Britain was aware, for example, that the Israeli army had introduced heavy weapons into its border settlements and that these were used during the exchanges of fire with Syria. It realized that the air strike was not a casual, impromptu escalation of the border incidents, but a well-planned operation, which was aimed at teaching the Syrians, as John Beith put it, a sharp lesson.[105] Nevertheless, and despite the seriousness of the Israeli action, Britain did not think that the Israeli government was solely responsible for creating this new and infinitely more perilous situation.

The Foreign Office believed Syria could claim more than its fair share of the responsibility for exacerbating the border incidents. Syria had, for a long time, been systematically harassing and provoking Israel. It had stepped up its provocative activities even further once the National Water Carrier had begun operating. Moreover, the Foreign Office maintained, Syria had yet to prove its claim that the Patrol Track passed through sovereign Syrian territory. Not, it pointed out, that Syria has shown any sign that it was willing to have a survey of the area carried out in order to verify its claim. Finally, and most tellingly, by shelling Israeli civilian settlements Syria was the first to open fire and escalate the border incidents. Syria also had a clear topographical advantage over Israel, which allowed it to shell the Israeli Kibbutzim, located close to the Syrian military outposts, easily, heavily and, so it thought, with impunity. John Beith drew the Foreign Office's attention to the Israeli settlements' topographic vulnerability. They were, he noted, "sitting ducks" on a plain commanded by Syrian gun positions. "It would be," he continued, "impossible to take action on the ground against these artillery posts except on a large scale."[106] An air strike was the only way to muzzle the Syrian guns.[107]

Although the Foreign Office agreed with the ambassador's judgment, it was loath to admit as much to the Israeli government. In official discussions with Israel's representatives, the Foreign Office took a much more neutral line. It emphasized that even though the British government supported the preservation of peace and stability along the cease-fire line, it did not think that any breach of the cease-fire accords by one side justified a violent reaction by the other. It pointed out that the United Nations Observation Force was the sole body authorized to deal with all cease-fire violations.[108] Privately, however, and between themselves, the British considered the Israeli air strike to be a fairly reasonable response to the Syrian artillery bombardments.

Topping Britain's list of priorities at the moment was to somehow prevent the conflict between Israel and the Arab states from accelerating any further. Both Israel and Syria had lodged complaints with the Security Council and this was, in Britain's opinion, a positive step, as it served to ease the tension a bit. The downside was that a discussion in the Security Council meant that Britain was faced with the unhappy prospect of formulating and stating publicly its views on recent events. To censor Syria, which according to UN reports had been the first to open fire, would bring down the wrath of the entire Arab world on Britain's head. In that Britain was already the target of Arab denunciations, owing to its presence in the area, this was really something it hoped to avoid. Yet Britain did not want to condemn the Israeli air strike. Although it acknowledged that the air strike presented a new and dangerous escalation of the conflict, Britain did not think that overall the situation in the Middle East had been made worse merely because, in this instance, the damage had been caused by bombs dropped from airplanes rather than by shells fired from cannon. Nor did it believe that the air strike was an unfair or disproportionate response to Syria's artillery bombardment of Israeli settlements. The British air attaché calculated that even though Syria had dropped 7 tons of shells on Israel, the Israel air force had dropped 10 tons of bombs on Syria. In any case, Britain was all too aware that one day it, too, might have to take similar action in the areas under its control, so that it had no wish to condemn and outlaw the use of air power against artillery batteries.[109]

So what should Britain do? What should its attitude in the Security Council be? How should it ultimately vote? These questions assumed even greater significance in view of recent political changes in Britain. On October 19, 1964, after thirteen long years in opposition, the British Labour Party had finally won the elections. Its leader, Harold Wilson, was known for his pro-Israeli views, and both the Arabs and Israelis regarded the stand Britain would take in the Security Council as a test case, an indication of the new government's policy in the Middle East. All waited with baited breath to see what course the British would adopt.

Surprisingly, or perhaps not, the Labour government decided to stick to the policy of its predecessor and maintain a low profile. The Foreign Office noted, with satisfaction, that the present government, like its Conservative predecessor, was inclined to avoid intervening in the dispute, other than minimally, and was quite content to leave all the dirty work to the Americans. In the Security Council, the United States tabled a balanced noncommittal resolution. The resolution expressed the Security Council's regret at the air strike. It also suggested that the Israeli-Syrian Mixed Armistice Commission reconvene and resume its discussions. Finally, it called for the final delineation of the Israeli-Syrian border. Britain endorsed the American resolution; the Soviet Union vetoed it.

Once again the Soviet Union had employed its veto for reasons of personal political advantage. The Soviet Union had, so far, benefited greatly from the Arab-Israeli conflict, and Britain, for one, was hardly surprised that instead of trying to find a reasonable solution to the dispute, it preferred to veto any constructive resolution to the dispute and, as Britain put it, to keep the pot boiling. It was after all the Soviet Union that had the most to gain if the tension increased or matters came to boil.[110] This was why the Soviet Union had vetoed the Security Council's resolution in August 1963, following the Almagor incident, and it was why it now did so again. By using its veto, the Soviet Union established itself as a loyal friend of the Arab states, committed to protecting Arab rights. This was in direct contrast to the United States and Britain who, despite the former's balanced proposal and the latter's efforts to maintain a low profile, appeared to the Arabs to be firmly on Israel's side.

The relative calm that had characterized the Middle East since the Cairo Summit Conference of January 1964 was swiftly dissipating. By the end of the year, relations between Israel and its Arab neighbors had taken a marked turn for the worse. The November 13 air-strike, far from being a random and isolated incident, was the culmination of a series of increasingly ugly border incidents that had taken place since the beginning of that month. Britain was under no illusion that the Israeli air strike and the destruction of counterdiversion equipment had in any way weakened Syria's resolve. The Syrians, it assumed, were still bent on and quite capable of stretching Israeli nerves and patience to the limit. The Israeli government, on the other hand, was plainly determined to stop the counterdiversion at all costs. The winds of war were beginning to blow—a war in whose growing shadow Britain now lived in fear.

NOTES

1. FO 371/170520, Brief by Secretary of State, December 11, 1963; Tessler, *Israeli-Palestinian Conflict*, pp. 362–363.

2. Rabinovich, "Conflict over the Jordan," p. 866.

3. Nimrod, "Conflict over the Jordan," p. 11; Shemesh, "Arab Struggle over Water," p. 128.

4. FO 371/175556, Amman to FO, January 2, 1964; FO 371/175574, Amman to FO, December 18, 1963 and Damascus to FO, January 7, 1964 and Guidance no. 25, January 13, 1964.

5. Ma'oz, *Syria and Israel*, p. 81; Shemesh, "Arab Struggle over Water," pp. 130–131.

6. Shemesh, "Arab Struggle over Water," p. 131.

7. Nimrod, "Water of Contradiction," p. 97; *Ha'aretz*, December 17 and 29, 1963; *Ruz al Yusuf*, December 16, 1963.

8. FO 371/175558, Damascus to FO, February 8, 1964; ISA, Hez/19/4327, Herzog to Israel's Representatives, December 31, 1963; *Al Ahram*, December 24, 1963; *Ha'aretz*, December 24, 1963.

9. The Egyptian government, fearing that Israel might respond aggressively to the summit conference, stationed an infantry division and an armored division east of Suez, between January 5–10. See FO 371/175558, Minute by Laurence, February 7, 1964 and Cairo to FO, February 28, 1964. Also *Ha'aretz*, January 11, 1964.

10. FO 371/175556, Cairo to FO, January 18, 1964 and Amman to FO, January 22, 1964; ISA, Hez/20/4322, Washington to Jerusalem, January 26, 1964.

11. FO 371/175556, Cairo to FO, January 18, 1964; FO 371/175557, Arab Summit Conference, January 28, 1964; Rabin, *Service Notes*, pp. 119–120; *Al Ahram*, January 18–19, 1964.

12. Sela, *Unity within Conflict*, p. 30.

13. FO 371/175555, Middle East Experts Report, October 22–23, 1964; FO 371/175556, Amman to FO, January 23, 1964.

14. CAB 133/247, Background Notes, January 31, 1964; FO 371/175574, Minute by FO, January 15, 1964.

15. FO 371/17554, Minute by Morris, January 2, 1964; ISA, Hez/20/4322, Jerusalem to Washington, January 23, 1964 and Washington to Jerusalem, January 26, 1964.

16. *Ha'aretz*, January 16, 1964.

17. *Knesset Debates,* 38, January 20, 1964; Lowi, *Water and Power,* p. 123.

18. FO 371/175860, Minute by Morris, February 28, 1964; *Ha'aretz,* January 21, 1964.

19. FO 371/175574, Minute by Morris, January 2, 1964; ISA Hez/10/4314, Minute by Kahana, May 1964.

20. ISA Hez/20/4320, Washington to Jerusalem, and Record of Conversation, January 24, 1964; and Washington to Jerusalem, January 26, 1964; and New York to Jerusalem, February 12, 1964; *FRUS,* 1964–1968, pp. 9–10.

21. FO 371/175574, Paris to FO, January 2, 1964; FO 371/175575, Paris to FO, January 27, 1964.

22. FO 371/175575, FO to Washington and Wright to FO, January 22, 1964; FO371/175806, Record of Conversation, March 9, 1964; ISA, Hez/20/4322, Jerusalem to London, January 16, 1964.

23. FO 371/175575, Tel Aviv to FO, January 22, 1964, and Minute by Morris, January 24, 1964; FO 371/175806, Record of Conversation, March 9, 1964; ISA, Hez,/20/4322, Jerusalem to Washington, January 23, 1964.

24. FO 371/175576, Minute by Harrison, February 21, 1964.

25. FO 371/175574, Guidance no. 30, January 14, 1964; FO 371/175576, Cairo to FO, February 13, 1964 and Record of Conversation, April 9, 1964.

26. FO 371/175574, Guidance no. 30, January 14, 1964.

27. FO 371/175576, Record of Conversation, April 9, 1964.

28. FO 371/175574, Minute by Morris, January 2, 1964 and Broomley to FO, January 7, 1964.

29. FO 371/175574, Guidance no. 30, January 14, 1964.

30. *Ha'aretz,* February 24, 1964.

31. FO 371/175574, Broomley to FO, January 7, 1964; FO 371/175576, Minute by Morris, February 20, 1964; FO 371/175557, Cairo to FO, February 1, 1964.

32. *Ha'aretz,* April 30, 1964.

33. FO 371/175575, Minute by Goodison, January 6, 1964 and Minute by Sinclair, January 7, 1964.

34. FO 371/175574, Tel Aviv to FO, January 10, 1964.

35. Ibid.

36. FO 371/175574, Guidance no. 25, January 13, 1964; FO 371/175576, Guidance no. 119, February 11, 1964; FO 317/175577, Review of Development, May 30, 1964.

37. FO 371/175574, Minute by Morris, January 22, 1964.

38. CAB 133/247, Minute by the FO, January 31, 1964; FO 371/175576, Minute by MacLaren, February 2, 1964; PREM 11/4876, Lists of Briefs, March 1964.

39. FO 371/17552, Minute by Crawford, April 13, 1964; ISA, Hez/20/4322, London to Jerusalem, January 16, 1964.

40. FO 371/175843, Washington to FO, February 6 and 25, 1964 and Minute by Morris, March 31, 1964; FO 371175546, Minute by Morris, April 23, 1964; *FRUS,* 1964–1968, pp. 29–31.

41. PREM 11/4933, Macmillan to Secretary of State, June 2, 1964; FO 371/175806, Minute by Morris, February 28, 1964.

42. FO 371/175806, Tel Aviv to FO, March 27, 1964.

43. FO 371/175574, Minutes by Morris, January 2 and 13, 1964.

44. Ibid.

45. FO 371/175576, Guidance no. 119, February 11, 1964 and FO to Amman, 25 February 25, 1964.

46. FO 371/175576, Background Note by the FO, February 11, 1964; DEFE 13, Butler to Prime Minister, April 20, 1964; CAB 134/2302, Overseas Defence Committee, July 27, 1963; Abadi, *Britain's Withdrawal*, p. 196.

47. FO 371/175574, Guidance no. 31, January 14, 1964; FO 371/175806, Minute by Morris, February 28, 1964.

48. FO 371/175574, Minute by Crawford, January 3, 1964 and Views on the Jordan Water Problem, January 8, 1964; ISA, Hez/20/4322, Jerusalem to London, January 16, 1964.

49. O'Ballance, *Arab Guerrilla Power*, p. 23; FO 371/175557, Damascus to FO, February 24, 1964.

50. FO 371/17557, Damascusto FO, February 24, 1964.

51. ISA Hez/20/4322, Washington to Jerusalem, January 10, 1964; FO 371/175576, Minute by Morris, January 22, 1964 and Amman to FO, January 23, 1964; FO 371/175579, Beirut to FO, February 8, 1964.

52. FO 371/175574, Damascus to FO, January 7, 1964 and Minute by the FO, January 15, 1964; CAB 133/247, Background Notes, January 31, 1964.

53. PREM 11/4876, Talking Points, March 1964; FO 371/175554, Minute by the FO, January 1964.

54. FO 371/175558, Anglo-American Talks, January 29–30, 1964 and FO to Beirut, April 17, 1964.

55. FO 371/175574, Minute by FO, January 8 and 15, 1964.

56. FO 371/175558, Minute by Morris, March 10, 1964.

57. Ibid.; FO 371/151254, Minute by Beith, January 25, 1960 and Minute by Stevens, January 28, 1960 and FO to Washington, February 3, 1960.

58. FO 371/175556, FO to Amman, January 7, 1964; FO 371/175557, Minute by Morris, March 5, 1964.

59. FO 371/175558, Minute by Morris, March 10, 1964; FO 371/175546, FO to Amman, February 25, 1964.

60. FO 371/175550, Washington to FO, January 7, 1964; ISA, Hez/20/4322, Washington to Jerusalem, January 10, 1964; ISA, Hez/19/4387, Washington to Jerusalem, April 21, 1964; *FRUS*, 1964–1968, pp. 38–39.

61. *Ha'aretz*, December 19, 1963.

62. Khouri, "Jordan River," p. 49; *The Times*, January 22, 1964.

63. ISA, Hez/20/4322, January 24 and 26, 1964 and February 14, 1964; FO 71/175550, Washington to FO, January 24, 1964.

64. Bar-Siman-Tov, *Israel*, p. 88; Spiegel, *Arab-Israeli Conflict*, pp. 123–125; Smith, *Arab-Israeli Conflict*, p. 193.

65. Little, "Choosing Sides," p. 156.

66. ISA, Hez/20/4322, Washington to Jerusalem, February 3, 1964; FO 371/175501, Amman to FO, January 29, 1964; *Ha'aretz*, January 23, 1964; *Al Ahram*, January 23, 1964; Riad, *Struggle for Peace*, pp. 12, 15; El Hussini, *Soviet-Egyptian Relations*, pp. 123, 133.

67. FO 371/186857, January 28, 1964; FO 371/175560, September 12, 1964; Heikal, *Cairo Documents*, p. 200; Khouri, "Jordan River," p. 150.

68. Little, *Choosing Sides*, p. 156; El Hussini, *Soviet-Egyptian Relations*, p. 133.

69. Wehling, "Dilemma of Superpower," p. 177; Kass, *Soviet Involvement*, p. 92.

70. Bhutani, *Israel-Soviet Cold War*, p. 92; Khouri, "Jordan River," p. 49; FO 371/178589, Cairo to FO, May 13, 1964.

71. Little, "Choosing Sides," p. 157; Heikal, *Sphinx and Commissar*, p. 136; El Hussini, *Soviet-Egyptian Relations*, p. 154; FO 371/178589, Minute by Smith, May 27, 1964.

72. Bar-Siman-Tov, *Israel*, pp. 86, 88.

73. Rabin, *Service Notes*, pp. 127–128; NA, RG/2346, Circular no. 2255, June 3, 1964; Spiegel, *Arab-Israeli Conflict*, p. 123; *Ha'aretz*, June 3 and 19, 1964.

74. FO 371/175546, Minute by Cradock, June 12, 1964; FO 371/175570, Minute by Goodison, September 7, 1964; ISA, Hez/11/744, Lourie to Levavi, July 2, 1964.

75. FO 371/175550, Minute by Crawford, January 24, 1964; FO 371/175546, Minute by Morris, April 23, 1964.

76. Sela, *Unity within Conflict*, p. 38.

77. Ibid.; ISA, Hez/20/4322. Washington to Jerusalem, January 10, 1964.

78. Gilbo'a, *Six Years*, p. 40; Nimrod, *Waters of Contradiction*, p. 100; *Ha'aretz*, May 7, 1964.

79. FO 371/175818, Tel Aviv to FO, July 17 and August 3, 1964; NA RG59/2352, SD to London, July 10, 1964 and Talbot to Harriman, July 13, 1964.

80. FO 371/175560, Arab Summit Conference, September 15, 1964; FO 371/175561, Cairo to FO, September 30, 1964.

81. FO 371/175559, Cairo to FO, September 13, 1964; FO 371/175561, Damascus to FO, September 22, 1964 and Cairo to FO, September 30, 1964.

82. Khouri, "Jordan River," p. 52; FO 371/175546, Note by Crawford, September 22, 1964.

83. FO 371/175555, Brief by the FO, October 12, 1964; FO 371/175578, Cairo to FO, September 14, 1964; FO 371/175560, Minute by Cradock, September 15, 1964; Yaniv, "Brutal Dialogue," p. 370; Seguev, *Israel*, pp. 28–29.

84. Seguev, *Israel*, p. 29; *Davar*, February 12, 1964.

85. Sela, *Decline of the Arab-Israeli Conflict*, p. 62.

86. FO 371/175559, Cairo to FO, September 12, 1964; FO 371/175560, Minute by Cradock, September 15, 1964; *Al Ahram*, September 11–12, 1964; Shemesh, "Arab Struggle over Water," p. 141.

87. Interview with Eshkol, *Ma'ariv*, October 4, 1967; Lowi, *Water and Power*, p. 125.

88. *Ha'aretz*, September 14, 1964; *Knesset Debates*, 40, October 12, 1964.

89. Gilbo'a, *Six Years*, pp. 41–42; Haber, *War Will Break Out*, p. 95.

90. *Ha'aretz*, November 8, 1964; Seguev, *Israel*, p. 31; Bull, *War and Peace*, pp. 74–76; ISA, Hez/2/4320, Jerusalem to Washington, November 14, 1964.

91. FO 371/175560, Minute by Cradock, September 15, 1964; FO371/175561, Minute by Morris, October 19, 1964.

92. FO 371/175561, FO to New York, October 28, 1964.

93. FO 371/175569, Minute by Cradock, September 15, 1964; FO 371/175561, Minute by Morris, October 19, 1964; FO 371/175578, FO to Tel Aviv, October 14, 1964.

94. FO 371/175561, Beirut to FO, September 26, 1964, and FO to Beirut, October 10, 1964.

95. Naff, *Water in the Middle East*, p. 43; FO 371/17555, Brief by FO, October 12, 1964.

96. FO 371/175579, Tel Aviv to FO, October 26, 1964.

97. FO 371/175578, FO to Tel Aviv, October 14, 1964.

98. Shemesh, "Arab Struggle over Water," p.149; Rabin, *"Service Notes,"* p. 121.

99. Yaniv, "Brutal Dialogue," p. 272; NA, RG59/2353, Tel Aviv, to SD, November 16, 1964; FO 371/175818, Tel Aviv to FO, July 13, 1964.

100. Yaniv, *Politics and Strategy*, p. 188; NA RG/59/2353 Tel Aviv to SD, November 16, 1964; Bull, *War and Peace*, p. 75.

101. *Ha'aretz*, November 15, 1964; Blechman, "Impact of Israel's Reprisals," p. 156; Dupuy, *Elusive Victory*, p. 224. Haber, *"War Will Break Out,"* pp. 41–43.

102. Bull, *War and Peace*, p. 76; Shemesh, "Arab Struggle over Water," p. 151; *Ha'aretz*, November 15, 1964.

103. Schelling, *Arms and Influence*, pp. 165–166; Haber, *War Will Break Out*, p. 43.

104. FO 371/175577, Minute by Morris, March 15, 1964.

105. FO 371/175820, Damascus to FO, December 17, 1964; FO 371/175819, Tel Aviv to FO, November 14, 1964.

106. FO 371/175819, Record of Conversation, and FO to New York, November 16, 1964.

107. FO 371/175820, Damascus to FO, December 17, 1964; FO 371/175819, Tel Aviv to FO, November 14, 1964.

108. FO 371/175819, December 1, 1964.

109. FO 371/175819, New York to FO, November 17, 1964; FO 371/175820, FO to New York, December 3 1964 and Tel Aviv to FO, December 15, 1964.

110. FO 371/175820, FO to Damascus, January 29, 1965.

3

The Winds of War
The Threat of a Conflagration between Israel and Its Arab Neighbors

---

ISRAELI POLICY

The air strike on November 13 offered clear evidence of the water dispute's dangerous potential. Syria, undeterred, was clamoring for war against Israel. Convinced that the deterioration of Israeli-Syrian relations served its interests, Syria was more than happy with the way things were developing. It hoped that a large-scale military confrontation with Israel would finally compel the Arab states, and, above all, Egypt, to come to its aid, and that meant war. Accordingly, shortly after the air strike the Syrians defiantly dispatched new engineering equipment to the counterdiversion site and began the sizable and costly operation of leveling the land on both sides of the River Banias.[1]

It was then that Lebanon surprised everyone. In the beginning of 1965, having, until now, obstinately refused to carry out the counterdiversion scheme, the Lebanese parliament voted unanimously in favor of actively joining the project. How did this sudden turnabout occur? The answer the question lies in the Arab Summit, which convened in Cairo, on January 9–10, 1965. At the summit conference, Lebanon was ordered to start to implement immediately the three counterdiversion projects it had been allotted at the Alexandria Summit Conference. The pressure on Lebanon was so great that it feared that were it to keep up its refusal both it and its newly elected President Charles Hilu would become the targets of an extensive and brutal propaganda campaign, which, by provoking strong nationalist feelings, both within and without Lebanon, would undermine if not shatter Lebanon's delicate, tenuous intercommunal balance. Consequently, and against its better judgment, the Lebanese government yielded to Arab pressure and agreed to do its part in the counterdiversion scheme.

The Lebanese government knew that its decision meant trouble with Israel. The Alexandria Summit Conference had ordered Lebanon to build a pumping station alongside the Wazzani Springs, which would divert Springs's water to the River Banias and from there southward to the Mukheiba Dam in Jordan.

This project would seriously reduce the amount of water pouring into the Jordan River. It is hardly surprising, therefore, that Lebanon was exceedingly nervous about Israel's response to its announcement that it would commence work on the pumping station. Hoping to ally Israel's anxieties and avoid an aggressive Israeli reaction, the Lebanese turned to France for help. They asked the French government, with whom they enjoyed close relations, to intercede on their behalf and explain their predicament to Israel, requesting that France tell the Israelis that Lebanon had tried and failed to withstand Arab pressure over the counterdiversion scheme. They also asked France to make it clear that for Lebanon to continue to resist would prove both fruitless and dangerous. As a result, Lebanon had simply been left with no choice but to bend to the Arab states' demands and start to build a pumping station alongside the Wazzani Springs.[2]

The Lebanese were right to worry. Their decision did trouble Israel. Coming on top of Syria's activities, the Lebanese announcement provoked growing and serious concern in Jerusalem. Until now, Israel had been fairly confident that other than issuing splendid sounding declarations, the Arab states would not take any active measures to disrupt the flow of water reaching the Jordan River. It banked on the fact that the Arab states knew that Israel would, as Eshkol had told the Knesset only a year ago, defend its water rights to the very end. But, by the beginning of 1965, a new wind was blowing through the Arab world, and things no longer looked so certain. The traditional Arab strategy—to weaken and ultimately destroy Israel—had clearly moved up a gear and was about to be put into action or so Israel feared. Hence, the heinous counterdiversion scheme was to stop water from reaching the Jordan River and cut off Israel's water supply. If further proof were needed that this was indeed the case, Israel had only to turn to the words of Nasser himself, who repeatedly emphasized that the water dispute was an integral part of the battle to liberate Palestine.

In response to these latest developments, Eshkol underlined, once more, the fact that Israel's economy depended on water. Water was vital to Israel's survival. Israel, he reminded the world at large, considered water to be akin to the very blood that runs through human veins. He emphasized that Israel had warned, time and again, that its policy and future actions would be based on these very elementary facts. Israel would regard any attempt to prevent it taking its fair share of the Jordan River's water as tantamount to an attack on its borders. Appealing to the Arab states, Eshkol expressed the hope that "they will think twice before taking any foolhardy and adventurous measures."[3] But he also warned that if, despite everything, they persisted in pushing through their schemes, a military confrontation was not out of the question.[4]

Not that Eshkol was anxious to take military action. On the contrary, a military operation was a risky business, both militarily and diplomatically, especially one that, for example, sought to put an end to the Arab scheme by seizing the counterdiversion sites. Accordingly, Israel decided that before taking military action it would launch a diplomatic offensive, with the aim of clarifying its position to the Western powers, as well as its views on the Arab counterdiversion and its estimate of the grave damages that would accrue as a result of the scheme. It was to be a diplomatic campaign on an unprecedented scale that would either encourage the West to do something itself to dissuade the Arab states from carrying out the counterdiversion, or ensure that Israel had Western support, if worse came to worse, and it was forced to take military action.

When speaking to the British, French and American governments, Israel underlined the crippling effect the counterdiversion scheme would have on its water economy. It singled out, in particular, the Lebanese plan to build a pumping station to divert the Hasbani River. According to Israeli calculations, the Lebanese project would deny Israel between 130–150 mcm of water a year. Syria and Lebanon, on the other hand, would obtain much more than the 55 mcm of water allotted them by the Johnston Plan. Moreover, the diversion of the Hasbani would produce a sharp rise in the saliency levels of Lake Tiberias, rendering the water completely unfit for use.[5] Mordechai Gazit, the Israeli consul in Washington, damned the entire Arab counterdiversion scheme as an unmitigated disaster, deeming its completion a calamity equal to Nasser capturing the West Bank.[6]

Britain was sympathetic, but, nevertheless, advised Israel against taking any hasty, precipitate action. Instead, Israel should keep the powder dry and wait until Syria and Lebanon had completed their counterdiversion project. Only then, it argued, would it be possible to determine if the Arab states were indeed expropriating water beyond their allotted ration.[7] Israel rejected Britain's advice out of hand. Foreign Minister Golda Meir inquired, sardonically, whether Britain meant that Israel should wait until Lake Tiberias was bone dry and full of salt. Then, just in case the British missed the point, she emphasized that the Israeli government would not be willing "to wait until the Arab states completed the counterdiversion, until after they finished surveying and started pumping, in order to ascertain whether the amount of water they divert warrants action."[8]

Israel rejected Britain's advice for two reasons: First, destroying the counterdiversion installations, once they were up and running, would be extremely difficult and would demand a great many more resources. In other words, it would be much more risky militarily and much more expensive financially to wait until the Arab states completed the counterdiversion scheme. Moreover, it was a risk Israel could ill-afford, especially, if, as seemed likely, the Arab states exceeded the Johnston Plan's quotas. The Arab states had constantly declared that the object of the counterdiversion scheme was to deprive Israel of every possible drop of water, which hardly accorded with the notion that they would stay within the limits proscribed by the Johnston Plan. Second, action to destroy the Arab installations, once they were completed, would probably turn world opinion against Israel. In other words, it was equally risky diplomatically.[9]

Accordingly, Eshkol made no bones about the fact that Israel would take all the steps necessary to ensure that the Arab states did not complete the counterdiversion. The only way to avoid a military confrontation, the Israeli government stressed, was for someone to tell the Arab states that they must abandon their policy of harassing Israel and threatening it on the subject of the Jordan River. Walter Eytan, Israel's ambassador to Paris put things more bluntly. When talking to Quai d'Orsay, he warned, ominously, that once the Arab states started work on the counterdiversion scheme, "there would be war."[10]

Meir told the British much the same. This time, she warned, Israel was not willing to compromise. It regarded the counterdiversion scheme to be a matter of life or death. In the past, she reminded Britain, the Western powers had often urged Israel to adopt a flexible and conciliatory position in the cause of peace, and, she emphasized, Israel had complied. However, it was manifest that the sole result of acceding to the powers' request had been that Israel lived in a climate of growing belligerence while awaiting the final Arab onslaught. Meir warned John Beith, that if the Western powers were

not prepared to warn the Arab governments concerned that they consider Israel's water programme reasonable and are opposed to the punitive diversion of the Jordan headwaters, then we shall be on our own.[11]

To reinforce her point, Meir warned, when speaking in the Knesset, against there being any illusions "in regard to our determination not to permit anyone to sabotage our water project. We will defend our natural and just rights just as we defend our territory and settlement."[12]

Meir suggested that if Britain genuinely wanted to prevent the water dispute igniting a military conflict, then it and its fellow Western powers should promise publicly to uphold the status quo in the Middle East. A Western commitment to deter aggression, in either direction, across the Arab-Israeli borders, was, she emphasized, the best way to prevent war erupting. It would also help solve many of the problems that currently plagued the region. In short, Meir was asking for a Great Power guarantee, something Israel had asked for several times in the course of 1963.

Britain's answer remained the same as before. It claimed, as did the Americans who had received a similar request, that the Kennedy and Macmillan May 1963 statements met Israel's demands in full, as both talked of preserving the status quo and proscribed aggression. Nothing more was needed. On the contrary, anything more, for example, a clear and unequivocal pledge in support of Israel, would only make things worse. It would heighten the water dispute, undermine the West's interests in the region and encourage further Soviet infiltration of the Middle East. None of which, Britain pointed out, was in Israel's interest.

With a public guarantee or a commitment to maintain the status quo out of the question, Israel fell back on its second-best option. It asked the British government to use what influence it had among the Arab states and dissuade them from carrying out the counterdiversion. To this end, it suggested that Britain should make clear to the Arab states that it supported the Johnston Plan and unequivocally and thoroughly disapproved of their punitive counterdiversion scheme. Britain was no happier with this proposal than it had been with the idea of a public guarantee. Trefor Evans, Britain's ambassador to Damascus, observed that the Arab states would regard a British endorsement of the Johnston Plan as proof of the existence of an anti-Arab Anglo-American conspiracy. Fear of provoking Arab wrath was not the only reason why Britain refused to publicly underwrite the Johnston Plan. "We do not," the Foreign Office explained,

want to commit ourselves to the view that any deviation from its provisions would be an international delinquency, which would justify violent action by Israel. . . . Moreover, all that is meaningful of the plan that survives is its allocation of water and the Americans who are its sponsors have been careful to say that it provides only "guidelines" on this.[13]

The most Britain was prepared to do was hold private talks with the Arab states and note that the Johnston Plan offered a reasonable basis for the equitable distribution of the Jordan River's water.

Behind Israel's belligerent pose and its threats to stop the counterdiversion by force, even at the cost of war, lay a great deal of fear and consternation. It was manifest that the Arab states had raised the stakes in the water dispute. They had finally taken practical and active measures to thwart Israel's water project and were they to succeed, the consequences would be very serious indeed. The flow of water to Lake Tiberias would be disrupted. Egypt's chances of uniting the Arab states and convincing them that they should cooperate, both with regard to the water dispute and the Arab-Israeli conflict in general, would improve tremendously. The successful completion of the counterdiversion, Israel worried, would underpin and consolidate Nasser's preeminent status and dominating influence within the Arab world. This was immensely disturbing as Nasser's power was on the ascent, and not only in the Arab world. To wit, as a result of Nasser's threats, West Germany had only just announced that it was reneging on its agreement, signed as recently as October 1964, to sell tanks to Israel.[14] All these points, but particularly the last, worried Britain no less than Israel.

Israel's threat to take military action was closely linked to the political and diplomatic situation in the Middle East. According to Israeli intelligence sources, war was still a distant prospect. This was in part because there was still no end in sight to Egypt's involvement in the Yemen civil war, which was currently 50,000 soldiers strong. Israel was also encouraged by the United Arab Command's lack of response to the November air strike against Syria. Hence, Israel's threats were less a bid to provoke a war than an attempt to strike fear in the Arabs hearts and weaken their resolve even further. As long as Egypt was bogged down in Yemen, Israel would continue to purse this brinkmanshiplike strategy of threatening the Arab states, and especially Syria, with military action. It was a dangerous strategy, especially in the volatile, unpredictable Middle East, and there is little question that Israel's threats played their part in propelling the region toward the ultimately inevitable military confrontation of 1967.

THE BRITISH DILEMMA

Britain saw, with horror, how a military conflict between Israel and the Arab states was rapidly beginning to take shape before its eyes. Since the beginning of 1965, its representatives in Washington, Paris and Tel Aviv had filed numerous reports, all of which left no doubt that Israel was determined to stop the Arab counterdiversion on its tracks. It would certainly not wait to see whether the Arab states were capable of putting the scheme into effect and was already contemplating a preventive strike. Eshkol's water and blood simile and Israel's forceful warnings all underlined just how dangerous the situation was. Reports received from France reinforced this impression. According to the French, Israel had declared that there were limits even to its patience, moderation and self-restraint. The Arab counterdiversion, had, in fact, stretched its patience to its very limits and would eventually lead to war.[15]

The U.S. assessment was much the same. The United States told Britain that to the best of its knowledge the view that Israel had better launch a preventive attack during the early stages of the counterdiversion operation was slowly gaining ground within the Israeli military and political establishment.[16] It pointed in particular to Moshe Dayan's recent statement, urging the Israeli government to declare categorically that the diversion of the Jordan River's headwaters meant war.[17] Dayan, Israel's former chief of staff and minister of agriculture, was, as both the Americans and British knew, a figure of immense influence in Israel in all matters relating to defense and security. In U.S. opinion it was manifest that Israel was becoming more anxious and more nervous by the hour. Consequently, it was likely to provoke a Syrian artillery barrage, which would give it the excuse it needed to launch a preemptive attack, while Syria was still militarily weak and unable to respond. The Americans did not rule out the possibility that Israel would either carry out an air strike or seize the Syrian counterdiversion site.[18]

Curiously, despite all these rather alarming reports, Britain was not particularly worried that a war might erupt. It assumed that the Israeli threats were little more than a scare tactic aimed at frightening the Arab states. It was, it judged, a way to deter them and convince them not to carry out the counterdiversion. Britain did not rule out the possibility that Israel might take violent action against the counterdiversion operations. But, it assumed somewhat naively that Israel, for practical reasons, would not attack the counterdiversion sites before the diversion installations were at least partially complete. After all, Israel, Britain thought, perhaps a bit complacently, would be hard pressed to justify a military offensive to world opinion, with Syria having done little more than dig few holes in the ground and Lebanon, for all intents and purposes, still sitting on the fence.

Britain believed that the Israeli threats were designed primarily to "make the Americans' (or French or British) flesh creep by impressing on us the likelihood of violent action," with the result that we would be more likely "to put restraint [and] pressure on the Arabs."[19] In short, Israel's threats were a way to manipulate the Western powers. This being the case, Britain saw no reason to abandon its policy of maintaining a low profile. It saw no need to intervene in the water dispute.

Nor was this too much of a gamble, as Britain could always rely on the United States, which was sufficiently fearful of an Israeli attack, to do everything necessary to prevent a conflagration, should one seem likely. France, like the United States, also found the situation exceptionally menacing and could also be trusted to take the appropriate measures to prevent a war from erupting. What is more, as France enjoyed friendly relations with both the Arab states and Israel, its endeavors were much more likely to be crowned with success than any comparable effort of Britain's. Finally, were Britain to intervene on top of the efforts made by its two fellow Western powers, the Arab states might well suspect that they were the target of a new anti-Arab, Western plot. Accordingly, the British government instructed its Middle East representatives to limit their references to the water disputes to the demand that their respective hosts exercise a goodly measure restraint and self-control.[20]

John Beith totally disagreed with the Foreign Office's view of Israel's policy. Beith stressed that according to his information the Israeli government was not simply intent upon frightening the powers and provoking them into action. The Eshkol government, the ambassador explained, deemed the National Water Carrier a vital political and economic enterprise. Thus, after weeks of intense political and military debate, it had formulated a deliberate and carefully calculated plan to put an end to the counterdiversion scheme. Having considered all possible repercussions and consequences of its action, it had, nevertheless, reached the conclusion that it would be a mistake to allow the Arab states to carry on with the counterdiversion scheme. This decision, Beith emphasized, was not the work of a small, if influential, minority. Although it was true that Eshkol was under great deal of pressure from both the military and activist coterie that surrounded Ben Gurion, the decision, nonetheless, reflected the prevailing opinion in government and military circles, as well as in the Israeli public at large.

In order to bear out his appraisal of Israeli policy, Beith referred to a number of conversations Britain's military attaché had held with senior Israeli military figures, including the head of military intelligence and the commander of the Northern District, which, the ambassador claimed, afforded some idea of current climate of opinion in Israeli military circles. The army, Beith observed, considered the Jordan River dispute as simply the most recent manifestation of the Arab threat to Israel's existence. He also mentioned in his report the Israeli military spokesman's official statement to the effect that Israel was considering several military options in response to the counterdiversion. Immediate action against the Arab diversion equipment and workforce was one. Another was to wait until a pumping station or an aqueduct was in place and then strike. Nor had the possibility of invading the areas adjacent to the counterdiversion sites, which lay approximately 5 km from the Israeli border, and staying put until all work on the scheme ceased or the Arab states accepted the Johnston Plan quotas, been ruled out. Finally, the ambassador recorded Yitzhak Rabin's, now Israel's chief of staff, boast that an order to advance toward the counterdiversion sites would not be one of the more difficult tasks the Israeli army had had to discharge to date. It was evident, Beith concluded, that the Israeli threat to take military action was no empty threat. There was a very real danger that Israel would, if not in the immediate future then in time, launch a military operation to thwart the Arab counterdiversion scheme.[21]

Beith's assessment was backed by a report received from the British embassy in Washington. The United States had told the embassy that according to Israeli sources, the Israeli government was in all probability planning a preventive strike against one or more Arab states, though Syria was the most likely target. Moreover, the United States believed that the Arab counterdiversion scheme was only an ostensible excuse for Israel's belligerent policy. The true motive behind the Israel's actions was its fear that the balance of power in the Middle East was rapidly shifting in the Arab states' favor. This was in part because the credibility of the IDF was being undermined, with the result that the Arab states were becoming more bold, aggressive and self-confident by the day. The growing number of border incidents was clear evidence of this process, and Israel thought that it was high time that the Arab states were taught a lesson. Hence, the Americans concluded, its desire to strike a military blow against one or more Arab states. The United States, the Washington embassy reported, was sufficiently worried that Israel would carry out its threat to suggest convening NATO's political committee to discuss the crisis.[22]

Following these two reports, the Foreign Office changed its appraisal of Israeli policy. It admitted that there was growing evidence that the Israeli government was seriously contemplating military action were the Arab states to persist in carrying out the counterdiversion scheme. The Foreign Office assumed that Israel had two military options: It could either wreck the preparatory groundwork and engineering equipment or it could invade and seize the counterdiversion sites that lay only a short distance from the Israeli-Syrian border. It did not much matter which of the two options Israel ultimately chose; either way British interests in the region would be seriously undermined, as both had the potential of setting off a dangerous chain reaction ending in a general conflagration.

The Foreign Office agreed with Beith's assessment that even if Israel took action, at this stage there was no danger of a general conflagration. For one thing, the Syrian army was in a shockingly poor state. For another, Nasser would refuse to go to war as long as the bulk his army was tied down in Yemen. Yet the possibility that Israeli action would provoke a wide-scale Arab military response could not be entirely ruled out. The United Arab Command, which, Britain conceded, had become, albeit slowly, a relatively competent and effective body, might order retaliatory action against Israel. Furthermore, while the Egyptian president certainly wished to prevent a situation whereby Syria dragged Egypt into an untimely war, he might, nonetheless, find himself forced to wage war, however reluctantly. The Foreign Office estimated that Nasser could not risk standing aside if the border incidents between Israel and Syria got worse or if Israel attacked a neighboring Arab country. The shame and subsequent political repercussions would be too great. This proved to be a fairly accurate prognosis of the future developments. At present, however, the situation was sufficiently serious that Michael Stewart, Britain's foreign minister, saw fit to send his Cabinet colleagues a detailed memorandum, containing a list of recommendations on how to tackle the complex problems currently plaguing the Middle East.[23]

Given the extraordinarily tense situation in the Middle East, Britain thought it essential that it act before an explosion occurred. But before deciding in favor of one particular course of action or another, the Foreign Office thought that another review of Britain's interests in the Middle East, its standing in the region and its ability to influence the parties to the dispute was in order. Britain's interests had, by and large, remained the same. The export of oil to Western Europe and Britain remained one its primary interests, as did the operations of the British petroleum companies and Britain's expanding trade relations with the oil-producing countries, both of which made a vital contribution to Britain's economy. All these interests, most of which centered on countries such as Iran, Kuwait and the Gulf States, were predicated on the maintaining peace and stability in the region. And this, too, was one of Britain's principal, perhaps its overriding, interest in the region.

It was here that the Soviet Union posed a particular threat, as it was tension and not stability that served Soviet interests. Accordingly, it was essential to prevent the Soviet Union from further undermining the region's precarious stability. In October 1964, there had been a change in the Soviet leadership, following Khrushchev's removal from power. Unfortunately, this did not produce a corresponding change in the Soviet Union's Middle East policy. The new ruling triumvirate of Leonid Brezhnev, Aleksei Kosygin and Nikolai Podgorny was clearly approved and abided by their predecessor's Middle East policies. In December 1964, they sent Alexander Shelepin, a senior member of the Politburo, to Egypt on a visit, which was intended to mark the Soviet Union's continued high regard for Egypt. It was a signal that there would be no change in its policy toward Egypt.

The Soviet Union still sought to undermine Western influence in the Arab world, drawing it into the Soviet orbit instead. Hence, its efforts were to excite Arab opposition to Britain's remaining Middle East bases. The Soviet Union also continued to offer the Arab states economic and military aid, having discovered that this was a very effective way of advancing its goals in the Middle East. The Soviet Union, Britain realized, saw aid, particularly military aid, as pivotal to its efforts to increase and consolidate its influence in the region. This was equally true of the Arab-Israeli conflict. In the Foreign Office's view, the conflict furnished the Soviet Union with ample scope for troublemaking. The more support the West offered Israel, the more openly the Western powers identified with the Israeli cause, the easier it was for the Soviet Union to, opportunistically, back the Arab states and promote its own interests. What Britain feared, above all, was that as a result of this process the Middle East would become increasingly polarized between East and West. If, the Foreign Office fretted, "complete polarisation ever came about, then there would be no chance of protecting our interests in the Arab countries and we should have given the USSR an easy opening into this important area."[24]

There was a very real chance that owing to the tension produced by the water dispute, hostilities would soon erupt in the Middle East. This was something the British government sought earnestly to prevent, which, in turn, meant that Britain was now faced with the unhappy choice of deciding whether to protect its interests in the Middle East and check Soviet expansion or support what it believed to be Israeli's legitimate position on the water dispute. In the end, British interests won out. As Crawford, the undersecretary of state, explained, Britain's

dilemma is that the steps we can take to prevent it [war] are conditioned by the basic fact that the protection of our interests entails preserving the best possible relationship with the Arab countries, in which the bulk of Middle East oil lies, with which we do a much great [sic] volume of trade than we do with Israel, valuable though that is, which control many transit routes through the area and whose relations with the (Soviet) bloc might develop in a way gravely detrimental to the West.... If we are to preserve the friendship of the Arab governments, which we need to protect out interests, including those in the Gulf and elsewhere in Arabia we must avoid giving that degree of overt support to Israel.[25]

Britain's decision not to offer Israel public support on the water dispute did not imply that it had abandoned its moral duty to stand by Israel if Israel's existence were under threat. Were such a threat to emerge, Britain, like the other Western powers, would automatically take whatever action was required to thwart it, regardless of the consequences. If, as a result, British interests suffered, so be it. It is worth noting, in this context, that it was Britain's commitment to Israel's existence that accounted, to some degree, for its wish to avoid war. Britain was genuinely worried that should war erupt, Israel might find itself fighting for its very survival. Of course, the fear that war would allow the Soviet Union to further penetrate the Middle East was also a major consideration.[26]

Beith was quite frank when explaining to Meir why Britain would not endorse Israel's position on the water dispute, or guarantee its borders. The ambassador admitted that in Britain's view the Israeli government was acting both legally and fairly. But, unfortunately, Western fears of bolstering the Soviet Union's position in the Arab world and Britain's own vital interests in the region made it impossible for it to offer Israel the support it wanted. The most Britain could do was to offer private assurances of goodwill. That, however, was as far as Britain was willing to go, in the hope that such assurances would, as the Foreign Office put it, be sufficient to deter the Israelis from taking desperate measures against the Arab states. In short, the policy of nonintervention and keeping a low profile, which was considered the best way to safeguard Britain's interests in the Middle East, still held sway.[27]

Britain's exchanges with the Arab states over the water dispute accorded with its policy of maintaining low profile. Britain impressed upon the Arab states, once again, that its primary and sole interest in the matter was to maintain peace and stability in the region. Its representatives, emphasizing the danger of a counterdiversion scheme, which failed to respect the vital needs of all riparian states, warned that such a scheme might provoke armed hostilities. Britain exercised most of its persuasive skills on the Lebanese in part because it had been the Lebanese decision to build a water pumping station that had prompted the Israeli government to threaten to take preemptive action and in part because Lebanon, unlike Syria, had joined the scheme under duress and with the utmost reluctance, causing it to be considered the weakest link in the chain and so, Britain hoped, the most open to influence. Britain hammered away at the Lebanese, underlining the danger of a war erupting as a result of its counterdiversion operation. They revealed that Israel was very, very nervous and meant business.[28]

Britain was careful to distance its, albeit moderate, efforts to dissuade the Arab states from carrying out the counterdiversion scheme from similar American and French efforts. In this way, it hoped to avoid creating the impression that the three Western powers were in cahoots and had coordinated their policies in Israel's interests. It was a forlorn hope, reflecting Britain's occasionally ostrich-like tendency to ignore reality and burrow its head in the sand. In this instance, Britain totally ignored Egypt's and Syria's instinctive assumption that the West, and above all the United States and Britain, sided with Israel. How else, for example, were they to explain the fact that the West supplied Israel with arms, providing it with the means to pursue its aggressive anti-Arab policies. In any event, Britain's appeals fell on deaf ears. Even the Lebanese proved obdurate. Lebanon might be afraid of Israel, but it dreaded the prospect of an internal uprising, which might well erupt, with Egypt's active support, should it continue ignore the United Arab Command's orders.

Britain's endeavors came to nothing, and a military conflict remained a distinct possibility. Were the Arab states to continue to carry out the counterdiversion scheme and spurn the Johnson Plan's water quotas, Israel, as Britain knew, would inevitably take action to defend its water rights. Accordingly, having failed to convince the Arab states to abandon the counterdiversion scheme, Britain began to exert massive pressure on the Israeli government in an attempt to convince it not to take action, which would exacerbate the already tense situation. A report on the water dispute composed by British hydraulic experts came to the Foreign Office's aid and indeed persuaded it that to press Israel was the right course to take. Based on the data provided by experts' reports, the Foreign Office, while emphasizing the dangers of using military force, advised Israel that it really had very little fear from the Arab counterdiversion scheme.

Britain noted that it would be a mistake to assume the Arab states could realize their grandiose counterdiversion scheme in the near future. For one thing, they had neither the technical expertise nor engineering ability required for the swift and efficient execution of such a scheme. Nor did they have the large sums of money needed to finance the project. Equally, the Arab states' claim that they would divert huge amounts of water was little more than an empty boast. Without first-rate foreign technical expertise, which, Britain pointed out, had not to date been forthcoming, they will be able to divert at the most 100 mcm of water, per annum, which is less than a fifth of the water supplied by the Jordan River's headwaters. If worse came to worse and they did, by some chance, get outside help, then the amount of water diverted would rise to 150 mcm. This was not very much, and would hardly, Britain pointed out, effect the amount of water Israel drew from Lake Tiberias. What is more even that much would take ten years to achieve.

Britain admitted that according to the Johnston Plan, the Syrians and Lebanese were only supposed to pump 77 mcm of water from the Jordan River's headwaters each year. But it drew Israel's attention to the fact that under the Johnston Plan, Israel was required to permit 100 mcm of water to proceed southward from Lake Tiberias to the Lower Jordan River. Accordingly, Britain hinted, if worse came to worse and the Arab states exceeded their allotted water quotas so that Israel's own water ration was substantially reduced, all Israel had to do was block the flow of water southward to Jordan. Britain elaborated upon this latter point, suggesting that, in this sense, the counterdiversion might even work to Israel's advantage. Were the Arab states to exceed the Johnston Plan's water quotas, then Israel itself would no longer be bound by the plan and would be free to do whatever it wished with the water of Lake Tiberias. It could, for example, reduce the water levels in the Lake and channel salt-filled water down the river to Jordan. Harold Wilson advised Eshkol, during the latter's visit to London in March 1965, that Israel has the perfect means to retaliate against the Arab states: if the Arabs cut its amount of water Israel received, all Israel had to do was turn off the tap and prevent water from reaching the Lower Jordan River.

Britain realized that diverting the Banias River meant that the salt content of Lake Tiberias would rise. Israel claimed that saliency levels in the lake would rise to a point where the water would be rendered unusable. Britain was less pessimistic, and in any case supposed that should a problem of saliency emerge, Israel would easily overcome it.[29] A British hydraulics expert confirmed that according to

the information available to us ... it would appear that it [Israel] is capable of engineering a solution even if the Arabs do succeed in partially diverting the Upper Jordan water and that it should be possible to improve the quality of the water despite the Upper Jordan diversion.[30]

Britain informed Israel that the United States agreed with this assessment. The United States did not think that higher saliency levels would hamper Israel's exploitation of Lake Tiberias especially because Israel had already embarked upon a project to divert the salty streams flowing into Lake Tiberias.

Britain also revealed to Israel that not even the Arab states had much faith in the counterdiversion scheme or attributed much importance to it. Ahmed Salim, the Egyptian engineer heading the project, had nothing but contempt for the

Arab states' technical abilities. Hassan Sabry al Khouly, the head of the Palestine Office in Egypt, had assured Sir Humphrey Middleton, Britain's ambassador to Cairo, that there was no intention to tamper with Israel's water quotas. The sole purpose of the counterdiversion scheme, he claimed, was to allow the Arabs to exploit their water resources independently, without having to cooperate with the Israeli government or submit to any kind of international authority. In point of fact, al Khouly revealed, thanks to the Arab scheme Israel would be able to enjoy an even larger portion of water than that it had been allotted under the Johnston Plan. Quite how it would do so, he didn't explain. Nasser, too, assured the American undersecretary of state, Philip Talbot, that the Arabs would not exceed the water quotas prescribed by the Johnson Plan.[31] Whether Britain was truly taken in by these Arab protestations of innocence or took them with a pinch of salt, it certainly took full advantage of them to try and persuade Israel that it had nothing to fear from the counterdiversion scheme.

There was one final point. According to Britain's information, the Lebanese government was most unhappy at being forced to participate in the scheme, especially as none of the conditions it had posited at the Cairo Summit Conference for joining the scheme had been fulfilled. Consequently, Britain thought, one could expect that Lebanon, once the first stages of its diversion installation were complete, would try to avoid finishing the project and perhaps even postpone it indefinitely. What is more, it would probably manage to do this successfully. All in all, Britain concluded happily, "the actual victory [in the water dispute] is an Israeli one, since despite Arab threats Israel will have put onto effect her own water scheme, subject only to a possible minor loss of water imposed by the Arabs at great expense."[32]

Given the above, there really was no reason, Britain thought, why Israel should take military action against the Arab states. Such action would be completely unjustified. Preemptive action would also, as both Wilson and Michael Stewart warned Eshkol, gravely damage British and Israeli interests. It was, the two stressed, in the interest of Britain and Israel, both, that the Arab world remains divided, as this served to erode Nasser's leadership. Military action, the British warned, would persuade the Arab states to rise above their differences and unite in common purpose to defeat Israel and its Western patrons. All this occurred precisely at a time when Arab discord was at its height and several Arab leaders were intent on challenging Nasser's leadership.

The British were right. The Arab world was in turmoil and deeply divided. Two events, in particular, had combined to deal a severe blow to the Arab world and to Nasser personally. The first concerned West Germany. As mentioned, in early 1965, West Germany had been forced to bow to Egyptian pressure and revoke its agreement to supply Israel with arms. But Bonn, loath to leave Israel in the lurch, announced that it would reimburse Israel for its breach of the agreement, thus enabling it to purchase arms elsewhere. This was not at all to Nasser's liking, and it was no coincidence that on February 24, 1965, Walter Ulbriecht, head of the German Democratic Republic, arrived in Egypt on a state visit at

Nasser's express invitation. There is little doubt that the invitation to the East German leader was extended, in part, at the Soviet Union's behest, the ties between the Soviet Union and Egypt having become closer than ever. It seems equally reasonable to assume that the invitation was extended in order to exact a petty revenge on the West Germans and to punish them for their special relationship with Israel. If this was case, then Nasser's scheme backfired.

In line with the Hallstein Doctrine, Bonn denounced Ulbriecht's state visit, which amounted to Egyptian recognition of East Germany, as an unfriendly act and announced that it was stopping all economic aid to Egypt.[33] In the beginning of March, it declared that it had decided to establish diplomatic relations with Israel. The West German decision, which came into force on March 12, 1965, shocked and infuriated the Arab world. Ahmed Shukairy, the head of the Palestine Liberation Organization, demanded that the Arab states sever immediately all relations with West Germany. Egypt proposed a less extreme course of action, and suggested that the Arab states recognize East Germany and impose an economic embargo on West Germany. At a meeting of the heads of the Arab states, on March 15, 1965, ten of the participants declared that they were severing relations with West Germany. Saudi Arabia, Libya, Morocco and Tunisia, however, refused. The first two, who luckily for West Germany also happened to be two of the region's principal oil producers, were equally opposed to the idea of an oil embargo. They waged a successful battle against the proposal, which was eventually abandoned.[34]

It was about this time that a furious, virulent quarrel broke out among the Arab states. On March 6, 1965, the Tunisian president, Habib Bourguiba, exploded a bombshell. Bourguiba called for a change in the Arab states' attitude toward the Palestinian question, urging them to abandon the emotionalism and fiery passion, which had, until now, dominated their response to the problem, and to adopt a more moderate reasoned approach, instead. After all, he emphasized, far from resolving things wars tended only to spawn greater, more complicated problems. The Arab world, Bourguiba counseled, should adopt a moderate policy and seek a solution to the Palestinian problem free of bloodshed. To start with, Bourguiba suggested the Arab states might accept the UN's November 1947 resolution. The decision admittedly divided Palestine into two states, Jewish and Arab, but it also called for the return of the Palestinian refugees home. Bourguiba proposed that the Arab states should recognize Israel within the borders proposed by the partition plan.

The Tunisian president's courageous initiative came to nought. In fact, all it earned him was a violent campaign of hate and vilification. Egypt and the other progressive Arab states branded him a turncoat. They damned him for stabbing the Arab nation in the back and betraying cause of pan-Arab nationalism. So great was the fury against the Tunisian president's heresy that Egyptian protestors ransacked the Tunisian embassy in Cairo and set it alight. Bourguiba, in turn, castigated Nasser for sowing hatred and dividing the Arab world. Bourguiba also refused to take part in the Arab Summit Conference that was to be held in Casablanca that September. Interestingly, despite Bourguiba's bold, revolutionary proposals, not all the Arab states reacted so savagely. Some, notably

Saudi Arabia, Lebanon and Morocco, refused to censure or condemn the Tunisian president.[35]

With the Arab world at daggers drawn, Britain observed that Israel, by launching a wide-scale military attack, would merely be helping the Egyptian president to unite the deeply divided and squabbling Arab world. Preemptive military action might also have several unforeseen, adverse consequences. For example, it might have a negative effect on the policies of, so far, moderate countries such as Lebanon and Jordan. Finally, by resorting to military action, Israel would weaken its wholly justified case on the water dispute and thus turn world opinion against it. Surely, John Beith remarked, Israel did not want to start something it could not end.[36]

Back in Britain there was some discussion as to whether to involve the United Nations in the dispute. There were several arguments against doing so. First, it was fairly certain that the Soviet Union, instead of helping to find a reasonable solution to the dispute, would exploit the Security Council discussions to advance its personal interests. The Soviets would probably veto any constructive proposal, whether pro-Israel or even-handed. Second, Britain suspected that any British initiative to raise the water dispute in the Security Council would provoke Arab animosity. Far from seeing Britain's initiative as an attempt to preserve peace and security, the Arab states would interpret it as a British stratagem designed to help Israel prevent them from carrying out the counterdiversion. Third, Britain would be forced to abandon its low profile and state its views on the water dispute, which, on the whole, favored Israel. All this meant that the Security Council would be split into two, with the three Western states supporting Israel and the Soviet Union supporting the Arabs. In short, other than to further polarize the East-West and Arab-Israeli conflicts, a discussion in the Security Council would achieve nothing.[37] There was also the fact that Israel did not want the matter raised in the United Nations. It did not want any international body interfering with its water policies, least of all the United Nations, which it suspected, with some justice, of having a strong anti-Israeli bias. Israel was particularly worried lest, as had happened in 1954, the United Nations would force them to adopt a new and more costly diversion plan.

Britain obviously did not have much faith in the United Nations, but it also thought, not unreasonably, that given the tense situation in the Middle East, perhaps it would be better if the United Nations took action before rather than after hostilities erupted. Furthermore, one never knew, and a debate in the Security Council might, after all, prevent an armed conflict. This was certainly the opinion of Sir Humphrey Middleton, Britain's ambassador to Cairo, who was strongly in favor of the United Nations intervening in the dispute. In any case, UN involvement, even if it led nowhere, was infinitely preferable to the catastrophic alternative of Israeli military action. In addition, there was some, albeit limited, value to the UN's intervention. The United Nations could make the facts of the water dispute public. These would prove that Israel's diversion "involve[d] neither the taking of so much water nor the possibility of settling so many new immigrants that the Arabs have a justifiable *causes belie.*" Conversely, it would demonstrate that the threat to Israel presented by Arab plans, if it existed at all, was utterly insignificant.

This would have the double effect of removing the ground from under the feet of those Israelis who argue that Israel's vital interests demand retaliatory action against the Arabs' diversion works and of showing the hollowness of much of the Arab bluster about the damage to Israel that their plans are supposed to be designed to achieve. [38]

After reviewing the pros and cons of the case, Britain decided that its best option was to suggest to Israel that it appeal to the United Nations itself. After warning Israel, once again, that military action would only damage Israeli interests, Britain tried to convince it of the importance and benefit of making an appeal to the United Nations. If Israel considered the Arab counterdiversion schemes to be a serious threat and a deliberate act of provocation, or if, as the Foreign Office put it, the situation became intolerable, Britain urged Israel to appeal to the Security Council. What it should not do is attempt to resolve the water dispute unilaterally, and it should certainly not try to resolve it by force. George Thomson, Britain's pro-Israeli undersecretary of state for foreign affairs, was sufficiently honest to admit to the Israeli ambassador, Arthur Lourie, that it was highly unlikely that the United Nations would offer Israel a satisfactory solution to the water dispute. But Thomson emphasized Israel would be making a grave mistake if it tried to take on both the Arab states and the United Nations at once. In Thomson's opinion, the best course for Israel to follow was to appeal to the Security Council, while reserving its freedom of action should the Security Council's discussions reach a deadlock.[39]

Eshkol was unwilling to divulge what Israel's would do next. He would certainly not commit himself to making an appeal to the United Nations. Yet it should be noted that Israel had begun to consider how it could sabotage the counterdiversion equipment without precipitating a further escalation in the conflict. In order to leave Israel in no doubt as to how Britain would react if it launched a military strike, Wilson warned Israel several times not to initiate a war. If it did, Wilson asserted that it would find itself fighting alone without Britain's support. In order to press the point home, the Foreign Office drew Israel's attention to the fact that were Britain to support Israel it would find itself facing a solid Arab, Afro-Asian, communist bloc front, just as it had during the Suez situation, and then left Israel to draw its own conclusions.[40]

Britain concluded that if Israel stuck to its guns despite, to its mind, the strong arguments against military action, there must be other reasons behind its decision to launch a preemptive strike. Otherwise, how else was it possible to explain Israel's rejection of the conclusive evidence Britain had laid before it proving that it had little or nothing to fear from the counterdiversion and that the damage the scheme would inflict on Israel's water economy would be minimal? How else to account for Israel's refusal to consider an appeal to the United Nations, should it emerge that the counterdiversion scheme did, after all, undermine its water policies? It seemed that Israel was using the water dispute as a handy and timely excuse to take military action, and the reason Israel wanted to take action was, Britain thought, less practical and more political. What worried Israel was the political effect or rather psychological impact the successful execution of the counterdiversion scheme would have on the Arab world. Arab prestige and self-confidence would soar, and the Arab states would believe the United Arab Command capable of anything, including crushing Israel to the ground.

To this must be added Israel's sense that it had been left to face of Arab hostility alone. "We," Golda Meir told the British ambassador, "must see ourselves standing alone in face of all the dangers to our security."[41] Israel's sense of isolation had deepened after West Germany had yielded to Arab pressure and reneged on its deal to supply arms to Israel and following Ulbreicht's visit to Egypt. Israel seriously doubted whether it would receive effective Western support in an emergency. Britain thought it was this profound feeling of isolation rather than any actual fear for its water supply that had led Israel to adopt its belligerent policy.[42]

Arthur Lourie, Israel ambassador to London, made no effort to hide Israel's fears of what the future held. On the contrary, he told the Foreign Office that the Arab states had changed their tactics. They now relied on joint long-term planning and coordinated their military efforts. He pointed to the establishment of the United Arab Command, which, he claimed, had increased the tension in the region. The Arab states, he observed, also sought to actively undermine Israel's international position. Then there was Egypt and Egypt, as the Israeli ambassador emphasized, was a particular threat. Thanks to Soviet aid, Egypt had more than doubled its military power over the past few years. Its domination of the United Arab Command enabled it to gain control over the military forces of its fellow Arab states. West Germany's surrender to the Egyptian dictate and its agreement to stop supplying arms to Israel had not only raised Nasser's standing in the Arab world, but also had other serious practical and psychological repercussions. These were all, Lourie emphasized, alarming developments. They encouraged the Arab states to adopt an increasingly intransigent attitude toward the water dispute. They placed the future of the Middle East and Israel, in particular, in grave jeopardy.

In light of the above, Lourie summed up, it was not surprising that Israelis entertained somber thoughts about the future. Nor was it surprising that those who argued that Israel should take action, rather than wait until the Arab states crushed it, were slowly gaining the upper hand. This last point was verified by independent British sources, according to whom the Eshkol government was being subjected to a great deal of pressure, especially from the coterie of young politicians surrounding Ben Gurion and known as the "Young Turks." This latter group included such influential figures as Shimon Peres and Moshe Dayan, all of whom favored a preemptive military attack. It was no secret that Dayan had argued in favor of Israel taking military action during the first stages of the counterdiversion. Finally, the 50,000 trained and experienced Egyptian soldiers currently bogged down in Yemen, also, Britain thought, presented a huge temptation for Israel to act now before it would be too late and these soldiers, having finished their task in Yemen, returned home to confront Israel.[43]

There was an enormous gulf between Britain's appraisal of Israel's ulterior motives and the true facts of the case. Britain failed to realize that when Israel claimed that it regarded its water supply as a matter life and death, it meant precisely that. Britain underestimated the extent to which water dominated Israel's thoughts and actions. It did not appreciate, therefore, that Israel, in all consciousness, believed that the Arab counterdiversion presented a genuine and fundamental threat to its existence. Accordingly, Israel had never intended to wait until the counterdiversion project was complete, and only then to assess the damage it caused; that was simply too dangerous. Yet, despite some very belligerent Israeli voices, taking action did not necessarily mean that Israeli government was intent upon launching an immediate preemptive military strike. What is more, even if it were considering a preemptive attack, the chances of the Israeli government deciding in favor of one were small owing to American intervention, to be discussed shortly. To this extent Beith's assessment that Israel would not embark on military action in the near future was correct.

Nonetheless, the Foreign Office thought the possibility of a conflagration in the Middle East was as great, if not greater, than ever. Other than the water dispute, there were two additional developments, which, to its mind, increased the odds of an armed conflict. First, there was the unprecedented arms race in the Middle East, with all the states in the region busy buying huge quantities of sophisticated weapons. Second was Israel's nuclear program. As to the first issue, high-quality arms were continuing to pour into the region and in increasingly large quantities. Competing for power and influence, the United States and the Soviet Union had become the patrons of Israel and the Arab states, respectively, and each superpower made certain that its client had all it needed, not least in terms of military equipment. It was a sure sign that the Middle East had finally and irrevocably joined the Cold War.

Not that Britain had suddenly stopped supplying arms to Israel. Britain regarded the preservation of a military balance between Israel and the Arab states, and especially Egypt, as one of the keys to preserving peace and stability in the Middle East. To this end, it continued to sell weapons to Israel, including submarines and, most recently, 250 Centurion tanks, in addition to the tanks Israel had already received from West Germany. France, too, kept on equipping Israel with Mirage fighter jets. But, it was the United States, who, thanks to its recent arms deals with Israel, was rapidly emerging as Israel's number one arms supplier. Meanwhile, the Soviet Union was busy furnishing Egypt with mammoth quantities of modern weapons. In principle, preserving the military balance might be a recipe for peace and stability, but in practice it produced a massive influx of weapons in to the Middle East and served to increase the firepower and self-confidence of the local states, to the point where a military confrontation became almost inevitable.

Clearly there was a need to examine the regional arms race afresh. And this is precisely what Britain did, despite having reviewed the issue a mere year ago. In fact, until the outbreak of the 1967 War, the British Cabinet would periodically discuss the possibility of stemming the flood of arms pouring into the Middle East. In 1965, having reexamined the issue again, it reached the inevitable, if frustrating, conclusion that nothing had changed; the Soviet Union still had no interest in bringing the arms race in the Middle East to an end.

First, Soviet influence in the Middle East, as both it and Britain knew, owed much to the fact that it supplied the Arab states with arms and offered them diplomatic and other support in their conflict with Israel. The most effective way to extend and consolidate that influence was to continue to furnish the Arabs with weapons. Second, the Sino-Soviet conflict obliged the Soviets to prove, unequivocally, their anti-imperialist credentials.[44] The Chinese would be quick to pounce on any arms limitation agreement between communist Russia and the capitalist West and accuse the Soviet Union of conspiring with the West against the Third World countries. Major Soviet clients, such as Cuba or Indonesia, might also react badly to such an agreement. Finally, perpetuating the Arab-Israeli conflict, continuing to supply arms to the Arab states, allowed that tension in the region to remain high, and this, as far as the Soviet Union was concerned, was a good thing. It would, for instance, help it reduce and eventually eliminate Western influence in the Middle East. Accordingly, Britain concluded, the policy of tension without explosion remained the Soviet Union's policy. The Soviet Union had no interest in settling the Arab-Israeli dispute or even promoting some kind of modus vivendi between Israel and its Arab neighbors.[45] As for the arms race, the Foreign Office acknowledged, that

there is no prospect of successfully negotiating with the Soviet Union any formal agreement for the limitation of arms supplies to the Middle East on terms that would be acceptable to us and that we could suffer serious political loss if we were to take the initiative in starting such negotiations.[46]

In other words, even if by some miracle the Soviet Union were willing to consider an agreement limiting the arms race in the Middle East, it would insist on reciprocal concessions, including, for example, the evacuation of all foreign military bases in the region, which would seriously undermine Western interests. The Foreign Office also noted that there was no guarantee that other Western states would agree to join an arms limitation agreement, particularly as most of them regarded the Middle East as a highly lucrative and profitable market.

Britain also knew that the Arab states were absolutely opposed to any plan designed to limit their supply of weapons. Nasser had often stated that his government strongly objected to any attempt to curb Egypt's, or any other Arab state's, arms arsenals. The Arab world was intent on acquiring a significant, overwhelming military advantage over Israel, which would enable it to finally liberate Palestine. Limiting its supply of arms would thwart its plans. It would also, from the Arab perspective, give Israel an unfair military advantage, to the point where it might launch a surprise military attack, either to impose a political settlement on the Arab states or extend its borders.[47] In view of the above, Britain concluded that any arms limitation agreement would provoke an extremely hostile Arab reaction. Further, though both East and West would become the targets of Arab wrath, it was Britain who would suffer the most, certainly more than either of the two superpowers. The reason was simple: "our greater material interests in Arab countries," as the Foreign Office dryly observed, "make us so much more vulnerable."[48]

All in all an agreement to restrict the supply of arms to the Middle East appeared to be out of the question, which was much the same conclusion Britain had reached a year ago. In the present circumstances, there seemed to be no way out of the arms race. Yet this worrying issue remained on Britain's agenda with the British government returning to it from time to time.

Britain was equally concerned with the prospect of Israel manufacturing nuclear weapons. In Britain's opinion the basic problem was that Israel's nuclear program threatened the nuclear status quo in the Middle East. Like the United States, Britain had no doubt that Israel, if it wanted to, could manufacture a nuclear bomb within two or three years, having both the ability and technical means to do so. Not so the Arab states who had neither the means nor the knowledge required to produce nuclear weapons. An Israeli bomb meant more than the proliferation of nuclear weapons, an undesirable thing in itself. It would also produce a sharp deterioration in the Middle East. Regarding it as a life and death issue, the Arab states would never agree to Israel acquiring nuclear weapons. Nasser had already said that he considered it as a legitimate reason for war and warned that Egypt would take preemptive action if Israel were ever to be on the verge of producing a bomb. Egypt would, for example, Nasser threatened, invade Israel and destroy its nuclear bases before they were turned against the Arabs.

Should Israel appear to be on the brink of manufacturing nuclear weapons, the Arab states would probably ask the Soviet Union for nuclear arms to counter the Israeli threat. But Britain thought it unlikely that the Soviets would accede to their request. What they would do was offer the Arabs a nuclear guarantee against a nuclear attack by Israel. This had the advantage of neutralizing the Israeli nuclear threat. On the other hand, it would increase the chances of an East-West confrontation in the Middle East. It is instructive that Britain ruled out the possibility of reaching an agreement with the Soviet Union regarding the presence of nuclear weapon in the Middle East. It assumed that the Soviet Union would refuse to limit the discussion to the specific countries concerned and demand the inclusion of all existent military systems active in the region, including CENTO, the 6th fleet and local British forces.[49]

It seemed that Britain's best option was to appeal to Israel and underscore the dangers inherent in developing nuclear weapons. It was hardly in Israel's interest, Britain pointed out, either to provoke Nasser into launching a conventional preemptive strike, or to force him to appeal to the Soviet Union for nuclear aid. True, the Soviets might refuse Nasser's request, but Egypt could always turn to the Chinese who were sure to say yes. Eshkol, however, was unwilling to offer any commitments regarding Israel's future nuclear program or its prospective manufacture of nuclear weapons. Instead, while taking great care to appear accommodating, Eshkol faithfully maintained Israel's opaque policy on the subject.

Eshkol reassured Wilson that, at present, Israel had no intention to produce or purchase nuclear weapons. He was even willing to subject the Dimona nuclear plant to some form of international supervision. At the same time he also questioned, in passing, the effectiveness of international supervision over Egypt's nuclear policy. Finally, if the Western states were genuinely interested in regional arms control, Israel would be willing to consider such an agreement, but on two conditions. First, that the agreement covered both nuclear and conventional weapons; second, that China and East Europe were also parties to the agreement.[50] Israel and everyone else knew that the prospects for such an agreement were zero. Hence, Britain assumed that the Israeli offer was not seriously meant and that Israel was intent on keeping its nuclear option in reserve. This assumption was reinforced by Eshkol's rather evasive reply when asked about Israel's nuclear option. The Israeli government, he remarked obliquely, "had to watch her position in the absence of reliable Western guarantees to her security."[51] Israel, which had very little faith in any international measures designed to prevent the proliferation of nuclear weapons, was resolved to maintain its nuclear option.

Among the plethora of problems that beset the Middle East, it was Israel's accelerated nuclear program, the flood of arms pouring into the region and the water dispute that combined to produce a state of affairs, which would, Britain feared, lead inevitably to war. Not that Britain could do much to stop this downward spiral. Its ability to influence either side to the conflict was severely limited. It was limited, for example, by its fear of provoking an angry Arab reaction and damaging British interests. Thus, pressure, even gentle British pressure on the Arab states, was ruled out. Britain did try to influence Israel, and to this end initiated an intensive and ongoing dialogue with the Israeli government. But here, too, its efforts met with little success. Eshkol was less interested in hearing what the British had to say, whether on the water dispute or nuclear weapons, and much more interested convincing the British of the justice and legitimacy of Israel's policies. That left the Americans as the only ones capable of exercising some influence over Israel. Luckily, in the beginning of 1965, the United States, which of late had become more and more involved in the Middle East's affairs, decided to intervene personally and reduce the tension that overshadowed the region.

THE UNITED STATES INTERVENES

The first issue on the U.S. agenda was the arms race. It was also one of the more complicated issues on its agenda because of all the Western powers, the

United States faced the greatest dilemma when it came to deciding its attitude toward the arms race. Before discussing the evolution of U.S. policy on the arms race, it should, however, be noted that economic considerations played a very small part in shaping American policy on this issue. In principle, the United States, which opposed the arms race, wanted to avoid becoming the chief supplier of offensive weapons to any of the Middle East's countries, Israel included. This did not mean that the United States was indifferent to the region's military balance or Israel security. But it hoped to, as it were, both have its cake and eat it. Hence, in 1964 it was willing to supply Israel with tanks, but only indirectly through the West Germans. Likewise, it was constantly pressing Britain to furnish Israel with a sufficient number of modern tanks to allow Israel to maintain its security. Britain refused, explaining that it could only supply Israel with weapons at the expense of the British army, which was obviously out of the question. The truth, however, was that Britain, like the United States, simply did not want to become Israel's chief source of tank supply.[52]

Both Presidents Kennedy and Johnson believed that the United States was committed to maintaining a military balance between Israel and the Arab states. This meant ensuring that Israel maintained a qualitative military edge over its Arab neighbors. The United States assumed that a militarily weak Israel, which lacked sufficient weapons, posed two dangers. First, lacking a secure and regular supply of weapons, Israel might be forced to adopt warlike measures, simply in order to maintain its power to deter the Arab states. Second, a weak Israel might tempt the Arab states, which would regard its military weakness as a golden opportunity into launching a war to destroy Israel once and for all.

In view of all the above, and because the Soviet Union was busy supplying Egypt with arms, the United States felt that it had no choice but to meet Israel's military requirements, itself. Dean Rusk, the American secretary of state for foreign affairs, explained to Britain that the United States had agreed to furnish Israel with tanks in order to close the arms gap, which had opened up between Israel and the Arab states. The U.S. Joint Chiefs of Staff had advised that owing to the sharp increase in Arab military strength, it was essential to augment Israel's supply of tanks.[53] Clearly, the United States was gradually being drawn into the arms race. In fact, it would find it impossible to escape its destiny as Israel's chief arms supplier, as evidenced by the chain reaction provoked by its decision to supply Jordan with arms.

The United States had decided to sell Jordan weapons as part of its policy of supporting its more moderate allies in the region. Of course, Jordan's threat to turn to the Soviet Union if the United States refused to supply it with the tanks and planes it needed for its defense also had something to do with the American decision. The Americans assumed that owing to the tension resulting from the water dispute, Jordan might make good its threat and buy arms from the Soviet Union. They further assumed that the Soviets would not miss such a wonderful opportunity to gain another foothold in the Arab world. However, by supplying weapons to Jordan, the United States disrupted the military balance between Israel and its Arab neighbors, and Israel, not surprisingly, demanded that the Americans redress the balance. Hence, the decision to supply Israel with tanks. This, in turn, triggered an immediate Egyptian response, with Nasser announcing that owing to heavy pressure from his military, he was forced to ask the Soviet Union to supply Egypt with similar weapons.[54]

One of the reasons the United States agreed to supply Israel with arms— first tanks and then airplanes—was to stop it from manufacturing nuclear weapons. Strange as it might seem, the prospect of an Israel bomb worried the Americans even more than it did the Egyptians.[55] The United States had long been convinced that it must take effective action to prevent Israel from developing a nuclear bomb before it was too late and Israel present it with a fait accompli. In 1965, with the water dispute at its height, it was considered more imperative than ever. There is no question that U.S. endeavors to convince Israel to give up its plans to manufacture nuclear weapons were bound with its effort to reduce the tensions produced by the Arab counterdiversion scheme.

U.S. views on the water dispute were much the same as those of its British ally. It had no more faith than Britain did in the Arab states' ability to carry out the extremely complicated counterdiversion scheme. Its estimate of the time it would take to complete the scheme, the amount of water that could be diverted, was also the same as Britain's. So, too, was its appraisal of the damage the Arab scheme would cause the Israel water economy. It did not, for example, think that saliency would be much of problem. Unfortunately, Israel's threats to take widescale military action did not arise from the water dispute per se, or so the Americans, again like the British, thought. The Israeli government was well aware that counterdiversion would hardly effect its water quotas, and so, like Britain, the Americans believed that what truly concerned Israel were the psychological implications of the scheme. It feared, for instance, that the successful completion of the counterdiversion would prove, above all to the Arabs themselves, that the Arab states were capable of taking concerted action.[56] Accordingly, the Israeli government wanted to put an end to the counterdiversion and strike before the 50,000 Egyptian soldiers returned home from Yemen.

There was, however, one thing on which the Americans took a different view from their British ally. They were certain that the Middle East was on the verge of a military confrontation. Robert McNamara, the secretary of defense, advised the Combined Forces Committee that owing to the diversion and counterdiversion of the Jordan River, the Middle East might explode at any moment. The Americans feared that an open armed conflict between Israel and its neighbors would accelerate the polarization of the Middle East, a development from which only the Soviet Union could benefit. There was also, of course, the danger that polarization would lead to a direct confrontation between the two superpowers. Accordingly, the United States sought to prevent the onset of open hostilities, not an easy task given the endless stream of Soviet military and economic aid received by Egypt, Syria and Iraq.[57]

In order to ease the tension, and especially, as the Americans put it, calm Israel's nerves, the Johnson administration decided to send a special two-man mission to Israel. Robert Komer, a member of the National Security Council and Averell Harriman, acting as President Johnson's special envoy, were charged with extracting from Israel a commitment that it would not take preemptive military action against the Arab states; if that proved impossible then, at the very least, to dissuade it from launching such an attack. The two were also to discuss several issues, which were currently of interest to both two states, including Israel's development of nuclear weapons and the military balance between Israel and its neighbors, which was being disrupted owing to the huge quantities of high-quality arms the Soviets were pouring into Egypt as well as the U.S. decision to sell Jordan advanced aircraft and tanks. Komer and Harriman's mission signaled U.S. growing involvement in the Middle East. By revealing U.S. willingness to recognize and meet Israel's security needs, it was also a mark of the closer relationship between the two countries.[58]

Not that the Israeli conversations with Komer and Harriman were always amiable or smooth—anything but. They were, in fact, among the most difficult and painful discussions ever to have taken place between the two countries. The two Americans adopted a firm, even aggressive attitude, from which the element of threat was not entirely absent.[59] During their talks with the Israelis, Komer and Harriman habitually mixed threats with inducements, alternately brandishing the carrot and the stick, and so set the pattern of future American-Israeli relations. Threats were made in the event that the Israeli government refused to act in line with American policy, which was then offset by a growing willingness to meet Israel's security needs, to open up the American arms markets and to offer Israel economic and diplomatic support, should it play ball.

Komer and Harriman both stressed that the United States was fundamentally committed to Israel's security and that the United States was, accordingly, willing to consider favorably the possibility of supplying Israel with weapons in order to maintain its deterrence capacity. All this was music to Israel's ears. Not that this was the first time the United States had impressed upon Israel its commitment to Israeli security. Prior to Komer and Harriman's visit, the Israeli chief of staff, its deputy defense minister and the head of the Israeli Air Force were given an official demonstration of the might and power of the 6th fleet. Stationed in the Eastern Mediterranean, the 6th fleet was a mighty military force, which included, among other things, eighty offensive fighter jets. More important, it was ready, at all times, to come to the defense of Israel if its existence came under threat.[60]

Yet, American favors came at a price. U.S. willingness to open the American arms market and investigate the dangers inherent in the United Arab Command was dependent on an Israeli commitment not to launch a preemptive attack or take any kind of military action against the counterdiversion of the Jordan River. The two Americans underlined that the United States was totally opposed to the use of violence to solve the water dispute, and they insisted that the Israeli government seek a peaceful solution to the dispute, including an appeal to the United

Nations. They added that by making threats, Israel was acting contrary to its own interests, as threats weakened the ability of the moderate Arab countries, such as Lebanon for instance, to withstand the pressure of extremist elements both from within and without.[61] They concluded a peaceful solution was the best solution, and in the U.S. view the Johnston Plan still offered the most equitable and just basis for the distribution of the Jordan River's waters.

The next major issue on the Americans' agenda was the manufacture of Israeli nuclear weapons. This proved to be no less a complex an issue than the water dispute. According to U.S. information, the Dimona nuclear plant had already gone critical. There were also reports that the Israeli government had recently decided to develop a medium-range surface-to-surface missile. Both these developments gave rise to serious American concern, which, surprisingly enough, the Egyptians did not share. Feeling very strongly about the subject, the United States reacted accordingly. Komer and Harriman warned that if Israel were to develop nuclear weapons, it might provoke the most serious crisis between the two states to date. They demanded an explicit commitment on Israel's part that it would not acquire nuclear weapons and would subject all its nuclear facilities to the scrutiny and safeguards of the International Atomic Energy Authority.[62]

Israel, however, adhered steadfastly to its opaque policy on nuclear weapons. It explained to the two Americans that in view of the changed circumstances in the region, the best it could do was promise not to be the first country in the Middle East to acquire or develop nuclear weapons. In any case, Israel pointed out, the United States was abreast with the latest developments in the Dimona plant, its inspectors having visited it only recently, whereas the Nahal Sorek nuclear plant was under the supervision of the International Atomic Energy Authority in Vienna.[63] Unconvinced, the United States continued to pressure Israel, but to little avail. Israel stuck to its guns, and the United States failed to dissuade it from developing nuclear arms. Israel, in fact, managed to have its cake and eat it. It had extracted a promise from the Americans that they would supply Israel with arms, having promised in return only that it would not be the first to introduce nuclear weapons into the region. It could continue to develop nuclear weapons, if it so wished, with impunity.

Israel proved more accommodating on the subject of the water dispute. Although unwilling to limit its future options or promise not to take preemptive military action, Israel did agree to try to resolve the water dispute peaceably, before it resorted to force, though it drew the line at making an appeal to the United Nations. The reason was that the Israeli government was well aware that it could not just ignore the American demand that it not launch a preemptive strike or take wide-scale military action. Israel knew that if it took military action without American approval, it was likely to find itself in the unhappy situation of facing the Arab states, who were certain to have the benefit of full and unqualified Soviet support, alone and without the backing of the Western superpower. Israel's appreciation of just how much it needed American support in case of an armed conflict was to, henceforth, underlie its policy, particularly during the May crisis, which led directly to the Six-Day War.

The Israeli government could not risk open discord with the United States, for fear that the Americans might end or at least put on hold its policy of supporting Israel and supplying its needs. Israel believed that Komer and Harriman's visit marked a watershed in Israeli-American relations. It was visible proof that the United States was resolved to stand by Israel, and the Israeli government was unwilling to do anything that might weaken that resolve. Consequently, and in order to reassure the United States, Israel emphasized time and again that it would only take military action after it had carefully thought the matter through. It also assured the Americans that it would not, in as far as it could, drag the region into an all-out military conflict. "Israel," Prime Minster Eshkol reassured, "is not preparing for war, but there would be some shooting."[64] Indeed, despite its belligerent declarations, both during and after the Komer-Harriman visit, when it actually took action Israel destroyed the counterdiversion equipment, but was deliberately refrained from doing anything that would result in the region going up in flames. Consequently, the United States concluded that although it would not expressly commit itself, Israel would not launch a preemptive attack.

The United States thought that the Komer-Harriman mission was, on the whole, a great success. It had soothed Israel's nerves and assuaged its fears, so that for the time being, at least, the danger of an armed conflict had passed. In a conversation with King Hussein, shortly after the Komer-Harriman visit, the American ambassador to Jordan informed Hussein that "the likelihood of an Israeli preemptive strike had been reduced by the agreement reached at Tel Aviv." John Beith was even more optimistic, though he was probably exaggerating a bit when he reported to the Foreign Office that thanks to the pressure exerted by Komer and Harriman, it did not appear that Israel would, in the foreseeable future, dare to retaliate against the Arab states by contriving a specious incident before the counterdiversion scheme was complete.[65]

It is instructive that though the United States was firmly opposed to Israel launching a preemptive strike or taking any kind of wide-scale military action against the Arab counterdiversion, it did not totally reject the possibility that Israel sabotage the Syrians' diversion equipment. The United States, like Britain, considered the Syrians troublemakers, intent upon stirring up the Israeli-Syrian border and provoking a conflagration in the Middle East. Consequently, the United States hoped to isolate Syria. Nor would it, as it told the Israelis, shed any tears if Israel were to strike at the Syrians.[66] In short, without ever admitting it publicly, United States was quite happy to allow Israel to employ a limited amount of force if it was directed against Syria.[67]

Luckily, this coincided with the Israeli government's own inclination, which was to wreck the Syrian counterdiversion equipment without having to send in ground troops. Accordingly, Israel was soon to embark upon a series of limited military operations against the Syrian counterdiversion equipment. These were successful in that they removed the water dispute from the Middle East's agenda. But, what they did not do, nor could they have, was erase the dispute's harmful, adverse consequences. Tension and strife continued to bedevil the region, becoming, in fact, much worse. Stability, other than for one brief moment, did not return to the Middle East.

THE END OF THE WATER DISPUTE

So far Lebanon, having declared that it was ready to join and implement the counterdiversion scheme, had taken no practical steps to implement its decision. It remained faithful to its policy of doing its best to avoid a conflagration between itself and its Israeli neighbors. Not so Syria. At the start of 1965, Syria, ignoring the Israeli threats, began to work on the counterdiversion project at an accelerated pace. It did so independently, without bothering to consult or coordinate its steps with the rest of the Arab world. In Syria's view it was imperative to carry out the counterdiversion, as soon and as quickly as possible. It was the only way to recover the water that Israel, or so Syria accused, had stolen from the Arabs. The counterdiversion was also an integral part Syria's plan to liberate Palestine from the clutches of the Zionist enemy.

On the other side of the border, Israel, determined to strangle the counterdiversion scheme at birth, was looking for a way to destroy the Syrian diversion equipment, without igniting an all-out conflagration. It thought the best plan would be to provoke the Syrians into opening fire on Israeli targets, which was not in itself a very difficult thing to do, and then to retaliate by attacking the counterdiversion equipment.[68] Accordingly, in 1965, Israel began to farm the demilitarized zone, something it had not done since 1951. At the same time, a growing number of army patrols suddenly began to march down the Patrol Track. The United States immediately asked Eshkol to limit the number of patrols or, even better, cancel them all together. The Israeli patrols, the United States argued, were both unnecessary and dangerous. Eshkol disagreed. He contended that the patrols were essential to protect the Jordan River's headwaters from Arab interference. The Israeli army patrols would continue.[69]

Between January and March 1965, the Syrians managed to develop an area the size of 15 km. Israel decided that Syria had gone far enough and that it was time to destroy the diversion equipment. Accordingly, it stepped up its provocative actions, which became more and more frequent. Israel also mustered an array of tanks along the Israeli-Syrian border and put its air force on full alert, in case the fighting should spread to the nearby civilian settlements. This was a mere precautionary measure. The Israeli government hoped that it would not have to use its air force, as it did not want to provoke a wide-scale conflagration with the entire Arab world. The Israeli plan worked, with Syria playing its part to perfection. On March 17, the Syrians fired on an Israeli patrol making its way down the Patrol Track. In response, the Israeli tanks opened fire and, aiming at the diversion equipment, destroyed it completely.

The Syrian government did not give up; it introduced more equipment into the diversion site and continued to develop the land. It did, however, take one precaution and moved the entire operation to the Gisr Banat Yaacub area, which lay about 5 km from the Israeli border. The new site had two advantages: it gave Syria a topographic advantage over Israel and afforded it the protection of a series of closely knit and well-fortified military forts, as well as its armored forces. Once again, working at an accelerated pace, Syria managed to develop another 5 km plot of land. Israel tried again to provoke the Syrians into opening fire on an Israeli patrol. But, Syria, it seemed, had learned its lesson and refused to fire upon the Israeli soldiers. Accordingly, on May 13 Israel initiated a shooting incident itself, which ended with Israeli tanks, once more, destroying Syria's diversion equipment.[70]

The Syrian government was helpless. Faced with the powerful combination of Israeli military might and determination, it could not hope to carry on with the counterdiversion without Arab military aid. If it did so, it might find itself at war with Israel, alone. On May 26, at a gathering of the Heads of the Arab states, Syria demanded, and not for the first time, that the Arab states assemble a strong air force capable of intervening and neutralizing Israel's air superiority, should the need arise. It also insisted that all Israeli military actions be met with a blistering response. These were not necessarily to take place in the site of the initial incident and the exact location would be left to the discretion of the United Arab Command. Finally, Syria called on Egypt to expel the United Nations Emergency Force from Sinai and the Gaza Strip and replace it with Egyptian troops.[71] Hoping to goad Egypt into action, Syria accused it of cowering behind the United Nations' skirts.

Nasser was unmoved. He stuck to his policy of avoiding a confrontation with Israel until the time was ripe. In a speech given on May 31, at the opening of the second PLO conference, Nasser listed one by one the reasons why Egypt was, as yet, not ready to embark upon a war with Israel. First, it still had 50,000 troops fighting in Yemen. Second, the Arab states still refused to allow foreign Arab troops to be deployed in their territory. Third, he would not let Israel drag Egypt into war at its pleasure. He was not, Nasser scornfully proclaimed, willing to go to war at a time and place of Israel's choosing, merely because the IDF had wrecked one or two of the Syrian tractors used to divert the Jordan River's headwaters. As for the counterdiversion, it was plain that without adequate military protection, work on the scheme could not continue. Nasser proposed postponing the counterdiversion scheme until the Arab armies could guarantee its safety.[72]

Nasser's speech amounted to an Israeli victory; Israeli resolve and military power had clearly won the day. In Israel, it reinforced the prevailing assumption that as long as Egypt was busy fighting in Yemen, Nasser would not dare risk a war with Israel. The Israeli government further concluded that in the current favorable military and strategic circumstances it could afford to adopt a firm and strict policy addressing many of its problems, which affected its relations with the Arab world. It could even, if necessary, employ force to resolve some of these problems. In a speech in the Knesset, Eshkol declared that Israel would crush any attempt to violate its sovereignty or undermine the basis of its existence.[73] Britain, needless to say, was far from happy with Eshkol's new, tough and, apparently, uncompromising stand.

Britain had, for sometime, been troubled by the rising number of incidents along the Israeli–Syrian border. When these finally culminated in Israel's destruction of the Syrian diversion equipment, it became more than a little panicky, fearing that this event might finally push the region into war. Ultimately, however, the Israeli action elicited a sigh of relief from the Foreign Office. According to the Foreign Office's information, some of it derived from Israeli military sources, Israel had contrived the border incidents purely in order to wreck the Syrian equipment. Admittedly, the operation was evidence that Eshkol's government would not allow the counterdiversion scheme to get off the ground.[74] It equally proved that Israel was standing by its oft-repeated promise to take action to preserve its rights yet, at the same time, do all it could to prevent a general conflagration from erupting between itself and its neighbors.

The Foreign Office was honest enough to admit that the Arab failure to respond to Israel's action had vindicated, and in full, Israel's strategy of refusing to wait until the Arabs completed the counterdiversion of the Jordan River's headwaters. "We have to recognise," John Beith conceded, that "the Israelis were right in thinking that a limited response, before work got underway, was wiser and safer than a total response once the work was complete."[75] More than that, not only did Israel's military action not exacerbate the conflict, but it also actually served to reduce the tension produced by the water dispute. In Beith's opinion, it was Eshkol's government's essentially moderate character and its genuine desire to avoid an unwanted escalation that had dictated the limited, and ultimately successful, Israeli response.

Britain assumed that after having had their equipment destroyed by the Israelis, not once but twice, Syria would no longer pursue the counterdiversion project, or at least not in any serious manner. At the most, it would make a few minor symbolic efforts in order to save face. Syria knew that if it dared to bring any more equipment into the counterdiversion site, the Israeli government wouldn't hesitate before launching an attack similar to those carried out in March and May. Britain further assumed that the Arab states were incapable of militarily challenging Israel. Something Nasser's speech on March 31 had made abundantly clear. During his speech Nasser had warned the Syrians, in no uncertain terms, that if they wanted to carry on with the counterdiversion they could expect no help from Egypt or any other of its fellow Arabs states.[76]

U.S. reaction to the events of March and May 1965 was identical to Britain's. Although there was some lingering fear of escalation, the Americans were, on the whole, relieved and satisfied with the way things turned out. The Israeli-provoked border incidents, which had resulted in the destruction of the Syrian diversion equipment, had worried the administration mostly because it feared that they might escalate the conflict. It was why the United States had warned Israel against initiating such incidents, arguing that they might serve to unite a divided and split Arab world. It also warned Israel that it should not expect American support if these or other future incidents turned out to have serious consequences.[77] However, once it was evident that none of the Arab states, above all, Egypt, were going to respond to Israel's assault, the Americans were finally persuaded that a limited Israeli response did not contain the danger of general conflagration—something they had, in fact, suspected all along. As noted, some kind of limited military action was precisely the policy the United States had rather slyly alluded to when it had remarked that it would shed no tears if Israel wrecked Syria's bulldozers.

In the United States, the May 13 incident produced a general, all-round sense of relaxation, particularly as compared to the tense atmosphere that pervaded the corridors of Washington in the beginning of 1965. The United States no longer believed that counterdiversion scheme had the potential to ignite a general conflagration. Patrick Dean, Britain's ambassador to Washington, offered an accurate assessment of the American administration's state of mind, observing that "the State Department are somewhat less alarmist ... although they may not be willing to admit it, and I suspect the reason is that the limited Arab reactions to the last two Israeli attacks have suggested that a wider conflagration is less likely than they expected."[78]

Yet, though pleased with the outcome of the two Israeli attacks, the United States was not sufficiently blasé to entirely rule out the possibility of a future conflagration. It sought, therefore, to, as it put it, restrain the Israelis and dissuade them from taking further military action against the Arabs. British policy was much the same. There was, however, one big, fundamental difference between the two powers: the United States had incomparably greater influence over Israel than Britain, so that its efforts were much more likely to be crowned with success.

Although the March 17 and May 13 incidents did not ignite a military confrontation between Israel and the Arab states, they did, in Britain's opinion, serve to escalate the conflict. John Beith, having admitted that Israel's decision not to wait until the counterdiversion project was complete was correct, also acknowledged this strategy had the potential of exacerbating the situation. For one thing, Syria would never agree to a situation whereby Israel had total control over the Jordan River's headwaters. For another, Israel, having proved that it had the ability to destroy the Syrian diversion equipment and thus bring the counterdiversion project to a halt rather than seek a diplomatic solution to the affair, might be tempted to make further use of its military power in order to resolve the water dispute on its own terms.

Nor were Britain's suspicions unfounded as proved by subsequent events in Lebanon. In the beginning of March, the Lebanese government began to work on its counterdiversion project at an accelerated pace and at three different sites.[79] By doing so it hoped to demonstrate to the Arab world and, above all to Egypt, who had of late subjected Lebanon to some particularly vicious attacks, that it was faithfully executing the Alexandria Summit Conference's decisions. The counterdiversion, Lebanon thought, would be its entry ticket to the forthcoming summit conference, which was to take place in Casablanca that September.[80]

Lebanon had been charged with diverting the waters of the Hasbani River to the Banias in Syria from where the water would be channeled to the Yurmuk in Jordan. Undeterred by Israel's twin attacks on the Syrian diversion equipment and working at breakneck speed, Lebanon managed within a relatively short time to develop the area that lay between the Hasbani River to the Syrian border, dig a 4.5 km–long canal and to start building a dam on one of the Hasbani's offshoots.

None of this meant that Lebanon was indifferent to the possibility of an aggressive Israeli reaction. Quite the contrary. When it decided to push forward the work on the counterdiversion, the Lebanese government was banking on the fact that Israel would not wish to strengthen the hands of extremists in Lebanon, something that was bound to happen if it attacked the counterdiversion sites. In addition, in order to reassure Israel and prevent any untoward military response, the Lebanese government discretely divulged that the counterdiversion was principally intended to provide Lebanon's own water needs. It further promised that it would not exceed the quotas set by the Johnston Plan. As for the canal linking the Hasbani River to the Banias in Syria, the Lebanese government pointed out that the canal was useless until the Syrians completed their part of the project on the other side of the border, which, they hinted, seemed unlikely. In any case, they had no intention of finishing the canal. All in all, Lebanon concluded, Israel had no reason to attack it.[81]

It is hard to judge whether the Lebanese assurances were sincere, or simply a tactical measure. As the Lebanese were divided among themselves in respect to the scheme, it appears that they were most likely a mixture of both. Charles Hilu, the Lebanese president, and his Christian colleagues certainly hoped to keep the border with Israel quiet and as a result were careful to ensure that work on the scheme was kept to an absolute minimum. Not surprisingly, it was also Hilu who delivered these soothing messages. His prime minister, Hasin al Ayuni, like other Moslems in the Lebanese ruling establishment, took a different view. Eager to join the Syrian efforts, they pushed for the immediate and swift execution of the counterdiversion projects.

Whatever the truth of the matter, Britain took Hilu at his word. It credited his claim that the Lebanese counterdiversion was a minor project, intended to meet Lebanon's own irrigation requirements. It accepted that Lebanon had no intention of linking its diversion project with that of the Syrians. And it believed Lebanon's statement that it would not exceed the amount of water allotted it by the Johnston Plan. Lebanon, Britain applauded, had managed to avoid wrecking the Israeli water program while preempting Arab criticism of its attitude on this issue. Israel clearly had nothing to worry about, and Britain sincerely hoped it would do "nothing to harm the Lebanese whose moderate attitude in Arab counsels is to Israel's advantage."[82]

The Israeli government, however, was less inclined to give credence to Lebanon's reassurances. Not that this made much difference, as Israel, in any case, regarded all the counterdiversion projects, whether Syrian or Lebanese, as a threat to its vital national interests. Moreover, close inspection of the actual work carried in the counterdiversion sites proved beyond doubt, at least to Israel's mind, that Lebanon, far from seeking simply to supply its own water needs, was bent on diverting the Hasbani to Syria. Why else, Israel asked, would it be digging a canal only 200 meters from the Syrian border? The damage to Israel's water economy once the Lebanese canal was linked to the Syrian canal would be enormous. According to Israeli estimates, Lebanon intended to divert something between 100 and 140 mcm of water from the Hasbani to the Banias in deliberate defiance of the Johnston Plan, which had allocated only 35 mcm of water to Lebanon.[83] To strengthen its case, Israel quoted Lebanese Prime Minister Hasin al Ayuni, who, on June 14, had informed the Lebanese Parliament "that the work of diverting the tributaries continues according to the [sic] plan. Lebanon is working seriously for the implementation of the diversion of the Hasbani."[84]

Israel thought that Lebanon was behaving in a totally irrational manner, especially in view of the fact that Israel had twice attacked and destroyed the Syrian counterdiversion equipment. The general verdict was that Lebanon, having been pushed against its will into the cold water, now insisted, for better and for worse, upon swimming. The Israeli government appealed to the Western powers, time and again, to use their influence and convince the Lebanese to stop working on the counterdiversion. It warned Lebanon, and, parenthetically, the Western powers, too, that if diplomacy did not work, Israel would resort to the same kind of action that had proved so successful with Syria. On July 15, Yitzhak Rabin, the Israeli chief of staff, observed that "a second country, bordering on Israel, is proceeding with its diversion operations" and, he continued on a rather threatening note, "it will have to bear the responsibility for the consequences."[85]

All the Western powers were suspicious of the true motives behind Israel's aggressive and uncompromising stance. The United States doubted the veracity of Israel's information on the Lebanese counterdiversion in general, and on the canal project in particular. The Americans admitted that work on the canal was proceeding in full swing, but only, they thought, because the Lebanese knew that Syria would never complete its section of canal. The United States was firmly convinced that the canal was intended solely for internal Lebanese use. Nevertheless, in order assuage Israeli fears, justified or not, and to make doubly sure that the Lebanese did not link their canal to the Syrian canal, the Americans were willing to warn the Lebanese that merging the two canals would have grave consequences, indeed. At the same time, the United States advised Israel that to attack Lebanon would be to play straight into the hands of extremist elements in Lebanon and might even increase the chances of the Nasserist faction capturing power.[86]

Israel had repeatedly asked France, the Western power with the most influence over Lebanon, to intervene and warn the Lebanese against continuing the counterdiversion. The French, however, did not believe that the Lebanese project posed a serious threat to Israel's water supply. A French expert was sent to examine the Lebanese diversion sites, and his conclusion was that projects were indeed intended to supply Lebanon's own internal needs. Accordingly, France suspected that the Israeli government was deliberately exaggerating and embellishing its reports on the Lebanese counterdiversions. The reason? "Possibly because they themselves have in mind to establish a pipeline from Gisr Banat Yaacub to Tabgha pumping station to reduce the saliency of Lake Tiberias."[87] Israel was planning no such thing, and this utterly mistaken surmise is evidence of France's strong doubts regarding Israel's true motives. It also reflected France's total lack of understanding of Israel's life and death attitude toward its water supply.

As for Britain, the British government believed that thanks to the success of the action against Syria, military thinking had usurped diplomacy as Israel's way to resolve the water dispute. In fact, Britain assumed that Israel's relative military power, in general, formed the basis of its attitude and policies toward the Arab world. This judgment was not far wrong. Eshkol, unlike Ben Gurion, had little understanding of military or security matters. His public career to date had been limited to domestic affairs: finance, immigration, agriculture and the development of Israel's water sources. Accordingly, if Ben Gurion had the military and security establishment firmly under his thumb, the military establishment ruled Eshkol.

In government, Eshkol, as well as being prime minister also held the defense portfolio. But, to all intents and purposes, Israel's actual defense minister was Eshkol's chief of staff, Yitzhak Rabin. Israel Lior, Eshkol's military attaché, observed, rather discerningly, that Rabin acted as the prime minister's beacon on all matters relating to the army and security.[88] It had been Rabin who had suggested using the air force on November 13, and that Eshkol agreed to this revolutionary, provocative step was a measure of Rabin's immense influence over the Israeli prime minister. In the course of the water dispute, Rabin constantly threatened first Lebanon and later Syria with Israeli military action, and he would continue to do so in the future. The Egyptian slogan "Nasser awaits Rabin," coined on the eve of the Six-Day War, when Egypt thought an Israeli preemptive attack was in the offing, reveals exactly who the Egyptians thought was in charge, and it certainly wasn't Eshkol.[89]

Despite the doubts and reproaches of its three Western patrons, Israel stood its ground. In its opinion, the Lebanese authorities had managed to pull off a successful full-scale bluff.[90] Israel remained adamant that the work carried out in the Lebanese counterdiversion sites seriously threatened its interests. It warned that if the Lebanese refused to terminate the project, Israel would have no choice but to destroy the equipment and counterdiversion sites. The Israeli threats, direct and indirect, together with the albeit tepid pressure exerted by the Western powers, had their effect. The Lebanese government ordered the cessation of all work in the counterdiversion sites. But, in order not to give the impression that it had yielded to Israeli threats, Lebanon issued a statement explaining that it had been forced, temporarily, to stop the operations owing to lack of funds.

The Israeli threats, the Lebanese capitulation and the subsequent calm along the Israeli-Lebanese border, were, in Britain's opinion, conclusive evidence that Israel's policy was and would be in the future based on military force:

The Israelis have shown beyond doubt that they are not prepared to wait and see what Arab diversion [is] capable of carrying before resorting to limited military action. The success of this policy so far seems likely to encourage them to apply it to any diversion that could be represented as capable of exceeding the Johnston Plan allocation.[91]

When Israel, once again, attacked and destroyed Syrian counterdiversion equipment on August 12, it removed any lingering doubts Britain might have had about Israel's attitude toward the counterdiversion and its determination to use, or to threaten to use, force to resolve the water dispute. After the May 13 incident, Syria had again moved its counterdiversion site, this time to a location about 11 km from the Israeli border. The Syrian government, having calculated that the new site lay outside the range of Israel's artillery, banked on the fact that Israel was not reckless enough to escalate the dispute by using its air force to attack the site. It was proved right, but only in part.

Israel believed the Syrian and Lebanese governments had closely coordinated their work on the counterdiversions projects. Indeed, it only had to point to the fact that both countries were busy digging a canal on either side of the border. True the Lebanese had put their project on hold, but the Syrians were as busy as ever. As a result, the world was soon to witness to a repeat performance of the events of March and May. Israeli farmers began to farm the land in the disputed demilitarized zone, which provoked the Syrians into firing upon an Israeli tractor; in a flash, Israeli tanks and battery units, which had been stationed along the border in advance, fired and, to the Syrians' dismay, hit the counterdiversion equipment. The Israeli Foreign Ministry informed the British, somewhat tongue in cheek, the principal goal of the operation had been to neutralize the Syrian artillery units, though the possibility that "some shells may also have fallen amongst Syrian water diversion equipment," had been considered.[92]

Having successfully used force against Syria and Lebanon, not once, but several times, with the Arabs helpless to respond, Britain feared Israel would be tempted to continue along this aggressive road. The result would be continual friction along Israel's borders, in the form of recurrent incidents, which might drag the entire region into war. This was the last thing the Foreign Office, haunted by the possibility of war, wanted, as it believed Britain and British interests would suffer the most from a war in the Middle East.

There was one ray of hope. Britain assumed that neither side would deliberately provoke a war, especially not Egypt. True, the inevitable war of annihilation against Israel was one of Nasser's pet themes. But Nasser also insisted that such a war demanded careful preparations if victory was to be assured. For the moment, as far as Nasser was concerned, Israel's military might, the 6th fleet and Arab disunity combined to rule out the possibility of war, especially the latter. A successful war for the liberation of Palestine depended on the Arab world uniting and acting as one, something that did not appear likely to happen, at least not in the foreseeable future. Yet, even if some of the Arab states, Egypt, Syria, Iraq and Jordan, for example, were able to patch together some form of unity, Israel would regard such a development as a threat to its existence and would take preemptive action, attacking before the union had a chance to consolidate.[93] In light of these facts, Britain concluded that "the real danger lies in a war by accident, an unpremeditated confrontation in which the United Arab Republic government feels it cannot draw back without suffering unacceptable political defeat."[94]

In other words, Britain predicted that a situation might develop where, unless Nasser was willing to risk losing his standing in the Arab world, he would have no choice but to adopt measures that might lead to war. This was a more or less accurate assessment of the dynamics of Arab-Israeli relations, and the events of the next few years would bear out the Foreign Office's analysis to a remarkable degree.

Britain was also afraid that all this talk of inevitable wars, together with the establishment of the United Arab Command and the Palestine Liberation Organization and with the arms race hovering in the background, increased greatly the changes of war erupting. Nor was Arab talk of an inevitable war mere talk. The idea of Israel's annihilation was, as Willie Morris, the head of the Middle East Section in the Foreign Office, noted, a deep-rooted and intrinsic part of Arab, especially Egyptian, ideology and strategy. It formed the basis of the Arab states' policy toward Israel and other countries. Sir Humphrey Middleton, in Cairo, agreed and commented that the idea of Israel's destruction was

so embedded in the minds of the Egyptians that it will come more and more to influence U.A.R. policy. The same may already be happening over the ideas of using Arab oil as a weapon against the West and regulating the Arab's relations with third countries in accordance with those countries' attitude to Israel.[95]

Both sides were bent on policies that would, Britain feared, result in war by accident. Israel's uncompromising water policy had prompted it to use a limited measure of force to stop the counterdiversion of the Jordan River's headwaters. The Arabs, or more precisely the Egyptians, who, admittedly, hoped to prevent a war from breaking out before they were ready, nonetheless, set on a policy that forced Israel to take military measures. Neither side's policy left much room for diplomatic maneuver, resulting in repeated confrontations and clashes. Therein lay the danger of war.

The United States thought Britain's assessment that a single or series of border clashes might push the Middle East into war was, in essence, correct. It did not, however, think that the occasion would be the water dispute, which, in its opinion, was gradually petering out. It thought that in the future the Arab states would, at most, "proceed with only token or face saving projects, such as the local irrigation schemes, which would be dignified with the title of

Diversion Projects."[96] Hence, it was not the counterdiversion of the Jordan River's headwaters that would lead to war, but the growing number of guerrilla raids perpetrated from Syrian and even Jordanian territory.[97] The Americans based this surmise on the fact that Syrian-inspired border incidents between Israel and its Arab neighbors, which did not necessarily originate in the water dispute, were on the rise. The water dispute was, indeed, being pushed to the margins, but only to be replaced by the deadly activities of irregular Palestinian units, as Arab terminology had it, or terrorist units, as the Israelis called them.

Once the Syrian government had realized that the counterdiversion scheme was a dead letter, that none of the Arab states were willing to join it and wage an uncompromising battle against Israel, it decided to attack the problem of Israel by adopting an indirect strategy, by proxy as it were. It began to nurture and support Palestinian guerrilla units, which were to carry out raids across the border, disrupt life in Israel and, above all, sabotage Israel's water installations.[98] The Palestinian units were drawn from Al Fatah, a Palestinian organization that was independent of Ahmed Shukairy's PLO. Al Fatah, established in 1959, was led by Yasser Arafat and had a military arm known as Al Asifa (the storm). In the beginning of 1965, Al Asifa launched a series of raids against Israel. Syria saw Al Fatah as a means of advancing its interests in the Arab world and furthering its struggle against Israel. This did not quite fit in with Al Fatah's own strategy of a "Popular Armed Struggle," according to which the Palestinians must entangle the Arab states in a war with Israel against their will. This was the ultimate goal of the their activities, which would, Al Fatah hoped, ignite a general conflagration in the Middle East.[99]

Although enjoying Syrian patronage, the Palestinians units did not operate from Syrian territory alone. Raids were also conducted across the Lebanese, but, above all, the Jordanian border. The Israeli-Jordanian border was the longest and most vulnerable of all Israel's borders. Jordan also housed the largest number of Palestinian refugees, which provided Al Fatah with a goodly source of recruits, as well as making it relatively easy for it to build up the infrastructure it needed to carry out its operations.

Israel refused to tolerate Al Fatah's raids, even for a single moment, and it adopted a tough, fiercely uncompromising policy known as "Reprisals," in order to combat Palestinian guerrilla attacks. Eshkol emphasized that even though Israel knew that Syria was the driving force and inspiration behind the Palestinian attacks, no country from whose territory the attacks were launched would escape responsibility for the raids. Jordan was the first country to suffer the full force of Israel's resolve. At the end of May 1965, Israeli forces attacked several targets in Jordan, in retaliation to guerrilla attacks perpetrated from Jordanian territory.

The United States thought that the Israeli reprisals were the logical extension of Israel's earlier assaults on the Syrian counterdiversion equipment. As a demonstration of Israeli military might, the reprisals were intended to drive home to the Arabs that Israel still maintained its full power of deterrence.[100] Unfortunately, Jordan, who had been tacitly cooperating with Israel over the Jordan River, was forced, as a result of Israel's tough policy, to adopt a more extreme attitude toward Israel. Israel had demanded that Jordan put a stop to, or at least circumscribe, Palestinian activity, and this proved to be beyond Jordan's ability.[101] Helpless, and impotent, Jordan found itself trapped between the hammer of Israeli demands and the anvil of Palestinian activities. It was an impossible Catch-22-like situation, which not only established the dynamics of the two countries' future relations, but also would ultimately push Jordan, on the eve of the Six-Day War, into Egyptian arms.

Unhappy at this new turn of events, Britain warned the Israeli government that reprisals against Jordan—even if they were legitimate acts of retaliation—were not in Israel's interests.

We believe it is in Israel's best interest that we should have in Jordan a moderate government, interested in constructive development and the preservation of Jordan's independence. There is such a government at present; action ... can only force it to take a more extreme nationalist attitude and waste its energies on preoccupation with defence.[102]

Britain, like the United States, fully accepted Hussein's increasingly frantic claims that as anxious as he was to preserve peace along Jordan's border with Israel, he was incapable of sealing the border hermetically and preventing the Palestinian raids. Sir Roderick Parkes, Britain's ambassador to Amman, was not far off the mark when he likened Hussein's efforts to prevent Palestinians from infiltrating Israel to trying to do battle with the tentacles of an octopus.[103] In conversations with Israel, Britain constantly underlined its opposition to the use of force and urged Israel to exploit UN supervision mechanisms to resolve its problems with its neighbors.

Britain agreed with the American prognosis that the current cycle of attacks and counterattacks, especially if they escalated, might drag the Middle East into war. Indeed, this appeared to it to be a highly likely scenario. Accordingly, from mid-1965 onward, British-Israeli discussions were dominated by the problem of Palestinian guerrilla activities, which gradually replaced the water dispute as the hot issue of the day. Not that Britain had abandoned its estimate of the water dispute's menacing potential, but it was acutely aware that the numerous border incidents resulting from the Palestinian raids added a new and possibly even more catastrophic dimension to the Arab-Israeli conflict.

Revising its previous assessment, Britain now believed that a war between Israel and its neighbors might erupt for one of several reasons. These included an escalation of the border incidents precipitated by terrorist attacks on Israel; an increase in the border incidents sparked by the water dispute, though these were confined to Syria alone and finally there was the possibility that Egypt, if Nasser believed that Israel was on the verge of acquiring nuclear weapons, might decide to launch a preemptive strike.[104] None of this was helped by Israel's tough, aggressive policy, which left almost no room for diplomatic maneuver. Believing that military force was the answer to all its problems, Israel was intent upon deploying a limited amount of force to dictate or impose its views and solutions on the Arabs. Until now this policy had paid off, to wit, the suspension of the counterdiversion scheme. In some respects, Britain thought Israeli policy closely resembled that of the Soviet Union, albeit that the logic behind it was different: to keep the pot boiling or maintain a state of high tension.

The Casablanca Summit Conference was, to Israel's mind, further proof of the effectiveness of its new policy. The summit conference, which convened between September 13–17, 1965, offered an accurate reflection of the state of affairs in the Middle East following Israel's military strikes. The summit conference had originally intended to assess the progress made on the counterdiversion scheme, the strengthening of the Arab countries' military forces, and, especially, the buildup the United Arab Command. When it finally convened in mid-September, the original purpose of the summit conference was forgotten, and it all turned out very different from planned.

Even before the summit conference met, Nasser had made it very clear that Egypt would adhere to its policy of avoiding a precipitated armed conflict with Israel. The Egyptian president was, at present, pursuing a generally moderate foreign policy. On August 27, he signed an agreement with the Saudi King, Ibn Saud, who supported the monarchist faction Yemen, to end the civil war in Yemen. According to the agreement, known as the Jedda Agreement, a plebiscite, to be held no later than November 23, was to determine Yemen's future regime. In addition, Saudi Arabia was to stop assisting the monarchist faction in Yemen, while Egypt would start evacuating its troops from Yemen within three months of signing the agreement, a process, it promised, that would take ten months to complete.[105] It is hard to say to what extent Nasser intended to fulfill his side of the agreement, particularly as he had signed the agreement mainly as a result of American pressure. Indeed, there is little question that Nasser's sudden willingness to resolve his differences with Saudi Arabia were closely linked to the ongoing discussions between the United States and Egypt about a new aid package to Egypt.[106]

Nasser arrived in Casablanca determined to stick to his policy of avoiding an untimely war with Israel. In this, he had the support of Jordan, Lebanon, Morocco and Saudi Arabia. He also, and more crucially, had the support of General Ali Ali Amer, the commander in chief of the United Arab Command, though this was hardly surprising given that General Amer was Nasser's direct subordinate. Amer made no attempt to hide just how weak and unprepared the United Arab Command and the forces at its disposal were. Not only, he declared, were the Arab states not ready for a military confrontation with Israel, but also they were not even capable of protecting the counterdiversion scheme against Israeli attacks. In Amer's estimation it would take about four years and 150 million pounds sterling before the Arab armies would be fit to challenge Israel.

As a result of Amer's revelations, the summit conference decided to continue to build up and consolidate the United Arab Command. But until this was achieved the Arab states were to avoid provoking Israel, so that these provocations could not be used to its advantage. In addition, the summit conference agreed that each state was at liberty to decide, at its own discretion, whether to carry out the work on the counterdiversion scheme on the sole condition that the diversion sites were outside of the range of Israeli commando attacks.[107] These two decisions meant that Syria, who still demanded an immediate and uncompromising struggle against Israel, was completely isolated. The Syrian government finally realized that were it to continue with the counterdiversion scheme it would be left to face the terrors of the Israeli artillery alone. As far as the counterdiversion scheme was concerned, Israel, as Syria knew and Britain noted, had no intention of taking anything on trust or to playing any kind of waiting game. It would react instantly.[108]

Perhaps the Casablanca Summit Conference's crowning achievement was the signing of the Arab Solidarity Convention. In the Convention the Arab states promised to cease all mutual recriminations and refrain from interfering in each other's internal affairs. Egypt, for example, was to respect the integrity of all the Arab regimes. Unfortunately there was a huge gulf between the Convention's praiseworthy goals and the bitter reality of discord, divisions and disharmony that characterized the Arab world.

Other than the Convention, the Casablanca Summit Conference appeared to be a perfect example of Arab political and diplomatic realism. The Arab states had plainly recognized that they were currently unable to vie with the Israeli military power or execute the counterdiversion scheme. Britain's ambassador to Morocco offered a slightly different interpretation of Arab realism. He reported that after having talked with several of the summit conference's participants, he was certain that what the Arabs really wanted was to prevent a conflict from erupting before they had made significant progress toward developing a nuclear bomb of their own. It was this concern, the ambassador stressed, that truly lay behind the summit conference's moderate, realistic stance. The ambassador pointed out that the four years of military preparations General Amer had demanded were, precisely, "the period within which he hopes to have at his disposal an atomic bomb developed by German scientists."[109] The Arab states, aware that Israel was on the verge of developing a nuclear bomb, were very much afraid that if unduly provoked Israel would threaten to use the bomb. Hence, they concluded that they must avoid provoking Israel until such a time as they had a bomb of their own. The ambassador might well have been right, but until all the Casablanca Summit Conference's protocols were open for inspection, it would be impossible to estimate the veracity of his information or conclusions.

Britain regarded the Casablanca Summit Conference as a mixed blessing. It removed the water dispute from the Middle East's agenda, and on the other hand, it reinforced Israel's inclination to resolve its problems with the Arab world by force. Israel had discovered that in dealing with its neighbors, military force was an enormously effective instrument. Moreover, in both Britain and the U.S. estimation, Israel, at present, was, in military terms, more powerful than any possible combination of Arab forces, an assessment that would remain in force until the eve of the Six-Day War.

Israel's obvious military power served to reinforce Britain's judgment that there was little danger of the Arabs beginning a war in the near future. This meant that the region would have a much needed "breathing space for a few years before a deliberate confrontation is again seriously considered."[110] Not that Britain had abandoned the assumption, first voiced during the Cairo Summit Conference in January 1964, that an escalation of the border incidents might lead to a military confrontation. Furthermore, although Israel's military strength might prevent the Arab states from intentionally embarking upon war, Israel, who was wielding its power in an extremely reckless manner, without due consideration of the possible consequences of its actions, might inadvertently provoke a war. Israel certainly did not seem to take into account the possibility that its actions would unite and consolidate the currently divided Arab world. In sum, Britain feared that the border incidents and Israel's unruly use of force might hasten a conflagration.

Nevertheless, British apprehensions apart, the Casablanca Summit Conference did signal the beginning of a period of relative calm. The water dispute was no longer something of a time bomb, and the border incidents arising from dispute were on the wane. The Palestinians, disappointed with the results of the summit conference, had, admittedly, increased the number of guerrilla raids, but these, too, soon dwindled in number. In October 1965, having suffered several Al Fatah raids from Lebanese territory, Israel took retaliatory action against Lebanon and put an end to that. At the end of 1965, Syria advised the Americans that Israel was contemplating a military strike against Syria owing to its support of Al Fatah. According to Syria, Israel was, to this end, concentrating its forces along its northern border. This was a complete fabrication. If Israel did at one point consider a retaliatory attack against Syria, it no longer did so in view of the decline in Al-Fatah activity. It certainly was not concentrating its forces along the Syrian border.[111]

In 1965 the water dispute dominated the situation. That year opened with the fear that Israel would launch a preemptive military strike against the Arabs, and closed with a general all-round abatement of tension. The winds of war, which had blown so strongly at the start of 1965, had, by the end of it, died down. But if the water dispute no longer dominated the Middle East's agenda, fueling the Arab-Israeli conflict, it nonetheless contributed a great deal to the conflict's dynamics. It marked the beginning of an ever-growing number of border clashes between Israel and it neighbors. It also paved the way to Al Fatah guerrilla activities, and Al Fatah, though it benefited from Syrian patronage, had its own agenda and strategy. Its self-imposed mission was to propel the Arab states into war with Israel even against their will. Its ability to fulfill this strategy, however, was strongly in doubt, and by the end 1965, the number of guerrilla attacks against Israel had fallen significantly. The Middle East, Britain believed, perhaps a bit optimistically, was plainly entering a period of relative calm. As evidence of this, it pointed to the decline in Soviet meddling, stressing that peace and tranquillity did not offer the Soviets many opportunities to expand their influence. This much was true, so perhaps the Britain did have grounds for at least some cautious optimism.

NOTES

1. FO 371/180666, Military Attaché to Ministry of Defence, January 21, 1965.

2. Shemesh, "Arab Struggle over Water," pp. 142–143; FO 371/180666, Paris to FO, February 4, 1965.

3. *Ma'ariv*, January 17, 1965; *Ha'aretz*, January 12 and 20, 1965.

4. BBC, *Panorama*, March 29, 1965; *Ha'aretz*, January 17, 1965.

5. ISA, Hez/12/744, Lourie to Herzog, March 18, 1965; FO 371/180666, Washington to FO, February 4, 1965.

6. FO 371/180666.

7. ISA, Hez/7/3526, Jerusalem to London, February 16, 1965; FO 371/180865, FO to Tel Aviv, February 26, 1965.

8. FO 371/180666, Kellas to Goodison, May 5, 1965.

9. ISA, Hez/7/3526, Jerusalem to London, February 16, 1965; FO 371/180666, February 11, 1965.

10. FO 371/180666, February 4, 1965.

11. FO 371/180666, Tel Aviv to FO, February 16, 1965.

12. *Knesset Debates*, 42, March 29, 1965.

13. FO 371/180865, Minute by Morris, March 17, 1964; FO 371/180666, Damascus to FO, February 9, 1964.

14. Bar-Siman-Tov, *Israel*, p. 89; Spiegel, *Arab Israeli Conflict*, pp. 131–133; Hez/7/3526, London to Jerusalem, February 19, 1965.

15. FO 371/180666, Paris to FO, February 4, 1965.

16. FO 371/180666, Washington to FO, February 8, 1965.

17. *Ha'aretz*, November 6, 1964.

18. FO 371/180653, Washington to FO, January 22, 1965.

19. FO 371/180666, Minute by Morris, February 9, 1965.

20. Ibid.

21. FO 371/180666, Tel Aviv to FO, February 11, 1965; FO 371/180667, Tel Aviv to FO, February 9, 1965.

22. FO 371/180666, Washington to FO, February 18, 1965.

23. CAB 129/120 Memorandum by Secretary of State, March 24, 1965; FO 371/180666, Minute by FO, February 18, 1965.

24. FO 371/180651, NATO Expert Working Group, March 11, 1965.

25. FO 371/180865, Minute by Crawford, March 1, 1965.

26. CAB 129/120, Memorandum by the Secretary of State, March 24, 1965.

27. ISA, Hez/7/3526, Jerusalem to London, February 16, 1965; FO 371/180665, Minute by Morris, March 19, 1965.

28. ISA, Hez/12/744, Jerusalem to London, March 16, 1965; FO 371/180666 Washington to FO, February 8, 1965.

29. FO 371/180666, Minute by the FO, March 1, 1965 and Minute by Grehan, February 13, 1965; ISA Hez/7/3526, London to Jerusalem, February 16, 1965.

30. FO 371/180667, Comment on the Record of Meeting between the Secretary of State and the Israeli Ambassador, March 16, 1965.

31. FO 371/180667, Cairo to FO, March 23, 1965; FO 371/180664, Minute by Crawford, April 6, 1965; ISA Hez/9/4317, Washington to Jerusalem, April 20, 1965.

32. FO 371/180667, Minute by FO, February 18, 1965.

33. The Hallstein Doctrine, named after its author the West German Foreign Minister Walter Hallstein, came into force in 1955. The doctrine stated that the West German government considered any recognition of East Germany to be an unfriendly act. Recognizing East Germany, it declared, implied the recognition of Germany's division into two states, for which there was, according to West Germany, no legal basis. Moreover, as the only government freely elected by the German people, Bonn claimed the sole legal right to represent Germany in the international arena. See Bark and Gress, *Democracy*, p. 374.

34. Ibid., p. 27; Sela, *Decline of the Arab-Israeli Conflict*, pp. 79–80.

35. Sela, pp. 80–81; *Ha'aretz*, March 7, 1965; Seguev, *Israel*, pp. 40–41.

36. FO 371/180666, Tel Aviv to FO, February 16, 1965; FO 371/180648, Brief by the FO, April 22, 1965.

37. FO 371/180667, Minute by FO and Minute by Morris, February 18, 1965.

38. FO 371/180667, FO to New York, March 9, 1964 and New York to FO, March 11, 1965 and Cairo to FO, March 17, 1965; FO 371/180666, New York to FO, March 6, 1965.

39. CAB 133/269, Brief by FO, March 29, 1965; ISA, Hez/12/744, London to Jerusalem, April 13, 1965; Parliamentary Debates, 5th series, vol. 709, cols. 1975–1979, April 1, 1965.

40. FO 371/180648, Minute by the FO, April 22, 1965; *Ma'ariv*, October 4, 1965.

41. ISA, Hez/7/3526, Jerusalem to London, February 19, 1965; FO 371/180865, FO to Tel Aviv, February 26, 1965.

42. FO 371/180651, NATO Expert Working Group, March 11, 1965; FO 371/180677, Paris to FO, March 15, 1965.

43. FO 371/180667, Minute by Morris and Minute by FO, February 18, 1965; FO 371/180651, North Atlantic Committee, March 15, 1965; ISA, Hez/7/3526, Jerusalem to London, February 19, 1965.

44. The Sino-Soviet split developed between 1957–1959, following ideological and strategic differences between the two communist mammoths. The spilt deepened at the beginning of the 1960s and reached its zenith when the two began to quarrel over the exact position of the border between northeast China and the Soviet Union. See Nogee and Donaldson, *Soviet Foreign Policy*, pp. 229–239.

45. FO 371/1800660, Permanent Under-Secretary Steering Committee, February 17, 1965.

46. Ibid.

47. Ibid.

48. Ibid.

49. CAB 129/120, Memorandum by the Secretary of State, March 24, 1965; FO 371/180655, Washington to FO, March 23, 1965; PREM 13/292, Record of Conversation, July 19, 1965.

50. CAB133/269, Brief by FO, March 29, 1965; PREM 13/415, Minute by the FO, September 20, 1965.

51. Ibid.; FO 371/180660, Draft Aide Memoir, May 6, 1965; ISA, Hez/5/4328, London to Jerusalem, March 28, 1965.

52. PREM 11/4934, Note of Meeting and O'Shaughnessy to Timotey and Dodds and Secretary of State, May 4, 1965.

53. FO 371/180665, Washington to FO, March 23, 1965; FO 371/180894, Minute by Morris, February 11, 1965; PREM 11/4934, Note of Meeting, May 4, 1965; El Hussini, *Soviet-Egyptian Relations*, p. 149.

54. See in this connection: NA RG59/2356, Memorandum of Conversation, February 25, 1964; FO 371/180664, Minute by Crawford, April 6 and Cairo to FO, April 25, 1965; *FRUS, 1964–1968*, pp. 66–68; Rabin, *Service Notes*, p. 129.

55. Cohen, "Cairo, Dimona," p. 196; NA RG59/2349, Talbot to Harriman, June 2, 1964.

56. ISA, Hez/6/3689, Gazit to Herzog, April 6, 1965; FO 371/180667, Noted for Meeting, March 29, 1965 and Memorandum of Conversation, April 1, 1965.

57. *Ha'aretz*, February 19, 25, 1965.

58. CAB 129/130, Memorandum by the Secretary of State, March 24, 1965; FO 371/180856, Washington to FO, March 4, 1965; NA RG/1888, SD to Tel Aviv, March 2, 1965 and Memorandum of Conversation, March 3, 1965.

59. Rabin, *Service Notes*, p. 130; FO 371/180856, Tel Aviv to FO, March 31, 1965.

60. Spiegel, *Arab-Israeli Conflict*, p. 134; Rabin, *Service Notes*, p. 128; FO 371/180856, Washington to FO, March 4, 1965; Peres, *David's Sling*, p. 85.

61. Little, "Choosing Sides," pp. 163–164; Ma'oz, *Syria and Israel*, p. 87; Bar-Siman-Tov, *Israel*, p. 90; Rabin, *Service Notes*, p. 129.

62. Aronson, *Nuclear Weapons*, pp. 20 and 41–42; Cohen, "Battle over Dimona," p. 195; Cohen, "Balancing American Interests," pp. 293–294; FO 371/180856, Washington to FO, March 4, 1965.

63. FO 371/180894, Washington to FO, March 15, 1965; Rabin, *Service Notes*, p. 130.

64. Rabin, *Service Notes*, p. 129; Ma'oz, *Syria and Israel*, p. 87; FO 371/180651, North Atlantic Council, March 10, 1965; FO 371/180856, Washington to FO, April 24, 1965 and Tel Aviv to FO, March 31, 1965; *FRUS, 1964–1968*, pp. 373–375.

65. FO 371/180856, Washington to FO, March 4, 1965; FO 371/180655, New York to FO, March 12, 1965; FO 371/180894, Washington to FO, March 15, 1965; FO 371/180668, FO to Washington, May 10, 1965; *FRUS, 1964–1968*, pp. 330–332.

66. ISA Hez/6/3689, Gazit to Herzog, April 6, 1965.

67. Lenczowski, *American Presidents*, p. 106.

68. FO 371/180879, Damascus to FO, May 14, 1965 and Tel Aviv to FO, May 20, 1965 and Air Attaché to FO, May 19, 1965; Zisser, "Between Syria and Israel," pp. 206–207.

69. FO 371/180877, Washington to FO, January 6, 1965.

70. FO 371/180878, Damascus to FO, March 17, 1965 and Tel Aviv to FO, March 19, 1965 and Minute by FO, March 27, 1965; FO 371/180879, Washington to FO, May 14, 1965; NA RG/2353, Jerusalem to SD, May 16, 1965 and Memorandum of Conversation, May 19, 1965; Bull, *War and Peace*, pp. 77–78; Shemesh, "Arab Struggle over Water," pp. 152–156.

71. FO 371/180668, Damascus to FO, June 19, 1965; Shemesh, "Arab Struggle over Water," pp. 156–157.

72. FO 371/180646, Anglo-French Discussion, July 2, 1965; Neff, *Warriors for Jerusalem*, p. 53; Gilbo'a, *Six Years*, p. 48.

73. *Knesset Debates*, vol. 43, May 15, 1965; Yaniv, *Brutal Dialogue*, p. 373.

74. FO 371/180878, Damascus to FO, March 23, 1965; FO 371/180879, Damascus to FO, May 14, 1965.

75. FO 371/180668, Tel Aviv to FO, June 2, 1965.

76. FO 371/180646, Anglo-French Discussion, July 2, 1965.

77. FO 371/180879, Minute by Morris, May 19, 1965; FO 371/180668, Washington to FO, May 21, 1964.

78. FO 371/180668, Washington to FO, May 21, 1964; FO 371/180668, FO to Washington, May 19, 1965.

79. Lebanon was allotted three counterdiversion projects. The first entailed building a canal from the Upper Hasbani to Hasbia from where the water would be diverted to the Litani River. The second involved two counterdiversion sites in the Middle Hasbani, the first on the river itself, the second on Wadi Sarid, which together were to channel the waters of the Hasbani and Wadi Sarid to the Banias River and from there to the Yarmuk. The third project entailed constructing a canal on the Lower Hasbani, which was to exploit the river's water for local use. The Lebanese were also instructed to build three pumping stations to convey excess waters from the Wazzani Spring in Lebanon to Syria, by means of the Sarid-Banias canal. FO 371/180668, Remez to Thomson, July 7, 1965; Shemesh, "Arab Struggle over Water," pp. 144–147.

80. Shemesh, "Arab Struggle over Water," p. 144; FO 371/180669, Beirut to FO, July 22, 1965.

81. FO 371/180668, Beirut to FO, May 28, 1965; FO 371/180669, Beirut to FO, July 24, 1965.

82. FO 371/180865, Brief on Special Matters by Morris, July 6, 1965 and Beirut to FO, July 9, 1965.

83. FO 371/180669, Tel Aviv to FO, July 7 and 12, 1965 and Beirut to FO, July 16, 1965; Shemesh, "Arab Struggle over Water," p. 146; FO 371/180668, Remez to Thomson, July 7, 1965.

84. FO 371/180668.

85. *Jerusalem Post*, July 15, 1965.

86. FO 371/180668, Washington to FO, July 8 and 9, 1965; FO 371/180669, Washington to FO, July 19, 1965; NA RG/2353, Talbot to Secretary, July 14, 1965.

87. FO 371/180668, Paris to FO, July 8, 1965.

88. Haber, *War Will Break Out*, pp. 42, 67, 97.

89. In this connection, see Nasser's speech to the Egyptian officers on May 22. Nakdimon, *Approaching H-Hour*, p. 43; Parker, *Politics of Miscalculation*, p. 8.

90. FO 371/180669, Tel Aviv to FO, July 7, 1965.

91. FO 371/180669, FO to Beirut, August 10, 1965; Lowi, *Water and Power*, p. 127.

92. FO 371/180880, Tel Aviv to FO, August 13 and Damascus to FO, August 14, 1965; Yaniv, *Politics and Strategy*, p. 189; Golan, "Conflict over the Jordan," p. 857.

93. FO 371/180668, FO to Cairo, May 20, 1965.

94. FO 371/186830, Morris to Middleton, May 21, 1965; FO 371/180668, Amman to FO, June 11, 1965 and Damascus to FO, June 19, 1965.

95. FO 371/180668, Cairo to FO, April 23, 1965.

96. FO 371/180830, Minute by MacLean, July 28, 1965.

97. FO 371/180668, Washington to FO, June 21, 1965.

98. Yaniv, *Politics and Strategy*, p. 189; Bulloch and Darwish, *Water War*, p. 39.

99. Yitzhaki, *Arab Eyes*, p. 30; Ohana et al., *PLO*, p. 34; Sela, *Decline of the Arab-Israeli Conflict*, pp. 77–78.

100. NA RG/59/2350, Talbot to the Secretary, June 1, 1965.

101. *Knesset Debates*, 43, May 18, 1965; Gilbo'a, *Six Years*, p. 49; ISA, Hez/12/744, Jerusalem to London, June 1, 1965,

102. ISA, Hez/2/748, Remez to Jerusalem, May 31, 1965; FO 371/180879, Minute by FO, May 31, 1965.

103. ISA, Hez/2/748, Remez to Jerusalem, May 31, 1965 and Anug to Jerusalem, September 8, 1965; FO 371/180879, Amman to FO, May 29, 1965; FO 371/180880, Amman to FO, August 6, 1965; FO 371/180881, Washington to FO, September 7, 1965; NA RG/2347, Memorandum of Conversation, May 28, 1965.

104. FO 371/180646, Anglo-French Discussion, July 2, 1965; FO 371/180653, Minute by McLean, September 27, 1965.

105. FO 371/180652, Holliday to Stewart, September 30, 1965; Sela, *Decline of the Arab-Israeli Conflict*, p. 82.

106. Sela, *Decline of the Arab-Israeli Conflict*, p. 82; Burns, *Economic Aid*, pp. 82–83; FO 371/180646, Anglo-American Talk on the Middle East, November 29, 1965.

107. FO 371/180652, Holliday to Stewart, September 30, 1965; FO 371/180651, FO to the United Kingdom Delegation, NATO, October 7, 1965; Shemesh, "Arab Struggle over Water," p. 160.

108. FO 371/186439, FO to Tel Aviv, February 15, 1966.

109. FO 371/180652, Holliday to Stewart, September 30, 1965.

110. FO 371/180646, Anglo-American Talks, November 29, 1965.

111. ISA, Hez/2/748, Remez to Jerusalem, November 2, 1965; FO 371/180883, Washington to FO and Tel Aviv to FO, November 21, 1965.

4

A Brief Respite and Rapid Escalation

A TEMPORARY CALM

Britain was not alone in thinking that there were grounds for optimism about the future of the Middle East. The United States and France thought that there was reason for at least some cautious optimism. After the Casablanca Summit Conference, there appeared to be a toning down of the tense relations between Israel and the Arab states. Furthermore, several developments combined to indicate that this relative calm and stability would continue. First, and most important, the Arab states had postponed indefinitely their plan to divert the Jordan River's headwaters. Second, the number of border incidents had declined significantly. Accordingly, the Western powers concluded that for at least the next four years, there was no danger of war erupting as a result of the river dispute. According to the United States, this new atmosphere of temperance and restraint in the Middle East was part of the general wave of moderation that was sweeping over the entire international system.[1]

The year 1966 began well. The borders were relatively tranquil. There were few sabotage operations or raids, and these, too, soon stopped altogether. It is hard to say whether it was the Syrian government's fear of Israeli reprisals or King Hussein's vigorous efforts to circumscribe Al Fatah's activities in Jordan that were responsible for the cessation of the Palestinian attacks. Most probably it was a mixture of both. Britain believed that it, too, had a share in this positive development and was convinced that the pressure it had exerted on Hussein to curb the raids against Israel had paid off. Not that Britain, as it was the first to admit, had to apply too much pressure, as the king himself was anxious to live in peaceful coexistence with his Israeli neighbors.[2] In any event these were, in Yitzhak Rabin's phrase, months of tranquillity.

The resumption of inter-Arab squabbling was another encouraging sign. The decision at Casablanca to postpone the military showdown with Israel until all the military preparations were in place did not herald the resumption of Arab unity. Nor did the Convention of Solidarity, signed at the summit conference, signal the beginning of a new era of Arab solidarity. Quite the contrary. Within days of the summit conference, the Arab states reverted to their habits of old and the disputes, divisions and splits that had characterized the Arab world before the Cairo Summit Conference in January 1964 ruled the roost again. Ironically, or perhaps not, Egypt stood at the center of the most serious of these inter-Arab feuds. Relations between Syria and Egypt had reached a new all-time low, with the Egyptian president refusing to cooperate with the Syrian Ba'ath regime. He refused, for example, to support or even offer encouragement to Syria's strategy, which sought to liberate Palestine now.

Relations between Egypt and Saudi Arabia were not much better. The ink on the Jedda Agreement had barely dried before the two were again up in arms over Yemen. Neither side had fulfilled its part of the agreement. The Saudis insisted that before they did anything Egypt must first evacuate its forces from Yemen. Egypt, on its part, refused. Although according to the Jedda Agreement it was supposed to have begun the evacuation process in November 1965, Egypt now insisted on the establishment of a transition government and a republican regime before the Egyptian soldiers returned home. In truth, the Jedda Agreement had been a dead letter even before it was signed. The Egyptian-Saudi clash over Yemen was both a symptom and a part of a wider, deeper conflict between Egypt and Saudi Arabia. The conservative Ibn Saud was intent upon challenging Nasser's radical leadership of the Arab world. In the beginning of 1966, for instance, he raised the idea of a Summit of the Heads of the Moslem states. Ibn Saud's proposal was probably little more than a blind to create a coalition of conservative Arab governments with American backing, and Nasser was not far wrong in assuming that the Saudi king was seeking to create an antirevolutionary, pro-Western coalition reminiscent of the 1955 Baghdad Alliance.[3]

While busy quarrelling with several of its fellow Arab states, back home, Egypt was in the throes of a severe economic crisis. Although its relations with the Soviet Union were better than ever, the Soviet Union was incapable of solving Egypt's economic problems. It could offer Egypt vast amounts of arms, and on terrific terms of credit, but it could not meet Egypt's food requirements, let alone provide it with the vital financial and economic aid it needed to survive. The only power who could do that was the United States. In the beginning of 1966, after months of arduous negotiations, Egypt and the United States finally signed an economic aid agreement. Nasser was desperate enough for American assistance that he was willing to display a more moderate stance toward Israel, as well as the Middle East in general. In short, Nasser was ready to keep the peace, but only temporarily. Nasser's newfound moderation was a provisional, tactical affair; he never, for one minute, abandoned his strategy of ultimately destroying the Zionist entity.

Britain, unfortunately, did not enjoy the fruits of Nasser's moderation. It remained the target of a vicious Egyptian propaganda campaign, which sought to eject it from its bases in Aden and the Federation of Southern Arabia.[4] Nevertheless, in early 1966, the long-suffering British government was quite satisfied with the general turn of events. It assumed that as long as Egypt was busy quarrelling with the other Arab states, as long as its soldiers were bogged down in

Yemen and as long as it was burdened by weighty economic problems, Egypt would not nor would it allow others to deliberately go to war with Israel. As no Arab state would dare to launch a war without Egypt, the Egyptian president's unwillingness and inability to consider a military confrontation with Israel, other than in the distant future, was an excellent guarantee that war would not erupt.

The current state of affairs in the Arab world confirmed Britain's assessment that the water dispute would not provoke a military conflagration. True, the Arab states did not abandon but merely postponed the counterdiversion scheme. Nevertheless, in Britain's opinion, they were, at present, little inclined to provoke Israel by a diversion inimical to Israeli interests.[5] Even Syria, who for reasons of national pride was still carrying out some low-scale work on the scheme, had no intention of igniting a military conflict with Israel. It was why Syria had moved the diversion site far from the Israeli border, why the work at the diversion site proceeded at a snail's pace and why any progress made was minuscule, if that.

Syria secretly admitted that it was incapable of challenging Israel, and its insistence upon carrying out the counterdiversion in however low key a manner owed more to pride and self-respect, a refusal to capitulate completely to Israeli military power. In fact, far from contemplating war, Syria, in light of past experience and aware that Israel would destroy the engineering equipment at the first opportunity that presented itself, was afraid of finding itself the victim of yet another Israeli strike. Accordingly, from the end of 1965, Syria began to complain about the concentration of Israeli forces along its border. Perhaps its fear was genuine. Or perhaps it sought to force Egypt to confront Israel directly, always a possibility as long as the water dispute was still on the agenda.[6]

Lebanon and Jordan, too, resumed work on the counterdiversion scheme. Lebanon began laying down the groundwork in a diversion site in the south of the country. Jordan started to build the Mukheiba Dam. Yet Jordan was very careful to uphold its tacit agreement with Israel regarding their allotted quotas of water. Lebanon, on its part, reassured the Western powers that once its diversion project was complete it would not divert more than the 35 mcm of water Lebanon had been allocated by Johnston Plan. Accordingly, Britain assumed, neither project would result in anything more than a minor deviation from the Johnston Plan, certainly nothing that might affect the Israeli water economy. Israel apparently agreed and did not consider either Lebanon or Jordan's activities as a threat.[7] Israel, nevertheless, thought it necessary to alert Britain and the United States to the possible dangers inherent in both counterdiversion projects, especially the Lebanese. Why? Perhaps it was afraid that the Arab states were still intent upon completing the counter-diversion, but by other, less obvious, means.

Disconcerted and somewhat irritated by Israel's complaints, Britain refused to pursue the Israeli allegations. As far it was concerned, the Arab states had plainly postponed their plan to divert the Jordan River's headwaters. Willie Morris gave voice to Britain's exasperation, grumbling that

[the] Israelis seem to regard themselves as entitled to complain at any abstraction of water by the Arabs from the tributaries of the Jordan, but we should not accept this, as long as Arab water is roughly within the limits of the Johnston Plan.[8]

Between March 10 and 17, the Arab states' prime ministers gathered in Cairo for yet another Summit. There were three topics on the agenda: inter-Arab relations, the Arab states' relations with Israel and the counterdiversion scheme. Other then a regurgitation of previous summit conference decisions, the Cairo Summit Conference produced nothing of consequence. For instance, it reconfirmed the decision to postpone the counterdiversion scheme; a decision that had, in fact, been ratified only six months earlier. Abdel Rahman al Bazzaz, the prime minister of Iraq, tried to inject some fresh meaning into the decision by adding that the Arab states directly concerned with the scheme would do their utmost to overcome all the obstacles in the way of completing the project and that once they had strengthened their military forces they would be able to execute the scheme in full.[9] The only decision of any value to emerge from the Cairo Summit Conference was to convene another summit conference in September, this time in Algeria.

"The significant feature of the meeting was that the participants found it unnecessary to [even] seriously pretend that it had any significance at all" was Israel's rather caustic verdict on the Cairo Summit Conference.[10] Wit apart, the summit conference had clearly underlined the divisions and splits that characterized the Arab world at present. The summit conference had very quickly developed into an embarrassing exhibition of acrimonious and bitter verbal altercations, which, by now, had become symptomatic of most inter-Arab gatherings. Divided interests rather than unity of purpose was the order of the day. Britain saw the summit conference as further evidence of Arab discord, on the one hand, and of the Arab states' sober attitude toward the counterdiversion plan on the other. As a result, the Foreign Office noted with some satisfaction that the Middle East was, in many respects, much quieter than it had been for years and that Britain could look forward to a period of relative calm in the Arab-Israeli Conflict.[11]

Arab, and especially Egyptian, strategy toward Israel was determined largely on the basis of Israel's relative military power. This was why the Arab states continuously and obsessively added more and more weapons to their already swollen arms arsenals. But then so did Israel and in an even more vigorous manner, thanks to which it had managed, so far, to maintain its qualitative edge over the Arab states. In Britain's estimation the military balance in the region would remain in Israel's favor for at least four years. The United States disagreed and thought that Israel would be able to maintain its military advantage for at least seven years. Britain and the United States also differed over the question of why Israel was continuously asking for more weapons, with special emphasis on aircraft. Walworth Barbour, the American ambassador to Israel, in an attempt to get to the bottom of Israeli military thinking, suggested that Israel might be contemplating an air battle over Cairo. Britain, however, believed that Israel was simply trying to increase its military strength to the point where the Arab states would feel totally incapable of defending themselves against an Israeli attack.[12] Israel's aim, Britain assumed, was to achieve absolute security.

Despite enjoying the temporary calm that enveloped the Middle East, Britain still believed a military conflagration possible. The possibility of an accidental escalation of the conflict or following a desperate preemptive attack launched by the Arabs in the belief that Israel was on the verge of producing a nuclear bomb were both equally realistic and frightening scenarios.[13] In the latter case, Britain could draw some comfort from Israel's nuclear policy. The Israeli government had of late, though admittedly only after having been subjected to a great deal of pressure, made a genuine effort to reduce the tension provoked by its nuclear program. This, however, was offset by the fact that the Arab states, and Egypt in particular, had begun to show signs of increasing nervousness at the prospect of an Israeli nuclear bomb.

Between the end of 1965 and beginning of 1966, Israel's nuclear capability was the hot topic of the day. Numerous articles and reports were published on the subject, the majority claiming that Israel was on the brink of producing a nuclear bomb. This was not something that the Arab world and, above all, Egypt could ignore. Egypt deemed an Israeli nuclear bomb to be an out-and-out threat to the Arab world. Accordingly, Nasser began to threaten Israel with a preemptive attack. Throughout the first months of 1966, Nasser warned, time and again, that if Egypt had the slightest reason to believe that Israel was manufacturing atomic weapons it would immediately launch a preemptive attack. Nasser, it should be emphasized, was not threatening Israel with total war. He was talking of some kind of limited action to destroy Israel's nuclear installations in Dimona, which were capable of producing nuclear weapons.[14]

It is difficult to judge whether Nasser meant what he said, or whether these were empty threats whose chief aim was to underline and underpin Nasser's leadership of the Arab world and Egypt's military strength. In view of Egypt's involvement in Yemen and its fear of Israeli reprisals, it is the latter possibility that seems the more likely of the two. But Britain did not rule out the possibility that Nasser might risk a limited attack on Dimona[15] "if the Arabs really believed Israel to be on the brink of developing nuclear weapons."[16]

Britain did not think the Arab states' fears were completely groundless. Britain was convinced that Israel was capable of manufacturing nuclear weapons the moment it decided to do so. Whether it decided to do so was largely dependent on the willingness of the Western powers to guarantee its security and borders. But, in view of the West's desire to maintain reasonable relations with the Arab world, there was no chance that the West would offer Israel an explicit and public guarantee. Any hope Israel might have entertained in this respect was, as it ultimately realized, totally unrealistic. Consequently, and according to its information, information whose sources still remain secret, Britain concluded that Israel would go ahead with its nuclear program, so that by the end of 1966 and the beginning of 1967 it would be ready to conduct its first nuclear test.[17]

Britain was right. As long as the West refused to grant it a guarantee, Israel would continue to develop the bomb. In the absence of a Great Power guarantee, Israel believed that nuclear weapons offered it the best guarantee for its future existence. Hence, Israel's nuclear policy remained the same. At most, it was willing to repeat its cryptic promise not to be the first country to introduce nuclear weapons into the region. Abba Eban, who in January 1966 had replaced the hawkish Golda Meir as Israel's foreign minister, declared that Israel "has not initiated and will not initiate the introduction of new arms or any sorts of new weapons, into the Middle East, whether conventional or non conventional."[18]

This was far from satisfactory. Britain was certain that behind these ambiguous statements lay a determination to put Israel in the position of being able to manufacture a bomb at will, even though, thankfully, Israel had not yet taken the final decision to actually make one. Britain would have much preferred it if Israel, rather than indulge in enigmatic, vague statements about not being the first to introduce nuclear weapons into the area, took concrete action to prevent the proliferation of nuclear arms in the Middle East. In an effort to dissuade Israel from manufacturing a bomb, Britain constantly drove home the point that the possession of nuclear weapons would not ensure Israel's safety. On the contrary, Britain warned, if Israel appeared to be on the verge of acquiring a bomb, the Arab states would feel compelled either to launch a preemptive strike or to turn to the Soviets or Chinese for help, whether to acquire a bomb or to provide them with a nuclear umbrella. In Britain's opinion, Israel's interests would be best served by joining the nonproliferation agreement and subjecting its peaceful atomic energy program to international safeguards and supervision.[19]

Britain's ability to influence Israel on the question of Israeli nuclear policy proved no greater than its ability to influence Israel on any of the other issues relating to the Arab-Israeli conflict. Nor did Britain have any illusions in this respect. It knew that its influence over Israel was extremely limited, if indeed it existed at all. A memorandum sent by the Foreign Office to Michael Hadow, Britain's new ambassador to Tel Aviv, described Britain's position in a nutshell:

We have neither the physical power, nor the economic weapons, nor the consequent political influence, which the Americans can deploy, and if any Western power can achieve something it is the US.[20]

The Foreign Office was, in effect, admitting that the only country that possessed sufficient economic, military and political clout to influence Israel was the United States. And it was right.

Israel stubbornly preserved its nuclear option. The United States, however, was just as determined, and it exerted a great deal of pressure on Israel in an effort to persuade it to modify or abandon its nuclear policy. To this end, the United States, as before, combined threats and inducements, the carrot and the stick. The stick took the form of warning Israel that by refusing to open its nuclear plants to inspection teams, whether American or international, it was jeopardizing American-Israeli relations. Dean Rusk advised Abba Eban that although Israel's nuclear policy was the sole issue, it could have a totally disastrous effect on American-Israeli relations. Nor, he added, was opacity a solution. The adoption of an ambiguous policy, Rusk emphasized, would equally undermine the relations between the two countries.[21]

Although the American threats certainly had their effect, it was the carrot, that is, the U.S. agreement to meet Israel's conventional arms requirements, that ultimately convinced Israel to allow American inspection teams into its nuclear plant. The United States assumed, correctly, that Israel's nuclear lobby would find it much more difficult to promote their views if Israel were able to satisfy its bona fide conventional arms requirements, and vice versa. Robert Komer, U.S. national security advisor, explained to the British that a generous arms policy was one way of preventing Israel from manufacturing a bomb.[22] Of course, supplying Israel with advanced weapons also had the advantage of allowing Israel to better deter the Arab states and convince them that it was not in their interests to launch a war against it.

On March 23, 1966, Israel and the United States signed a new arms deal. The United States agreed to sell Israel forty-eight Skyhawk tactical aircraft plus related armaments, ammunition, spare parts and other goods and services, as to be agreed upon mutually. All this was for the bargain price of $72 million, which was to be paid on very easy credit terms. In Israel's view the deal marked a watershed in its relations with the United States, and in return for this extraordinarily generous agreement, it was willing to let an American inspection team into the Dimona plant. It was also willing to declare for the first time publicly, from the Knesset podium, that Israel would not be the first country to introduce nuclear arms into the Middle East.[23]

The decision to allow an American inspector team into the Dimona plant created a minor uproar in Israel. Eshkol's critics, the most vocal of whom was his predecessor Ben Gurion, accused him of undermining Israel's security. Professor Ernest Bergmann, a key member of Israel's nuclear establishment, was utterly opposed to any kind of international supervision of Israel's nuclear plants and resigned in protest from the Israeli Atomic Energy Commission. But Eshkol stuck to his guns. In the beginning of April, a team of American inspectors visited the Dimona plant. Like their colleagues who had inspected the plant a year earlier, they found no evidence pointing to the existence of a plutonium separation plant, or of any activity linked to the development of nuclear weapons.[24]

The United States was pleased with the results of the inspection team's visit. The United States was not naïve, and, like Britain, it was well aware that Israel had the ability, should it so decide, to develop a nuclear bomb within two or three years. Nevertheless, it believed that by reassuring the Arab states that Israel was not on the verge of manufacturing a bomb, it would help prevent the proliferation of nuclear weapons in the region. Accordingly, the United States passed on the team's findings to the Egyptians. In fact, the Americans had kept in close touch with the Egyptian government. It seems that the American report laid Egypt's fears to rest. Otherwise, it is difficult to explain why Nasser's threats to launch a preemptive strike against Israel's nuclear plant stopped almost immediately.

The Americans also appraised Britain of the inspection's team's findings and Britain agreed with the United States that the inspection's principal achievement was that it diffused the tension provoked by Israel's nuclear policy. It is, however, instructive that neither power ruled out the possibility that Israel, unbeknown to them, had hidden nuclear plants where it was secretly developing the bomb. It was a possibility that neither Britain nor the United States, for obvious reasons, shared with the Arab states.[25]

The reduction in tension that followed this minicrisis was consistent with the general calm that befell the region at this time. The United States assumed that the relative tranquillity currently enjoyed by the Middle East was part of the more relaxed, more moderate atmosphere, which, in general, characterized the international arena at the time and was personified by the "Tashkent Spirit" named after the city of Tashkent in Uzbekistan. It was in Tashkent that India and Pakistan, under Soviet sponsorship, had signed an agreement bringing an end to the war, which had been raging between them since September 1965.

The prime minister of the Soviet Union, Aleksei Kosygin, had personally invited the leaders of India and Pakistan, Bahadur Shastri and Ayub Khan, to meet on Soviet soil and resolve the long-standing conflict between their two countries. The three met in the city of Tashkent on January 4. The summit conference lasted six days until January 10, when, after a great deal of Soviet cajoling and pressure, an agreement was finally signed. Both sides declared their "firm resolve to restore normal relations and peaceful relations between their countries and to promote understanding and friendly relations between their peoples."[26] They also agreed to an effective cease-fire under which India and Pakistan were to withdraw their troops to their positions prior to the outbreak of war.

Israel believed that the events in Tashkent were a sign that the Soviet Union had turned over a new leaf. It thought it immensely encouraging that the Soviet Union had worked hard to convince, if not actually bulldoze, warring India and Pakistan into signing an agreement. When one added Kosygin's recent declaration that the Soviet Union was interested in the peaceful settlement of conflicts and the establishment of peaceful coexistence everywhere to this equation, then there was, Israel thought, room for the hope that Soviet policy was taking a new and better turn. Israel assumed that this new moderate, pacific Soviet policy was not confined to the Indian subcontinent alone but extended to the Middle East and Israel as well. Eshkol's new government, established on January 12, 1966, was certain that it stood on the threshold of a new, happier era of Soviet-Israeli relations, with the Soviet Union adopting a friendlier and more sympathetic attitude toward Israel.

Eshkol and Abba Eban hoped to take advantage of Tashkent Spirit to resolve or, at least, ease the Arab-Israeli conflict. To this end, Abba Eban began to tour the capitals of the West in an attempt to convince the Western powers, and above all Britain and the United States, that the Soviet Union must be allowed to play a part in the effort to resolve the Arab-Israeli conflict. He explained to Britain that "the Soviets did not seem to want to become completely identified with one side or the other in area's quarrels. Their support for the Arabs seemed to end at a point where it was bound to lend to violence."[27] What is more, he was convinced that the Soviets were most probably the only ones capable of persuading the Arab states to adopt a more moderate and realistic attitude with regard to the Arab-Israeli conflict. In this sense, Eban believed the Soviet Union had a crucial role to play in maintaining the region's stability.[28] Soviet intervention in the "Spirit of Tashkent," he concluded, was akin to pouring water and not oil on all the troubled waters, including that of the Middle East.

In February 1966, during a meeting with Harold Wilson, Eban urged the British prime minister to invite the Soviet Union to join the three Western powers—the United States, France and Britain—and hammer out a four-power accord on the Arab-Israeli conflict. The accord would include a joint statement to the effect that all four powers upheld the independence and territorial integrity of all the countries in the Middle East. It would also underline the four's opposition to the use of force as a means of resolving disputes or upsetting the status quo. As for the arms race, Eban acknowledged that, at present, an arms reduction was impossible, but, on the other hand, the four powers could set some sort of ceiling, limiting the sale of arms to the Middle East, which would check the spiraling arms race.[29]

Israel disliked the arms race. It was, however, troubled less by its destabilizing effects and more by the fact that buying weapons was a very expensive business. Israel, with only limited economic resources, was not a rich country. The endless acquisition of more and more modern weapons imposed a massive economic burden, which Israel only bore thanks to outside financial help. Britain's ambassador to Tel Aviv noted:

The Israelis would really much prefer not to have a very heavy defence budget. Unlike the Arabs they see no point in having arms for prestige reasons.... They would therefore prefer to spend their money on developing their country.[30]

Throughout his trip, Eban harped on the expense of purchasing arms. The arms race, he complained, mostly to the United States, placed an enormous burden on Israel, without which it would have long since have achieved its economic independence.[31]

All this begs the question: How did Eban's proposal to limit the arms race accord with Israel's policy of seeking to acquire advanced American weapon systems? Apparently Israel saw no contradiction between the two. It wanted to reduce the huge amounts of weapons pouring into the Middle East, which not only imposed an impossible economic burden on its treasury but also could lead to a general conflagration. On the other hand, it hoped that by harping on about the difficulties and dangers of the arms race, it would finally convince the Americans to change their policy, dating from 1965, which did not allow them to supply Israel with offensive aircraft. In other words, Israel wanted to limit the arms race but not absolutely. Moreover, by pointing out the extent to which the acquisition of arms by the Arab states increased the burden on its defense budget, Israel hoped to procure additional American economic aid.

Eshkol and Eban were confident that the Soviet Union would not reject the proposal of a four-power meeting out of hand. Since the end of 1965, and in marked contrast to its behavior in previous years, the Soviet Union had, of late, shown a marked a degree of moderation toward Israel. It did not attack Israel at every opportunity, not in international forums, not even during meetings with Arab leaders. There had been an improvement in Soviet-Israeli economic relations. The Soviets had also expressed an interest in concluding scientific and cultural agreements with Israel and holding joint sporting events. The impending arrival of both the Russian Philharmonic Orchestra and a delegation of Soviet authors to Israel was symbolic, Israel believed, of these new, warmer Israeli-Soviet relations. But in Israel's eyes the most telling and hopeful sign of the change in Soviet policy was the Soviet Union's willingness to permit some limited Jewish immigration to Israel.[32]

The British Foreign Office, whose members had a very high opinion of Eban's rhetorical skills, did not doubt for a moment his ability to come up with the perfect, seductive turn of phrase to describe the situation as he saw it. But there lay the problem. To Britain's collective thinking, Eban saw it all wrong. Neither he nor Eshkol had any understanding of Soviet foreign policy, whether in general, or in the Middle East. Tashkent was an isolated case. The reasons that had led the Soviet Union to bring the war in the Indian subcontinent to an end did not apply to the Middle East. The Tashkent Summit Conference served Soviet interests in a way that a similar development in the Middle East could not. Consequently, Britain was certain that the Soviet Union had no intention of embarking on an analogous course in the Middle East.

If this was true, why then had the Soviet Union been considerably less active in the Middle East since the end of 1965? The lull in Soviet meddling had certainly contributed to the overall calm that characterized the region at the time. Britain thought the answer was simple: It was merely a temporary lull, partly due to the fact that the Soviet Union was in the process of reviewing and reassessing its foreign policy as a whole, including in the Middle East. Britain based its judgment, among other things, on the fact that not once in any of their recent meetings with the British, including Wilson's visit to Moscow in February 1966, had the Soviets offered a clear-cut position on any of the questions currently on the international agenda.[33] As for the Middle East, it is hard to pinpoint the specific reasons behind this hiatus in Soviet aggressive troublemaking. Perhaps it was the result, as the Americans believed, of the power struggle that had followed Khrushchev's removal from power. One thing, however, is certain: The reevaluation of Soviet policy did not signal a turning point or, indeed, any kind of change in Soviet policy, with regard to the Middle East or anywhere else. Rather, as Britain correctly surmised, the Soviet Union was busy reviewing its standing in the communist world and its conflict with China, as well as various internal developments within the Soviet Union itself. True, these were all factors that would, in the future, affect the Soviet Union's policy in the Middle East, but not, unfortunately, in the direction Israel had hoped.[34]

Actions speak louder than words, and though the Soviet Union had not, of late, offered a definite or explicit opinion on the Arab-Israeli conflict, it continued to cultivate economic, scientific and cultural relations with the "progressive" Arab states, most notably with Egypt. Nor did it cease supplying weapons to the Arab states. The Soviet Union had no intention of forfeiting its hard-won position of influence in the Arab world. It knew that if it publicly supported the status quo, as Israel effectively wanted, it would be throwing away years effort and expense. The Soviet Union's policy in the Middle East remained one of promoting tension, while carefully avoiding anything that might precipitate a major conflict. It was a policy that advanced Soviet interests in the region, while reducing, if not eliminating, Western influence in the Arab world.[35]

Britain concluded that the Soviet Union also, as it had done many times in the past, had no interest whatsoever in curbing the arms race and for much the same reasons. Soviet influence in the region was dependent on the steady supply of Soviet-made weapons to the Arab states, as well as Soviet diplomatic support. Moreover, any arms limitation agreement would expose the Soviet Union to Chinese accusations of collusion with the imperialist powers, something it was very anxious to avoid. Finally,

[the] sort of price which might interest them as a quid pro quo for giving up the advantage of their present position would be the removal of Western bases from the area and the inclusion of Iran and Turkey in any agreement.[36]

And that, the Foreign Office admitted, was "too steep a price" to pay.[37]

Britain's impassive appraisal of Soviet policy was much more realistic than Israel's wishful thinking, as the latter was now to discover. While Israel was busy singing the praises of the Soviet Union, the Soviet Union, in a complete a *volte face*, at least to Israel's mind, began to tighten its relations with the "progressive" Arab states. The Soviet Union sought, as it had always done, to bolster its political influence in the Arab world, which shattered Israel's illusions in the process. This renewed burst of Soviet activity was, in part, a response to local, regional developments. It also helped exacerbate the turbulent, violent relations between Israel and its Arab neighbors, thus pushing the region further along the road to war.[38]

On February 22, 1966, Denis Healy, Britain's minister of defense, announced that in two years' time, Britain would grant the British colony of Aden its independence and evacuate all its military bases from the area. This would be the same year (1968) that Britain's defense agreements with the Southern Arab Federation expired. In a memorandum to the British Cabinet,

Healy explained that from 1968 onward Britain would have no more official commitments either in Aden or in the South Arab Federation.[39] This is not to say that Britain was abandoning the Gulf to its fate. The decision to grant Aden its independence had been made, in part, in order to enable Britain to reduce and redeploy its forces in the region in a more rational manner. It would still maintain bases in the Gulf in places like Bahrain and Sharja, which were considered vital to the stability of the region. The remaining British bases would also reassure Iran, an important regional ally, that Britain would continue to defend its independence and territorial integrity in face of the Soviet threat.[40]

Healy's sensational announcement was preceded by lengthy discussions in the cabinet and between Britain and United States. The problem was that Britain, beset by economic difficulties, simply could not afford to keep all its bases in the Gulf region. The Labour government, as Foreign Minister George Brown, attested, "had inherited a position, which we could not afford to maintain indefinitely. We must therefore complete a gradual and orderly withdrawal from the Middle East."[41] Accordingly, from its first days in office, in October 1964, the Wilson government had discussed the possibility of reducing Britain's presence in the Gulf. It had by no means been an easy decision. Leaving Aden and cutting down the number of British forces in the Gulf was tantamount, as the government knew, to reducing Britain's commitment to defend the Gulf States, not the least from the Soviet threat. In other words, the decision would be both an admission and reflection of Britain's declining strength in this part of the world and of its slowly diminishing responsibility. Britain had, as George Brown, Britain's foreign minister, confessed, no special role to play in the Middle East.

The diminution of Britain's imperial commitments was part of a process that had begun in the immediate aftermath of the Second World War. Indeed, Britain's decision to quit Aden and limit its presence in the Gulf was in many ways similar to its decision, twenty years earlier, to evacuate Britain's forces from Greece.[42] Britain, who had dominated the Middle East for so long, was being slowly replaced by the two superpowers. This process accelerated after the Cairo Summit Conference. The summit conference had escalated the longstanding conflict between Israel and the Arab states, and consequently the two superpowers had become more closely involved in the affairs of the Middle East. They became the chief arms suppliers for the Middle East countries. They provided the economic aid to the rival sides, as well as, on occasion, diplomatic support. After Cairo, the Middle East, like Europe and the Far East before it, became an integral part of superpower and Cold War rivalry. With its power on the wane, Britain was no longer able play a major role in the East-West competition for the Middle East. Unable to maintain its commitments in the region, it was unable to take a fair and equal share in the battle against Soviet incursions. Britain was turning inward. We prefer, at present, Wilson told the American President Lyndon Johnson, when they met in December 1965, to concentrate on revitalizing Britain's economy.[43]

Only one day after Healy had made his dramatic announcement, the Middle East underwent a minor upheaval. In Syria, the left-wing faction of the ruling Ba'ath party seized power in a bloody coup. The coup was the work of a group of young army officers, most of whom were in their thirties and members of the Syrian Alawi minority. They were led by Salah al Jadid, Hafez al Asad and Ahmed Sweidani, better known as the Sphinx. Asad became the new regime's defense minister and head of the Syrian Air Force, and Sweidani became his chief of staff. The new ruling triumvirate decided to install three civilians in the country's three major political posts: Dr. Nur al Din al Atassi became president, Dr. Yusuf Zuyin was appointed prime minister and Ibrahim Makhos became Syria's new foreign minister. Perhaps it is not surprising that the new government soon became known as the Doctors' Government. With its members mostly in their thirties or forties, the new Syrian government, which was controlled by the army and almost exclusively Alawi in composition, enjoyed the narrowest sociopolitical base and most tenuous legitimacy of any government in the history of modern Syria.[44]

The new government's policy toward Israel was even more extreme than that of its predecessor. It cultivated the ideology of a war for the liberation of Palestine, turning it virtually into a religion. At the center of its creed stood the concept of the perpetual armed struggle, which was, the Syrian government believed, the best and shortest way to victory. According to this doctrine, the land stolen from the Arab nation could only be liberated through a constant unceasing struggle. The only way to ensure victory was to relentlessly and brutally confront Israel, day in and day out. In this struggle, the Palestinians would act as the vanguard of the Arab nation, to be joined eventually by the rest of Arab world.

There was very little correlation between this militant, warlike ideology and the new Syrian regime's actual power and capabilities. These were in fact poles asunder. Aware of its weakness, and seeking to extend its domestic power base and garner more support for the regime, the government's leaders were willing to cooperate with the, until now, pariah Syrian Communist Party. As a result, and for the first time in Syria's history, two communist ministers were brought into government. Moreover, in an effort to gain external backing, the new regime abandoned Syria's traditional neutralist policy and openly identified itself with the communist bloc. The Young Officers coup manifestly destabilized the Middle East. Some historians have even gone so far as to call it "a coup for war."[45] Although the epithet coup for war is, perhaps, overly dramatic and slightly exaggerated, there is little doubt that the coup helped pave the way to war.[46]

Israel, not surprisingly, regarded these two events—the British announcement and the Syria coup which occurred literally within days of each other—as the harbingers of evil tidings. It was afraid that Britain's decision to evacuate some of its bases in the Middle East would lead to growing instability in the Gulf area. Surely, Israel thought, it was no coincidence that Britain's announcement was almost immediately followed by Nasser's declaration that Egypt had no intention of implementing the Jedda Agreement. Nasser had announced Egypt would remain in Yemen and would not implement the agreement until the entire Gulf region was free of Britain's presence. Israel also believed that the Syrian coup and the new regime's bellicose declarations presaged the escalation of aggressive Syrian anti-Israeli activity, after a period of relative calm. The Israeli premonitions proved right. The Middle East, having enjoyed a brief interval of tranquillity, now experienced a rapid escalation of the Arab-Israeli conflict. Its focus was the Syrian-Israeli border. This, in turn, would be exploited by the Soviet Union, who suddenly became very attentive of Syria and Syria's needs.

SYRIA ESCALATES THE STRUGGLE

One of the first things the new Syrian regime did, once it settled down, was to promote Palestinian raids against Israeli targets. Nor did it make any effort to hide its activities. On the contrary, Syria's leaders repeatedly declared that the only way to destroy the hated Zionist entity was a popular war of liberation. Hafez al Asad, Syria's minister of defense, announced that Syria was facing an uncompromising and brutal war to liberate Palestine and expel the Zionist invader. His chief of staff, Ahmed Sweidani, condemned the current "Arab strategy, which consisted of increasing their [the Arab states'] military power by purchasing more aeroplanes and tanks ... as distorted and fallacious." The exaggerated purchase of arms, he rebuked, "by placing a heavy burden on their budget does not allow countries to develop internally. Nor will a guerrilla war based on superiority in manpower and arms lead anywhere, as it is utterly ineffective. The Ba'ath party's strategy was the best and only way to victory. We must," the Sphinx concluded, "take inspiration from the examples of Algeria and Vietnam and adopt the strategy of a popular war for liberation."[47]

Under Syrian patronage, Palestinian guerrilla units, from Lebanon and, above all, Jordan with its large concentration of Palestinian refugees, began infiltrating Israel on a daily basis. Nor did Syria limit itself to simply supporting Al Fatah activities; the Syrian Army, too, began to conduct raids into Israeli territory, and Syrian soldiers routinely fired upon Israeli farmers working in the disputed demilitarized zone. According to the British Embassy in Tel Aviv, not since the tension-filled days prior to the outbreak of the Suez War 1956 had the region suffered so dangerous a combination of events as the Al Fatah raids and the renewed round of Israeli-Syrian border incidents.[48]

Syrian provocations and Palestinian guerrilla activities did not go unanswered. Although it knew that Syria alone made no attempt to check Al Fatah and actively supported the Palestinian organizations, Israel held all its neighbors equally responsible for not curbing the Palestinian operations. If they did not comply with the Israeli government's warning, Israel would respond appropriately. And so it did. On the night of April 29–30, Israeli forces attacked two Jordanian villages, north and south of the Jordan River, in retaliation to guerrilla activity perpetrated from Jordanian territory. In the course of the operation, several Jordanian soldiers were killed, and fourteen houses were blown up. The reprisal was intended to signal to King Hussein that if he did not stop the Palestinian infiltrations, he would be subjected to strong Israeli disciplinary action.

The Israeli reprisal frustrated and angered Jordan. Having made a great effort to curb guerrilla activity, it could not understand why Israel saw fit to strike yet another blow at Jordan. Britain and the United States were also annoyed. Britain branded the reprisal a foolhardy action, which played straight into the hands of the Soviet Union and Syria. It allowed the Soviets to increase the tension in the region and the Syrians to persuade Jordan to actively join the Arab-Israeli conflict. In point of fact, it was not so much that Israel took retaliatory action that infuriated Britain, but its choice of target. Without actually saying so, Britain would have preferred Israel to have taken action against Syria and not Jordan. Britain's ambassador, Michael Hadow, murmured in Abba Eban's ear that were Israel to find it necessary to take forceful and aggressive action against the Syrians, Britain, though naturally observing the familiar ritual of condemning the reprisal, would in fact understand and indeed sympathize with Israel's dilemma.[49]

Syria viewed the raid on Jordan as a bad omen. Having pointed an accusing finger at the Syrian regime as the inspiration and driving force behind the terrorist attacks on Israeli territory, Israel had made it abundantly clear that it knew exactly who was responsible for the terrorist activities. Nor had it left any room for doubt that these attacks would not go unavenged or unpunished. "I want to make it absolutely clear to the rulers of Damascus," Eshkol declared from the Knesset podium, "that this situation cannot continue."[50]

Not unreasonably, Syria was quick to assume that Israel was planning another military strike against it. The Syrian leaders had few illusions about Syria's ability to withstand a full-blown Israeli offensive; Syria, they knew, was far too weak to face the full brunt of Israeli military might. Hoping to dissuade Israel from taking military action, the Syrians denied any knowledge of or connection with Al Fatah's military organization. This, as everyone knew, was completely fallacious. The Syrians' denials were even less believable in view of the fact that not only did Al Fatah continue its guerrilla activities, but also the Syrian army joined in the raids on Israeli territory. At the same time, Syria launched a diplomatic campaign to discredit Israel. The regime almost hysterically began to accuse Israel of concentrating forces along its border with Syria, drawing the Security Council's attention to this "fact." It told Britain that Israel, or those who pulled Israel's strings, was planning an attack on Syria.[51]

Britain did not rule out the possibility that Israel was considering taking reprisal action against Syria, but it found no evidence that Israel was concentrating its forces along the border.[52] The Soviet Union, by contrast, fully endorsed the Syrian accusations. This was a new and ominous development. The Soviet press began to publish reports that described in vivid detail how Israel was busy concentrating its forces along the Syrian border in order to overthrow the new Syrian regime. Then, on May 25, the Soviet Union's deputy foreign minister, Vladimir Semyenov, handed Israel's ambassador to Moscow, Katriel Katz, a note, which claimed that the Soviet government had concrete evidence that Israel was concentrating its forces along its northern border. When coupled with Israel's hostile propaganda campaign against Syria, this development, the note accused, assumed an even more dangerous and threatening character. The note concluded with the hope "that the Israeli government would not allow external forces to determine the fate of its people and country" and reassured Israel that "in expressing these thoughts, the Soviet Union is motivated solely by its honest desire to promote peace and tranquillity." The Soviet Union was accusing Israel not only of concentrating its forces but also of deliberately taking provocative action against the Arab states and warning it that the Soviet Union "could not remain indifferent to these attempts to rupture the peace in a region bordering the Soviet Union."[53]

This was a slap in the face for the Israeli government, who still harbored some hope that the Soviet Union had changed its policy toward Israel. The note marked the end of any illusions Israel might have still had in this respect. With the Soviet Union firmly supporting Syria, it was crucial that Israel acquire similar backing from the United States. But first of all the Israeli government set about refuting the accusations listed in the Semyenov Note. It flatly denied that it was concentrating forces along its border. In fact, it claimed, if any one was concentrating their forces along the border it was Syria and not Israel, and it invited the Soviets to help ease the tension along the border. It asserted that Israel was nobody's puppet. It acted solely in its own interests, which were determined only by its desire for peace along "its borders and the preservation of the sovereignty and integrity of all Middle East States."[54]

Denials were all very well, but Michael Hadow thought that Israel should have done more. In his opinion Israel had missed a trick. It had lost a golden opportunity to suggest to the Soviets that if they were genuinely worried about the tension along the Israeli-Syrian border then they should initiate a Tashkent-style summit conference between the Israeli and Syrian foreign ministers in order to discuss ways of reducing the tension between the two countries.[55]

The Soviet Union's overt and unqualified support of the new Syrian regime was closely linked to its decision to step up its involvement in the region. The period from the end of April to the beginning of May 1966 saw a frenzy of Soviet activity. On April 18, 1966, Yusuf Zuyin, the Syrian prime minister, arrived in Moscow on a rather hastily organized visit. In a joint statement issued after the visit, both countries affirmed their continued solidarity with the Palestinian Arabs and hailed fighting Zionism as a legitimate right. Zionism, they declared, was no more than the tool of imperialist forces, which sought to increase the tension in the Middle East. The battle against it was a just one. Two weeks later Syria and the Soviet Union signed an agreement for economic cooperation, which in practice meant the provision of more Soviet military aid for Syria. Indeed, over the next year Soviet military and economic aid to Syria increased tenfold and far exceeded the sum total of aid Syria had received from the Soviet Union over the past ten years. The Soviet Union also sent hundreds of officers and military instructors to Syria. Nor was Egypt neglected. In mid-May, a high-level Soviet mission, led by Prime Minister Aleksei Kosygin, Foreign Minister Andrei Gromyko and Deputy Defense Minister Sergei Gorshkov arrived in Cairo on an official visit. Trefor Evans, Britain's ambassador to Damascus, dubbed this burst of Soviet activity as the Soviet Union's new policy.[56]

All this intense Soviet activity worried the Israeli government. There was a growing sense of alarm and urgency—if not outright panic—that affected the Israeli government and public alike. It was evident that Soviet policy toward Israel had undergone a fundamental change, and precisely in the opposite direction Israel had hoped. Israel assumed that this outburst of Soviet activity had been inspired both by Britain's announcement that it would quit Aden in 1968 and the coup in Syria. It presumed that the Soviet Union saw an opportunity to move southward and fill the vacuum created by Britain's announcement of its impending evacuation of the region, something it had, so far, been prevented from doing thanks to the combined front of Britain, Iran and Turkey.

There were two countries that could help the Soviet Union achieve its age-long ambitions in the Middle East: Iraq and Syria. This was especially true of the latter, which could act as a bridgehead for further Soviet penetration of the region. It was, therefore, not all that surprising that the Soviet Union was devoting so much time and effort, both political and economic, to curry favor with the new Syrian regime and ensure its stability. Its description of an aggressive Israel manipulated by the imperialist powers, like its tales of vast concentrations of Israeli forces along the Syrian borders, were all designed to prove to the Syrian regime that it could totally rely on the Soviet Union's patronage and protection. The fact that the Ba'ath regime had allied itself to the Syrian Communist Party merely added to Syria's attractions, acting as an added incentive.[57]

In an effort to deal with these disturbing new developments, Israel appraised Britain and the United States of its new, revised view of Soviet policy and its deleterious consequences. Israel explained to the two powers that it was Britain's announcement that it was evacuating Aden which had prompted the Soviet Union to resume their political offensive in the Middle East. Unfortunately, it continued, at present, there was no power in the region capable of dealing with this renewed Soviet drive. This was all the more worrying as the Soviet Union, seeking to advance its aims, might provoke a conflagration between Israel and its Arab neighbors. In view of all this, Abba Eban told Walworth Barbour, the American ambassador to Israel, it was essential that the United States "reaffirm her presence in the area and ... reaffirm her guiding principles relating to the area."[58] Playing on U.S. Cold War predilections, Eban, or rather Israel, was hoping to convince the United States to assume an explicit commitment to defend those countries it considered its allies from the perils of Soviet expansion.

The United States agreed with Israel's analysis. It, too, believed that Britain's announcement had had several unfortunate repercussions, which had manifested themselves even before Britain had actually quit Aden. However, it reminded

Israel that Britain was not intending to abandon the Gulf, but merely to redeploy its forces in the region. There was, therefore, no need for anyone to fill the so-called vacuum created by the British evacuation. Certainly, the United States had no intention of doing so. It absolutely refused to accept any new and, to its mind, totally unnecessary, commitments East of Suez. Moreover, it reminded Israel that the war in Vietnam was in full swing and consuming enormous resources, so that both Congress and the American public would firmly oppose the United States from taking on any more military commitments. Dean Rusk, civil, but to the point, remarked that if Israel hoped that the United States would assume additional commitments the answer will be: "No. Thank you very much."[59] The Americans softened the blow by adding that none of this meant that the United States would not help strengthen the armies of local friendly states.

Unlike Israel, Britain was not particularly alarmed by this latest spurt of Soviet activity. It was still convinced that the Soviet Union, firmly wedded to the policy of tension without explosion, a policy that had, so far, served its interests well, had no intention of provoking an armed conflagration along the Israeli-Syrian border or, indeed, anywhere else in the Middle East. Nevertheless, the British government did try and allay some of Israel's fears. Although its decision to quit Aden was irreversible, it assured Israel that it had no intention of abandoning the Gulf to Soviet devices. It would remain in the Gulf and even increase the number of forces stationed in the region. Furthermore, Israel should not give up hope on the United States, as there was always the chance that it would, in time, reconsider the possibility of filling the vacuum created by Britain's evacuation of Aden. The United States, it observed, might very well reverse its decision, once it had reduced its involvement in Vietnam and the "process of educating American official and public opinion was complete, something to which Britain was devoting a great of effort."[60]

Israel was disappointed with what it considered to be the complacent American and British responses. Israel thought that their insouciant reaction opened the way for further hostile Soviet activity in the region. It encouraged the Soviet Union to support Syria's policy of exacerbating the conflict, so that they could exploit the resulting tension and increase Soviet influence in the region. Thus, with no American guarantee in the offing, Israel had no choice but to try and reduce the tension along its border with Syria. Thus, Eban asked Britain and the United States to exercise what influence they had over Syria in order to calm the Syrians down. Eban explained to Hadow that Syrian provocations were bound to produce a military collision between the two countries, and even though Israel had no desire or intention to take action against Syria, if Syria continued to attack Israeli farmers, if "the position would become intolerable . . . Israel might have to take action whatever the consequences."[61] The British and Americans should reassure Syria that it was not the victim of an imperialist plot. They should seek to convince it that Israel had nothing against the present Syrian regime and in fact couldn't care less who ruled in Damascus. Finally, they should note that Israel hoped that Syria would view its failure to respond to the Almagor incident as a sign of its genuine desire to keep the border quiet.[62]

Britain refused Israel's request to intercede with Syria on its behalf. It did so not because it had any sympathy with the new Syrian government; on the contrary, Britain considered it an unruly and unbridled regime, lacking in any self-restraint. It did so because, as Hadow told Israel, "we had ... absolutely no influence in Syria. Our position there was so weak that anything we said would have no effect and would only prejudice the standing of our Ambassador."[63] In fact, none of the Western powers had any influence over Syria. The Soviet Union had some influence, but, unfortunately, was bent on using it to Israel's detriment. The Soviet Union continued to falsely accuse Israel of concentrating forces along its borders. It consistently denounced Israel for pursuing aggressive policies in the service of imperialism. These and other examples of unequivocal Soviet support helped raise Syria's self-confidence. It certainly encouraged Syria to step up the number of border incidents and guerrilla attacks. As events were soon to prove, all this was a recipe for further escalation.

Ever since the Almagor incident, the Israeli-Syrian border had been relatively calm, as Syria had significantly curtailed the number of border incidents. On the other hand, Syria continued to pursue the counterdiversion scheme, albeit in sites located at some distance from the Israeli border. At the end of April, seeking to accelerate the pace of the operations, it brought additional engineering and mechanical equipment to the counterdiversion sites and soon managed to prepare an area 35 km in size.[64] Meanwhile, on the other side of the border, Israel was waiting patiently for an opportunity to punish Syria for the border incidents and guerrilla attacks, as well as, per usual, to destroy the Syrian counterdiversion equipment. It did not have long to wait.

On July 13, an Israeli vehicle drove over a mine near Kibbutz Almagor. As a result two solders and one civilian were killed. Israel was quick to respond, and the very next day the Israeli air force attacked and destroyed the Syrian engineering equipment at a site located 12 km from the Syrian border. The Israeli air strike caught the Syrians by complete surprise. It had never crossed their mind that Israel would attack a target that lay deep in Syrian territory. Believing that it had no choice, Syria sent several fighter jets to challenge the Israeli planes. In the succeeding air-battle, Israel managed to shoot down one Syrian MIG fighter.[65]

The object of the Israeli strike was to demonstrate to Syria, and everyone else, that Israel was as determined as ever to stop the counterdiversion scheme at whatever the risk. Its action was obviously effective as from that time on work in the Syrian counterdiversion sites effectively came to a halt. Israel justified its action by pointing out that the restraint and self-control it had previously shown in the face of repeated Syrian provocations which had, as evidenced by the tragic events of July 13, proved utterly useless. Syria clearly needed to be taught a lesson, and steps had to be taken to make it realize that the Israeli government would not tolerate these recurrent acts of violence on its territory and against its population.[66] Not that Israel was particularly worried that it would be censured as a result of the air strike. It assumed that the West, and especially the United States and Britain, were cognizant of Israel's topographic handicap vis-à-vis Syria, which made an air strike the only effective way of retaliating against Syrian aggression and violence.

Certainly Britain was not surprised by the Israeli air strike and even justified it. According to Willie Morris:

There is nothing surprising about the decision of the Israelis to lay on a retaliatory raid after the last incident near the Syrian border. Since it is common knowledge that the Syrian government has been permitting terrorist action against Israel to be organised from Syria, it is more logical ... that the Israelis should retaliate against Syria rather than against Jordan and Lebanon, whose governments do their best to keep the border quiet. The Israelis have chosen to attack by air ... rather than by land because the terrain gives Syria great tactical advantages against ground forces.[67]

In fact, Britain was quite possibly relieved and even pleased that Israel chose to retaliate against Syria rather than Lebanon or, worse, Jordan.

The Israeli air strike added to the tension in the region and helped further escalate the conflict. Until now, Israel had not used its air force other than in response to Syrian shelling of Israeli settlements, as had been the case in November 1964. Consequently, Syria, knowing that Israel would not think twice before launching an air strike if it shelled Israeli settlements, had been very careful not to bombard civilian Israeli settlements. In this respect, therefore, the July 14 incident marked a new stage in the Arab-Israeli conflict. It was the first time Israel had used its air power not in response to an attack on its settlements, but in order to dictate the rules of play. These were quite simple, as Rabin, Israel's chief of staff, explained: "If there will be no quiet on our side of border, there will be none on the other side." Israel and "Israel alone," he emphasized, "will decide by what means to retaliate."[68] Rabin's declaration was a signal to Syria that Israel would not hesitate to respond Syrian provocations, nor would its response necessarily be a limited one.

The air strike neither weakened Syrian resolve nor persuaded it to modify its policy. The guerrilla attacks continued unabated, while Hafez al Asad, determined to prevent Israel from ruling the skies of the Middle East, decided to initiate a series of Syrian attacks in Israel's own air space. It was an explicit and deliberate Syrian effort to escalate the conflict. Asad's opportunity to implement his decision came on August 15 when an Israeli coast guard ship ran aground in Lake Tiberias. According to Britain's information, the Israeli ship had been sailing along the Lake's Eastern shore, which was controlled by Syria, and had opened fire on a Syrian fishing boat. Having first cleared its action with the local United Nations forces, Israel sent an Israeli rescue ship to salvage the coast guard ship. But the salvage operation failed after four Syrian MIG fighter jets opened fire on the rescue ship, and Syrian forces shot at the grounded ship from the shore. Israeli jets were immediately rushed to the scene and shot down one Syrian MIG. Another MIG was hit by Israel armored cruisers and fell into Lake Tiberias.[69]

The Syrian air offensive was a turning point in Syrian military thinking and marked the birth of a new Syrian strategy. Asad boasted that for the first time since 1948, Syria had moved from a defensive to an offensive strategy. Syria's president, Nur al Din al Atassi, echoed his defense minister, adding that Syria "would not confine itself to defensive action but would attack defined targets and bases of aggression within the occupied area [Israel]."[70] Syria was now waiting for another opportunity to implement its new offensive strategy, that is, to use its air force to prove to the Arab world that Israel's boast that it enjoyed air superiority lacked all foundation. The Syrian leaders emphasized that in the future they would not hesitate to initiate steps to counter Israeli aggression. Although it was not Syria, they were careful to stress, that would be responsible for escalating the situation and endangering world peace.

Israel regarded Syria's attack on its salvage operation as an act of deliberate provocation. Rabin denounced the Syrian offensive as a grave incident, which constituted a clear act of aggression. Eshkol warned Syria that "if Israel were attacked by the Syrian airforce, the latter would not be able to retreat safely behind its border. The border was no defence. Self-defence comes first."[71] As Rabin put it: no border will protect the Syrian aggressors.[72] There was no great distance between these menacing statements and the specter of an air battle in Syrian air space. Yet the Syrian government, undaunted, rather than try to reduce the tension, deliberately escalated the conflict even further. Within days of the Lake Tiberias incident, it announced that it considered sabotage operations and acts of terrorism, including the sowing of mines, legitimate activities and that Syria had no intention of doing anything to stop them. On the contrary, it would encourage and promote all such action. Syria was true to its word. Not a day went by without a road mine blowing up in Israel, water pipes and electrical transformers being sabotaged or bombs being planted in Israeli residential buildings. Not surprisingly, the population in Israel subsequently became agitated, nervous and angry. By now these almost routine attacks had, as the British could see, a profoundly adverse psychological effect on the Israeli population's state of mind.[73]

The Israeli government began to seriously consider the possibility of a wide-scale retaliatory action against Syria. In an interview given on September 12, 1966, to the army journal *Bamahane* (The Camp), Rabin, a known proponent of the strategy of taking sweeping military action against Syria, explained Israel's position in light of the recent Syrian-Palestinian unrelenting campaign of terror and sabotage. He emphasized that Syria was the only Arab state that supported Al Fatah's terrorist activities. He admitted that in the case of Jordan and Lebanon, confining Israel's reprisals to the destruction of property in villages harboring Al Fatah guerrilla units had proved an effective method. But, he pointed out, it would not, however, work in Syria's case, as in Syria the authorities were in league with the terrorists. The Syrian government had, in Rabin's opinion, definitely decided upon war. Consequently, Israel's "response to Syria's activity must be both against those who carry out the terrorist attacks and against the regime which supports them and is still executing the counter-diversion scheme. Israel must induce the Syrian regime to change its policy and remove any possible motivation it might have to implement its schemes."[74]

Rabin was hinting, in fact, demanding, that Israel intervene in Syria's internal affairs. This was, to say the least, an extravagant, excessive and intemperate demand. That he made it at all was a sign of Rabin's self-confidence and commanding position within the Israeli political establishment. This time, however, Eshkol decided to call Rabin to order. He upbraided Rabin for his reckless remarks and, attempting to repair the damage caused by the interview, explained that Rabin had not meant to imply that Israel wanted to depose the Syrian regime or interfere in anyway in Syria's internal affairs. Yet, Eshkol's own angry and threatening statements did not fall far short of those made by his chief of staff. Syria, Eshkol charged, was constantly making bloodthirsty threats against Israel. It had taken the Palestinian organizations under its wing and was training them to carry out their murderous attacks on Israel. Eshkol avowed that Israel took the Syrian threats and activities very seriously and "will hold the Syrian government responsible for any acts sabotage and terror perpetrated from Syrian territory."[75]

These belligerent statements reinforced Britain's suspicions that Israel was definitely contemplating wide-scale action against Syria. Moreover, Israel had pointed out to Britain on more than one occasion that the policy of limited retaliatory raids, with relatively few casualties, would not work with Syria. Britain, not unreasonably, concluded that Israel was contemplating "something more than a localised retaliatory raid or air strike, but ... less than a full a full-scale attack."[76] Britain speculated that Israel was thinking along the lines of a large-scale operation to conquer the area immediately adjacent to the Syrian border, including the high ground dominating the Hula Valley, and, at the same time, to destroy as much Syrian military equipment and get rid of as many Syrian soldiers as possible. The aim of the operation would be to ensure a prolonged period of peace along the Israeli-Syrian border, such as currently existed on Israel's border with Egypt.[77]

Israel's bellicose statements, warnings and threats did not deter the Syrian Ba'ath regime. The sabotage operations continued, while the number of border incidents and Palestinian infiltrations actually increased. One Al Fatah unit managed to infiltrate West Jerusalem and plant a bomb in one of the city's heavily populated residential neighborhoods. The bomb exploded, wounding five Israeli citizens and severely denting the government's prestige. After this incident, the Syrian government gloated that it would continue to train Palestinian units and to wage an uncompromising war against Israel. The Israeli government, for its part, warned the Syrian regime that it was much too early to indulge in self-congratulations. Israel would, at its convenience, decide when and how to respond to the terrorist attacks; Syria would soon realize that respond it would. Eshkol advised Syria that until then "the score-book is open and a record is being kept." This, perhaps Eshkol's most famous warning, has since become a popular, idiomatic Hebrew phrase.[78]

Fearing a large-scale attack, Syria began once again to complain that Israel was concentrating forces along its borders. Its charges were no truer this time than the last. The actual purpose behind these spurious Syrian accusations was to mobilize Arab and especially Egyptian support. Egypt had of late begun to draw closer to Syria. In September, an Egyptian military mission visited Damascus to begin the process of coordinating the two countries' armies. Abdel al Hakim Amer, Egypt's vice president, declared that Egypt would consider an attack on Syria as an attack on Egypt and that the Egyptian army would not hesitate to stand by Syria's side.[79] In truth, however, Nasser had yet to decide whether to offer Syria a definite guarantee against an Israel attack. He was well aware that such a commitment would give Syria the power to force Egypt into a confrontation with Israel before the time was ripe. It was a Syrian trap Nasser had, so far, managed to avoid.

In the end, it was the Soviet Union, rather than any of the Arab states, that came to Syria's aid. On October 3, *Pravda*, the official organ of the Soviet Communist Party, published an article signed by R. Petrov. Its title, "Rabin: The Warmongering General," said it all. According to the article, the Israeli government, not content with provoking incidents along the Israeli-Syrian border, was plotting to overthrow the Syrian regime by means of military intervention.[80] Clearly, Israel's denials had fallen on deaf ears.

The Western powers were convinced that an Israeli strike was in the cards. The United States urged Israel not to use force but to first seek a diplomatic solution. This powerful combination of American pressure and the Soviet Union's unequivocal support of Syria persuaded Israel to defer its plans to take military action against Syria and to put its trust, temporarily at least, in diplomacy. It decided to launch an extensive diplomatic campaign, pleading its case against Syria and Palestinian guerrilla attacks. First, however, it saw fit to inform Britain that should its diplomatic efforts fail to restrain Syria, Israel would not and could not allow the current state of affairs to continue. Otherwise, "we might as well stop being a Government as far as the public is concerned." Moreover, it warned, if Israel were forced to take military action against Syria, it would not limit itself to a small, trifling reprisal but would, regardless of the consequences, strike a blow against Syria which would teach the Syrians a lesson for years to come.[81]

One of the first things Israel did was ask both Britain and the United States to speak with the UN Secretary General, U Thant and persuade him

that the most useful step would be some declaration by him as Secretary General to the effect that Syria should try to stop these border incidents. It would also be useful if the Great Powers themselves could condemn Syrian provocations.[82]

Britain refused. Its policy of keeping a low profile demanded that it intervene as little as possible in the Arab-Israeli conflict. Moreover, Britain suspected that a Western appeal, which led to a one-sided Security Council resolution condemning Syria, would only fuel Soviet and Syrian propaganda to the effect that there was indeed an imperialist conspiracy in the Middle East.[83] Hardly, Britain thought, the desired outcome.

On October 12, 1966, Israel submitted a complaint to the Security Council. Israel still had very little faith in the ability of the United Nations to resolve its problems with Syria or the Arab world. It appealed to the Security Council mainly because it hoped that by doing so it would be able to refute the sham accusation that it was concentrating forces along the border as part of some kind of general plan to launch a wide-scale offensive against Syria. Israel also calculated that even if the Security Council were to prove unable, as seemed likely, to resolve the problem of Syrian-inspired guerrilla attacks or curb these attacks, then, at least, the appeal, by laying the facts of the case before the world, would sway world opinion in Israel's favor and engender support for a limited offensive against Syria. In this context, what Israel wanted, above all, was American approval and support. It knew that American backing in the international arena was vital if Israel was to embark upon any kind of limited military operation. In sum, the Israeli appeal to the Security Council was a tactical move. What Israel really hoped to get was a green light to take direct action.[84]

In the Security Council, Israel highlighted the fact that it had become the victim of a brutal terrorist campaign carried out under the guise of a war of liberation. It proved its case by quoting Syrian Prime Minister Yusuf Zuyin, who had stated that Syria was not the guardian of Israel's security and would do nothing to prevent the Palestinian Liberation Movement from carrying out its activities. Moreover, Zuyin warned, if Israel dared to take any action in response, Syria would turn the region into a battlefield.[85] Eshkol, speaking to the Knesset on October 17, reiterated Israel's views on Syria, underlining that of all the states in the Middle East, Syria, the "Sick man of the Middle East," held the record for internal instability and the pursuit of an intemperate, unrestrained foreign policy. He emphasized that Syria today stood at the heart and center of Al Fatah terrorism. It was, Eshkol exclaimed, the source of the malignant tension that cast its shadow over the Middle East.[86]

As part of its diplomatic campaign, Israel also turned to the Soviet Union, asking it to kindly restrain its Syrian allies. An extremely skeptical Britain doubted whether the Israeli appeal had any chance of success. The Soviet Union sought to squeeze the utmost political benefit from the current tense situation. Curbing Syria was certainly not on its agenda. The problem with the Soviet Union, Britain lectured, was that it was not interested in lowering the temperature in the Middle East. Although it might not be desirous of a full-scale war, it was certainly eager to stir troubled waters and thus increase its influence in the region.[87] The Soviet response to Israel's overtures bore out the British assessment of Soviet policy in full.

The Soviet Union, far from acceding to Israel's request, accused Israel, as was its wont, of being an agent of Western imperialism. Tchouvakhine, the Soviet ambassador to Israel, sent the Israeli Foreign Office a note, later described by Michael Hadow as "a silly message," stating that according to Soviet information Israel was mustering a large army along its border with Syria. Furthermore, Israel was clearly preparing to launch an air strike along its northern border. The air strike was to provide air cover for Israeli ground forces, which were to cross the border and penetrate deep into Syrian territory. "These measures," the note accused, "are indicative of the relentless efforts of radical circles in Israel to take violent action against its Arab neighbours, and especially the Syrian Republic, who simply are intent upon pursuing an independent policy."[88]

Eshkol's response to the note was to suggest to Tchouvakhine that he accompany him to Israel's northern border and see for himself whether there was any truth to the Syrian accusations. The Soviet ambassador, not surprisingly, turned the proposal down. It should be pointed out, however, that even though Israel was not concentrating forces along it northern border, it could, given its small geographic size, mobilize and deploy its forces along the Syrian border in a relatively short time. Thus, it could launch, at extremely short notice, an eighty to one hundred aircraft-strong air strike, which is precisely what it did only a few months later.

With the Soviet Union pointing an accusing finger at Israel, and a Soviet veto in the Security Council in the air, it was obvious that no relief would come from the United Nations. The Security Council was clearly not the body to compel Syria to modify its aggressive policy. Nonetheless, and though still skeptical of the Soviet Union's willingness to cooperate and reduce the tension in the Middle East, Britain thought it worth trying to harness it to joint five-power resolution. The United States joined the British initiative. Having pressured Israel into taking diplomatic action, it saw itself as obligated to work toward a Security Council resolution that would effectively restrain the Syrians. The two countries formulated a resolution calling upon Syria to fulfill its obligations under the cease-fire accords and to take all the measures necessary to prevent its territory from being used as a base for activities that would violate the cease-fire agreements. As Britain suspected, the Soviet Union refused to cooperate. It had no intention of paring down its support of Syria's intransigent policy. The only resolution the Soviet Union would support was one that would satisfy the Arabs. All others would be subject to a Soviet veto.[89]

On the assumption that the guerrilla attacks would continue and more Israeli lives would be lost, Britain believed a Soviet veto meant an inevitable Israeli military strike. Both Israel and Syria remained firmly entrenched in their respective positions. Eshkol warned, time and again, that there was a limit to Israel's patience and that his government would do everything necessary to check Syrian-inspired terrorist activity. It was, he declared, what the Israeli public demanded and expected, as it had every right to. The Israeli government, Eshkol stated, would not hesitate to use its air force against Syria or trespass into Syrian airspace. Syria, on its part, continued to make aggressive and provocative statements to the effect that terror was a legitimate weapon of war and that Syria would take action against all bases of aggression—in other words, Israel.

It would have hardly been surprising if Britain had been worried that an escalation, which might drag the entire region into war, was in the cards. But, in actual fact, it wasn't. Although assuming that Israel would probably launch a massive air strike against Syria, it did not think this would have disastrous military consequences. None of the Arab states, certainly not Lebanon or Jordan, wanted to be involved in a conflict between Israel and Syria. Nasser, preoccupied with Egypt's economic problems and the civil war in Yemen, had other, more immediate things on his mind. A conflict with Israel was certainly not a pressing priority, and Nasser adhered to his strategy of not becoming involved in an untimely confrontation with Israel.[90] In these circumstances, Britain thought that an Israeli air strike might actually be a good thing. It might serve to restrain the problematic and unstable Ba'ath regime. "Nothing," the British Foreign Office noted, "could be worse than the present [Syrian] regime."[91] Other than waiting for Syria to change its regime of its own volition, an unlikely event, an air strike was perhaps the only way to restrain the unruly Syrians.

The United States disagreed with Britain's assessment on all counts. It was even doubtful whether a change of regime would produce a more moderate Syrian policy. Accordingly, the United States felt obliged to warn Israel against resorting to force whatever the outcome of the Security Council's discussions. It emphasized that in the currently confused state inside Syria no one could foresee the consequences of an Israeli raid and that the United States would not support a retaliatory attack on Syria.[92] Israel did not ignore U.S. warnings, but they were not in themselves enough to prevent the launching of an attack against Syria if it was thought to be necessary. Its decision of whether to retaliate against Syria had to take into account not only U.S. policy, but also the Soviet Union's support of Syria and, above all, Egypt's changed relationship with Syria.

On November 4, 1966, after four days of high-level discussions, Egypt and Syria signed a Defense Agreement. The agreement posited that an armed attack against one of the two signatories would be considered an attack against both. In the case of a war erupting, the Syrian and Egyptian armies would operate jointly under the command of the Egyptian chief of staff. There was to be a joint Defense Committee, composed of Egypt and Syria's defense and foreign ministers, which would meet two times a year. There was also to be a Military Command Headquarters, which would meet once every three months. Egypt, it seemed, had finally assumed an obligation to automatically come to Syria's aid. However, there was one loophole in the agreement, which could help it to evade its commitment. According to the agreement, Syria and Egypt's security policies must be the product of joint consultations. This meant that unless Egypt first agreed to all Syria's initiatives and actions, especially those that might lead to a conflagration, the agreement was null and void. In short, the Egyptian commitment would take effect only after joint policy consultations.[93]

This loophole apart, the Defense Agreement was plain evidence that Syria had finally managed to force Egypt to assume a more active role in the Arab-Israeli conflict. But, had it also, at long last, contrived to drive Egypt into the trap of an untimely war, a trap the latter had until now managed to successfully evade? The Egyptian answer was a resounding no. One of the reasons Nasser had agreed to sign the agreement was precisely to prevent Syria, and its policy of supporting terrorism, from dragging Egypt into an ill-judged, ill-timed war against Israel—hence the loophole, which Nasser hoped to use to control Syrian policy and tie Syria's hands.

In Nasser's view, like that of the Soviet Union, the Defense Agreement marked the union of the region's two "progressive" forces. Its aim was to help the region's radical regimes coordinate their efforts and resolve the Palestinian problem by revolutionary means. In this sense, the Defense Agreement was a substitute and a slap in the face to the United Arab Command. The agreement also reflected Egypt and Nasser's preeminent, commanding position within the Arab world. It made it clear that Nasser, and no one but Nasser, determined the rules of the game in the Arab world as, for example, did the cancellation of the fourth Arab Summit Conference, due to convene at the end of August, merely because Egypt would not be participating.[94]

Regardless of Nasser's own reasons for signing the Defense Agreement, there is little doubt that his decision to conclude the agreement was partly a result of Soviet pressure. According to one source, the Soviet Union had promised to meet all Egypt's arms requirements forthwith if Nasser agreed to sign the agreement.[95] It was a timely offer, and Nasser was more than happy to receive additional Soviet aid, particularly as relations between Egypt and the United States had reached a new, all-time low. The United States had recently announced that it had decided to stop all economic aid to Egypt, while Nasser, probably in order to save face, declared that he had no need and no desire for American aid. None of this, the Americans thought, augured well for the future. By the end of 1966, the U.S. embassy in Cairo was reporting that a conflict in the Middle East was not far off. Nasser's determination to preserve his leadership of the Arab world, his economic difficulties and his deteriorating relationship with the United States might all encourage him to instigate a war with Israel.

Israel was more optimistic. It hoped that the Egyptian-Syrian Defense Agreement would curb the Syrian aggression. It did not think that Egypt would allow itself to be dragged behind the chariot wheels of the unstable, unruly Syrian regime. Unfortunately, it soon became clear that whatever Israel, or even Egypt, believed the aim of the agreement was, Syria took the opposite view. In its opinion the Defense Agreement allowed it to escalate its provocative, warlike activities, and so the guerrilla raids continued unabated. As a result, the Israeli government decided, on November 9, 1966, to extend the compulsory military service period from twenty-four to thirty months. The extra six months, Eshkol explained, were intended to improve the army's military preparedness and allow it to carry out its basic duties more efficiently.

Two days after the conclusion of Egyptian-Syrian Defense Agreement, the Soviet Union, as expected, vetoed the joint British and American proposal calling upon Syria to take firm action to prevent incidents that violated the cease-fire agreement. Abba Eban took some comfort from the fact that, despite the Soviet veto, it was manifest that the other members of the Security Council all held the Syrians responsible for the disturbances along the Israeli-Syrian border. The ball, Eban declared, was now in Syria's hands, and Israel would, in the future, assess Syria's actions in the light of the Security Council's discussions.[96]

The Soviet Union was quick to react. On November 9, Katriel Katz, the Israeli ambassador to Moscow, was handed another Soviet note. This one stated that the Soviet government had registered Eshkol's declaration that the Israeli government desires peace. Regrettably, however, it was forced to conclude that, in practice, Israeli policy stood in complete contradiction to these pacific statements. The Soviet Union believed that Eshkol's statements were a ruse designed to confound the world before Israel launched a military attack against Syria. Finally, the note trotted out the by now routine accusation that Israel was being exploited by imperialist forces intent on waging war against the Arab states.[97] It is difficult to estimate whether and to what extent Israel was alarmed by the Egyptian-Syrian Defense Agreement or the Soviet note. Britain thought that neither had much effect on Israel's policy. It was plain that an offensive was inevitable and that Israel had decided to strike a blow against Syria whatever the consequences. Britain was almost, but not quite right. Israel did attack, but its chosen target was Jordan, not Syria.

THE SAMUA RAID: ISRAEL CHOOSES THE WRONG TARGET

> I said it was madness to strike at Jordan, but the scale of the operation shows
> that the scale of the madness was far greater than we thought.
>   Willie Morris, Head of the Middle East Desk
>   in the British Foreign Office.[98]

On the night of November 11–12, an Israeli army vehicle carrying nine soldiers drove over a mine, just south of the town of Hebron. Three soldiers were killed and six wounded. A serious incident in itself, it was also one of a series of mounting guerrilla attacks that had taken place between the end of October and beginning of November, all perpetrated from Jordanian territory. An explosive device planted on the rail tracks on the route between Tel Aviv to Jerusalem had exploded, blowing up several carriages of a transport train; a water pipe next to Ein Gedi had been wrecked; there had been an attempt to sabotage a building in Jerusalem; and an Israel army patrol had been shot at.[99]

Israel had had enough. On November 13, Israeli armed forces raided the village of Samua, located 16 km south of Hebron, in Jordan itself. The Israeli force, which was about the size of brigade, attacked in broad daylight. It was accompanied by tanks and artillery units and enjoyed the benefit of air cover. It was the biggest Israeli reprisal action since the 1956 Sinai campaign. The raid had a dual objective: to punish the villagers, whom, the Israeli government believed, were harboring and abetting the Palestinian units, by blowing up their homes, and to deter others from doing the same. Unfortunately, the raid did not quite go according to plan. Jordan immediately sent reinforcements to the area, and instead of a simple retaliation operation, Israel now had a full-fledged battle on its hands. During the fighting, twenty-eight Jordanian soldiers were killed, and fifty-four were wounded. In addition, an Israel jet downed a Jordanian Hunter airplane. Nor was the raid's original purpose forgotten—the Israelis demolished 120 of the village's houses.[100]

Both the fact and scale of the Israeli raid stunned the Western world and, above all, Britain and the United States. The Americans thought that physical damage apart, the raid had dealt King Hussein and the Jordanian army a devastating and humiliating psychological blow.[101] Britain, which had never doubted that Israel would launch a retaliatory raid against Syria once the Security Council discussions ended in a Soviet veto, had never dreamed that when it came, the blow would be directed against Jordan. And why should it have? The Israeli government had stated time and again that it held the Syrian government responsible for terrorist attacks perpetrated from Jordanian and Lebanese territory. It had, accordingly, focused its attention and activities on the Syrian border. All of which begs the question, Why did Israel ultimately decide to launch a massive retaliatory strike against Jordan?

The Israeli raid is even more puzzling in light of its relationship with Jordan, which was one of tacit coexistence. It is doubly mystifying considering that both the United States and Britain held King Hussein and his policies, as Israel well knew, in high regard. Britain, like the United States, had repeatedly told Israel that King Hussein and his government were doing all they could to apprehend the terrorists and prevent the guerrilla raids. Moreover, the Jordanians had done so with some measure of success, a success that was all the more impressive in light of the local population's orientation and sympathies and the length of the Israeli-Jordanian border.[102] Michael Hadow made sure that Israel fully appreciated Britain's position with regard to Jordan and its efforts to curb Palestinian terrorism. Shortly before the Samua raid, the ambassador told Eshkol:

We ourselves, and the Americans, were fully satisfied that the Jordanian government was very bravely doing all it could to prevent the terrorists from operating from their territory. It was just as difficult for the Jordanians to stop the infiltrators from Syria entering Jordan as it was for the Israelis to prevent the infiltrators entering Israel.[103]

Furthermore, Britain argued, it was against Israel's own interests to attack Jordan. To do so would be to play straight into the hands of Syria and the Soviet Union. King Hussein, too, asked Israel to act with restraint and limit its retaliatory responses. He did so both directly in the course of clandestine meetings with Israeli representatives and indirectly through the United States. If Israel did not, he explained, shock waves would spread throughout the kingdom, weakening Jordan and creating the most appalling problems for him and his regime.[104]

Israel, in fact, had never ruled out the possibility of a retaliatory raid against Jordan. Only days before the Samua raid, the Israeli consul in London had told the Foreign Office that were the terrorist raids from Jordan to continue, he was very much afraid that the Israeli government would have no choice but to mount a retaliatory raid against Jordan, and it would do so even though it was well aware that this was precisely what the Palestinian units wanted.[105] Back in Israel, the Israeli population was going through an extraordinarily stressful and traumatic period. The public was nervous and bewildered. The attack on the night of November 11–12 was the most serious guerrilla attack to date: Three soldiers had been killed, and the army now demanded action. The Israeli government was not prepared to resign itself to this utterly intolerable situation and for some time had plans ready to mount an attack against Syria. Eshkol was too weak or insecure to oppose the army's demand for action. Least of all was he able to stand up to his chief of staff, Rabin, who by now totally dominated Israel's security and defense policies.[106]

The Israeli government had three options. First, it could make an another appeal to the Security Council. This option, however, was quickly ruled out in light of past experience. None of the previous appeals to the Security Council had produced anything but lengthy, nerve-racking discussions, which had ended with the Soviet Union vetoing even the more moderate American-British resolutions. Moreover, Israel believed that the Arab states would interpret another appeal to the Security Council as a sign of Israeli weakness and that the Palestinian units might, as a result, actually step up their attacks.

Israel's second option was to launch an attack against Syria. This was what the Israeli public preferred. It also accorded with the Israeli government's accusations that it was Syria that inspired, directed and equipped the Palestinian terrorist organizations. Two things, however, weighed against this option. The first was practical. The local terrain was such that the Israeli ground forces would find it extremely difficult to move through the area freely and quickly. The string of heavily fortified Syrian posts along the Israel-Syria border would also hamper the smooth execution of the operation. Consequently, an attack on Syria would result in a great many Israeli casualties. Second, there was no way to predict the wider consequences an assault on Syria might have, particularly as Syria not only enjoyed unqualified Soviet support, but also had just concluded a Defense Agreement with Egypt.

This left the third option: retaliatory action against Jordan. As a straightforward "cause-and-effect" solution, it was no doubt the most attractive of the three options. Furthermore, as Jordan would probably not react to the Israeli action, it held few military risks. Nor would there be, or so Israel assumed, many, if indeed any, political, diplomatic repercussions. In view of the above, Eshkol, ignoring the British and American appeals, as well as those of King Hussein, elected to go with the "Jordanian Option." Action against Jordan, he felt, would satisfy the army, while proving to the Arab world that Israel would not sit quietly and submit to Arab terrorism. And it would do all this at very little risk.

As subsequent events were to prove, Eshkol had seriously miscalculated. It seems that neither he nor his government had given sufficient thought to the raid's consequences.[107] After the raid and in an attempt to mollify Britain and preempt any forthcoming British criticisms, Israel emphasized that following the failure of its appeal to the Security Council, the government simply could not have carried on unless it had taken action. Moreover, the combatants who planted the mine that had blown up the army vehicle were members of a terrorist organization that was independent of Al Fatah and based in Jordan. The local population and the local Jordanian forces were aware of and supported this organization's terrorist activities, and both had to be taught a lesson. Finally, Israel suggested, the reprisal actually served Jordan's interests as well as its own, as Jordan had clearly lost control over the Hebron region.

The Israeli government concluded by expressing its regrets that the operation had escalated beyond its original parameters. Its object had been simply to punish the villagers in the region of Hebron for aiding and abetting terrorists. But Israel, unfortunately, had failed to foresee the way things would develop.[108] Indeed, perhaps it hadn't. What is certain is that its belief that it had to retaliate against the guerrilla raids was carved in stone. Yet the decision to mount a large-scale raid against Jordan, which combined ground forces, tanks, artillery units operating under air cover, was a mistake and had been from the start. Jordan, in a sense, was no less a victim of the Palestinian units than Israel.

The raid, as Hussein had predicted, shook Jordan to the core. Riots spread throughout the kingdom, and were particularly violent in the West Bank cities of Hebron, Jenin, Ramallah and East Jerusalem. The PLO, calling for a revolt against the king, demanded the establishment of an independent Palestinian state in the West Bank. Syria and Egypt helped poured oil over the troubled waters. Their propaganda machines went into action, depicting Hussein as an agent of Western imperialist forces and styling the Israeli raid as an Imperialist-Hashemite-Zionist plot. Hussein was accused of betraying the Palestinian cause, just as his grandfather, Abdullah, had done before him. His regime in danger, the king was forced to call out the army in order to quell the disturbances and return order to the Kingdom.[109] But the army posed no less a threat to Hussein than the Palestinian riots in the cities. Humiliated by its inability to frustrate the Israeli attack and strike back, the army was in ferment. According to British intelligence sources, Hussein was "facing one of the most serious crises in his career. Within the army, members of the officer corps are displaying open disaffection towards the King and Royal family."[110] Truly, the head of Jordanian intelligence was not exaggerating when he claimed that a military conspiracy against the king had been born on the morn of the Samua raid.

Britain and the United States came quickly to their Jordanian ally's aid, hoping to contain and limit the damage wrought by the Israeli raid. President Johnson declared that the United States was committed to Jordan's safety and security. Amer Khammesh, Jordan's chief of staff, was invited to Washington to discuss Jordan's security needs, especially its arms requirements. The United States, aware that the raid had dealt a severe blow to the Jordanian's army morale, thought that furnishing it with arms was one way to help it recover. The United States asked Britain to help it equip the Jordanian army. Britain, however, refused on the grounds that its difficult economic situation meant that it could not help Jordan more than it was already doing. Instead, Britain sought other ways to soften and minimize the adverse effects of the Israeli raid. Phillip Adams, the British ambassador to Jordan, assured the king that the Israeli government fully understood that the Samua raid had been a mistake. It realized that the raid had undermined its own interests of keeping the peace in Jordan and preserving the regime's stability.[111]

The king was not convinced. Israel's ex post facto justifications and explanations sounded hollow to his ears. As far as Hussein could see, his country had become little more than the Israeli army's punching bag. Despite all his efforts to stop the Palestinian infiltrations and despite his attempts to maintain a positive relationship with it, Hussein felt that Israel evidently made no distinction between Jordan and the other Arab states. As far as Israel was concerned, they were all tarred with the same brush. He was, Hussein told Adams, utterly disillusioned. His efforts to "live with Israel" had come to naught.[112] Hussein suspected that the real aim of the Israeli raid was to bring Jordan to its knees and spark a serious crisis, which would allow Israel to seize the West Bank. In a meeting with Amman's diplomatic corps, Hussein, while reviling Zionist aggression, stated with some conviction that

[it] was now clear that the Israelis thought the time was ripe to expand their territory to include the whole West Bank of the [sic] Jordan. Sunday's incident should be seen as the first battle in a campaign with that objective.[113]

In view of these facts, Hussein concluded that he had no choice but to seek the protection of the Arab world. There was no great distance between this conclusion and Hussein's subsequent decision to join the Egyptian-Syrian Defense Agreement. Thanks to the Samua raid, Jordan had now discarded its goal of living in peaceful coexistence with Israel and adopted a tough, inflexible and antagonistic stance toward its Israeli neighbor instead.[114]

Despite its attempt to mollify Hussein, Britain, too, was shocked and outraged by the Samua raid. It pilloried the Israeli action, branding it a wildly reckless act, lacking in all intelligence. To Britain's mind it was a regrettable, foolhardy action and a serious error of judgement that was based on sheer folly.[115] Britain simply could not understand how Israel could have been stupid enough to sanction such a harebrained military operation. American intelligence sources were equally baffled, and wondered whether there were not perhaps other, hidden, motives behind the raid.[116]

Perhaps one of the things that upset Britain most was that only a few days before the raid it had, for once, deviated from its policy of keeping a low profile and had personally intervened in the Arab-Israeli conflict, all, it now seemed, to little effect. It had asked the Jordanians to take strong action against the terrorist groups. It had constantly impressed upon Israel Hussein's unflagging efforts to prevent terrorists from crossing the border into Israel, which meant that any Israeli retaliation against Jordan would be totally indefensible. More than that, Britain contended, it would be sheer madness to retaliate against Jordan. Then came the Samua raid, a reprisal on an unprecedented scale, which proved just how mad it was.[117] Britain was angry with the Israeli government for ignoring both its and U.S. appeals not to take action against Jordan. Not that the Israeli government had appeared to have taken any more notice of its own public, which had wanted Israel to retaliate against and punish Syria, not Jordan, for the guerrilla raids.

As far as Britain was concerned, Israel's attempts to justify the raid and explain away its clash with the Jordanian army were the last straw. It found the Israeli claim that the raid ultimately served Jordan's own interests particularly infuriating. No less galling were Abba Eban's efforts to throw the blame for the whole fiasco on the army, which, he claimed, had departed from its assigned task of punishing the villagers.[118] Britain thought all this was so much humbug and double-talk. In its opinion, Israel had simply chosen the soft opinion of attacking Jordan, rather than risk a military confrontation with Syria. Nor was it far wrong. As noted, Israel was well aware that, unlike Jordan, Syria possessed a topographic advantage over Israel, that is, a string of fortified posts along the border, a defense agreement with Egypt and Soviet support, all of which made the idea of attacking it an extremely unattractive proposition.

In sum, Britain thought the Samua raid a gross example of political and military recklessness and irresponsibility. Israel had chosen the wrong the time, the wrong place and the wrong target. Yet, despite its withering criticism, and angry as it might be, Britain sought to minimize the damage wrought by the Israeli raid, not only to Jordan but also to Israel as well. It had no doubt that the raid had seriously undermined Israel's standing in the international community. Having emerged from the last Security Council session in a very strong moral position vis-à-vis Syria and the guerrilla attacks, it had now, thanks to its foolhardy action, thrown it all away, losing all the sympathy and support it had previously gained. The raid had also limited the British government's ability to support Israel in the international arena.[119] Britain couldn't have put it better then Dean Rusk who, in the course of upbraiding the Israeli ambassador, remarked, "What you have done in the name of your security seems in fact to have undermined your security."[120]

What worried Britain above all was the raid's destructive effect on King Hussein's regime. The raid had undermined and destabilized the Jordanian Kingdom. Accordingly, in addition to offering the king verbal and moral support, Britain thought it necessary to help him stabilize his country in some more practical, concrete way. The question was how? The United States, for example, had considered the possibility of placing an embargo on the sale of arms to Israel. It had, however, quickly discarded the idea and was content, instead, to warn Israel that a similar action in the future might lead to a reassessment of the American arms policy.[121] The United States did suggest to Britain that it might place an arms embargo on Israel, but Britain refused even to consider the idea. Willie Morris explained why:

We believe a balance of defensive capacity is necessary in the Middle East if stability is to be maintained. We believe that there is particular danger that if Israel feels that she is

being abandoned by the West, she will either embark on some desperate military enterprise to destroy Arab [*sic*] armies before she is overwhelmed, or go nuclear.... A British
embargo by itself would harm Anglo-Israel relations and do us commercial harm while
accomplishing nothing.[122]

If the situation in Jordan got worse, Britain might consider the possibility of
an arms embargo but only as a last resort.

Having dismissed both the idea of an arms embargo and the possibility of increasing British military aid to Jordan, the only practical measure left open to
Britain was to support a Security Council resolution condemning Israel for the
Samua raid. Jordan had already lodged a complaint in the Security Council, so
that a debate in the Security Council was, in any case, inevitable. Britain believed
that it had little choice but to support the Jordan complaint. If it did not, the Arab
states would accuse it of observing a double standard—one for the Jews and one
for the Arabs—and of being willing to support a decision condemning Syria for
minor attacks yet refusing to condemn Israel for launching a large-scale raid
against Jordan.[123] That this was the best Britain could do reveals just how limited was its influence in the region. Indeed, other than to support a resolution
condemning Israel, Britain was left with little to do but watch helplessly and
with growing concern as the relations between Israel and its Arab neighbors
went from bad to worse.

Israel was well aware of Britain's irate state of mind. Michael Hadow, Britain's
ambassador, did not mince his words when he reproved Israel for its madcap and
foolhardy actions. After one particularly difficult conversation with Abba Eban,
he reported to the Foreign Office, with some satisfaction, that "I am quite confident that Eban was in a mood to tell his colleagues quite how foolish they had
been."[124] Israel, of course, was not happy with the British response. It particularly disliked Britain's willingness to support the Jordanian complaint and the
Security Council resolution roundly condemning Israel, particularly as the Soviet Union had only recently vetoed a moderate and balanced resolution against
Syrian aggression. Ironically, instead of the Arab states, it was Israel who now
accused Britain of adopting a double standard.

In a personal note to Harold Wilson, Eshkol confessed his alarm at the prospects
of Security Council resolution. While completely ignoring the need to stop guerrilla attacks against Israel perpetrated from neighboring Arab countries, the resolution condemned Israel, warning that similar action in the future would result
in appropriate steps being taken against it. Eshkol maintained that a lopsided resolution, which condemned Israel and no more, was particularly dangerous because

[on] the Arab side extremism would be encouraged and the guerrilla raids renewed and
in Israel a mood of frustration and disillusionment with international justice would
create a climate in which it would be difficult for steadfast, prudent councils to prevail.[125]

Wilson did not bother to reply to the Israeli prime minister's appeal directly.
This was a symbolic gesture, intended to impress upon Israel the extent of

Britain's displeasure and disapproval. Britain did not, however, totally ignore Eshkol's note. The Foreign Office mentioned to Israel's representatives, in a rather general and noncommittal way, that it had told Britain's ambassador to the United Nations to take into consideration the points raised in the Israeli prime minister's note. The ambassador, the Foreign Office assured, would continue to support the effort to reach an efficacious decision, which would discourage both sides from carrying out these grievous attacks. Yet, back in Israel, Hadow was constantly reminding Eban that British policy in the United Nations was ultimately determined by the need to stabilize Jordan, which was, he pointed out, in turmoil owing to the Israeli raid. This, of course, somewhat offset the effect of Foreign Office's lukewarm assurances.

So perhaps it did not come as a great surprise to Israel when the Security Council unanimously condemned it for the Samua raid. Censuring Israel for launching a large-scale military action against Jordan, the resolution emphasized that "it was impossible to condone retaliatory action of any kind and should it prove necessary the Security Council will examine what effective measures, consistent with the United Nations Charter, it should take to prevent the recurrence of such action."[126] All three Western powers—the United States, France and Britain—endorsed the resolution.

Israel may not have been surprised by the Security Council's decision, but it was, nevertheless, bitterly disappointed at the way its three Western allies had voted and believed that the resolution reflected a double standard on the part of the Security Council. Yet, fair or not, the resolution did persuade Israel to show more self-restraint in response to the guerrilla attacks. The angry reactions of Britain and the United States to the Samua raid were probably equally if not more responsible for Israel's newfound restraint although the fact that the number of guerrilla attacks had recently diminished might also have had something to do with Israel's self-restraint. Whether it was fear of an Israeli reprisal or the desire to wring every bit of advantage it could from Israel's international censure that encouraged Syria to temporarily stop aiding and abetting guerrilla attacks is a moot point. Israel, certainly, was not fooled, not even for a minute and knew that Syria would soon recommence the guerrilla attacks. Accordingly, Rabin continued to denounce Syria as the spiritual and practical patron of Arab terrorism. Rejecting the UN condemnation and refusing to tolerate Syria's policy of promoting guerrilla attacks, Israel was merely waiting for an opportunity to strike a military blow against Syria if and when the guerrilla attacks resumed.[127]

Britain was right in thinking that the Samua raid had radically and irrevocably altered the situation in the Middle East. The stability it had labored to achieve was floundering. As Britain predicted, the raid had played directly into the hands of those elements that wished to overthrow Hussein's regime. It also benefited those, like the Soviet Union, who sought to exploit the situation to increase the tension in the region. Moreover, there was little doubt that thanks to the raid, the Soviet Union had increased its influence and improved its position in the

Arab world. Thanks to the raid, the Arab states now appreciated the advantages of having the Soviet Union as a patron. Unlike Syria, who enjoyed Soviet protection, Jordan was allied to the West, and when it fell victim to an Israeli attack, its Western friends were powerless to help it. The conclusion was obvious: the only way the Arab states would be safe from Israeli attacks and acquire the power to confront Israel was to ally themselves with the Soviet Union. This unfortunate conclusion on the part of the Arab states was reinforced once it became known that only days before the Samua raid the Soviet Union had sent Israel a note warning it not to take action against Syria.[128]

Meanwhile, in Jordan the internal situation remained extremely ugly, and Hussein's regime was still under threat. Syria and the PLO fanned the flames of discontent, hoping to bring about the king's overthrow. Egypt, too, did its bit, and tried to exploit the volatile situation in Jordan in order to get rid of yet another reactionary regime. Jordan, in turn, attacked Egypt for evading its responsibilities and not coming to its aid. Egypt, Hussein charged, had once again abandoned an Arab state to the mercy of Israel's military power. Why, he asked accusingly, had Nasser not sent the Egyptian air force to help Jordan during its battle with Israel?

Nasser could not remain silent in face of these serious accusations. He justified Egypt's nonintervention by arguing that had the Israeli action constituted a wide-scale military operation, Egyptian military assistance would have been immediately forthcoming. He explained Egypt would provide the Arab states with air cover only in the case of a full-scale war. Isolated incidents such as the Samua raid did not warrant Egyptian air cover.[129] Hussein's accusations had, nevertheless, hit Nasser hard, putting his leadership of the Arab world to the test. This was, Nasser knew, the last time he could refuse to act in face of Israeli military action unless he wanted to undermine Egypt's standing in the Arab world and jeopardize his own leadership, which he most assuredly did not. Thus, the Samua raid, like the Egyptian-Syrian Defense Agreement, marked another step toward Egypt's greater and more personal involvement in the Arab-Israeli Conflict.

There is some, albeit unconfirmed, evidence to suggest that sometime in December 1966, hoping to defuse and deflect Arab criticism of Egypt's inaction, Egypt's vice president, Marshall Abdel al Hakim Amer, proposed that Egypt demand the evacuation of UN forces from Sinai and introduce Egyptian forces in their stead. He further suggested stationing an Egyptian force in Sharem el Sheikh, which overlooks and controls the sea route to Israel. He even went so far as to advise that Egypt declare the Straits closed to Israeli shipping. Nasser rejected his deputy's proposals. To his mind it was far too early to take such provocative action. The conditions, he pointed out, were not yet ripe.[130] But apparently they would ripen in only a few months, when Egypt would implement Hakim's proposals in full.

Britain viewed the rapidly deteriorating situation in the Middle East with growing concern. Looking back on the events of the past month, it could only conclude that the Israeli decision to raid Samua had severely and irretrievably

damaged Arab-Israeli relations. Jordan had been driven to adopt an openly antagonistic policy toward Israel. Syria, encouraged by the raid's international
repercussions, showed no sign that it intended to moderate its policy. On the
contrary, Syrian-inspired activities against Israel continued unabated.[131] The
Middle East was a time bomb waiting to explode. The only possible way to reduce the tension, Britain thought, was to enlist the help of the Soviet Union.
The fact that Britain was considering afresh the idea of Soviet cooperation, after
having previously rejected it as, to say the least, implausible, was a measure of
its helplessness and desperation. In truth, on the question of Soviet cooperation,
British policy was somewhat reminiscent of a pendulum, as time after time it
explored the possibility of cooperating with the Soviet Union, only to reject it.
Perhaps Britain preferred the frustration of being unable to obtain Soviet cooperation than to have to suffer the humiliation of having to admit that it was utterly impotent and unable to do anything to stop the escalation of the Arab-
Israeli conflict.

The possibility of appealing to the Soviet Union was first raised in connection with George Brown's prospective visit to Moscow. The United States
thought it a good idea, while Israel had, in fact, specifically asked Britain to appeal to the Soviets to help defuse the tension. Underlying the idea of approaching the Soviet Union was the assumption, spelt out by Trefor Evans, Britain's
ambassador to Damascus, that

the time when the West alone without the USSR could pursue its policies in the Middle
East is obviously past. Russian influence here [Damascus] and in Egypt is such that the
West can no longer act effectively even if tripartite co-operation is re-established.[132]

Having raised the idea of asking for Soviet cooperation, the Foreign Office almost immediately rejected it. There was absolutely no point, it explained, in
turning to the Soviet Union for help. It would be a completely useless and futile effort. Soviet and British interests in the Middle East were diametrically opposed. At present, the East-West competition was more bitter in the Middle East
than almost anywhere else in the world. The Soviet Union sought, and was still
seeking, to replace the West as the leading power in the Middle East and, to this
end, was busy gnawing away at the West's position in an attempt to undermine
its influence in the region. The Foreign Office admitted that the Soviet Union,
though intent upon exploiting the tension in the Middle East to advance its interests, did not want this tension to lead to a full-scale explosion. Yet it did not
think that this one interest the Soviet Union shared with the West offered a basis
for fruitful discussions, not to say a joint effort to solve the major problems of
the Middle East region. Any appeal to the Soviet Union, the Foreign Office concluded, would be made in vain.[133]

Unable or unwilling to cooperate with each other, the powers allowed events
in the Middle East to spiral out of control. Seeking to increase its influence in
the region, the Soviet Union backed the Arab states to the hilt. The West, hoping to preserve a measure of stability in the region and prevent an armed conflict from erupting, supported Israel. The result was that by the end of 1966, war

was closer than ever. Perhaps it was the awareness and fear, on the part of the sides to the conflict, that the Middle East was on the verge of a general conflagration that now led to a temporary calm. Short-lived and largely fortuitous, it soon ended leaving the region to continue its march along the road to war.

NOTES

1. ISA, Hez/16/3975, Gazit to Herman, January 16, 1966; FO 371/186830, FO to Tel Aviv, March 8, 1966.

2. ISA, Hez/9/3976, Washington to Jerusalem, February 8, 1966.

3. Sela, *Decline of Arab-Israeli Conflict*, p. 86.

4. FO 371/186422, Brief by FO, February 1966; Burns, *Economic Aid*, pp. 165–166.

5. FO 371/186429, NATO Middle East Experts Meeting, April 13–16, 1966.

6. Shemesh, "Arab Struggle over Water," pp. 161–162; Golan, "Conflict over the Jordan," p. 858.

7. FO 371/186439, Washington to FO, February 16, 1966.

8. FO 371/186439, Minute by Morris, January 25, 1966 and Washington to FO, February 26, 1966.

9. *Ha'aretz*, March 21, 1966; *Al Ahram*, March 20, 1966.

10. FO 371/186430, Minute by Morris, March 29, 1966.

11. FO 371/186422, Brief by FO, February 1966; FO 371/186429, NATO Middle East Experts, April 13–16, 1966.

12. ISA, Hez/9/3976, Gazit to Herman, January 16, 1966; FO 371/186422, Record of Meeting, February 3, 1966. See also NA, RG/59/2356, Hare to Secretary, December 28, 1965 and Memorandum of Conversation, February 9, 1966.

13. FO 371/186436, Minute by Morris, January 17, 1966.

14. Cohen, "Cairo, Dimona," pp. 196–197; Cohen, *Israel and the Bomb*, pp. 246–251. See, for example, *Ha'aretz*, February 21, March 30 and April 18, 1966.

15. FO 371/186430, Cairo to FO and Minute by Mclean, March 7, 1966.

16. FO 371/186864, Minute by FO, March 24, 1966.

17. FO 371/180646, Anglo-American Talk on the Middle East, November 20, 1966.

18. FO 371/186660, Minute by Morris, October 21, 1966; FO 371/186804, Tel Aviv to FO, April 21, 1966.

19. FO 371/180660, Minute by Morris, October 21, 1966; FO 371/186436, Fenn to Ministry of Defense, January 17, 1966.

20. FO 371/186420, FO to Hadow, January 5, 1966.

21. FO 371/186183, Washington to FO, February 1, 1965; NA, RG59/2356, Memorandum of Conversation, February 9, 1966; Cohen, *Israel and the Bomb*, pp. 185–221.

22. FO 371/186864, Minute by Morris, April 5, 1966; Little, "Choosing Sides," p. 168; Spiegel, *Arab-Israeli Conflict*, p. 135.

23. Little, "Choosing Sides," pp. 167–168; Hersh, *Samson Option*, p. 105; Yaniv, *Politics and Strategy*, pp. 172, 199; Cohen, *Israel and the Bomb*, pp. 210–213; NA RG59/2356, Memorandum for Rostow, April 30, 1966.

24. FO 371/186422, Record of Meeting, February 3, 1966; FO 371/186422, FO to Washington, April 27 and Washington to FO, May 20, 1966; NA, RG59/2351, Brewer to Davis, April 20, 1966.

25. Cohen, "Cairo, Dimona," p. 198; Aronson, *Nuclear Weapons*, pp. 36–37; FO 371/186864, FO to Washington, April 17 and Minute by McLean, July 11, 1966.

26. Wolpert, *History of India*, pp. 374–376.

27. FO 371/186813, Tel Aviv to FO, April 28, 1966.

28. FO 371/186429, Paris to London, March 23, 1966; ISA, Hez/18/7229, Eshkol to Wilson, January 20, 1966; NA, RG59/2359, Memorandum of Conversation, February 9, 1966.

29. FO 371/186422, Anglo-American Talks, February 1966; FO 371/186425, Tel Aviv to FO, January 19, 1966; ISA, Hez/9/3976, Washington to FO, February 8, 1966, No. 70; *Knesset Debates*, 45, March 23, 1966.

30. FO 371/186436, Tel Aviv to FO, December 28, 1965; ISA, Hez/9/3976, Washington to FO, February 8, 1966, No. 70.

31. ISA, Hez/9/3976; NA, RG/59/2356, Memorandum of Conversation, February 9, 1966; ISA, Hez/9/3876, Washington to FO, February 8, 1966.

32. FO 371/186813, Washington to FO, February 11, 1966, Tel Aviv to FO, April 28, 1966 and FO 371/186812, Hadow to Stewart, May 18, 1966; NA, RG59/2358, Memorandum of Conversation, April 24, 1966; Zak, *Israel and the Soviet Union*, p. 310.

33. ISA, Hez/18/7229, Eben to Eshkol, March 15, 1966; ISA, Hez/12/4005, London to FO, February 15, 1966.

34. ISA, Hez/12/4005; ISA, Hez/24/4048, Washington to FO, June 18, 1966.

35. FO 371/186429, NATO Middle East Experts Meeting, April 13–16, 1966.

36. Ibid.; FO 371/186436, Talking Points, January 17, 1966 and FO to Washington, March 29, 1966; FO 371/186422, Record of Conversation, February 4, 1966.

37. FO 371/186433, Middle East Heads of Missions Conference, May 16–20, 1966.

38. Wehling, "Dilemma of a Superpower," pp. 175–177; Kaufman, *Arab Middle East*, p. 50.

39. Kelly, *Arabia*, p. 25; CAB 129/24, Memorandum by Secretary of Defense, February 11, 1966; Balfour, *End of Empire*, pp. 84–85.

40. Ibid.; FO 371/186433, Middle East Heads of Missions Conference, May 16–20, 1966; ISA, Hez/12/4005, London to Jerusalem, January 14, 1966.

41. CAB 128/39/3, 49th Conclusion, September 23, 1966.

42. Kuniholm, *Cold War*, pp. 404–405.

43. FO 371/186426, Draft Talking Brief, December 17, 1965 and FO to Hadow, January 5, 1966.

44. FO 371/186904, Evans to Stewart, August 1, 1966; Ma'oz, *Syria and Israel*, p. 88; Seale, *Assad*, p. 144.

45. El Hussini, *Soviet-Egyptian Relations*, p. 163; Ramat, *Soviet-Syrian Relationship*, p. 38; Mo'az, *Syria and Israel*, p. 88.

46. Zisser, "Between Syria and Israel," p. 212.

47. Shemesh, *Palestine Entity*, p. 86; Heikal, *Sphinx*, pp. 162–163; *Ha'aretz*, March 9 and May 24, 1966; Seguev, *Israel*, pp. 52–53.

48. FO 371/186434, Minute by Morris, May 2, 1966; FO 371/186652, Tel Aviv to FO, June 14, 1966.

49. FO 371/186834, Tel Aviv to FO, May 11, 1966 and Amman to FO, May 3, 1966; ISA, Hez/2/4005, Jerusalem to London, May 27, 1966.

50. *Knesset Debates*, 45, May 18, 1966.

51. FO 371/186834, FO to Damascus, May 5, 1966; FO 371/186435, Damascus to FO, May 5 and 11, 1966.

52. FO 371/186435.

53. ISA, Hez/24/4048, Jerusalem to Moscow, May 12, 1966 and Moscow to Jerusalem, May 26, 1966; *Ha'aretz*, May 29, 1966; Katz, *Budapest*, p. 137; Rafael, *Destination Peace*, p. 114.

54. ISA, Hez/24/4048, Moscow to Jerusalem, May 29, 1966 and Draft Note to the Soviet Union, no date; Gurvin, *Israel Soviet Relations*, pp. 244–245.

55. FO 371/186435, Tel Aviv to FO, June 8, 1966.

56. FO 317/186904, Evans to Stewart, August 1, 1966; Cohen, "Balancing American Interests," p. 297; *Le Monde*, April 20, 1966.

57. ISA, Hez/24/4048, New York to Jerusalem, June 1, 1966; Rafael, *Destination Peace*, pp. 121–122.

58. ISA, Hez/12/3975, Jerusalem to London, June 19, 1966.

59. ISA, Hez/16/3977, Washington to Jerusalem, and Rafael to Eban, August 1, 1966.

60. FO 371/186435, Minute by McLean, June 8, 1966; ISA, Hez/16/3977, London to Jerusalem, no date.

61. FO 371/186435, Tel Aviv to FO, May 27, 1966.

62. The Almagor incident took place on May 16, 1966. Two Israelis were killed when their vehicle drove over a mine. It appears that the publication of the Skyhawk plane deal between Israel and the United States that was made public on May 20 and the planned visit of Eshkol in Africa was the reason why Israel did not react. Ibid.; NA, RG59/2353, Tel Aviv to SD, June 1, 1966; ISA, Hez/12/4005, Jerusalem to London, May 27, 1966.

63. FO 371/186435, Tel Aviv to FO, May 27, 1966.

64. ISA, Hez/13/3975, Jerusalem to Washington, June 24, 1966; Shemesh, "Arab Struggle over Water," p. 162.

65. FO 371/186435, Minute by Morris, July 24, 1966; NA, RG59/2359, Tel Aviv to SD, July 14, 1966; Seguev, *Israel*, p. 53; Gilbo'a, *Six Years*, p. 58.

66. FO 371/186435, Tel Aviv to FO, July 15 and 21, 1966.

67. FO 371/186435, Minute by Morris, July 15, 1966.

68. *Ha'aretz*, July 15, 1966.

69. FO 371/186436, Minute by Middle Eastern Department, August 18, 1966; Ma'oz, *Syria and Israel*, pp. 90–91.

70. Yaniv, "Brutal Dialogue," p. 376; Ma'oz, *Syria and Israel*, p. 91. See also NA, RG59/2354, Memorandum of Conversation, August 18, 1966.

71. *Ha'aretz*, August 16, 1966.

72. Ibid.

73. FO 371/186437, Tel Aviv to FO, October 12, 1966.

74. *Bamahane*, September 12, 1966; Gilbo'a, *Six Years*, p. 60.

75. *Ha'aretz*, September 19, 1966.

76. PREM 13/1617, Tel Aviv, October 18, 1966; FO 371/186429, NATO Expert Working Group on the Middle East, October 18, 1966.

77. NA RG59/2353, Memorandum of Conversation, November 2, 1966.

78. *Ha'aretz*, October 9, 1966.

79. *Ha'aretz*, September 8 and 19, 1966.

80. Gurvin, *Israel-Soviet Relations*, pp. 246–247; Zak, *Israel and the Soviet Union*, pp. 312–322.

81. FO 371/186437, Tel Aviv to FO, September 12, 1966, No. 417.

82. FO 371/186437, Tel Aviv to FO, October 12, 1966, No. 416.

83. FO 371/186437, FO to New York, October 13, 1966 and Tel Aviv to FO, October 12, 1966, No. 417.

84. ISA, Hez/12/4005, New York to Jerusalem, October 15, 1966.

85. FOR 371/186437, Tel Aviv to FO, October 12, 1966, No. 419.

86. *Knesset Debates,* 47, October 17, 1966.

87. FO 371/186426, Record of Conversation, October 13, 1966 and Minute by Allen, October 26, 1966.

88. Dagan, *Moscow and Jerusalem,* p. 187; FO 371/186426, Tel Aviv to FO, October 12, 1966, No. 419; Seguev, *Israel,* pp. 58–59.

89. FO 371/186438, FO to New York, October 26 and New York to FO, October 27 and FO to Moscow, November 1, 1966.

90. FO 371/186429, NATO Expert Working Group on the Middle East, October 18, 1966 and FO 371/186438, Washington to FO, October 26, 1966; ISA, Hez/12/4005, New York to Jerusalem, October 15, 1966.

91. FO 371/186425, Record of Conversation, November 2, 1966.

92. FO 371/186438, Tel Aviv to FO, October 25, 1966 and FO to Tel Aviv, October 26, 1966 and Washington to FO, October 26, 1966; NA, RG59/2354, SD to Damascus, September 16, 1966.

93. Gilbo'a, *Six Years,* p. 72; Yitzhaki, *Arab Eyes,* pp. 76–78.

94. Sela, *Unity within Conflict,* p. 65; Bhutani, *Israel-Soviet Cold War,* p. 105; Evron, *Middle East,* p. 72.

95. Ben-Tzur, *Soviet Factors,* p. 125; El Hussini, *Soviet-Egyptian Relations,* pp. 173–174.

96. FO 371/186438, Tel Aviv to FO, November 7, 1966.

97. Bhutani, *Israel-Soviet Cold War,* pp. 104–105; Guvrin, *Israel-Soviet Relations,* pp. 248–249.

98. ISA, Hez/11/1390, Anug to Jerusalem, November 13, 1966.

99. FO 371/186840, Tel Aviv to FO, December 21, 1966.

100. Seguev, *Israel,* p. 59.

101. NA, RG59/1888, Hare to the Secretary, November 16, 1966. See also NA, RG50/2352, Memorandum of Conversation, November 29, 1966.

102. NA, RG59/2350, Hare to Davis, August 6, 1966; NA, RG59/2351, Amman to SD, October 31, 1966.

103. NA, RG59/2351; FO 371/186438, FOR to Tel Aviv, November 13, 1966.

104. Garfinkle, *Israel and Jordan,* p. 43.

105. FO 371/186438, FO to Damascus, October 29, 1966; FO 371/186437, Tel Aviv to FO, October 12, 1966.

106. Yaniv, "Brutal Dialogue," p. 375.

107. FO 371/186840, Tel Aviv to FO, November 30 and December 21, 1966; Hammel, *Six Days in June,* p. 21; Yost, "How It Began," p. 307.

108. FO 371/186438, Tel Aviv to FO, November 14 and Washington to FO, November 16, 1966; NA, RG59/2356, Memorandum of Conversation, November 21, 1966.

109. FO 371/186839, Amman to FO, November 16; Mutawi, *Jordan in the 1967 War,* p. 80; Susser, "Jordan and the Six Day War," p. 106.

110. FO 371/186439, Current Intelligence Bulletin, December 15, 1966 and Amman to FO, December 16, 1966; NA, RG59/1888, Hare to Secretary, November 16, 1966.

111. FO 371/186439, FO to Amman, November 18, 1966; FO 371/186840, Washington to FO, December 1, 1966; *FRUS, 1964–1968,* pp. 683–685, 718–720; Little, *Choosing Sides,* p. 172.

112. FO 371/186439, Current Intelligence Bulletin, December 15, 1966; Mutawi, *Jordan in the 1967 War,* p. 77.

113. FO 371/186439, Amman to FO, November 17, 1966.

114. Evron, *Middle East*, pp. 73–74; Ma'oz, *Syria and Israel*, p. 91; Dayan, *Story of My Life*, p. 391.

115. FO 371/186423, Anglo-French Talks on the Middle East, November 15–16, 1966; FO 371/186439, FO to Amman, November 18, 1966; FO 371/186850, Minute by Morris, November 23, 1966.

116. FO 371/186830, Washington to FO, December 1, 1966.

117. FO 371/186436, FO to Damascus, October 24, 1966 and Draft Letter by the FO, November 1, 1966.

118. FO 371/186840, Tel Aviv, November 17, 1966.

119. FO 371/186438, Draft Telegram and Tel Aviv to FO, November 14, 1966; ISA, Hez/17/4005, London to Jerusalem, November 13, 1966.

120. NA, RG59/2356, Memorandum of Conversation, November 21, 1966.

121. Ibid.

122. FO 317/186850, Minute by Morris, November 23, 1966.

123. FO 371/186439, Damascus to FO, November 16, 1966.

124. FO 371/186840, Tel Aviv to FO, November 17, 1966.

125. FO 371/186840, Eshkol to Wilson, November 20, 1966.

126. Gilbo'a, *Six Years*, p. 75; *Ha'aretz*, November 27, 1966; FO 371/186840, Morphet to Palliser, November 22, 1966.

127. *Yediot Aharonot*, December 30, 1966; Gilbo'a, *Six Years*, p. 75; FO 371/186840, Tel Aviv to FO, November 30, 1966.

128. ISA, Hez/17/4005, London to Jerusalem, November 18, 1966; FO 371/186840, FO to Certain Missions, December 10, 1966.

129. Seguev, *Israel*, p. 60; *Ha'aretz*, November 25, 1966.

130. Ayalon, "Road to the Six Day War," p. 5; Hammel, *Six Days in June*, p. 23.

131. FO 371/186830, Washington to FO, December 1, 1966.

132. FO 371/186424, Minute by Roger Allen, December 15, 1966.

133. Ibid.; FO 371/186426, Minute by Morris, December 16, 1966; ISA, Hez/17/4005, London to Jerusalem, November 18, 1966.

5

Britain and the Road to War

THE CURTAIN RISES

After the Samua raid and the Security Council's subsequent condemnation of Israel, there was a marked rise in the number of Syrian-initiated border incidents. Syria's self-confidence had increased, and it was evident that it felt that it had a free hand to pursue its offensive strategy to the full. Syria also believed that thanks to events of the past month the Israeli government's hands were tied and assumed that after the Samua affair Israel would not dare launch a large-scale reprisal against it. The border incidents were also a way of giving lie to the erroneous belief, which had taken hold, in Israel above all, that the Egyptian-Syrian Defense Agreement of November 1966 was designed to curb aggressive Syrian activity on Israel's northern border.[1]

Syria did all it could to set the Israeli-Syrian border ablaze. It no longer confined its aggression to a single area along the border, but provoked incidents throughout the length of the border, so that now areas that had previously been more or less trouble free also came under Syrian attack. It bombarded numerous targets in Israel, using a variety of weapons including tanks and artillery. It planted mines in Israel and carried out sabotage operations. It fired upon farmers and tractors working in fields, as well as upon civilian cars, boats sailing in Lake Tiberias and, of course, military patrols and army posts. As a result, within the space of a mere couple of months, Israel logged no less than 800 border incidents.[2]

Most of the incidents occurred within the boundaries of the disputed demilitarized zone. Israel and Syria had since 1949 been at loggerheads over the question of who had the right to farm the zone. Now, almost twenty years later, there was still no sign that either side was willing to make any kind of concession over this extremely contentious issue. True, in 1965 things had calmed down a bit after Syria had reached an understanding with the chief of the United Nations Truce Supervision Organization, the Norwegian General Odd Bull, not to farm certain areas in the disputed zone. In 1967, however, General Sweidani, the Sphinx, informed the Israeli-Syrian Mixed Armistice Committee (ISMAC) that he had issued orders to start farming the Arab land within the demilitarized zone immediately, and regardless of Syria's unwritten agreement with General Bull. If, Sweidani warned, Israel dared fire upon the Syrian farmers working the fields, Syria would not hesitate to respond in kind.[3]

Syria was right about one thing: After the uproar created by the Samua affair, all the Israeli government wanted, at this point, was a little peace and quiet. It certainly was not interested in escalating the situation along its northern borders. But this did not mean that Israel had any intention of giving the Syrians a free hand to do as it wished with impunity. It was here that Syria erred; Israel would respond, and respond quickly and forcefully, to any and all cases of aggression along its borders, as well as to Syria's efforts to resume farming the disputed zone. Indeed, owing to rapid increase in the number of Syrian-inspired border incidents, Israel was soon convinced that the only way to deal with Syria was to strike and strike hard.

This time, however, Israel decided to prepare world public opinion for what increasingly appeared to be the inevitable strike against Syria. To this end, it initiated a diplomatic campaign to prove, especially to the United States and Britain, that self-restraint in the face of repeated Syria aggression was no longer a viable option. It sought to impress upon the two powers that no self-respecting country could tolerate Syria's belligerent provocations and to make it clear that Israel's sole alternative was to take military action, in the hope of bringing this intolerable situation to an end. In London, Israel's ambassador, Aharon Remez, having first expressed his grave concern at the recent bloody developments along the Israeli-Syrian border, stressed that Israel

expects friendly countries ... to understand that should Syria continue to disregard the highly explosive situation into which she manoeuvres herself, a situation could arise where the benefits of self-restraint will have to be weighed against Israel's international rights and national obligations of self-defence.[4]

In short, were Syria to continue to provoke incidents along the border, the Israeli government would be forced to take vigorous action against Syria. It was simply a matter of self-defense. Effi Evron, the Israeli consul in Washington, told the Americans much the same thing. Israel could not, he emphasized, afford to let the current situation along the Israeli-Syrian border continue unchecked.

Both Britain and the United States sympathized with Israel's plight, but neither approved of its solution to the problem. The Americans underlined that any retaliatory action by Israel would be a cause for deep concern.[5] The British insisted that after Samua, the use of force carried with it the risk of dangerously escalating the situation in the region and possibly even of engendering a war between Israel and the Arab states.[6] Perhaps. But the Israeli government was nevertheless determined to deal Syria a blow similar to the one it had delivered Jordan in Samua. It must be said that the Israeli government's resolve stemmed, in part, from the understandable, if not very worthy, desire to restore Israeli pride, which had been badly bruised by the overwhelming evidence that the Samua raid had been a horrible mistake. Whatever Israel's underlying motives, the upshot was that Israel, which had so far shown remarkable self-restraint in the face of Syria's aggression, would take action if peace were not restored to its northern border. Israeli restraint was not entirely a matter of goodwill. Its object was to let the Syrian-provoked incidents reach such proportions so as to justify Israel overriding the restraints placed on it following the Samua raid by both the Security Council's censure and American and British pressure.[7]

Anxious as ever to avoid a Middle East conflagration, Britain tried to defuse the tension. Aware that it had absolutely no influence over Syria, it fell back on its only viable alternative, which was to persuade Israel not to launch a wide-scale military assault against Syria. Britain impressed upon Israel the extremely dangerous consequences such action might have. Moreover, Michael Hadow warned Abba Eban that the Israeli government would be making a very grave mistake indeed if it assumed that either Britain or the United States would condone any sort of direct military action against Syria, simply because both, admittedly, found Syria an infernal nuisance. Hadow added, on a somewhat threatening note, that

As a result of the Samua raid there was now a Security Council resolution which, to my mind, pretty clearly indicated that the next time Israel took the law into its own hands there would be a case for sanctions against Israel. I hope he [Eban] would think about this very carefully.[8]

Britain suggested that the best policy Israel could adopt, in light of the border incidents, was one of self-restraint. A military response would play directly into the hands of those elements in the Arab world, like the Syrian government and the Palestine Liberation Organization, who preach violence against Israel, as well as the more moderate Arab states, whose continued existence was in Israel's own interest. The solution to Israel's problems lay in the United Nations, not the battlefield, and Britain urged Israel to make every effort to support the UN's efforts to keep the peace in the Middle East. After all, it pointed out, the United Nations was charged with keeping the peace, and was, in fact, the only forum capable of keeping the peace in the region.[9]

Britain also advised Israel to ask the Soviet Union to use its influence with Syria and help put an end to the border incidents. The Israeli government had, in fact, already approached the Soviet ambassador in Israel to this end, but to little avail. According to Abba Eban, in response to the Israeli request, Tchouvakhine had "merely trotted out the usual drivel."[10] By now the border incidents had become so serious, frequent and numerous that the British and American warnings made absolutely no impact on Israel. The only advice the Israeli government was willing to listen to was how to muzzle the Syrian guns once and for all.

The UN secretary general also intervened, hoping to check the rapidly deteriorating situation along the Israeli-Syrian border. U Thant could hardly have continued to ignore the numerous complaints submitted by Syria and Israel against one another; Israel alone had, within a couple of months, submitted 120 complaints to the Security Council. But there is no doubt that his intervention was also, in part, the result of continual and determined American and British prodding. Thant informed the Security Council that the large army concentrations along the Israeli-Syrian border, which included heavy weapons and armored vehicles, could produce a large-scale conflagration at any moment. He appealed to both countries to exercise maximum self-restraint. He also asked them to accept General Odd Bull's proposal to convene a special meeting of the Israeli-Syrian Mixed Armistice Commission in order to settle, once and for all, the dispute over the right to farm the land in the demilitarized zone.[11]

The Israeli government acceded to the secretary general's request. Eshkol explained that in view of the dangerous situation on the border, this was the UN's last chance to prevent a general conflagration. The Israeli government also hoped that ISMAC would be able to come up with a formula that, by settling the dispute over the demilitarized zones, would reduce the number of border incidents. Syria also said yes. Quite why was beyond, at least Israel's understanding, because it showed no sign of curbing, let alone suspending, its violent assaults on Israel.[12]

The Israeli-Syrian Mixed Armistice Commission met on January 25, 1967. It was the commission's first meeting after a long five-year interval. At the start of the meeting, it was agreed that during this and all subsequent ISMAC meetings the only issues discussed would be those directly connected to the problem of farming the land in the demilitarized zone. In addition, both sides pledged not to carry out acts of violence and aggression.[13] It all seemed very promising. But, at the second ISMAC meeting, which took place only a few days later, the Syrian delegation, probably owing to pressure by the radical faction of the Ba'ath Party, withdrew its promise to refrain from hostile action against Israel.[14] Liberating Palestine was the Syrian regime's chief priority, and Syria, the delegation declared, could not and would not guarantee Israel's security, particularly not against the Palestinian guerrillas. As a result, throughout the months of February and March, the Syrian government only moderated but did not stop its aggression against Israel. At the same meeting, Syria also went back on its agreement to limit the discussions to the question of farming alone. It now insisted that the whole issue of the demilitarized zone be discussed and on its terms. It demanded that the Israeli forces evacuate the area so that it would be under Syrian control and that its former Arab inhabitants return to their homes.

At the same time, Syria resumed its aggressive rhetoric, calling for an Algerian style war of liberation. Hafez al Asad threatened to escalate the border clashes with Israel. Syria, he thundered, "was not afraid of Eshkol and Rabin's threats. Extensive operations along the border will be the first stage of the liberation of Palestine." The Syrian government implored its fellow Arab states to embark immediately upon the campaign to liberate the Arab lands, which Israel had seized by force.[15] Not surprisingly, all this belligerent talk of war brought the ISMAC discussions to a halt. Nor were the talks subsequently renewed. It also, as Syria had hoped, escalated the conflict.

In mid-February, during a visit to London, Abba Eban told the British that "[t]he situation in the Middle East was relatively quiet at present ... looking back over the past two years things have gone reasonably well."[16]

But, he emphasized that although this assessment was true in respect to Egypt, and even Lebanon and Jordan, it certainly did not describe current Israeli-Syrian relations. Eban stressed that given Israel's tiny geographic size, no Israeli government could submit to an ongoing guerrilla war. Every attack inevitably threatened something—be it life or property. Abba Eban did not think it necessary to precisely spell out to Britain what Israel would do if the terrorist attacks, sabotage operations and border incidents continued. Instead, he was content to note that Israel would take appropriate action to protect its citizens and settlements.[17] Eban did, however, ask Wilson to appeal to the Soviet Union to restrain its Syrian clients, as one could not ignore the fact that the Soviet Union, thanks to its influence over Syria, was a key player in the Middle East.[18]

Britain, as noted, had already concluded that any approach to the Soviet Union would be a complete waste of time. Nor had it changed its mind. It was as certain as it ever had been that the Soviet government welcomed Israeli-Syrian tension and hoped that the border incidents would pay it handsome dividends in the future. This did not mean, however, that Britain now approved of the idea of an Israeli military strike. George Brown, Britain's foreign minister, cautioned Eban that with all Britain's sympathy for the intolerable situation Israel had found itself in, it did not think that a military strike, which "would have very grave consequences for us all," was a good idea.[19] Israel took a different view. With ISMAC discussions having failed and Soviet intervention ruled out, it concluded that it had no other choice but to strike a military blow against Syria. Perhaps it had also lost patience and was no longer interested in exploring other ways of restraining Syria. In any event, IDF officers informed Michael Hadow that a military strike against Syria was now simply a matter of time.[20]

Following the break in ISMAC's discussions and Syria's refusal to renew the talks over the question of farming the land in the disputed zones, the Israeli government decided that if Syria kept up its policy of encouraging guerrilla raids and attacks against Israeli targets, as it had done prior to the ISMAC meetings, Israel would launch a military operation against it. And, sure enough, Syria continued to encourage Palestinian guerrilla attacks, and Israel, as of old, sought to provoke Syria into opening fire on Israeli targets, thus giving it the opportunity to launch its planned military assault. Rabin assumed that farming the disputed demilitarized zones would, as it had before, do the trick.[21]

Until now, Israel, which did not wish to further exacerbate its relations with Syria and had hoped to create a positive climate around the ISMAC negotiating table, had not farmed the land in the disputed zone.[22] But the minute General Bull announced that Syria was officially withdrawing from the discussions, Israel resumed work in the disputed fields. Syria did not let Israel down and played its allotted part in the Israeli script to perfection. On April 3, 1967, Syria, using both cannon and submachine guns, opened fire on Israeli tractors plowing the fields in the disputed zones.

On April 7, four days after this shooting incident, the Israeli air force attacked Syrian artillery batteries. This led to a dramatic air battle, the first large-scale air fight between the two states, in the course of which Israel shot down six Syrian MIGs. The scale of the Israeli response was without precedence. The air strike was carried out in broad daylight. Generating earsplitting supersonic booms, 130 Israeli planes flew over Damascus; the air battle itself reached the outskirts of Damascus, so that other than being deafened by the Israeli planes, the Syrian capital's citizens also witnessed the downing of two Syrian fighter jets.[23]

Plainly, the Israeli air strike was, as it was meant to be, a terrible humiliation for the Syrian Ba'ath regime. It demonstrated just how vulnerable Syria was to Israeli military power. It also revealed the extent of Syria's isolation, as none of the Arab states had come rushing to its aid. Finally, it confirmed the hollowness of the Syrian regime's repeated calls for a war of liberation modeled after the Algerian war. Not that any of this prevented Syria's minister of propaganda, Mouhamed al Zuebi, from defiantly declaring that "we believe that yesterday's battle was neither the first nor the last. There will be more battles, more difficult and more brutal ... our goal is known: to liberate Palestine and destroy the Zionist entity.... There will be no peace in the area as long as this country of bandits and outlaws still exists."[24]

The unprecedented Israeli response raised the Arab-Israeli conflict to new heights and signaled the possibility of further escalation in the future.[25] Ever since November 13, 1964, when Israel had first used its air force against Syria, it had consistently expanded the use it made of its air force in its retaliation operations, thus contributing to the ever-escalating Arab-Israeli conflict. Nevertheless, there was a marked difference between the April 7 incident and previous operations involving the Israeli air force. Until April 7, Israel had limited its air attacks to Syrian targets, which lay relatively close to the border, be they counterdiversion installations, military posts or artillery batteries. Moreover, as a rule, the air force was employed only when Syria bombarded Israeli settlements or diversion equipment or had used its own air force, as had happened during the Lake Tiberias incident the previous August. Now, for the first time, Israeli planes had penetrated 70 km deep into Syrian territory, reaching the outskirts of Damascus. Nor did the air force confine itself to shooting down Syrian planes, but attacked numerous other targets on the ground. The air strike had manifestly added a new dimension to the conflict. Certainly Israel's already tense relations with Syria became much worse. The April 7 air strike, without doubt, heralded the coming war.[26]

Not every one in Israel was happy with this new turn of events. Moshe Dayan, the former Israeli chief of staff, was shocked at the scale of the air operation strike. He protested that there had been no need to use so many planes and then boast about it, declaring that it had been done deliberately. "Have you gone mad?" he asked Ezer Weizman, the head of Military Operations. Don't you realize that "you are leading this country directly into war."[27] David Ben Gurion, too, was appalled by the Israeli air strike. To his mind Eshkol had senselessly turned every reprisal into an act of war.[28]

The government, however, was pleased with the results of the operation. It saw the 130 aircraft strong air strike as further proof that none of the Arab states were willing to come to Syria aid, not even Egypt, with whom Syria had a defense agreement. It reinforced Israel's strongly held conviction that as long as Egyptian troops, which now numbered tens of thousands, were bogged down in Yemen, Egypt would not go to war. Moreover, the air strike had been such an overwhelming and stunning demonstration of the Israeli air force's capabilities that the government assumed that none of the Arab states would, in the future, seriously consider challenging Israel.[29] Hence, Rabin's triumphant claim was that Israel had the power and ability to deal with the Syrians in any way it chose, and Israel—not Syria—would have the privilege of choosing the kind of weapons that would be used in these encounters.[30]

Rabin's statement would be followed by fiercer pronouncements by other Israeli leaders and Rabin himself, all of which threatened Syria with even more ferocious attacks in the future. Clearly, the Israeli government was insensitive to or, at least, insufficiently alert to the shift that had recently taken place in Egyptian policy. Internal pressure, especially from its military, inter-Arab pressure, its deteriorating relationship with the United States and its blossoming relationship with the Soviet Union had combined to produce a change in Egyptian policy. Moreover, the air strike against Syria coming on top of the Samua raid meant that Egypt could no longer turn a blind eye to events and shun its responsibilities. It would have to take action.

Unlike the Samua raid, the British Foreign Office was neither surprised nor shocked at the scale of the Israeli air strike. Britain had been expecting Israeli action against Syria. Just days before the event, Hadow had reported that senior IDF officers were repeatedly and publicly underlining the need to teach the Syrians a lesson, a need that became twice as imperative once the ISMAC talks ended owing to Syria's refusal to observe the conditions set for the discussions. These were the conditions that they had agreed to.[31] Nor did Britain criticize the attack, despite the fact that according to British information, the Israeli strike, far from being a spontaneous affair, had been meticulously planned well in advance. The British military attaché, for example, reported that Israel had responded to the Syrian barrage almost instantly. No one here, he assured, was in any doubt that Israel expected Syria to fire on its farmers "and, as in the previous Dan incident, was ready and able to seize the opportunity to teach Syria a lesson."[32] Yet Britain appeared not only to accept the Israeli assault, but also even somewhat indifferent to it.[33]

All this was a far cry from Britain's vehement and angry response to the Samua raid. It underlined Britain's very different attitude toward Jordan with whom it enjoyed excellent relations, and the Syrian regime, which it disliked, especially because it believed that Syria sought to destabilize the region at any price. Moreover, even though Britain admitted that the air offensive was the most serious exchange of fire between Israel and Syria to date, it did not believe that it marked a serious escalation of the conflict. In Britain's view the air strike simply signaled the return to the tension-filled months that had preceded the ISMAC discussions.[34]

As far as Britain was concerned, the important thing now was to ensure that the air strike did not lead to a wide-scale military confrontation. Not that it believed that a general conflagration was very likely. The air strike had lasted several hours, yet none of the Arab states, not even Egypt, appeared even to have considered intervening. No one had come rushing to Syria's aid, and Syria had been left to suffer the full force of the Israeli attack, alone. Nonetheless, the possibility was always there. For example, in the aftermath of the attack, Israel began to concentrate forces along its northern border on a scale unknown since the 1956 Suez campaign. Its aim was twofold: to deter the Syrians from any further aggressive activity and to enable the IDF to respond quickly and effectively if Syria insisted on pursuing its warlike policies. Within a few days, when nothing much appeared to be happening, the Israeli forces dispersed. Once again the border was relatively tranquil.

Britain was also heartened by the thought that the Israeli air strike, precisely because of its massive scale, demonstrated to one and all, and particularly to the Arab world, that Soviet friendship did not offer very effective protection against Israel. Not that it thought that this would have much effect on the Syrians, who, undaunted, would continue to assault Israel and promote guerrilla attacks, as indeed they did. The air strike was also, Britain believed, proof that as long as Egypt was enmeshed in Yemen, Nasser would not risk war with Israel. Here Britain erred. Like Israel, it did not appreciate the impact the air strike had on Egypt or the changes that had taken place in Egypt in the weeks prior to April 7.

The downing of several Syrian MIGs, two of them directly above Damascus, had profoundly humiliated not only Syria but also its Egyptian ally, as well. Moreover, after the Israeli offensive, Nasser found himself in a particularly awkward and embarrassing situation. The air strike had exposed the hollowness of the Egyptian-Syrian Defense Agreement, which had been signed only a few months earlier. Loophole or no loophole, Egypt had plainly not lived up to what most Arabs saw as its duty to come to Syria's assistance. Saudi Arabia and Jordan enthusiastically attacked Nasser personally for refusing to send Egypt's air force to Syria's aid. Jordan reminded Nasser, in case he forgot, that he also had the power to block the Straits of Tiran and thus prevent Israel from importing weapons, trading and establishing relations with the African states. But, Jordan sneered, the Egyptian president was plainly hiding behind the United Nations' skirts.[35] In an attempt to justify his inaction, Nasser offered a few feeble, fumbling excuses in his defense, none of which convinced his Arab critics. Nasser claimed that the battle that had taken place on April 7 was not a real war and, what is more, was over before it began. He pointed out that the Egyptian fighter jets had a limited range, so that without bases in Syria—and we all know, he hinted, whose fault that is—Egypt found it very difficult to come to Syria's assistance.[36]

The Israeli air strike had no doubt struck a severe blow at Egypt's position as the preeminent Arab state and threatened Nasser's own position as the leader of the Arab world. Justifications and bluster apart, Nasser knew that he could not afford to ignore Israel's attack on a sister "progressive" Arab state. Moreover, the air strike, like the Samua raid, took place in broad daylight, revealing how vulnerable the Arab states were, Egypt included, to Israeli military power. In view of this, the Israeli threats that it would take further aggressive action against Syria left Nasser with, as he saw it, only one alternative: to come to Syria's aid if and when Israel attacked. It seems that Syria, at admittedly a rather high price, had finally managed to force Nasser into confronting Israel directly, something he had, so far, sought to avoid until he was ready and all the preparations for the ultimate showdown were in place. But Nasser was neither foolhardy, misguided nor vain enough to launch a suicidal war merely to reassert his leadership of the Arab world. As was his wont, Nasser would carefully consider all the possible consequences of his actions before moving against Israel. Accordingly, if Egypt now adopted a more overtly belligerent policy, it was because Nasser believed that the circumstances for action were ripe and the time for the ultimate showdown had, at long last, arrived.

In sum, far from dissipating the tension, the Israeli air strike had made matters far worse. The Middle East was rapidly moving toward the abyss of war. Not that the fault was Israel's alone; all parties to the conflict had contributed their share to the rapidly escalating conflict. Take Egypt, for example. Only days after the air strike, Sidqi Mahmoud, the head of the Egyptian Air Force, arrived in Damascus in order to coordinate the two countries' air strategy. A week later, a high-level Egyptian mission led by Egypt's prime minister, Sidqi Suleiman, and its foreign minister, Mahmoud Riad, visited the Syrian capital seeking to strengthen the ties between Syria and Egypt. In the course of the visit, Suleiman declared publicly that were Syria to fall victim to another Israeli attack the Egyptian and Syrian air forces would act in tandem to repel the assault.

It was, however, the Soviet Union who perhaps contributed the most to the swiftly deteriorating relations between Israel and its Arab neighbors. The Soviet Union, from the beginning, had stuck to its policy of tension without explosion. And why shouldn't it? It was a policy that had so far yielded, as Britain put it, very handsome dividends, and all at the West's expense. On April 21, about two weeks after the air strike, Katriel Katz, Israel's ambassador to Moscow, was, once again, summoned to the Soviet Foreign Ministry, though why it took the Soviet Union two weeks to respond to the Israeli offensive remains unclear. One possible answer is that the right-wing military coup, which had taken place in Greece that very same day, had raised all the old Soviet fears of imperialist plots and conspiracies. Seeing the two events as linked, they quite possibly believed that Israel had launched the air strike, with American connivance, in order to overthrow the pro-Soviet Syrian regime. In the Foreign Ministry, Katz was met by Yakob Malik, the deputy Soviet foreign minister, who proceeded to read to Katz the following strongly worded note:

Israel is playing with fire in an area close to the Soviet Union's borders. This extremely dangerous game has also been accompanied by statements, which serve to confirm that Israel is bent on resolving the Arab-Israeli conflict by force and from a position of power. The Israeli Chief of Staff had declared that the Israeli attack [April 7] would not be the last and that Israel alone would determine the time and nature of similar actions in the future. The Government of the Soviet Union believes that it is its duty to warn the Government of Israel, once again, that its traditional policy against its neighbours is immensely dangerous and that the responsibility for the consequences will be its alone.[37]

The tone and content of the Soviet note was harsh and uncompromising. Moreover, not content with pointing an accusing finger at the Israeli government and its policies, in general, the Soviets once again charged Israel with concentrating large forces along its northern border in order to launch a military offensive against Syria.[38] After the meeting, Malik refused to hand the Israeli ambassador the note. Instead, five days later the Soviet Union proceeded to publish it.

The combination of Egyptian support and the blatantly pro-Syrian Soviet policy explains why, despite having been thoroughly thrashed by the Israeli air force, Syria's self-confidence rose. Thanks to its two patrons, Syria was not worried about the possibility of a second Israeli retaliatory attack, and its aggressive policy toward Israel, the guerrilla attacks and border incidents, continued as before. Thus, Syria, too, played its part in escalating the conflict.

As did Israel. Unwilling to become the victim of daily guerrilla attacks, Israel threatened to retaliate forcibly. As time went by, these threats became more frequent, more vocal and more aggressive. On May 9, Eban warned Syria that it is "fundamentally mistaken if it assumes that its provocations will go unanswered. Any government, which possessed a modicum of international conscience would sympathise and understand Israel's refusal to submit to the despatch, day in and day out, of terrorists from Syria to Israel."[39] Eshkol impressed upon General Odd Bull that Syria alone was responsible for the growing tension along the border. He told the chief of the United Nations Truce Supervision Organization that in light of Syria's constant threats and provocations, Israel felt that it had every right to act in self-defense. An article published by the daily Ha'aretz, on April 10, revealed the army's reaction to the guerrilla attacks. According to the paper, the prevailing view in Israeli military circles was that "unless, the Syrians abandon their policy of actively supporting terrorism against Israel, Israel must, if it wishes to prevent a rise in the number of the terrorist attacks and stop them from spreading further, meet the Syrians face to face in open combat."[40] On May 11, Eshkol warned that "it is possible that Israel will have to respond [to the Syrian provocations] on a much larger scale than on the 7 April."[41] That same day the Israeli delegation to the United Nations submitted a note to the secretary general, advising U Thant that if the Syrian government did not change its unrealistic and aggressive policy, Israel considered itself fully entitled to take action in self-defense.[42]

Rabin, Israel's hawkish chief of staff, joined this chorus of Israeli threats and warnings. On May 13, he declared that "it is obvious to Israel that Syria lies at the heart of terrorist activity in the Middle East." But, he added menacingly, Israel "had framed itself one rule—we will chose the time, the place and the means to drive back Syrian aggression."[43] According to various unsubstantiated sources, Rabin had, in fact, been at his most ferocious only a day earlier, threatening to "carry out a lightening attack on Syria, occupy Damascus, overthrow the regime and return" home.[44]

The Israeli saber-rattling was widely seen as indubitable proof that Israel was planning a wide-scale military operation against Syria. Neither Egypt nor the Soviet Union could ignore Israel threats. The Soviet response has already been described.[45] On May 13, without any evidence to uphold its claim, the Soviet Union informed the Egyptian government that Israel was concentrating its forces along its northern border in preparation for an attack on Syria.[46] Egypt had already began to secretly redeploy its forces on May 11, though to what end was not yet clear.[47] On May 14, following the Soviet revelations, Egyptian forces marched into the Sinai Peninsula, beginning a chain of events that would ultimately end in war.

NASSER—QUO VADIS

On May 14, 1967, two Egyptian infantry divisions, accompanied by 200 tanks, began moving toward the Sinai Peninsula to join the single division already stationed there. These troops were the first of Egypt's forces to enter Sinai. From that point on, Egyptian forces began to pour into Sinai in ever-growing numbers. The introduction of Egypt's forces into the Sinai Peninsula received huge coverage in the Egyptian press, which claimed that the Egyptian government, having been informed by reliable sources that Israel was on the verge of attacking Syria, had been forced to take military measures in response.[48]

This was patently untrue. Admittedly, Israel could, if it wished, quickly and easily mobilize its forces in readiness for an attack against Syria. But Nasser had access to several reports from sources, no less, if not more, trustworthy than the Soviet Union that confirmed that Israel was not concentrating forces along its northern border. In a memorandum to the UN secretary general, General Odd Bull stated, unequivocally, that there was no evidence that Israel was concentrating its forces on either side of the Israeli-Syrian border. Lieutenant Commander L.P. Blasch, the American military attaché stationed in northern Israel, reported that he had seen no unusual movement of Israel forces. Most tellingly of all, Mouhamad Fawzi, the Egyptian chief of staff, following persistent Syrian complaints about the concentration of Israeli forces, had been sent to Damascus in order to confirm the Syrian charges and came back empty handed. Upon his return Fawzi told Nasser that he had seen no extraordinary movement of Israeli forces nor was there any indication that Israel was concentrating its forces.[49]

These reports were utterly at odds with those reports submitted by the Soviet Union in early May, accusing Israel of concentrating eleven or thirteen brigades along the border in preparation for an attack on Syria. Of course, this was not the first time that the Soviets had raised this particular alarm. They had done so in May and October 1966, and now, after having time and again refused Israel's suggestion that the Soviet ambassador travel north and see that there was absolutely no truth to their accusations, they were doing so again. In all likelihood, the Soviet Union was genuinely afraid that Israel was about to attack its Syrian ally, a fear compounded by the April 7 air strike, which had offered some very real evidence of Israel's military prowess. It is probable that the Soviet Union, by passing along false information about Israeli military preparations, hoped to galvanize Egypt into action. It hoped to push Egypt into fulfilling its obligations under the Egyptian-Syrian Defense Agreement, which, in turn, would deter Israel from carrying out its offensive plans against Syria.

Expecting a few, largely symbolic gestures on Egypt's part, mostly for deterrent effect, the Soviet Union seriously underestimated the scale of the Egyptian response. It certainly did not expect Egypt to take steps that would engender a serious escalation of the Arab-Israeli conflict, possibly to the point of war.[50] Tension was all very well, and, as Britain correctly observed, it suited Soviet purposes well. But the Soviet Union had no intention or desire to ignite a war between Israel and the Arab states. In fact, it considered even an open conflict to be too risky, as it contained the danger of a superpower confrontation. Yet, by disseminating bogus information about the concentration of Israeli forces, the Soviet Union was playing with fire and so must assume its share of the responsibility of pushing the Middle East into war.

One of the more interesting questions in this connection is what did Nasser hope to achieve by sending Egyptian soldiers into Sinai in broad daylight. Was it his sole intention to deter Israeli aggression? Did he consider the possibility, and accept the danger, that by moving such a large portion of his army into the Sinai desert he might provoke the very conflict he had, at least until recently, been hoping to avoid? Or, perhaps Nasser had, for some time now, been contemplating and planning the introduction of Egyptian forces into Sinai, with all the attendant risks, and it was all simply a question of timing. With Israel threatening to strike an even more powerful blow against Syria than the April 7 air strike, did Nasser think that the time for the final showdown with Israel had finally arrived?

There is another possibility. Some scholars maintain that there is no connection between Nasser's decision to move into Sinai and the events on the Israeli-Syrian border. They claim that Nasser, who had received information that Israel was on the verge of exploding a nuclear bomb, felt compelled to take action and prevent Israel from carrying out its plans.[51] As previously discussed, Nasser, in the course of 1966, had warned more than once that Egypt would launch a preemptive strike if Israel were on the brink of producing a nuclear device. Yet there is no convincing evidence linking Egypt's decision to enter the Sinai Peninsula and Israel's nuclear program. Throughout the crisis, from the time the Egyptian forces first set foot in Sinai, on May 14, until the outbreak of the Six-Day War, on June 5, none of the parties to the crisis, not Egypt, not Israel, not Britain, not the United States, not France and not the Soviet Union, raised the nuclear question even once. That being the case, why then did Egypt order air reconnaissance flights over the nuclear plant in Dimona on May 17 and 26, respectively. The answer is simple: during the crisis the plant was considered a strategic target that was to be attacked should hostilities erupt.[52]

Other, mostly Arab, scholars argue that Nasser had no intention to go to war and had sent his forces into Sinai solely in order to deter Israel from attacking Syria.[53] Hassanein Heikal, editor of the Egyptian daily *Al Aharm*, a highly influential figure in the Egyptian political establishment and, most important, one of Nasser's confidants, maintains that the decision to enter the Sinai was a purely defensive decision designed to draw off Israeli forces from Syria. The Egyptian president, Heikal contends, was convinced that the presence of part of his army in the Sinai desert would deter Israel from launching an assault against Syria. He insists that Nasser did not contemplate any kind of offensive operation against Israel.[54] According to Heikal and like-minded writers, Egypt was not ready for war. Certainly not with 50,000 soldiers, including the army's elite units, still busy fighting in Yemen. The way in which the Egyptian forces were deployed throughout the Sinai Peninsula was also, to their mind, proof that Egypt had no offensive intentions. Moreover, they point out, Nasser himself did not think very highly of his army's fighting capabilities. Nasser had always preferred a weak, highly politicized army rent with in-fighting, which posed little or no threat to his regime and helped him stay in power.

These writers conclude that the dramatic step of introducing forces into Sinai was made in order to, on the one hand, deter Israel and, on the other, demonstrate and underpin Nasser and Egypt's leadership of the Arab world. It was a move designed to show the Arab states that Egypt had not abandoned its obligation to defend the Arab nation. In this sense, Nasser's decision to return to Sinai was a public relations measure designed to reap him and Egypt huge political and psychological dividends in the Arab world.[55] Senior Egyptian army officers, including General Abdel Ghani al Gamasi, Egypt's chief of operations in 1973, confirmed these claims, insisting that Egypt was definitely not ready for war. They maintained that Nasser's decision to send Egyptian forces into Sinai was a political decision and moreover one that the armed forces, ill-prepared for war, was unable to execute.[56]

This view was endorsed by another quite unexpected source. When discussing the Egyptian decision, Rabin remarked that he seriously doubted whether Nasser had anticipated how things would develop when he decided to send his forces into Sinai, and he questioned whether Nasser had, at the time, intended to go to war. Rabin personally believed it to be far more likely that Nasser had merely wanted to improve his increasingly shaky position in the Arab world and prove, at little risk, that only he could stand up to and defeat Israel.[57] These arguments are certainly persuasive. But if the decision was intended purely as a deterrent measure, why did Egypt continue to pour forces into Sinai once the powers had intervened and prevented the situation from deteriorating further? Moreover, with no need for further deterrence, how does one explain Nasser's subsequent steps? For example, there was his decision on May 22 to close the Straits of Tiran to Israeli shipping.

Throughout the May crisis, and even after it was clear that Israel would not take action against Syria, that it had, in effect, been deterred, Nasser, inflexible and intractable, refused to do anything to reduce the tension. Quite the opposite, he sought, as evidenced by his decision to close the Straits to Israeli shipping, to escalate the conflict. It was this decision that would prompt the UN secretary general to visit Egypt before matters spiraled out of control. U Thant's visit, on May 23–24, combined with the American appeals for moderation and restraint, offered an opportunity to arrest the developing crisis. However, not too much should be made of this, as with Nasser in an obviously implacable and belligerent mood, things did not appear too hopeful. Even before U Thant's arrival, Nasser had made his position clear. Egypt, he declared, welcomed war. The forthcoming battle was expected to be a gigantic and sweeping one, and its aim was the destruction of Israel.[58]

The inescapable conclusion is that when Nasser decided to introduce Egyptian forces into the Sinai Peninsula, he had, finally, embarked upon his age-long ambition to destroy the state of Israel. To paraphrase Nasser's own words, 1967 wasn't 1956, and it seems that Nasser now judged that he had the military power and the diplomatic support he needed to successfully confront and vanquish Israel. One of the key factors in Nasser's calculations was the Soviet Union. Over the last few years, the Soviet Union had given Egypt unequivocal diplomatic support and more than generous military assistance. Nasser assumed that should a conflagration erupt, he could count on Soviet diplomatic and even military support to counterbalance such support as Israel might receive from its patron, the United States. Even better, on the basis of past experience, he was certain that the Americans would restrain Israel and that no Israeli government would dare to act without U.S. sanction. Moreover, and contrary to the Egyptian officers' claims, Nasser was convinced that he could defeat Israel. According to Hassanein Heikal, Nasser's vice president, Abdel al Hakim Amer, had assured him that the Egyptian army could withstand one or even two Israeli offensives and still be able to launch a counterattack.[59] Nor was this mere braggadocio. Since 1963, Egypt had acquired massive quantities of military equipment, with special emphasis on aircraft. It seems likely that one of the reasons Nasser was so confident that he could defeat Israel was that he now possessed a large, modern and well-equipped air force. Soviet arms plus Soviet diplomatic backing raised Nasser's self-confidence to new heights and contributed much to his decision to send forces into Sinai[60] just as Israel's freedom to buy arms from a variety of sources raised the Israeli government's self-confidence and encouraged it to adopt a firm, often uncompromising stand against the Arab states, including Nasser's Egypt.

In short, Nasser was too sober minded, too rational and too prudent to take hasty, ill-considered measures. Innately cautious, Nasser would only take action after he had carefully thought through the consequences of each step. It seemed Nasser had at long last decided that the time was ripe for the final showdown with Israel. This demanded extensive and scrupulous preparation, both military and diplomatic. Hence, his decision to continue sending forces into Sinai, as well as his efforts to isolate Israel and avoid a repetition of 1956, when Britain and France stood and fought by Israel's side. In May 1967, Nasser assumed that he could survive and defeat Israel, even in a lengthy confrontation. Perhaps he even hoped to defeat Israel before the first shot was fired.

The return of Egyptian forces to Sinai, worrying though it was, did not unduly alarm the Israeli government. It assumed that Nasser's decision was little more than a show of strength, a flexing of Egyptian muscles or at most an attempt to start a war of nerves. According to Israeli military intelligence, the Egyptian action was a repeat performance of "Operation Rotem," which occurred in February 1960 when Nasser, in order to deter Israel from attacking Syria, had ordered his army to secretly enter Sinai. Now Nasser was doing the same thing, only in public and on a larger scale. Accordingly, the Israeli government did not think the Egyptian maneuver posed any particular threat, especially as, at least at the beginning, it was still convinced that Egypt was not ready to go to war. Nevertheless, the government did take one or two precautionary measures, just in case things got out of hand. For example, it mobilized part of its reserve force and took steps to expedite the delivery of Israel's arms supplies.[61]

The United States also believed that Nasser's decision to send forces into the Sinai desert was primarily a political one. It assumed that Nasser, castigated by conservative Arab countries such as Saudi Arabia and Jordan for being soft on Israel, sought to reestablish his leadership of the Arab world and recover his severely damaged prestige by posing as Syria's protector.[62] British opinion was much the same. In the Foreign Office's judgment,

[the] Egyptian armed forces alert resulted from the Israel [sic] open warnings of further retaliation against Syria if terrorist attacks continued and the belief that this presaged an early large scale attack on Syria. Egyptian purpose would be partly deterrent.... to demonstrate to the Israelis that the U.A.R. (Egypt) would not stand aside this time ... i.e. to prepare for supporting action if Syria were attacked.[63]

Unfortunately, Britain pointed out, by sending forces into Sinai, Egypt had become so deeply enmeshed in the crisis that Nasser would find it virtually impossible not to take military action should Israel attack Syria. In sum, in Britain's opinion, the Egyptian decision marked an escalation, but not an unusually dangerous escalation, of the Arab-Israeli conflict. Accordingly, the Foreign Office saw no reason to deviate from its traditional policy of keeping a low profile.

Britain's representatives in the Middle East were instructed to avoid taking the lead in promoting international action of any kind to defuse the tension. Instead, Britain was to join forces with the United States and seek a way to prevent the onset of a series of dangerous confrontations in the Middle East.[64]

Britain had already ruled out the possibility of bringing the affair before the Security Council. It was certain that the Soviet Union, which saw the crisis as a wonderful opportunity to advance its interests, would be sure to exploit any discussion in the Security Council to demonstrate its loyalty to the Arabs. The Soviet Union would argue that it was the Israeli threats to take aggressive action against Syria that alone had given rise to the current crisis. Britain, in response, would be forced to raise the question of Syrian provocations and the unceasing Palestinian infiltrations and attacks on Israel. All of this meant that the discussions in the Security Council would soon degenerate into another sterile Cold War ritual. Moreover, the Foreign Office feared that if there was even the slightest hint that the Security Council was putting Israel in the dock, the Israeli government might be provoked into taking precisely the kind of action that Britain was seeking to a prevent.[65]

The Foreign Office thought that a direct and private appeal to the Soviet Union to help reduce the tension might stand a better chance of working than trying to convince it to cooperate within the framework of the Security Council. The Foreign Office presumed that the Soviet Union was not interested in a general conflagration, so that it seemed reasonable to assume that it would be willing to use its influence, behind the scenes, to restrain Damascus and Cairo. In addition, the British delegation to the United Nations was instructed to join forces with its American and French colleagues, and persuade the secretary general to issue a public declaration, in the name of the Security Council's permanent members, on the affair. In the declaration, U Thant was to warn the parties to the conflict of dangers inherent in the current situation and implore them to avoid taking any action that could lead to a serious explosion. He was to ask Syria to exercise more control and to prevent the Palestinians from infiltrating Israel from Syrian territory; he was to ask Egypt to withdraw its forces from Sinai and, finally, he was to ask Israel not to take the law into its own hands.[66]

The Foreign Office also thought it advisable to approach Syria and Israel directly and impress upon them the dangers of further escalation. Michael Hadow was instructed to lose no time in making it absolutely clear to the Israelis that "if they were to mount a raid on Syria in the present circumstances, the danger of escalation would be very serious" indeed. He was to emphasize that the British government expects Israel to act with all due restraint and underline the fact that by employing force, Israel would severely damage both its own interests as well as those of the West.

As for Syria, Britain hoped to convince it, once and for all, that Israel was not concentrating its forces along the Syrian border. When speaking with the Syrians, Britain also made a point of emphasizing that were the terrorist attacks to continue, Israel could easily and quickly mobilize its forces and send them north to strike at Syria. Britain asked Syria, as it had asked Israel, to show self-restraint. It urged the Syrian government to act in accordance with the cease-fire accords, which stated that no warlike or hostile acts should be conducted from territory controlled by one party against the other party.[67]

Israel, fearful that events would deteriorate and spiral out of control, was anxious to return to the status quo as soon as possible. Yet it was far from clear to Israel how it could disentangle itself from this increasingly complicated and dangerous crisis. Even if Egypt were to withdraw from Sinai, this did not solve the crisis along the Syrian border. There things would remain as tense as ever, particularly as Israel had no intention of promising not to take military action against Syria if the guerrilla attacks and provocation continued. What it was willing to do was to assure Britain that there was no concentration of Israeli forces along the Syrian-Israeli border, a claim verified by the United Nations' observers, and that it had no plans to attack Syria. But, under no circumstances, would it hesitate to launch a military offensive against Syria if one should prove necessary. Aharon Remez, the Israeli ambassador to London, explained why. The hotheads in Damascus, he informed the Foreign Office, might see the movement of Egyptian forces into Sinai as an opportunity to take precisely the kind of action that would result in a dangerous escalation of the conflict. Not that Israel was anxious to take action, which was why, Remez emphasized, the Israeli government sincerely "hoped ... that friendly Governments would all do what they could to restrain Syria from terrorist acts in Israel."[68]

It seems that both Israel and Britain understood that from the moment Egypt entered the Sinai Peninsula the rules of play had changed. What is more, it was Nasser, and only Nasser, who now determined the rules, and as far as he was concerned, the question of whether Israel was or was not concentrating its forces along its northern border was a moot point; he would continue to seek a confrontation with Israel, regardless. Thus, while Britain was busy trying to reduce the tension, the Egyptian president decided that it was time to escalate the crisis.

On May 16, 1967, Egyptian Chief of Staff Mouhamad Fawzi ordered Major-General Rikhye, the commander of the United Nations Emergency Force in Sinai, to recall the UN troops stationed along the Israeli-Egyptian border between Rafah and Eilat. The Egyptian government justified its demand by claiming that it merely wished to protect the UN soldiers should hostilities erupt. It seems more likely, however, that what Nasser really wanted was to refute the Arab accusations that he was hiding behind the UN's skirts.[69] To wit, even before Major-General Rikhye had time to respond to Fawzi's demand, Egyptian soldiers began to station themselves along the Israeli border. Fawzi, it should be noted, did not demand the evacuation of the entire Emergency Force, which numbered about 3,400 soldiers, from the U.A.R. and Gaza Strip.[70] Thus, the demand was the kind of carefully calculated, limited escalation, which was very much in keeping with Nasser's cautious nature. Nasser knew that to demand the withdrawal of the entire Emergency Force was to risk an Israeli attack before he had completed the concentration of Egyptian forces in the Sinai desert.

If Nasser had undoubtedly raised the stakes, the United Nations secretary general now managed to make things much worse. In U Thant's view, the Emergency Force was a single, integrated force. Accordingly and ignoring the fact that the Egyptian president had no right to issue orders to the United Nations, he told Nasser that although he could withdraw the entire force from Egypt, he was unable to order the evacuation of only a part of it.[71] The Egyptians were dumbfounded.[72] With this all or nothing message, the secretary general had contrived to put the fate of the Emergency Force directly into Nasser's hands, and the Egyptian president, seeing this as another test of his leadership, not surprisingly opted for the withdrawal of the entire Emergency Force. On May 18, Mouhamad Riad, the Egyptian foreign minister, summoned the representatives of those countries such as Canada, Yugoslavia and India, which had contributed soldiers to the Emergency Force, to the Egyptian Ministry, where he informed them that the Egyptian government had decided to terminate, forthwith, the presence of the Emergency Force in Egypt and the Gaza strip.

It would be a gross understatement, to say that Nasser's decision astonished, worried and infuriated Israel. The Israeli government immediately took steps to prevent matters from getting further out of hand. It warned Britain that it would be a grievous and dangerous mistake to withdraw Emergency Force from Sinai. Eban conceded that, for the past ten years, the Emergency Force had played a key role in preserving the stability in the Middle East, so that to withdraw it would undermine the status quo in the region. Moreover, Eban pointed out that the secretary general did not have the authority to accede to the Egyptian demand without first consulting and receiving the permission of the United Nations General Assembly. Eban emphasized that it was the General Assembly that had authorized the establishment of the Emergency Force in the first place, so that only it had the authority to reverse its decision. Furthermore, stationing the Emergency Force in Sinai had been part of the deal concluded in March 1957, whereby Israel agreed to evacuate parts of Sinai and Sharem el Sheikh, in return for the protection this Force was supposed to provide. What is more, Israel had agreed to this deal, as Eban reminded Britain's representatives, partly because Britain argued that the Emergency Force would safeguard its security interests. Finally, Eban criticized U Thant's decision as "maybe in the long run more disastrous to the United Nations than for Israel."[73] Nor was he exaggerating. Henceforth, U Thant's wretched decision apart, the United Nations, other than to issue various ineffectual statements and declarations, would take no active or constructive part in the conflict.

The United States was also shocked and mystified by U Thant's decision. It couldn't understand how the secretary general could have been so foolish as to agree to the withdrawal of the United Nations Force precisely at a time when it was needed more than ever—at a time when it was necessary to strengthen the United Nations' military presence in the region, not weaken let alone dissolve it. Perhaps, the Americans thought, Thant's decision had been inspired, in part, by the position of countries such as India and Yugoslavia, which had contributed soldiers to the Emergency Force and enjoyed a special relationship with Egypt.[74] But whatever Thant's motives, Egypt, in U.S. opinion, was clearly acting illegally. Having signed an international agreement, giving its consent to the presence of the Emergency Force, it could not now unilaterally revoke it.

Britain agreed with Israel's assessment of the situation. Instead of alleviating the tension, the secretary general had made matters worse. George Brown was flabbergasted, observing that the UN umbrella had been withdrawn as soon as it began to rain. "I shall never understand," he later commented, "how he [Thant] was advised to come so quickly to this ill-considered and, I feel absolutely sure, totally unnecessary and unexpected decision."[75]

Lord Caradon, Britain's ambassador to the United Nations, was instructed to meet with U Thant and, speaking in the name of both Britain and the United States, insist that under no circumstances was the Emergency Force to be withdrawn from the region.[76]

France did not add its voice to the Anglo-American protests. Roger Seydoux, the French ambassador to the United Nations, explained to Lord Caradon that he was prevented from doing so as he had not yet received any instructions on the matter from the Quai d'Orsay. In any case, he did not think the situation sufficiently grave to warrant all three Western powers from joining forces in the United Nations. France, Seydoux said, considered some form of independent four-power cooperation to be a much better course of action.[77] The French would raise the idea of four-power cooperation, once again at the height of the May crisis. Perhaps the French refusal to cooperate stemmed from de Gaulle's dislike of playing what he saw as third base to the Anglo-American coalition. On the other hand, a four-power forum, de Gaulle believed, would allow France to assume its natural role as one of the world's four leading international powers. But the French decision not to play ball also pointed to the fact that France was intent upon ending its special relationship with Israel and strengthen its ties with the Arab states, a process that, as noted, had began when de Gaulle first assumed power in 1958.

The secretary general defended his decision. U Thant contended that the consent of the host country was a basic principle, which applied to all the United Nations' peacekeeping operations. Practically speaking this meant that an Emergency Force could not stay or fulfill its tasks without the host country's (Egypt's) agreement and cooperation. Thant pointed out that the Emergency Force had been stationed in Egyptian territory as a result of an agreement concluded between Nasser and his predecessor Dag Hammerskjold. Therefore, Thant argued, it was manifest that once the United Arab Republic had withdrawn its consent to the presence of the United Nations, it was incumbent on the secretary general to order its evacuation. But explanations and justifications apart, it is clear that the secretary general, when confronted with a test of the United Nations' ability to fulfil its raison d'être and prevent a conflagration erupting in the Middle East, had ducked the challenge. He had shifted the burden of decision regarding the fate of the Emergency Force onto the shoulders of the Egyptian president, who gladly took up the challenge. It is telling that Thant concluded his explanations by expressing his concern as to the possible repercussions these latest developments might have upon the peace in the Middle East.[78]

As the Emergency Forces began the process of evacuating Egyptian territory, the advance of Egyptian forces into Sinai continued unabated. By May 18, Egypt had a total of three infantry and one armored division, which together numbered 70,000 to 80,000 soldiers, as well as 600 tanks, artillery units and air force units deployed throughout the Sinai Peninsula. It was an unprecedented concentration of forces. Moreover, some of these units were stationed as close as 20 km from the Israeli border. Israel, understandably, found all this extremely worrying. It grew even more nervous when Nasser continued to pour more forces into Sinai, even though he knew that the information about the concentration of Israeli forces in the north was patently false. Accordingly, in order to be prepared for any eventuality, including that of a three-front war, the Israeli government ordered the mobilization of a significant portion of its reserve force. The Israeli government, in fact, assumed that a confrontation was inevitable. "It is war," Eshkol exclaimed, "it is war, it is a war, I tell you."[79] Eshkol may have been jumping the gun as it wasn't quite war yet. But with the Israeli and Egyptian armies in the process of marshalling their forces against each other, war was a distinct possibility.[80]

The mobilization of its reserve force imposed a heavy economic burden on Israel, and its economy came to a virtual standstill. It also engendered a growing sense of siege and isolation. For the first time in its history, Israel found itself in the midst of a serious crisis, in which it might soon find itself fighting for its very life without the support of any of the Western powers. In stark contrast to the solid support the Soviet Union offered the Arab states, none of the Western powers did anything to indicate that they stood squarely behind Israel. None offered the slightest word of comfort or made the smallest gesture of support. Not surprisingly, Israeli policy makers, bewildered and confused, suddenly seemed overcome by a sense of helplessness. Confronted with a huge crisis, Eshkol's government appeared totally unable to lead the country. The prevailing feeling in Israel was that Eshkol was incapable of making any decision, let alone a constructive one. Rabin complained bitterly that he was not receiving explicit instructions from Eshkol, who, he accused, had no clear–cut policy.[81]

Israel assumed that having expelled the United Nations Emergency Force from Egyptian territory and deployed its own forces throughout Sinai, including Sharem el Sheikh, it was only a question of time before Egypt closed the Straits of Tiran to Israeli shipping. And it was absolutely right. The conservative Arab states had, for some time, been berating Nasser for refusing to close the Straits. To their, and indeed to Egypt's, mind once Egypt had replaced the

UN forces at Sharem el Sheikh, which overlooked the Straits, an absurd situation was created whereby Egyptian soldiers would sit and watch Israeli and foreign ships sailing calmly through the Straits carrying cargo to and from Israel.

Israel attached enormous importance to the principle of free passage through the Straits of Tiran. The port of Eilat, which lay at the end of the Straits, was Israel's gateway to Africa and the Far East. It afforded Israel the best and least expensive way to trade and cultivate relations with the countries of Africa and Asia. It was also the cheapest way to transport oil from Iran. Nor can it be forgotten that securing the principle of free passage had been one of the crowning achievements of the Suez Campaign.[82] Israel left no doubt as to how it would react if Nasser closed the Straits to Israeli shipping. It told everyone, including the United Nations secretary general, U Thant, that it would regard any interference with the principle of free passage through the Straits as an act of aggression and Israel would take action to defend this right at all costs. Closing the Straits, it warned, amounted to a casus belli.[83]

The French, bent upon ending their special relationship with Israel, remained silent.[84] Nor did the secretary general respond, at least not directly. What he did do, after a great deal of American pressure, was decide to visit Egypt and meet Nasser in person in an attempt to defuse the crisis. Thant decided not to include Syria or Israel on his itinerary, another sign perhaps that the crisis centered on Egypt and that it was the Egyptian president who determined the nature and pace of events.

Hoping to prevent a general conflagration, the United States did react. But it soon became clear that it had no idea, let alone a well thought-out policy, how to actually go about achieving this. On May 17, President Johnson wrote to Eshkol, impressing upon him that "I cannot accept responsibility on behalf of the United States for situations, which arise as the result of actions on which we are not consulted."[85] The State Department reinforced the president's warning, making it plain that U.S. fulfillment of its commitment to Israel's security was conditional upon Israel not taking action without the prior consent of the United States. This was, in effect, tantamount to an American demand for complete control over Israeli policy. Apparently, at this stage, the United States thought its best option was to restrain Israel and warn it against taking what was, in its opinion, hasty and ill-conceived action.[86]

One thing the United States did not want was to become directly involved in the crisis. Owing to its continued and escalating involvement in Vietnam, the United States was reluctant, fearful even, of becoming entangled in yet another crisis. Consequently, U.S. options were limited. Even if the Johnson administration had wanted to become more personally involved in the crisis, its hands were tied by Congress, which insisted that the United States act solely through the medium of the United Nations. This, of course, flew in the face of President Kennedy's promise that if Israel ever fell victim to aggression his government would personally take action to bring this aggression to an end. It also ran counter to the U.S. commitment made only months after the Sinai Campaign to maintain the freedom of passage through the Straits. A memorandum, dated February 11, 1957, had stated that

The United States believe[s] that the Gulf comprehends international waters and no nation has the right to prevent free and innocent passage in the Gulf and through the Straits giving access there to.[87]

In the memorandum, the United States had explicitly recognized Israel's right under article 51 of the United Nations Charter to open the Straits by force if they were closed by force.[88] Moreover, the Americans had repeated this commitment on more than one occasion, assuring Israel that "we have no intention of letting the Straits be closed."[89] They did, however, inform Israel that the United States would support all measures designed to uphold the principle of free of passage, both within or without the United Nations's framework, which should, perhaps, have lit a warning light in Jerusalem.

What the United States was really hoping for was that someone else, including Israel, would resolve the crisis and relieve it of this onerous burden. To this end, the United States was willing to consider all possible courses of action, including an Israeli military strike against the Egyptian forces in Sinai. Its preferred option, however, was that Britain take the lead in the resolving crisis, something that Britain, of course, sought to avoid like the plague. The last thing the British government wanted was to become involved in a military operation in the Middle East, particularly one independent of the United Nations.[90]

But although Britain might have liked to escape any involvement in the current crisis, it discovered, to its dismay, that it had little choice but to become fully engaged in the crisis, although not, thankfully, in any military sense. France refused to do anything. There was little hope that the United Nations would offer any constructive solution to the crisis. The United States, shirking its own commitments, sought to throw the burden of the responsibility onto Britain's shoulders. Yet what ultimately forced Britain into action was the fact that it was the most vulnerable power in the region, and the one that could least afford a general conflagration. Britain was in the midst of the delicate process of evacuating its bases in the Middle East while trying, at the same time, to safeguard its interests, particularly economic interests, in the region. A war was bound to upset the process of British withdrawal and undermine its political and economic interests. Accordingly, Britain realized that it had to do something about the Straits crisis, and quickly, before the worst, that is, war, happened.

Britain was also coming under heavy pressure from the Israeli government to stand by its commitment to maintain the principle of free passage through the Straits. Israel pointed out that Britain had undertaken to uphold this principle after the Suez Campaign. In March 1957, its representative to the United Nations had declared that

it is the view of Her Majesty's Government in the United Kingdom that the Straits of Tiran must be regarded as an international water through which the vessels of all nations have a right of passage. Her Majesty's Government will assert this right on behalf of all British Shipping and is prepared to join with others to secure general recognition of this right.[91]

Abba Eban now demanded that Britain fulfill its commitment. He made it absolutely clear that Israel had no intention of lying down and accepting the abrogation of this historical fact. Nor would it agree to become the victim of an Egyptian blockade, cut off from its friends in Africa and Asia.[92]

Israel also raised the painful subject of Soviet activity and troublemaking in the Middle East. It maintained that one reason, perhaps the chief reason, why both Egypt and Syria were showing such lack of restraint was that they were certain that they had the Soviet Union's support. Israel had appealed to the Soviet Union several times to help find a solution to this and other crises, only to be turned down. Instead of helping, all the Soviets did was restate their unqualified support of Egypt's policies and actions. Tchouvakhine, the Soviet ambassador to Israel, had simply trotted out the old line that the American Central Intelligence Agency (CIA) was sponsoring the terrorist activities and that the Soviet Union had conveyed its views on the matter to both the Syrians and the Egyptians. He also warned Israel not to take any action against the Arab states. The Soviet Union, Tchouvakhine remonstrated, views it as a very serious matter that Israel not only refused to act upon its open and friendly warnings, but also totally ignored them. It was all very disappointing and frustrating, and Israel was left with no choice but to conclude that the Soviet Union regarded this crisis simply as another chapter in its ongoing rivalry with the United States. The Soviet Union's sole aim in the affair was to score a political diplomatic victory over its arch Cold War foe.[93]

In light of Soviet policy, Eban maintained, the Western powers must declare forthwith their support for both the integrity and independence of Israel and the maintenance of the status quo. By doing so, he explained, they would be establishing a counterpoise to the Arab belief that while the Soviet Union would stand behind them and support any act of aggression they might undertake against Israel, Israel stood alone and isolated.[94] Eshkol sent Harold Wilson an urgent note, arguing that "the only counterweight to this factor," that is, the Soviet Union's open and unequivocal support of the Arab states, "would be an emphatic clarification to the Soviet Union of British policy in support of Israel's independence and integrity." This, he stressed, was the only way to check the Soviet Union's policy in the Middle East and its unfortunate consequences, if indeed this was what Britain desired. Eshkol also asked Wilson that he and his fellow powers take immediate steps to stop and reverse the endless stream of Egyptian troops pouring into the Sinai Peninsula.[95]

Britain sympathized with Israel's plight, which, of course, was nothing new. But it still thought that a public declaration endorsing Israel's independence and territorial integrity was far too extreme and dangerous a step to take. Such a declaration, signifying that Britain identified with Israel and its cause, would probably cost Britain dear in terms of its political and economic interests in the Arab world. But what Britain failed to understand, or perhaps simply refused to see, was that no matter what it did the Arab states would always believe that it was taking Israel's side. In any case, Wilson, or rather the Foreign Office, which at this stage of the crisis was still in charge of British policy, ignored Eshkol's appeal. Instead, Wilson's reply to Eshkol's appeal called into account Israel's policy over the last few years. He hoped that Eshkol would forgive his

recalling that we have always had serious misgivings about the dangers involved in forceful reprisals, not because we have lacked sympathy for your situation, but because we believe that it is not possible to predict or control the consequences.[96]

As did the Foreign Office only a few days earlier, Wilson also advised Eshkol against taking any measures that would further aggravate an already grave situation. Nothing, Wilson insisted, was irreversible, and he sincerely hoped that it would be possible if, of course, Israel was willing to play its part, to revert to the status quo ante. Wilson suggested that Israel, for example, consider the possibility of stationing a United Nations Emergency Force on its territory. Britain pointed out that the reason Nasser had been able to dictate the fate of the Emergency Force was because it had been stationed only on one side—the Egyptian side—of the border. George Brown admitted that the presence of a United Nations Force on Israeli territory would not in itself secure the principle of free navigation through the Straits or prevent terrorists from infiltrating Israeli territory, but, he maintained, it would be an extremely advantageous step to take politically. Israel would certainly benefit, and the whole situation would take a turn for the better once it were known that Israel accepted the idea as part of a package deal. But, to Brown's consternation, Israel rejected his proposal out of hand. It did not think that Nasser should be rewarded for having struck a colossal blow, perhaps the greatest ever, at the United Nations' prestige.[97]

Despite its disappointment at Israel's refusal to abide by its advice, the last thing Britain wanted was for Israel to think that its friends had abandoned it in its hour of need and so develop feelings of deep bitterness and animosity. Britain was willing, therefore, to secretly meet Israel's urgent requests for more weapons.[98] It was also careful to underline the fact that Britain completely agreed with Israel that the principle of free passage through the Straits must be upheld. Accordingly, George Brown assured Aharon Remez that Britain regarded the Straits of Tiran as an international waterway, and that the maritime powers would not and could not accept or permit any interference with the principle of free passage through the Straits. Britain was even willing to publicly endorse the principle of free navigation through international waterways, including the Straits of Tiran, and declare that it believed that Israel had the full right to defend this principle were the Straits blocked to Israeli shipping. Britain thus hoped both to reassure Israel and dissuade Nasser from carrying out his plan of blocking Israeli access to the Gulf of Aqaba.[99] Nevertheless, Britain stopped short of giving Israel a guarantee that it would take concrete action to ensure the freedom of Straits. Like the United States, Britain preferred to operate within the framework of the United Nations and support any appropriate measures that that organization saw fit to take. As Wilson explained to Eshkol:

the Straits of Tiran constituted an international waterway, which should remain open to the ships of all nations. If it appeared that any attempt to interfere with the passage of ships through the waterway was likely to be made we should promote and support international action through the United Nations to secure the passage.[100]

Remez tried to persuade George Brown of the merits of setting up a special international maritime task force to patrol the Gulf of Aqaba. A task force, the Israeli ambassador argued, would be the best way of preventing Nasser from blocking the Straits. Brown did not reject the idea out of hand, but he wasn't quite sure how to go about organizing such a force. It is interesting, however, that within days Britain would adopt Remez's proposal in full, and that for the remainder of the crisis the concept of a maritime task force would form the basis of Anglo-American cooperation.

Israel realized that, in one way or an another, all the Western powers were shirking their commitment to maintain the principle of free passage through the Straits. The French, as was their wont, remained silent, while Britain and the United States were sympathetic but impassive. Neither power was ready to stand by Kennedy and Macmillan's May 1963 declarations and take action to maintain stability in the Middle East. Not surprisingly, the mood in Israel was bitter, resentful and anxious. It felt that the Western powers had deserted it, abandoned it to its fate. Mindful of the climate of opinion in Israel, Britain assumed that, as a result and in order to avoid a similar situation in the future, Israel would step up its nuclear program and accelerate the process of developing a nuclear bomb.[101]

On May 22, Eshkol spoke to the Knesset. The tone and content of his speech was temperate, moderate and even conciliatory, perhaps because he was intensely aware that none of the powers were willing to fulfill their obligations and stand by Israel, thus leaving it to face the crisis alone. Israel, Eshkol declared, had no desire to attack the Arab states. It had no wish to threaten their security, invade their land or undermine any of their legitimate international rights. Nor, he reiterated, was there any truth to the rumor that Israel was concentrating forces along its northern border. Eshkol also emphasized the need to return to the status quo, on both sides of the Arab-Israeli borders. Finally, he announced that Israel was ready to take part in any effort to promote stability and peace in the Middle East. Eshkol made only one oblique reference in his speech to the situation in the Straits. He did not warn Nasser point blank against closing the Straits. Instead, he appealed to the powers to take action to maintain the right of free passage, a right, Eshkol reminded them, that applies to all states without distinction.[102]

Eshkol hoped that this highly placatory speech might stop the crisis from snowballing out of control. He believed that he had offered Nasser a creditable way out of the crisis, as Nasser could now boast that he had stopped Israel from attacking Syria. Unfortunately, Nasser interpreted Eshkol's speech as evidence that the Israeli prime minister lacked backbone and that he was a weak, second-rate leader. Nasser found this very encouraging especially when coupled with Israel's obvious international isolation. Unlike the Suez Campaign, where Israel had enjoyed British and French support, Israel now, Nasser deemed, stood alone. None of the European powers were willing to help it, whereas the United States, sunk deep in the mire of Vietnam, was unlikely to get involved in another conflict.[103] The time, Nasser believed therefore, was ripe to up the crisis.

On the night of May 22–23, Nasser declared the Gulf of Aqaba closed to Israeli shipping and to all ships carrying "strategic material" to Israel. Plainly, neither Eshkol's speech nor his own success in getting rid of the United Nations Emergency Force had deflected Nasser from his carefully planned strategy. Having waited until the last of the Emergency Force soldiers evacuated Sharem el Sheikh, Nasser now pronounced the Straits closed. It was all part of his plan to move steadily toward an open confrontation with Israel. Hence, his speech to the officers stationed at the Egyptian Air Force base in Bir Gafgafa, which was symbolically located in the Sinai Peninsula. Speaking on May 22, Nasser declared that "we are now on the verge of a confrontation with Israel. Unlike 1956, when Britain and France stood squarely behind Israel, today Israel hasn't the support of even one European country. While it is possible that the United States will stand by Israel, its support would be limited to offering Israel political backing and supplying it with weapons and military equipment." The Egyptian president added ominously that Egypt's return to Sharem el Sheikh was "proof of our sovereignty over the straits of Aqaba. The Straits of Tiran lie in our territorial waters and under no circumstances will we allow an Israeli flag to sail through the Straits. If the Jews threaten us war? I say to them 'Welcome,' we are ready for war."[104] It is manifest from this speech that Nasser knew that blocking the Straits meant war with Israel, and his decision to close the Straits of Tiran was tantamount to a public declaration that Egypt had decided to go to war.[105]

Nasser's decision to block the straits had, fundamentally and radically, transformed the situation. It hit Israel out of the blue. Although Israel had, for some time, suspected that Nasser was planning such a move, it was nonetheless surprised and shocked at Nasser's announcement. Perhaps, Israel secretly believed that when it came to it, Nasser would never dare take such a dangerous, inflammable step. As far as Israel was concerned, war was now simply a question of time. Even Britain didn't understand why Israel didn't attack Egypt the moment Nasser so brazenly violated its rights.[106]

Michael Hadow admitted to the Israeli Foreign Ministry that he, the embassy's military attachés and almost the entire Foreign Office were astonished that Israel had not taken action the minute Nasser had announced that he was closing the Straits and before he managed to consolidate his position in the Sinai Peninsula. Britain thought that Israel had a good case for taking action against Egypt. The withdrawal of the United Nations forces, the closing of the Straits and the presence of a massive Egyptian force in Sinai all posed a grave threat to its existence and demanded that it take immediate action in self-defense.[107] However, because Israel did not launch an offensive against Egypt, Britain saw it incumbent upon itself to try and prevent a war erupting in the future. As the crisis had now reached a new and more dangerous level, Wilson decided to take full charge of British policy. The move from Foreign Office to 10 Downing Street was symbolic of the shift that would soon take place in British policy from one of maintaining a low profile to one of total British involvement. But if the method was different, the aim remained the same: a stable Middle East. British policy, as directed by Wilson, hoped to revoke Nasser's decision to close the Straits, and thus restore a measure of stability to the Middle East.

TOTAL INVOLVEMENT

The Israel government believed that Nasser's action constituted just and ample cause for war. Since the end of the Sinai War in 1956, Israeli statesmen and representatives had warned that Israel would never submit to the closing of the Straits and would regard such a step as an act of war.[108] Now, its chief of staff, Yitzhak Rabin, head of Military Operations, Ezer Weizman and head of Military Intelligence, Aharon Yariv, as well as other senior military officers, were furiously insisting that Israel take action against Egypt at once. If it did not, they warned, Israel would lose its ability to deter the Arab states. The Arab world would interpret its inaction as weakness and believe that it had an opportunity to threaten its security even further. Rabin warned Eshkol that what was at stake was not simply the right of Israeli ships to sail freely through the Straits, but Israel's military credibility, its resolve and ability to act in self-defense. If Israel did not respond to the closing of the Straits, he remonstrated that the IDF's power to deter the Arab states would be severely undermined. The best and most effective course of action, he suggested, would be to attack and destroy the Egyptian air force at base, and, he added, in order for such action to be successful, Israel must act immediately.[109]

Eshkol disagreed and for once stood his ground. Eshkol believed that it would be a disaster to take military action without the support of the United States. If no one else, he was highly conscious of the American administration's warnings that Israel should not act hastily or, indeed, take any action without first consulting the United States. Moreover, following Nasser's announcement that he was closing the Straits to Israeli shipping, the United States had enjoined Israel not to take unilateral action, but to allow a forty-eight-hour pause, in order to assess the situation. Eshkol knew that were he to yield to his army chiefs' demands, Israel would find itself fighting a war, alone and friendless. Fearful of leaving Israel isolated, Eshkol agreed to the American request. Eshkol also knew that whatever steps Israel ultimately decided to take, American support was vital, particularly in light of the Soviet Union's unequivocal support of the Arab states. In a military confrontation, Israel would find itself in dire straits, politically and militarily, unless the United States acted to counterbalance and neutralize the Soviet Union's support of the Arabs. Eshkol was afraid that without American support, Israel, despite winning the war on the battlefield, would ultimately lose the victory.[110] This meant that before it took action, Israel must first modify U.S. steadfast opposition to military action.[111]

The Cabinet Defense Committee, which directed Israel's policy throughout the crisis, agreed with Eshkol. It declared the closure of the Straits to Israeli shipping an act of aggression, but agreed to delay its response for forty-eight hours. During that time the foreign minister would ascertain the U.S. position on the issue. In addition, Eban would meet and discuss the crisis with the Western European leaders. Finally, the Cabinet empowered the prime minister and foreign minister to decide whether circumstances demanded that Eban travel to the United States and confer directly with President Johnson.[112] As nothing could be done until Eban's return, these decisions meant that Israel had, in effect, delayed its response beyond the forty-eight hours demanded by the United States.

President Johnson, sensitive to Israel's difficulties—the closing of the Straits, the mobilization of its reserve forces—took several steps to help alleviate its plight. Johnson publicly affirmed that the United States deemed the Gulf of Aqaba an international waterway and that it regarded its closing to Israeli ships as an illegal act, which was, moreover, potentially disastrous to the cause of peace. The entire international community, the president emphasized, considered the right of free and innocent passage through international waterways to be a vital interest, not only of Israel's but also of all maritime and nonmaritime nations alike. Nor did Johnson limit himself to offering Israel verbal support only. He authorized an aid package to Israel, which included armored vehicles, spare parts for tanks, food supplies, information on how to repair and renovate hawk missiles and a $20 million loan.[113]

American officials echoed the president's declarations and reiterated U.S. resolve to stand by its commitment to keep the Straits open. But, at the same time, they also pointed out that, regretfully, given that Congress was nervous and overly sensitive to any kind of exclusive American involvement in the current crisis, the president could not take action until he had consulted with the leaders of the House. Even then, the United States would probably be able to honor its obligations to Israel only on the basis of a joint decision made by both Houses.[114] Because congressional consent to any kind of independent American involvement in the crisis seemed unlikely, this amounted to a not so subtle hint that the United States would not be able to stand by its obligations. All this gives rise to the thought that the forty-eight-hour delay the United States had requested was no more that a ploy to give it time to bulldoze other countries, Britain in particular, into taking action in response to the closing of the Straits.

Luckily for the Americans, Britain had already begun to search for ways to prevent a war erupting between Israel and the Arab states. Britain strongly suspected that once Israel declared war, the Arab states, regardless of Britain's attempts to maintain an even-handed, low-profile policy, would damn Britain as pro-Israeli and anti-Arab and react accordingly. Nasser might declare the Straits closed to British shipping; British oil supplies might be tampered with, either at the source or in transit, the Arab states might limit or even stop trading with Britain altogether, while the oil-rich Arab states, like Kuwait, for example, might close their sterling accounts in Britain's banks. A war would also disrupt the process of Britain's gradual withdrawal from the region, and Britain was acutely aware that in less than a year, in the beginning of 1968, it was supposed to evacuate Aden and redeploy its forces throughout the Gulf. The long and short of it was that war would gravely damage all of Britain's regional interests.

Not surprisingly, Britain sought earnestly to prevent war from breaking out, which meant at the very least safeguarding the principle of free passage through the Straits. Wilson who, as noted, had assumed control of British foreign policy for the duration of the crisis, was much more militant toward Egypt than the Foreign Office. On the morning of May 23, Wilson invited his foreign minister, George Brown, and his minister of defense, Dennis Healy, to 10 Downing Street to discuss the crisis and ways of resolving it. All three agreed that unless steps were taken to ensure the freedom of navigation through the Straits, Israel would go to war. Brown added that while, on the one hand, there was "a real danger of early military counter-action by Israel," there was, on the other, only a very slight chance that the Americans would take independent action to solve the crisis.[115] He therefore suggested that Her Majesty's Government:

would be prepared to join with the U.S. and any other maritime powers in organising an international naval force, the purpose of which would not be described as to help Israel ... but as to keep open and permit freedom of international passage through the Straits into the Gulf of Aqaba. Ideally, this should be a UN force; but if no agreement could be reached at the UN to set it up, it should be established independently.[116]

Wilson thought Brown's solution to the problem a good one. He agreed that, if possible, the task force should be organized within the framework of the United Nations, but if not, then Britain should independently seek to set up such a force, which would include as many states as were willing to join. Wilson was certain that the United States, having declared its commitment to keeping the Straits open, would welcome the idea of a naval task force. After all, the United States had told Israel on numerous occasions that it had no intention of allowing the Straits to be closed to Israeli shipping, while its representatives had assured Britain that the United States fully intended to stand by its obligations.[117]

Wilson's decision that Britain was to work toward the establishment of an international naval task force meant that he was, in effect, abandoning the low profile policy the Foreign Office had championed since the 1964 Cairo Summit Conference. Under Wilson, growing, personal and direct intervention in the Arab-Israeli conflict were the order of the day. Ironically, however, though Wilson was driven to intervene for fear that a war would undermine British interests in the Middle East, it was the fact of Britain's intervention itself that ended up endangering British interests. Together with the entire Arab world, Egypt considered Britain's tireless efforts to keep the Straits open as indubitable proof that Britain sided and sympathized with Israel. To their mind, it offered conclusive evidence that British policy was essentially anti-Arab. They saw Britain's activities as marking a return to the days of 1956, which had been distinguished by British-Israeli collaboration and collusion.

Before taking any steps toward establishing the naval task force, Wilson first needed his Cabinet's sanction. The crucial Cabinet meeting took place on May 23, immediately after the Wilson-Brown-Healy meeting, and was to prove, in Wilson's opinion, one of the gravest Cabinets of his entire experience. Brown explained to the Cabinet the rationale behind the idea of the naval task. There was, he stated bluntly, a very real danger that Israel would be tempted to launch a preventive war. This was because its relative strength would decline, especially once it was denied access to the port of Eilat. Having considered various ways of averting an Arab-Israeli military confrontation, Brown had reached the conclusion that the most effective method to avoid war would be to organize a naval task force. The United Nations, Brown confessed, was clearly of no use. Past experience had shown that discussions in the Security Council led nowhere, and even if the Council was to formulate some constructive decision, the Soviet Union was bound to veto it. Brown, therefore, appealed to the Cabinet to authorize the government to join forces with the United States and any other such maritime countries as could be mobilized, and announce the intention to establish a naval task force, either under the auspices of the United Nations or independently. Its object would be to keep the Gulf of Aqaba open, or, if necessary reopen it, to ships of all nations. Establishing a task force, Brown explained, would be tantamount to offering Israel a guarantee that the Straits will remain open, and once Israel was satisfied that the principle of free navigation was guaranteed, it would not, Brown assured, launch a preventive war.[118]

Much to Brown and Wilson's dismay, the majority of Cabinet ministers opposed the idea that Britain should set about organizing a naval task force. Wilson thought his ministers had suffered a collective and acute attack of jitters. Faint-hearted, they were, he gibed, terrified of the idea of Britain taking the lead in any kind of military action against Egypt. But, timid or not, the Cabinet, as a whole, strongly disapproved of Brown's proposed measure. The opposition was lead by the chancellor of exchequer, James Callaghan, and, to Wilson and Brown's surprise and indignation, Denis Healy. Apparently, the minister of defense had, within the space of a few hours, completely reversed his opinion on the task force. Callaghan asserted that the pound sterling and the British economy in general would suffer badly if Britain were to organize a naval task force. Moreover, the chancellor added, venturing into the realms of military strategy to allow British aircraft carriers to patrol so confined an area as the Straits would be a strategic disaster.[119] Healy agreed. It would, he pronounced, be pure suicide to mount a military operation in the Straits. Britain's ships would be completely exposed to the Egyptian air force, and in order to prevent an attack on its ships, Britain would be forced to gain control of Egypt's air bases in the region.[120] In a letter to the prime minister, sent the day after the fateful Cabinet meeting, Healy told Wilson that he had discussed the crisis with the chiefs of staff and his military advisers, all of whom fully endorsed his position and

have reinforced the view which I have expressed in the Cabinet that there would be strong military objection to any plan for concentrating our ships near the Straits of

Tiran in order to counter UAR threat to the Straits, so long as Egyptian air forces are in a position to dominate the area.[121]

The majority of the cabinet ministers thought Brown's proposal reckless and foolhardy. They did not believe that it was in Britain's interest to commit itself to using force to open the Straits, as this risked undermining its Middle East interests. Moreover, the ghost of the Suez campaign clearly hovered around the Cabinet table, and the ministers feared a repeat performance of 1956 when Britain and France were accused of carrying on an imperialist conspiracy. Only in this case, the ministers were aware, Britain might find itself alone in the dock without the French. In an explicit reference "to the Suez operation of 1956," the Cabinet noted that "it was in our interests not to be seen to be taking the lead in international action in the present situation."[122] Accordingly, the Cabinet was not willing to allow Britain to assume the lead in taking any kind of military measure in response to the closing of the Straits. Britain's role, if any, it decided, should be limited to following the lead of others. It may cooperate with other countries but that, the Cabinet thought, should be the extent of its commitment.

Seeking to quash Brown's, to its mind, ill-conceived proposal, the Cabinet proceeded to render it meaningless. It demanded that Britain take the backseat and act only within some kind of international framework. As there was no power willing to assume responsibility of pushing toward some kind of concrete military action against the blockade, this meant that nothing would be done. The Cabinet also decided that Britain should keep in constant touch with France, believing that the French proposal for a four-power meeting held hope of a solution to the crisis and should therefore be encouraged. Wilson thought this sudden enthusiasm for the French proposal a remarkable exercise in self-deception. It stemmed, he believed, from his ministers' desire to postpone the evil day when they might actually have to opt for some more robust action, such as, for example, Brown's task force.

The Cabinet did make one concession. It agreed that Britain was to try to secure an international declaration, signed by all the world's maritime nations, confirming the right of free passage through the Straits. The signatories would also declare their willingness to cooperate with each other, and with other governments, in seeking the general recognition of this principle. Finally, a naval task force, which would include as many nations as possible, would be organized and would be charged with breaking the Egyptian blockade and reopening the Straits of Tiran.[123] Cynics mocked the proposal for a naval task force, nicknaming it "Wilson's Red Sea Regatta," though it had originally been the idea of Aharon Remez, Israel's ambassador to London.

The Cabinet had managed to stop Wilson and Brown from involving Britain in any independent military measure, which would, in Callaghan's words, totally destroy Britain's economy. Nevertheless, it did agree, under extremely restrictive conditions, to the establishment of an international naval force and the publication of the joint international declaration on the freedom of the straits. So that even though, in essence, the Cabinet neutralized Brown's proposal, it did not quite revert to the Foreign Office's policy of keeping a low profile.

Of all the powers, Britain was the most anxious to defuse the crisis as quickly as possible and so it now began to step up its efforts to resolve it within the limits imposed Cabinet. First, however, in order to calm Israel's nerves, Wilson declared, in a speech given on May 24, that

It is the view of Her Majesty's Government in the United Kingdom, that the Straits of Tiran must be regarded as an international waterway [sic] through which the vessels of all nations have a right of passage. Her Majesty's Government will assert this right on behalf of all British shipping and is prepared to join with other [sic] to secure general recognition of this right.[124]

Wilson emphasized that Britain would be acting as part of a joint international effort, and would not take the lead in executing any military measure. He said much the same, in private, to Abba Eban, who had arrived in London that same day. The British Cabinet, Wilson informed Eban, had decided that Nasser must be not allowed to prevail so that Britain, in tandem with other states, would seek to reopen the Straits.[125]

Before coming to London, Eban had stopped over in Paris, where he had an extremely frustrating meeting with President de Gaulle. "Ne fait pas la Guerre," the president warned, adding that it would be an absolute catastrophe for Israel to attack Egypt. De Gaulle did not explicitly renounce France's commitment to uphold the principle of free passage through the Straits. But, he told Eban, 1967 is not 1957, and it was no longer possible to offer exclusively Western solutions to the problems of the Middle East. The Soviet Union must be a party to any effort made to resolve the current crisis. The best solution, de Gaulle suggested, was to allow the four powers to come together and devise a solution to conflict. Thus, however one looks at it, de Gaulle was tacitly abandoning France's commitment to Israel and the principle of free navigation. This becomes even more apparent when viewed in the context of some of the French government's recent decisions. One decision, for example, stated that France does not regard itself as associated with or committed to any of the rival sides in the Middle East and that the first side to employ force would automatically lose its support.[126] Clearly, having spent almost nine years, ever since de Gaulle first assumed power in May 1958, rehabilitating its position in the Arab world, France had no intention of sacrificing its hard-won achievement on Israel's account.

In his meetings with de Gaulle and Wilson, Eban drove home the fact that Israel will never allow Egypt to block the Straits. The port of Eilat, he emphasized, was vital to Israel's survival, and if it came to a choice between surrender and war, Israel would have no alternative but to opt for war.[127] Wilson proved more supportive and understanding than de Gaulle. He did not raise the question of whether Israel should fight, or who it was that fired the first shot in the conflict. But, like de Gaulle, Wilson did not see fit to offer Eban a guarantee that Britain would take concrete action to reopen the Straits. So that sympathy apart, Israel saw little essential difference between the two European powers' position; neither was ready to commit itself to stand by Israel's side. Nor did the Security Council appear to offer Israel any hope of salvation. The Security Council met on May 24, at the request of Denmark and Canada, but its discussions proved as futile and as fruitless as ever. It did not even set a date for its next meeting, which was quite remarkable in view of seriousness of the crisis.

Hoping to offer Eban some encouragement, Wilson mentioned the Cabinet's decision to help organize a naval task force. He also told Eban that George Thomson, the minister of state for foreign affairs, had been sent to Washington in order to sit down with the Americans and draw up an operational plan for the task force. Before Thomson left for the United States, the Cabinet had impressed upon him that he was not to commit Britain to any military or naval action. Furthermore, any action decided upon must take place within the framework of the United Nations. Thomson was also reminded that Britain was not to take the lead in promoting either the maritime declaration or organizing the task force. Finally, the Cabinet decreed any decision or action decided upon in Washington must first be subject to Cabinet scrutiny and sanction.[128]

Once Thomson arrived in Washington and the discussions over the naval task force began in earnest, it became apparent that neither side had a very good idea as to the exact nature of the force. Neither had given much thought to such basic questions as: What would happen if Egypt resists? Would the task force use military force? Would it, if necessary, bombard Egypt's airfields? Would additional forces be sent to the region? There was also the important question of what would happen after the task force reopened the Straits, as there was no guarantee that Egypt would not close them again later. One way to prevent this from happening was to provide Israel with a naval escort, which would accompany its ships to and from the port of Eilat. But this, too, was hardly a simple matter. First, there was the question of who would finance the escort. Second, this solution, which clearly nullified the achievements of the Sinai Campaign, would hardly meet with Israel's approval.[129] The British and American governments failed to consider these and other related questions. This all lends force to the suspicion that the proposal to establish a naval task force was dead from the word go, unless, of course, the two powers were prepared to come to blows with Egypt, regardless of the consequences, a highly unlikely scenario, as neither wanted a confrontation with the Arab world.

Thomson arrived in Washington armed with a two-part proposal to deal with the crisis. First, he suggested organizing an international declaration signed by all the maritime powers, which confirmed the right of free passage. Second, he proposed setting up a naval task force to force open the blockade. As the British plan extracted the United States from the embarrassing predicament of being unable to uphold the principle of free passage itself or to take any independent measures to stop the conflict from escalating into war, it was more than happy to embrace the both suggestions. The United States could now claim that it was fulfilling its obligation to maintain the freedom of passage through the Straits, and the notion of a naval force had the added attraction of giving the Egyptian president an honorable way out of the crisis.[130]

There was, however, Dean Rusk told Thomson, one small snag. The Senate had informed Johnson that it would only agree to U.S. participation in a joint multinational effort carried out under the auspices of the United Nations.[131] That was fine with Thomson. After all the British Cabinet had demanded no less. However, once the discussions began in earnest, Thomson discovered, to his dismay, two other far more serious snags. First, the Americans wanted Britain to take the lead in procuring the maritime declaration and organizing the naval force. Second, they had absolutely no idea what was involved in setting up and operating a naval force. The United States believed that, ideally, the powers should assemble a large and powerful fleet in the neighborhood of the Gulf of Aqaba, which would then mount continuous navel and air patrols. The Americans apparently forgot that the Gulf of Aqaba was a fairly narrow passageway and that as a result the naval force would be practically on top of Egypt's artillery units and air bases, and so vulnerable to attack. They certainly did not consider what would happen if the Egyptians were actually to attack the task force.[132] Obviously the United States had not given much, if any, serious thought to the task force's aim and composition. In all likelihood, it was hoping that Britain would, just as it later hoped Israel would, remove this unhappy burden from its shoulders and reopen the Straits itself by whatever means it saw fit.

Thomson did not give up and suggested to the Americans that it would be far better to send a modest naval force to the Gulf of Aqaba. Composed of small ships, the force would escort Israeli and other ships through the Straits of Tiran to the port of Eilat. True, the escort force would also be vulnerable to attack, but Thomson submitted the 6th Fleet and ships contributed by other maritime states would be sufficient to deter the Egyptians. The idea, of involving the 6th Fleet sent shivers down the Americans' collective spines, who rejected it out of hand. The composition and nature of the task force was not the only point of Anglo-American contention. The United States wanted Britain to take charge of the task force, most of whose ships, it argued, would in any case be British. The United States would assume the overall command of the naval operation. Now it was the British Cabinet's turn to shudder. It categorically rejected the idea that Britain should assume direct command of the task force. Britain, it insisted, was not to take the lead in using force against Egypt.[133]

In short, Anglo-American discussions on the naval task force had barely began before they had reached a dead end. Both Britain and the United States, rather than take any constructive steps to organize the task force, were intent upon throwing the burden of responsibility onto each other's shoulders. The most either was willing to do was to encourage other states to join the force. Unfortunately, so far, only Canada and Holland were willing to participate in the task force, and it did not seem likely that they would be joined by any other maritime power. This was the state of affairs when Abba Eban arrived in Washington.

In Washington, Eban was scheduled to meet President Johnson and senior administration officials. Originally he was supposed to discover where exactly the Americans stood on the question of the international naval task force. However, immediately upon his arrival in Washington, Eban received an urgent telegram from Eshkol changing the objective of his visit. Instead of focusing upon the closing of the Straits, Eban was to highlight the danger posed by the massive concentration of Egyptian forces in Sinai. He was to impress upon the Americans that the Arab world was preparing for a war to annihilate the state of Israel. As evidence of this, Eban was to point to the shift that had recently taken place in the deployment of Egyptian forces throughout the Sinai desert, that is, a shift that had indeed prompted Eshkol's telegram. He was also to draw the Americans' attention to the fact that the Syrian government had, at the same time, begun to concentrate its forces along Israel's northern border. In light of these recent developments, Eban was instructed to ask the United States to issue a declaration to the effect that it considered any attack against Israel as an attack against the United States itself.[134]

Having put his request to the Americans, Eban was told that, regretfully, the president could not offer such a commitment without first receiving Congress' permission and that, conversely, without the sanction of Congress, any presidential guarantee was meaningless. In any case, the administration officials observed they had no information pointing toward an imminent Egyptian attack. None of their intelligence sources suggested that Egypt was preparing a surprise attack. Nor did Egypt have any reason to attack Israel, as it had already achieved its aim by closing the Straits. Moreover, the United States did not think that the introduction of massive Egyptian forces into Sinai posed a threat to Israel. First, the Egyptian deployment in Sinai was defensive in nature. Second, it gave rise to some very complicated logistical problems, so that in the Pentagon's judgment, it was on Israel's side, with Egypt becoming weaker and more vulnerable with each passing moment.[135] Finally, if worse came to worst and Egypt were to attack Israel, American intelligence experts were certain that Israel could easily and quickly defeat the Arabs, even in the case of a three-front war. "You will whip the hell out of them," Johnson assured Eban.[136]

Their confident prognosis apart, the Americans were sufficiently concerned to convey a strongly worded warning to Egypt. President Johnson advised Nasser that if Egypt were to attack Israel the United States would act upon its commitment to defend Israel. The administration also asked the Soviet Union to restrain their unruly Middle East Ally.[137] It is worth noting that the Soviet Union itself had, only recently, warned Israel against embarking on a war. Kosygin had sent Eshkol a note asking him

to do everything in your power to avoid a clash of arms that will have serious consequences for the cause of peace and international security ... it is easy to light a fire, but to put one out is not so easy as may be imagined by those who are pushing Israel toward the abyss of war.[138]

During his meeting with Eban on May 26, Johnson admitted that Israel had the right to act as it saw fit, but warned that if it did decide to take unilateral action it would forfeit the support of the United States. "Israel," the president observed, "will not be alone, unless it decides to go alone." The president, Defense

Secretary Robert McNamara, Foreign Secretary Dean Rusk and other numerous American officials all impressed upon Eban the fact that the United States fully intended to stand by its commitments, but that, unfortunately, without the sanction of Congress any commitment to independent action meant naught. It was why, they explained, the United States wanted to, had to, explore and exhaust all other alternative courses of action, including working through the United Nations, though they admitted to sharing Israel's doubts regarding that organization's effectiveness. The United States, they promised, would also do all it could to procure an international maritime declaration and organize a naval task force to end the blockade.[139] All this demanded time and, once again, the Americans, like the British, asked Israel for more time to allow them to fulfill their obligations. In the meantime, Israel was requested to display maximum self-restraint.[140]

Eban returned home empty handed. Other than a promise to do something about the closing of the Straits, the Americans had failed to offer Israel the guarantee it so badly wanted and needed. Nor did it give Israel the hoped for green light to take action against the Egyptian forces in Sinai. George Thomson had also returned home with nothing to show. Nasser, by contrast, couldn't be happier. The past few days had revealed that the West was in the process of abandoning Israel, while he, by contrast, enjoyed the solid support of the Soviet Union. Hence, his triumphant speech to the Labour Unions, on May 26, in which he divulged that the Arab world was in the midst of a campaign to destroy the state of Israel.[141]

Britain did not limit its efforts to resolve the crisis to trying to organize a multinational task force in tandem with the United States. It also sought French and Soviet help to end the crisis. But here, too, as with its American allies, Britain was to be bitterly disappointed with the results of its efforts. While Thomson was busy getting nowhere in Washington, George Brown went to Moscow to elicit the help of the Soviet Union. Brown's visit, as noted, had been scheduled as far back as December 1966 and offered, or so Britain thought, an excellent opportunity to discuss the current crisis in the Middle East. Indeed, with the Middle East apparently on the verge of war, Brown's visit was devoted almost solely to the developing crisis.

In Moscow, Brown asked the Soviets to help arrest the region's mad dash into war. Britain assumed that despite the superpower or East-West rivalry in the Middle East, neither side wanted a military confrontation between Israel and the Arab states. Brown underlined the dangerous consequences accruing from Egypt's closing of the Straits. He warned that unless Nasser removed the blockade, a general conflagration might ensue. He pleaded with the Soviets to use their influence with the Egyptian president and defuse this explosive situation before it was too late. He assured them that the British government was doing its part and was pressing Israel not to take provocative action or to react hastily to provocations by the other side. And, he stressed, Israel was, so far, acting responsibly.[142] Unfortunately, the Soviet Union did not want to play ball. Indeed, a spectator sitting in on the talks between Brown and the Soviet leaders, Prime

Minister Kosygin, Foreign Minister Gromyko and President Nikolai Federenko, would be quick to conclude that the two sides were speaking about completely different events and in completely different languages.

Kosygin assured Brown that the Soviet Union had no wish or plan to provoke a conflagration in the Middle East. He asked Brown to tell Wilson that the Soviets "had no interest in a flare up and they would do all they could to prevent a conflict in the area."[143] Having said that, he immediately began to accuse everyone else of seeking to do precisely that. Just before the discussions with Brown began, the Soviet government had issued a statement that claimed that ever since Israeli troops had attacked the Syrian Arab Republic on April 7, Israel's ruling circles had been tirelessly engendering an atmosphere of military psychosis in that country. The statement also accused Israel of concentrating its forces in the north in preparation for a war against Syria.[144] During the discussions themselves, Kosygin went even further, and observed that Israel was far too weak to act in such provocative manner on its own volition. It could only afford to act aggressively thanks to the support it received from those countries that financed and supplied it with arms. These countries, or as Soviet terminology had it, certain imperialist circles, longed for the return of the era of colonial oppression, and regarded Israel as their principal weapon in their battle against the Arab world.[145]

Obviously, unless the Soviet Union wished to lose its hard-won position of influence in the Arab world, it had no alternative but to adopt this totally unhelpful and extremely contrary line. The Soviet Union knew that even the slightest hint that it was willing to cooperate with the West or work toward a common solution would enrage the Arabs and destroy its new and highly prized position. Nor should it be forgotten that the May crisis offered the Soviet Union an opportunity to increase its influence in the Arab world and finally achieve its ambition of becoming the preeminent power in the Middle East. The upshot was that the Soviet Union not only refused to cooperate with the West, but also that it shamelessly exploited the British and American efforts to end the blockade in order to depict the two powers as pro-Israel and anti-Arab.

Brown returned home convinced that even though the Soviet Union was worried about the situation in the Middle East, this did not mean that it was willing to cooperate to resolve the crisis, whether in the Security Council or in any other international forum. Soviet policy, Britain concluded, hadn't changed one iota, which was unfortunate, as it gave Nasser the confidence he needed to pursue his belligerent policies. To wit, only a few days after Brown's visit, on May 28, Egyptian War Minister Shams al Din Badran arrived in Moscow, where his Soviet counterpart was quick to assure him that Soviet help would be forthcoming the moment Egypt required it. Not surprisingly, the very next day Nasser was heard to declare, with enormous satisfaction, that the "Soviet Union supports us in this battle and will not allow any power to intervene."[146]

France, too, gave Britain no cause for joy. Britain had hoped to convince the French to join the Anglo-American efforts to end the blockade. Although acutely aware that French policy both in the Middle East and toward the Soviet Union had changed since de Gaulle came to power, Britain did not appreciate the extent of the change. Above all, it failed to realize the degree to which France's attitude toward Israel had altered, something, that, for example, had become very clear to Eban in the course of his talks with the French president.

When discussing the Straits crisis with the French, the British highlighted the imminent threat of war. They emphasized that the only way to prevent preemptive Israeli action was for the international community itself to take action to keep the Straits open. Britain agreed that any action must, in the first instance, be carried out within the framework of the United Nations. Nevertheless, it pointed out, there was no guarantee that the United Nations would succeed in resolving the crisis, so that it was essential to consider alternative courses of action. Sensitive to de Gaulle's prejudices, Britain was very careful to avoid giving the efforts to organize a multinational task force with an Anglo-Saxon hue. It stressed that any plan must be international in character and supported by as many countries as possible. Britain flattered France, that Britain was particularly interested in discussing with it the various possible courses of action to end the blockade. This much was true, not least because France had a fleet stationed in Djibouti, which, Britain suggested, might play an important role in any future naval operation.[147]

But the French did not want to play any kind of role in any kind of naval force, which seemed to them an exclusively Western and, for all Britain's efforts, Anglo-Saxon, initiative. It certainly had no intention of putting its Djibouti fleet at the service of such a force. Britain's ambassador in Paris wrote gloomily that the French would do anything to avoid taking a stand on the current crisis, and they would certainly refuse to participate in any joint physical intervention in the area should one become necessary. He pointed out that having made great efforts to reclaim France's position in the Arab world, de Gaulle would not be willing to sacrifice France's restored position on the altar of the Straits. Moreover, the ambassador continued, France feared that its participation in the naval task force might endanger its economic and, above all, oil interests in the Middle East. It would also wreck de Gaulle's efforts to pursue an independent French policy in the Third World.[148]

Despite the ambassador's discouraging, yet by and large accurate, analysis of French policy, France was by no means indifferent to the crisis in the Middle East. However, it insisted that the solution to the affair lay in the realm of a four-power settlement. By raising the idea of a four-power solution, yet again, France hoped to achieve two things. First, it hoped to avoid any involvement in an exclusively Western action and second, to highlight and underline its status as one of the world's great powers. In other words, France wanted to demonstrate that it was not playing second fiddle to the Anglo-Saxon powers.[149]

Britain didn't have much faith in the outcome of a four-power meeting on the assumption, of course, that the two superpowers would agree to such a meeting in the first place. The United States, for example, although it didn't rule out the idea of a four-power settlement, didn't really favor it either. It assumed that such a gathering contained the risk of Franco-Soviet collaboration, which, proving counterproductive, might have some very dangerous consequences indeed.[150] Nevertheless, Britain accepted the French proposal, though more as a tactical maneuver than anything else. It was, Wilson explained, one way "to get the French fully engaged in a process which, if the Russians refused to play, could lead to closer co-operation between the French and ourselves."[151] It would get the French involved in the Anglo-American efforts through the back door. It would also pull the carpet out from under de Gaulle's claim that, so far, all the solutions to the crisis suggested had been exclusively Western.[152] In any case, the four-power meeting just might work or, at the very least, alert the Soviet Union to the dangers of a confrontation with the West in a part of the world where neither side could confidently expect to control its respective clients.[153] Of course, the Soviet Union first had to agree to meet with the three Western powers, and, apparently, it was in no hurry to do so.

This was the situation when Eban returned home from Washington. Five whole days had passed since Nasser had declared the Straits closed, and there was still no solution to the crisis in sight. Britain, for all its efforts, had failed to persuade its fellow powers to take action. In Moscow, Brown had received naught but a cold shower. De Gaulle stubbornly refused to cooperate, other than on his own terms. The United States was more than happy to discuss ways of ending the blockade, but was extremely limited in the kind of action it could take. The Israeli Cabinet, which had originally agreed to delay its response for forty-eight hours, had now to decide what to do. Should it now grant a further extension, as the Americans and British requested, or should it take action to resolve the crisis itself?

Eshkol was by now under immense pressure from the army to do something. His military chiefs hammered away at Eshkol demanding that Israel go to war. Ezer Weizman, for example, the head of Military Operations, insisted that Israel had no choice but to wage war on Egypt. He admitted that it would be a tough and difficult war, but to wait would be far more dangerous and would only make matters worse. Rabin emphasized that the price of further delay would be a greater number of Israeli casualties, and in making this extremely sensitive point, he was very much representative of military opinion as a whole. Yet, Eshkol, surprisingly, once again managed to withstand this forceful and highly emotive military barrage. He informed his army chiefs that like it or not Israel could neither exist nor fight without the help and support of the West and, above all, of the United States. Accordingly, it must carefully consider the American reaction before it took any kind of military action.[154]

The Israeli government met on the night of May 27–28 to discuss the crisis. Having heard Eban's report on his meetings in Europe and especially with the American administration, the Cabinet was convinced that war was inevitable. Even Eshkol spoke of the need to hone Israel's weapons in preparation for the inevitable confrontation.[155] In course of the meeting, the Cabinet received several notes from both Britain and the United States. The British asked for more time to find a solution to the crisis. The State Department affirmed that the

United States was abiding by its commitments and that the president was determined to take action to end the blockade. Moreover, both Britain and the United States were busy implementing the plan to organize an international naval escort in the Gulf of Aqaba. President Johnson personally enjoined the Israeli government not to embark upon a war and to allow the United States to exhaust all the possible methods of solving the crisis peacefully. Unilateral action on Israel's part, he warned, would be both irresponsible and catastrophic. He advised Eshkol that Kosygin was claiming that the Soviet Union had information that Israel was embarking upon military preparations with the intention of carrying out an armed aggression against its neighboring Arab states, and had warned that if Israel were to attack the Arab states, the Soviet Union would support and aid its Allies to the full.[156]

It seems unlikely that it was Kosygin's threat that finally persuaded Israel to delay its response and allow more time for diplomacy to play its part. The main reason Eshkol and his ministers acceded to the British and American requests was to ensure that Israel had the latter's support should war break out. At the same time, the Israeli government decided to send the head of the Israeli Mossad, General Meir Amit, to Washington to discover exactly and firsthand the U.S. position on the crisis. Having agreed to postpone any independent Israeli action, Eshkol then wrote to Johnson, emphasizing that "it is crucial that the international naval escort should move through the Straits within a week or two."[157] Accordingly, the Americans assumed that they had a week or two to come up with a diplomatic solution before Israel would take action.

In his memoirs, Eban asserts that Israel's decision to defer its response was a sign of political acumen and moral sensibility.[158] In retrospect, there would appear to be some justification to Eban's rather self-congratulatory claim, at least as far as Israel's political acumen was concerned. However, it is impossible to ignore the fact that Israel was genuinely afraid that unless it acquired the active, material support of the powers, its very existence was at risk. This fear was later proved to be completely groundless. But Eshkol, like his predecessor Ben Gurion, was firmly convinced that Israel could not take any kind of action without first receiving the blessing and protection of the West.[159] Nor is it possible when considering why Israel agreed to a further delay to discount Eshkol's own hesitant and indecisive nature.

Whatever the reasons behind Israel's agreement to delay its response, Britain heaved a great sigh of relief. Not that it thought that there was any effective solution to the crisis in sight. Its own furious efforts to galvanize its fellow powers into action had come to nothing. Nor had it any interest in taking upon itself the task to end the blockade for fear of damaging British interests in the Arab world. But, of course, even Britain's modest efforts to terminate the blockade had convinced the Arab states that Britain stood by Israel and that its policy was geared to serve Israeli interests. How else were they to explain the fact that in the beginning of June, Wilson planned to travel to the United States to meet with President Johnson to discuss the crisis. Accordingly, Arab threats to cripple

Britain's interests became louder, more violent and more frequent. In the meantime, Britain was in the process of being slowly converted to the American view that, in the absence of a multinational naval task force, war was inevitable. And because a war would in any case undermine its interests in the region, then Britain would much rather see an Israeli victory than an Egyptian one.

A SHORT LULL AND THE FINAL DENOUEMENT

The Israeli decision to delay its response gave the two Western powers a much-needed breathing space. Yet, curiously, or perhaps not, their efforts to persuade other states to sign the maritime declaration or join the naval task force moved at a rather leisurely pace. This was particularly true of the United States. Nor, as Britain's representatives gathered from their ongoing conversation with the Americans, was there much chance of anything changing in the future. True, the United States was still committed to reopening the Straits and, more important, to Israel's continued existence. But Congress, living in fear of another Vietnam, had tied the administration's hands and insisted that the United States act only within some kind of official international framework. Throughout their discussions with the British, the Americans not only showed no particular sense of urgency, but also clearly preferred to throw the responsibility for opening the Straits firmly onto its ally's shoulders. Utterly at odds with British policy, it was a burden Britain refused to accept.[160] By the end of May to the beginning of June, the naval task force had become a dead duck. Yet it was obvious that unless a satisfactory way, satisfactory to Israel, that is, was found to open the Straits and keep them open, Israel, who would never accept the current situation, would take action to open them itself. But could a satisfactory solution be found?

Any return to the status quo ante was, Britain realized, completely unrealistic. The only settlement Nasser would agree to was one that gave Egypt total control of the Straits. On the other hand, Israel would utterly reject any settlement that didn't guarantee it the right of free passage through the Straits. In its eyes, anything less would be viewed as an ugly and dangerous defeat. Nevertheless, Britain toyed with the idea of a compromise agreement, according to which the Straits would remain under Egyptian control, so that Egypt would retain the right to inspect the ships sailing through the Straits and maintain forces in Sharem el Sheik. However, and this was the point, oil would be excluded from the list of strategic materials that could not be transported through the Straits. Britain hoped that this compromise would be acceptable to both sides, as it thought it would not undermine Nasser's prestige or entail a capitulation on Israel's part.[161] The British may have discussed this compromise among themselves and may even have considered raising it in the Security Council, which was to convene on May 29. There is, however, no evidence that they mentioned it either to Israel or Egypt. It seems likely that they personally had little faith in the compromise's chances of success, and the whole idea was no more of a desperate intellectual exercise.

Convinced that war was in the offing, Britain made one last-ditch attempt to convince the Soviet Union to help end the crisis. Apparently, the British government had still not assimilated the fact that the Soviet Union stood totally and unconditionally by Egypt's side, something that had, after all, been amply demonstrated in the course of Brown's visit to Moscow. Or perhaps it was simply a measure of Britain's desperation. Whatever the case, Wilson now appealed directly to Kosygin, and on May 28, he sent the Soviet prime minister a note, emphasizing that

the urgent problem confronting us today is the preservation of peace in the Middle East.... we are on common ground in the search for peace and all of us have a clear duty to make every effort in our power to prevent a situation from developing which could lead to a major confrontation between the great powers of the world.... I believe we are confronted with a situation of great urgency and great danger.[162]

Kosygin did not bother to reply to Wilson's appeal. Not that the British prime minister was left in any doubt as to how Kosygin would have answered his note. On May 29, the Soviet Union formally rejected the French suggestion that the four powers meet and discuss the crisis. Apart from anything else, the Soviets probably realized that the Arab states were less than enthusiastic about this course of action, which smacked of great power dictation. The Soviet Union also claimed that Israel and its aggressive policies, especially toward Syria, were responsible for the crisis, and accused certain circles in the United States of condoning and encouraging Israel's belligerent actions.[163] Accordingly, the Soviet government concluded that even though the Soviet Union was doing all it could to preserve the peace in the region, there was, in the circumstances, very little point in any four-power meeting.

Soviet obduracy was pressed home during the discussions in the Security Council, which had convened that same day. Britain and Canada had submitted a joint proposal to the Council. Their proposal, which had already won the approval of the secretary general, called for the establishment of an international force, which would be under the authority and control of the cease-fire committee. The force would be stationed on both sides of the border, that is, in Israeli territory, too. In addition, there was to be a demilitarized zone along the Egyptian-Israeli border, with both Israel and Egypt withdrawing their forces from the area.[164] The Soviet Union, who, throughout the Security Council's discussions, had adopted a blatantly pro-Egyptian and partisan stand and who did not want it to even appear as though it approved of a solution that lacked Arab support, promptly vetoed the British-Canadian proposal.

A few days earlier, Nasser put forward his own solution to the crisis. According to Nasser, the Straits of Tiran should be recognized as part of the United Arab Republic's territorial waters; all the cease-fire agreements, including the article calling for the demilitarization of the Nitzana, should be implemented in full; Israel was to withdraw from all the demilitarized zones that do not belong to it and the United Nations was to station its forces in these areas in its stead.

The Egyptian leader had no doubt that Israel would reject his proposal. And he was absolutely right. Israel considered Nasser's terms utterly unacceptable. They overturned the achievements of the Sinai Campaign. Worse, they validated and consolidated Nasser's latest aggressive actions.[165]

Nasser's "generous" proposal was in all likelihood little more than an exercise in public relations. It certainly did not mark the limit of Egypt's ambitions. The Egyptian president was well aware that Israel was suffering under the burden of international isolation. There was, to his mind, no evidence that the West, above all Britain and the United States, had offered Israel any practical or effective support. Nor was Israel's situation at home much better. It had had been forced to mobilize its entire reserve force, thus bringing its economy to an almost complete standstill. Its government was weak and indecisive, and the mood throughout the country was downcast and dejected. Not surprisingly, Nasser began to glory in Israel's impending destruction. In a speech before the Egyptian National Assembly on May 29, he proclaimed: "I have said in the past that we would decide the time and place and that we must prepare ourselves in order to win.... Preparations have already been made. We are now ready to confront Israel."[166]

In Nasser's view what the Straits crisis was really about was not the Gulf of Aqaba, but Palestine and the rights of the Palestinian people. That was what was really at stake. He saw Egypt's return to Sinai and the closing of the Straits as the return to the circumstances that had preceded the 1956 war and that he regarded, in turn, as the first step toward restoring the situation in Palestine as it had been before the founding of the state of Israel. All his recent actions had been part of a carefully designed plan to achieve this end. The American embassy in Cairo reported to the State Department that Nasser genuinely believed that the Arab states were capable of crushing Israel on the battlefield and that every single Egyptian official the embassy had spoken to shared this belief. This sense of power, the conviction that Egypt was able to confront and vanquish Israel, the embassy's report concluded, has been present for some months now.[167] Nasser bore out the embassy's analysis by ordering the Egyptian air force to fly over Israeli airspace in a clear demonstration of his resolve and confidence in Egypt's power.

In stark contrast to Nasser's fierce determination, the mood in Israel was one of tense and anxious expectation. Unaware of just how indeterminate Britain and U.S. efforts to promote the naval task force were, it still waited for some progress on this issue. The British government was very much aware of the fact that Israel was, by now, close to panicking. It knew that Prime Minister Eshkol, who served as a defense minister also, was under enormous pressure; that his army was pressing him to go to war; that a large part of the Israeli political establishment was demanding his replacement, or that he, at least, give up the Defense portfolio—in short Eshkol's leadership was under threat.[168]

Eban met with Michael Hadow. He told the ambassador that Israel expected immediate international action to reopen the Straits. Statements and declarations of support were all very well, but that in absence of concrete action they meant absolutely nothing. Time, Eban urged, was of the essence, and Israel must know what Britain and the United States planned to do.[169] Yigal Allon, Israel's minister of labor and one of the more powerful figures in Cabinet, also spoke to Hadow, underlining Israel's resolute, uncompromising position vis-à-vis the Straits. He told the ambassador that even though Israel was willing to assume that substantial measures have been taken to organize the naval task force, it could only wait so long for these to take effect.[170]

The mood in Israel, once it had decided to accede to the U.S. request for another, second delay, was a mixture of confusion and bewilderment. It had no clear idea how to secure free passage for its ships through the Straits, short of war. On the other hand, it was becoming more and more apparent the neither the British nor the Americans were willing to take the lead, either together or separately, to form a naval task force or implement any kind of independent measure to end the blockade. The two states stuck firmly to the principle that all action to free the Straits must take place within an international framework.

With each passing day, the United States and Britain appeared more feeble and more impotent, totally incapable of resolving the crisis. Conversely, and perhaps not surprisingly, the Arab threats to damage Western interests became more frequent and more vocal, with Britain and British economic interests topping the list. Britain, Nasser thundered, had obviously failed to learn the lesson of Suez 1956, and in so saying was very much representative of the general feeling in the Arab world. One of the more aggressively outspoken Arab states, Kuwait threatened to end the export of oil to the West and to end the operations of British petroleum companies. This was extremely worrying, as Britain assumed that once Kuwait acted upon its threat, Libya and Iraq would be quick to follow suit. This was a nightmare scenario. The Wilson government had gone a long way toward stabilizing the British economy. It had lowered taxes, cut the budget and pared down its airspace industry, reducing the number of airplanes and aircraft carriers Britain manufactured yearly. Nevertheless, the British economy could ill-afford the Arab states to carry out their threats. Although the interruption of Britain's oil supply would, admittedly, be less of a problem in the immediate future, it would have a disastrous effect on Britain's oil reserves. Moreover, if Arabs forced the British oil companies out of the Middle East and the oil-producing countries closed their accounts in England's banks, Britain's balance of payments would soon collapse.[171] All in all, Britain would experience such severe economic difficulties that it would be forced to do the inconceivable and devalue the pound sterling.

The question facing the British Cabinet was what should it do now. Should it continue along the lines decided in Cabinet on May 23? Or should it, in light of the changed circumstances, take independent measures to end the blockade? On May 30, the Cabinet gathered to discuss these questions. Wilson and Brown, who had again conferred beforehand, agreed that Britain must uphold the principle of free passage through the Straits of Tiran, though Wilson did emphasize that he opposed the idea of Britain going it alone.[172]

In Cabinet, Wilson found that he now enjoyed the full support of his minister of defense. Healy brandished a report by the Chiefs of Staff Committee, which examined the whole question of reopening the Straits. In its report, the Committee highlighted the fact that Egypt's air, ground and naval forces had full control of the Gulf of Aqaba. Accordingly, any action to reopen the Straits entailed grave military risks, and required careful and detailed military planning. In the Committee's view, the most appropriate course of action for Britain to take would be to organize a small naval force that would escort merchant shipping through the Straits of Tiran and Gulf of Aqaba. As the naval escort would need direct and indirect air and naval support, the Committee suggested forming a support force in the Eastern Mediterranean. It added that, in its opinion, it would be advisable, at least during the first stages of the operation, to station an additional combined air and naval force in the Gulf of Aden. Finally, the Chiefs of Staff's report emphasized that the composition of both the naval escort and its support forces must be international.[173]

In Cabinet, Healy raised some doubts about the American commitment to act jointly with Britain. Banking on the Americans, he thought, was a gamble and not a very safe one at that. There was no guarantee that in the final count the United States would not desert Britain and leave it in the lurch. Healy then proceeded to underline the risks involved in Britain assuming the lead in the effort to end the blockade. Britain, he argued, would look like a pathetic, has-been imperial power trying in vain to reassert its suzerainty, at a time when it lacks all power to do so. Moreover, its activities would line up all the Arab states plus the Afro-Asian bloc against it.[174]

George Brown took the opposite view. The foreign minister argued that no matter what Britain did, the Arabs, who assumed that Britain acted solely and exclusively in Israel's interests, would damn it. Even if Britain stood aside and did nothing "we should be widely believed in the Arab world to be on Israel's side, a belief already being forged in Soviet propaganda."[175] It was manifest, Brown concluded, that it was beyond Britain power to prevent the Arab states from undermining its interests. He elaborated that it could do little to prevent the closing of the Suez Canal to British shipping, the disruption of Britain's oil supply or the termination of Britain's oil companies operations. Nor could it stop the oil-producing countries from withdrawing their money from Britain's banks. But, at least, he admonished his fellow ministers, it could do something constructive to stop the war.

Brown failed to convince the Cabinet. In the duel between the foreign and defense ministers, the latter won the day, not the least because he had the prime minister's support. The Cabinet decided to stick with its previous decision that Britain must not take the lead in any action to reopen the Straits. Likewise, it confirmed that Britain should from now on limit its efforts to enlisting as much support as possible for an international maritime declaration, asserting the right of innocent passage through the Gulf of Aqaba. Although the Cabinet acknowledged that recent developments in the Middle

East and especially Israel's predicament were worrying in the extreme, on balance, it elected to give priority to Britain's interests in the Arab world. It noted that:

Whatever our sympathies with Israel might be, our economic interests lie primarily in the Arab countries; in particular we were heavily dependent on their oil. Bearing in mind both these interests and our wider interests in avoiding a conflict in this area as elsewhere, it was therefore of crucial importance to us that we should avoid either participation in a solely or primarily Anglo-American force to assert effectively the freedom of navigation in the Gulf of Aqaba, or even in taking the lead in seeking to organise a fully multinational force for this purpose. If one were organised we might play some part in it. But it seemed doubtful whether in fact such a force could be established.[176]

Evidently the Cabinet preferred a policy that, to its mind, would keep to a minimum the damage inflicted upon British interests. It is worth noting, however, that if no solution to the crisis were found and war erupted, the Cabinet much preferred an Israeli victory. Admittedly, an Israeli victory would have several deleterious consequences, but the Cabinet realized that an Egyptian victory, and not necessarily a victory on the battlefield, would have far worse repercussions. True, the Straits issue would be resolved, but on Nasser's own terms. As a result, Nasser's prestige and standing in the Arab world would rocket. This, in turn, would pave the way to the collapse of the pro-western Arab regimes such as Kuwait and Saudi Arabia, countries in which most of Britain's interests were concentrated. An Egyptian victory would also advance and consolidate the Soviet Union's influence in the region. Although the supply of Middle East oil to the West would probably continue, it would do so under much more onerous financial terms and presumably be dependent on the predilections of basically hostile and pro-Soviet regimes. Finally, an Egyptian victory meant that the threat to Israel's existence remained, that the Arab states would inevitably embark upon a war for its destruction.[177]

While Britain and the United States were slowly but surely abandoning the idea of joint action to open the Straits, the Middle East continued its headlong rush into war. Israel appreciated the two powers' expressions of sympathy and understanding, but it could hardly ignore the fact that, so far, they had done nothing to resolve the crisis. As far as Israel could see, things had come to a complete standstill. Even the prospective maritime declaration now seemed little more than a sterile expedient; after the United States had informed Israel that as it wished to secure the largest number of signatures possible, the declaration would not contain the threat to use force.[178] Yet just when matters seemed to have reached an impasse, several events occurred that brought the situation to a head and forced Israel to reach a decision one way or another.

As noted, the Israeli government had decided to send the head of the Mossad, General Meir Amit, to Washington to ascertain the precise views of the United States on the crisis. Neither Eban's reports nor the reports of the Israeli embassy in Washington had provided the government with a sufficiently clear picture of American policy. Ambassador Herman, Consul Evron and, it seems, Eban himself had all assured Eshkol that President Johnson had promised to take all the measures necessary to open the Straits of Tiran to international shipping. The Americans themselves, however, informed Eshkol that the president had no authority to give such a commitment, and that the foreign minister's report did not accord with what Johnson had actually said in his meeting with Eban.[179] General Amit's task was to learn, prima facie, where the United States stood on the crisis and what it meant to do about it. Was it going to organize an international naval force or was it all just empty talk? Most crucially, Amit was to discover how the United States would react if Israel took independent action.[180]

Amit arrived in Washington on May 30. He left behind him an Israel rent by grave economic and political difficulties. The mobilization of its entire reserve force had by now brought the Israeli economy to a complete standstill. There was enormous internal pressure to change the political system. The public was on the verge of hysteria and clamoring for action. The army, angry and distraught at Eshkol's stubborn refusal to go war, was possibly close to a revolt. Day in and day out without fail the General Staff reminded Eshkol that with every passing minute the number of Israeli casualties would mount, once war, as it surely will, came.

In Washington, General Amit met with various Pentagon and administration officials, and it was not long before he realized that no progress whatsoever had been made toward organizing a naval task force. Richard Helms, the head of the CIA, told Amit quite bluntly: "There is no task force, there is no armada of maritime powers and there is no constructive plan of action."[181] Nor was there any chance of the United States or indeed of anyone else taking independent action to reopen the Straits. The task force had sunk without a trace, without even having left the drawing board. On the other hand, though nothing was said, at least not in so many words, Amit got the strong impression that the Americans would not object to Israel taking independent action to bring the blockade to an end. In fact, he concluded that they would welcome a successful Israeli military offensive against Nasser. How else was he to explain Secretary McNamara's response after Amit had revealed to him that he was going to go home and recommend to his government that it go to war; "I really understand you," McNamara had exclaimed.[182]

American policy had manifestly undergone a swift and drastic transformation. Only days earlier, President Johnson and other administration officials had warned Israel against going to war on its own initiative, lest it find itself alone, isolated and without American support. Yet, not once during Amit's entire visit did the Americans, on their own initiative, raise the question of war. Nor did they seem particularly perturbed by the prospect of war. Two factors had contributed to this sudden and surprising change of heart. First, the United States had finally given up on the naval task force, not the least because by the time Amit met with McNamara, still only two countries—Canada and Holland—had agreed to join the force. Britain, of course, had long suspected, and was by now firmly convinced, that the United States itself had been, at best, half hearted about the whole project. Second, and more significantly, May 30, 1967, was the date Jordan and Egypt had signed a joint defense agreement.[183]

With war seemingly drawing ever closer, King Hussein was fast becoming convinced that in order to survive Jordan must join forces with Egypt. Ever since the Samua raid, his kingdom had been in turmoil. Suffering under the burden of widespread riots and political agitation, the threat to Hussein's rule grew daily. In these circumstances, the king was convinced that by failing to join the war, if and once it broke out, he would, in effect, be signing his and the Hashemite regime's death warrant. What is more, it made absolutely no difference whether the war ended in victory or defeat, the end result, as far as Jordan was concerned, would be the same. If the war ended in defeat, Hussein would be held personally responsible for the debacle. He would be accused of refusing to open a third front against Israel and thus ensuring Israel's destruction. He would be damned as the servant of imperialism and condemned as a traitor to the Arab cause. But if Egypt won, he would be reviled for refusing to support both the principle of Arab unity and the Palestinian cause. Either way, civil war would erupt in Jordan. In short, Hussein assumed he was facing a choice of fighting a war against Israel or a civil war at home.[184]

The Jordan-Egyptian Defense Agreement was signed on May 30, 1967, in Cairo. According to the agreement, an armed attack against one of the signatories would be regarded as an attack on both, and during a war the two would use all the means available, including their armed forces, to assist one another. It was further agreed that, in case of war, the Egyptian chief of staff would assume the overall command of all military operations. The Defense Agreement was valid for five years and subject to automatic renewal.

On his journey home, Hussein was accompanied by one of his bitterest and most ruthless enemies: the PLO Chairman, Ahmed Shukairy. Like the fact that the agreement was signed in Cairo, Nasser's capital, this was a symbolic gesture, intended to signal the revival of Arab unity under Nasser's leadership. The Defense Agreement underscored Nasser's power and prestige within the Arab world. Conversely, the fact that Jordan, one of the West's traditional regional allies, had aligned itself with Egypt, weakened and undermined the West's already waning prestige and influence in the Middle East. The United States took a very serious view of the Egyptian-Jordanian Defense Agreement, which, in its opinion, had raised Arab militancy to new and alarming heights. It had created a frightening situation in the Middle East from which the only way out appeared to be an Israeli military initiative.

For Israel the Egyptian-Jordanian Defense Agreement was the last straw. It now found itself struggling under the burden of a blockade and surrounded on all three sides by an alliance of bitter enemies, all of whom seemed raring for a fight. According to Rabin, Israel was being slowly strangled to death by an Arab military and political noose, which no one was willing to help it remove.[185] Clearly, if Israel wished to avoid destruction it had to save itself. A decision had to be made and made now.

Moshe Dayan, Israel's chief of staff during the Suez Campaign and one of Israel's most admired military heroes, now entered the picture. On June 1, Eshkol finally reshuffled and expanded his government. He included two members of the opposition in the government, one of who was the opposition leader Mena-chem Begin. This was a revolutionary step in itself. Much more significant was Eshkol's decision to relinquish the Defense Portfolio and appoint Dayan in his stead. The appointment did wonders for public morale, and the army, which had been hankering for a resolute and decisive leader, capable of making difficult de-cisions, was delighted. More crucially, Dayan's appointment meant that the decision to go to war now gathered momentum.[186] Dayan took it for granted that the United States would not stand by its commitment to Israel. He further assumed that the discussions between the Americans and British were so much empty talk and led nowhere. War, Dayan insisted, was the only solution, and Is-rael must go to war soon, either on June 4 or 5.

It is possible that one of the reasons the decision to go war now kicked into a higher gear was the reports Israel had recently received to the effect that the United States was considering some kind of compromise deal with the Egyptian president. It is hard to judge what exactly the United States had in mind or how serious it was, as the talks between the Americans and Egyptians ended almost before they begun. In the last week of May, in an effort to relieve if not resolve the crisis, the Johnson administration sent a two-man mission to Egypt. It con-sisted of Charles Yost, a senior American diplomat and special adviser to the State Department, and Robert Anderson, who had been secretary of the trea-sury under Eisenhower and was on reasonably friendly terms with Nasser.[187] During their talks with the Egyptian president, it soon became clear to both Americans that Nasser, intractable as ever, would not compromise over the Straits. As far as he was concerned, they were to remain under exclusive and ab-solute Egyptian sovereignty.[188] Nasser's inflexible position was also apparent in a note he sent President Johnson, listing Israel's sins one by one. Nasser de-nounced Israel's aggression against Syria and its violation of the 1949 cease-fire agreements. He justified the introduction of Egypt's troops into the Sinai Penin-sula as a precautionary measure designed to combat Israel's aggressive policies. Finally, he raised the issue of the rights of the Palestinian people and the refugee problem.[189] It seems likely that Nasser's intransigent note only reinforced John-son's growing belief that military action was the only solution to the crisis.

Nonetheless, in one final last-ditch effort, Johnson decided to send Vice Pres-ident Hubert Humphrey to Cairo to reason with Nasser. It was also decided that on June 7, at the same time that Humphrey would be meeting Nasser, Egyptian Vice-President Zakaria Muhieddin would go to Washington, D.C. On June 3, Cairo released an announcement to this effect. Richard Nolte, the U.S. ambas-sador to Cairo, believed that Muhieddin's visit offered a genuine opportunity to find a constructive solution to the Straits problem.[190] Israel, however, feared the sole result of these talks would be a compromise at its expense. Effi Evron, the Israeli consul in Washington, warned presidential adviser Walter Rostow that the only solution acceptable to Nasser would be one that amounted to an ab-solute Egyptian victory. Such a solution would contain even greater dangers than those present in the current situation, as it meant that, one way or another,

Nasser would gain control over Jordan, Lebanon and the Arabian Peninsula. The only valid solution, Evron insisted, is one that demonstrated to all that Nasserist aggression had failed and failed miserably.[191]

Back in Britain, with the Middle East rapidly moving toward war, Wilson decided to go Washington and discuss the crisis with President Johnson personally. On the face of it, it seems a curious decision, as by now it was apparent, even to Britain, that there was no peaceful solution to the Straits crisis. The Security Council, which had met on May 29, had proved no more able to resolve this crisis than any other of the crises that afflicted the region. Its discussions, rather than reflecting any common desire to settle the problem of the Straits, had quickly degenerated into another tiresome and futile Cold War wrangle. With the Soviet Union promptly vetoing any resolution that offered even a glimmer of a solution, there was clearly no reason to look to the Security Council for salvation or, for that matter, to the United States.

Britain, like Israel, had, at least initially, failed to understand the actual position of the United States. There was an enormous gulf between the Americans' theoretical commitment to the principle of free navigation through the Straits and their willingness or ability to do something about it. U.S. efforts to organize a naval task force were halfhearted at best. It certainly wasn't prepared to assume any military obligations itself. Throughout their talks with Britain's representatives, the Americans displayed a combination of feebleness and indifference and were obviously much more interested in throwing the burden of reopening the Straits onto Britain's shoulders. In light of the above, Wilson's journey to Washington was probably a last minute and desperate gamble to resolve the crisis and prevent a war that, regardless of who fired the first shot, would gravely undermine British interests.

The changes in the Israeli political scene—Dayan's appointment and the inclusion of the right-wing Menachem Begin in the government—were clear evidence that Israel, too, preferred a military solution. Yet it is worth emphasizing that the British government, perhaps influenced by Hadow's optimistic reports, did not think that the political changes in Israel necessarily meant that Israel would opt for war. Quite the reverse. Britain believed that Dayan's appointment might have a positive, calming effect. The appointment, by reassuring the Israeli public, served to strengthen and stabilize the government, so that certain of strong public support, it would have the confidence to pursue a more moderate and restrained policy. The new Israeli government would think very carefully before embarking upon another reckless military adventure.[192] The British government hoped this would give diplomacy another eight or ten days to come up with a solution. Hence, perhaps, Wilson's decision to go to Washington. If so, he was to be gravely disillusioned on all counts.

Before meeting Johnson, Wilson first conferred with Canadian Prime Minister Lester Pearson. Canada's policy had, so far, been in complete accord with Britain's. The two countries had tabled a joint resolution regarding the Straits to the Security Council. Canada had also been one of the two countries that had endorsed the maritime declaration and was willing to join a naval task force. In the course of his meeting with Wilson, Pearson suggested a new solution to the crisis. He proposed leaving the whole question of Egypt's sovereignty over the Straits of Tiran open, provided that Egypt did not enforce its professed rights over the Straits. Instead the United Arab Republic, perhaps jointly with a UN representative, would inspect ships passing through the Straits. Israel, on its part, would accept the presence of UN forces on its territory.

Wilson thought Pearson's proposal might just work, because it offered enough room to maneuver and allowed both sides to save face. But there was, sadly, one stumbling bloc: the Soviet Union. "The Russians," Wilson sighed, "seemed to have no incentive for negotiations."[193] The Soviet Union refused to sit down and hammer out a constructive solution to the crisis. But, if not a solution to the crisis, Pearson did, at least, offer Wilson some useful advice, warning him that it was virtually impossible to pin down the American president on the subject of this crisis. This was, at least, Pearson's own impression, having discussed the crisis with President Johnson only a week earlier.[194] Wilson was soon to experience firsthand the president's wavering indecision.

Wilson's talks with President Johnson and other administration officials proved a tremendous disappointment. President Johnson was painfully pessimistic, insisting that there was no solution to the crisis. He had clearly completely given up on the maritime declaration and naval task force. "Who," he asked rhetorically,

would enforce this declaration? Who would provide the ships for any maritime force, which might be created to implement it? The United States and presumably the United Kingdom might be counted on; but who else was there?[195]

Secretary of State Rusk echoed his president's gloom and added a few doubts of his own, telling Wilson that the decision to escort the ships through the Straits was likely to result in a confrontation with Egyptian military forces. An attack by the Egyptian air force, in such a narrow sea passage, would demand a counterattack, with the result, Rusk confessed, that the administration would be hard pressed to get Congress to sanction any kind of military operation. The president also admitted to being horribly worried that Israel would, in the next day or two, take matters into its own hands and, without any prior warning, go it alone. It seems that Johnson, as General Meir Amit had rightly concluded, had reconciled himself to the fact that the solution to the crisis lay in an Israeli military offensive.

Curiously, the Americans were all the while careful to reassure Wilson that they would keep up their efforts to persuade more countries to adhere to the maritime declaration and join the naval task force. However, Wilson realized that these were little more than empty promises, which the United States had no intention or ability to carry out. Wilson left Washington with the sense that the Americans need the British more than British needed the Americans.[196] He summed up his visit as follows:

In general, my impression was that the Americans are as yet far from clear in their own minds about their policy, both political and military. L.B.J. [Johnson] is still asking very pertinent questions to which neither Rusk nor McNamara seem to have very clear or convincing answers; and the President is clearly very worried about this. As a result, there is a clear tendency to try and push us into the lead.[197]

Wilson returned home empty handed. The visit's sole achievement had been to confirm Arab suspicions about the existence of a Suez-like conspiracy. The Arab states assumed that Wilson had all along been working toward the institution of an anti-Arab coalition designed to serve Israeli interests. Egypt, for example, aware that General Amit had been in Washington at more or less the same time as Wilson, took it for granted that Britain, the United States and Israel were busy hatching a Suez-style plot.[198]

Like Thomson, Wilson returned from Washington with nothing to show. Moreover, Britain's independent efforts to convince more countries to join the maritime declaration had failed. The result was that Britain, too, lost heart. If prior to Wilson's meeting with Johnson Britain had alternately demanded and implored Israel to act with moderation and restraint, now it remained silent. Other than waiting to see if and how many other countries would be willing to join the maritime declaration, not in itself a very likely prospect, it did nothing. Like the United States, Britain had finally accepted that the only possible solution to the Straits crisis was an Arab-Israeli military confrontation.

The fruitless outcome of the Wilson-Johnson talks strengthened the hands of the prowar lobby in Israel. It confirmed Dayan's claim that there was no naval task force in the offing and that even if one were to be established it would achieve nothing. The conversations between the two Anglo-Saxon leaders proved the extent of the West's impotence, and with neither power able to resolve the crisis, war remained Israel's sole alternative. Israel, Eshkol informed his Cabinet, had exhausted all viable political and diplomatic options.[199] As a result, Israel began to prepare in earnest for the forthcoming war.

While Israel was busy getting ready for war, President Johnson, rather surprisingly, sent Eshkol a note. In his note, dated June 3, 1967, Johnson assured Eshkol that the United States was still trying, both through the United Nations and jointly with Britain, to secure a declaration signed by all the principal maritime powers, upholding the right of free passage through the Straits. The United States, Johnson told Eshkol, was also exploring Britain's proposal to establish a naval task force to patrol the Straits. Johnson concluded by emphasizing that the United States regarded it as its duty to continue its efforts to mobilize international support for these goals.[200] Was the note intended to exculpate Johnson in the eyes of history? Or was it another glaring example of Johnson's inconsistency? Probably a bit of both.

The Israeli government, relying, among other things, on Amit's appraisal of his Washington visit, did not think that Johnson's final message constituted a subtle warning against military action. On June 4, 1967, it finally decided to cut the Gordian knot. It would itself, by its own efforts, free Israel from the Arab noose that was slowly strangling it to death. It would launch a preemptive war and go on the offensive before the United Arab Command could put into operation its imminent plan to attack Israel. The date of the decision was June 5, 1967.[201]

The government kept its decision secret. Instead, over the next twenty-four hours, it pursued a policy designed to deceive the Arabs and the West alike. The plan was that Israel would continue its diplomatic efforts until the very last moment, and so lull the Egyptians into a sense of false confidence. At the same time, it would strive to create the impression that, despite having established a National Government with Dayan as minister of defense, Israel was not about to open war. This carefully planned ruse proved complete success. Hadow reported that Dayan, both in an official press conference and while speaking to IDF officers, had admitted that Israel could not afford to lose President Johnson's goodwill and launch an attack while the Americans were still trying to sort out the freedom of passage issue.[202] Hadow concluded happily

that the days of [the] firebrand in the Israeli Defence Force are over. They are now preparing for the long haul, but at the same time [they] must be ready for decisive action should some unfortunate incident make this inevitable.[203]

The next day Israel struck. It launched an air offensive against Egypt and Syria's air forces and within two hours destroyed the larger part of both. The Six-Day War had begun—the war Britain had tried so hard to prevent.

NOTES

1. ISA, Hez/17/4005, Jerusalem to London, January 6, 1966; *Ha'aretz*, January 9, 1967.
2. Gilbo'a, *Six Years*, pp. 77–78; Seguev, *Israel*, p. 60.
3. FCO 17/437, Damascus to FO, January 7, 1967.
4. FCO 17/437, FO to Tel Aviv, January 17, 1967.
5. FCO 17/437, Washington to FO, January 17, 1967.
6. FCO 17/477, Minute by Morris, January 18, 1967.
7. FCO 17/437, Tel Aviv to FO, January 8, 1967, and Minute by Morris, January 12, 1967.
8. FCO 17/437, Tel Aviv to FO, January 5, 1967.
9. FCO 17/477, Minute by Morris, January 18, 1966.
10. FCO 17/473, Tel Aviv to FO, January 5, 1967; NA, RG59/2230, SD to Tel Aviv, January 6, 1967.
11. Ma'oz, *Syria and Israel*, p. 92; Parker, *Politics of Miscalculation*, p. 41; NA, RG59/2230, SD to Damascus, January 16, 1967.
12. FCO 17/473, Tel Aviv to FO, January 18, 1967; *Ha'aretz*, January 17–18, 1967.
13. Gilbo'a, *Six Years*, pp. 78–79.
14. Ma'oz, *Syria and Israel*, p. 92.
15. Draper, *Israel and World Politics*, pp. 42–43; *Ha'aretz*, February 15, 1967.
16. PREM 13/1582, Palliser to FO, February 20, 1967.
17. PREM 13/1617, Record of Meeting, February 21, 1967; ISA, Hez/17/4055, Remez to Lourie, February 22, 1967 and Raviv to Lourie, February 23, 1967.
18. PREM 13/1582, Palliser to FO, February 20, 1967.

19. PREM 13/1617, Record of Meeting, February 21, 1967; FCO 28/362, Brief by the FO, January 26, 1967; FCO 17/538, Minute by the FO, February 17, 1967.

20. FCO 17/467, Tel Aviv to FO, January 3, 1967; FCO 17/473, Tel Aviv to FO, January 18, 1967.

21. Haber, *War Will Break Out*, pp. 141–143; Cuau, *Israel Attaque*, p. 47; NA, RG59/2230, Katzenbach to Amman, April 18, 1967.

22. Gilbo'a, *Six Years*, p. 83.

23. Smith, *Palestine*, p. 195; Glassman, *Arms for the Arabs*, p. 38; Gurvin, *Israel-Soviet Relations*, p. 252.

24. Draper, *Israel and World Politics*, p. 47; Mutawi, *Jordan in the 1967 War*, p. 85; ISA, Hez/2/644, Jerusalem to New York, April 9, 1967.

25. Wehling, "Dilemma of a Superpower," p. 188.

26. See in this connection Ze'ev Sieff's article in *Ha'aretz*, April 14, 1967.

27. Dayan, *Story of My Life*, p. 391; Weitzman, *On Eagles' Wings*, p. 254.

28. Bar-Zohar, *Ben Gurion*, p. 1588.

29. Interview with Rabin, *Ma'ariv*, June 2, 1972.

30. Bhutani, *Israeli-Soviet Cold War*, p. 139; *Ha'aretz*, April 9, 1967.

31. FCO 17/473, Minute by Morris, April 12, 1967.

32. FCO 17/473, Tel Aviv to FO, April 10, 1967 and Minute by Morris, April 12, 1967.

33. FCO 371/473, Minute by Morris, April 12, 1967; ISA, Hez/12/1390, London, to Jerusalem, April 19, 1967.

34. FCO 17/473, Minute by the FO, April 11, 1967.

35. Mutawi, *Jordan in the War*, p. 34.

36. Bhutani, *Israeli-Soviet Cold War*, p. 139; Parker, *Politics of Miscalculation*, p. 41.

37. FCO 17/474, Tel Aviv to FO, May 4, 1967; ISA, Hez/6/7228, Moscow to Jerusalem, April 21, 1967; ISA, Hez/3/6444, Moscow to Jerusalem, April 27, 1967.

38. Glassman, *Arms for the Arabs*, pp. 38–39; Zak, *Israel and the Soviet Union*, p. 327.

39. Gilbo'a, *Six Years*, p. 97.

40. *Ha'aretz*, May 10, 1967.

41. Gilbo'a, *Six Years*, p. 97; *Ha'aretz*, May 12, 1967; Yost, "How It Began," p. 307.

42. Parker, *Politics of Miscalculation*, p. 41.

43. Seguev, *Israel*, p. 69.

44. There are those who claim that Rabin made the statement on Israel radio that Israel should advance toward Damascus and overthrow the regime. See Cockburn, *Dangerous Liaison*, p. 135; Shamir, "Origin," pp. 65–66; Eilts, "The Six Day War," p. 89; Riad, *Struggle for Peace*, p. 30.

45. ISA, Hez/27/4048. Moscow to Jerusalem, May 16, 1967.

46. This information was passed on as early as April 29 through the offices of Anwar Sadat, who was, at the time, the chairman of the Egyptian Parliament. See Sadat, *Identity*, p. 172; Heikal, *The Cairo Documents*, p. 217 and *Sphinx*, p. 174.

47. In this connection see an article in *Ha'aretz*, May 10, 1967; also see Segeuv, *Israel*, p. 71; Wehling, "Dilemma of a Superpower," p. 189; FCO 17/474, Damascus to FO, May 13, 1967.

48. Bar-Siman-Tov, *Israel*, p. 174; Dayan, *Story of My Life*, p. 392; Hammel, *Six Days in June*, p. 26.

49. Parker, "The June 1967 War," p. 181; Yost, "How It Began," p. 309.

50. Zisser, "Between Syria and Israel," pp. 178–184; Parker, *Politics of Miscalculation*, pp. 43–44; Parker, "The June 1967 War," p. 181.

51. Aronson, *Nuclear Weapons*, vol. 1, pp. 32–34 and vol. 2, pp. 26–39.

52. Cohen, "Cairo Dimona," pp. 198–201, 204–205.

53. Tibi, *Conflict and War*, pp. 70, 73–74; Hisham, "Prelude to War," p. 53.

54. Heikal, *Cairo Documents*, p. 217.

55. Fahmi, *Negotiations*, p. 21; Sharabi, "Prelude to War," p. 53; Tibi, *Conflict and War*, pp. 73–74; Quandt, *Decade of Decisions*, p. 39.

56. Yariv, "Background," p. 20.

57. *Ma'ariv*, June 2, 1967, interview with Rabin.

58. FCO 17/479, Washington to FO, May 17, 1966 and Tel Aviv to FO, May 18, 1967; Mutawi, *Jordan in the 1967 War*, pp. 94–95.

59. Mutawi, *Jordan in the 1967 War*, pp. 94–95; Vatikiotis, *Nasser and His Generation*, pp. 255–256; Whetten, *Canal War*, p. 40; Cohen, "Cairo, Dimona," p. 201.

60. Glassman, *Arms for the Arabs*, pp. 35–36; Vatikiotis, *Nasser and His Generation*, p. 256.

61. Bar-Siman-Tov, *Israel*, p. 86; Rabin, *Service Notes*, pp. 134–135.

62. Quandt, *Decade of Decisions*, p. 201.

63. FCO 17/479, FO to New York, May 16, 1967.

64. PREM 13/1617, FO to Washington, May 16, 1967; ISA, Hez/5/4080, Jerusalem to London, May 16, 1967.

65. ISA, Hez/5/4080; NA, RG59/2230, SD to Tel Aviv, May 16, 1967.

66. PREM 13/1617, FO to Washington, May 16, 1967.

67. PREM 13/1617, FO to Tel Aviv, May 16, 1967; ISA, Hez/5/4080, Jerusalem to London, May 16, 1967; FCO 17/479, FO to Washington, May 16, 1967 and Damascus to FO, May 17, 1967.

68. FCO 17/479, FO to Tel Aviv, May 16, 1967.

69. Heikal, *Cairo Documents*, pp. 217–218.

70. Dayan, *Story of My Life*, p. 392; Rabin, *Service Notes*, p. 136.

71. Geist, "The Six Day War," p. 62; Brecher, *Decisions*, p. 364.

72. PREM 13/1617, Washington to FO, May 22, 1967; FCO 17/481, Record of Conversation, May 21, 1967.

73. PREM 13/1617, FO to Tel Aviv, May 22, 1967; FCO 17/479, Tel Aviv, May 18, 1967; ISA, Hez/5/4080, Jerusalem to London, May 18, 1967.

74. PREM 13/1617/Washington to FO, May 18, 1967; ISA, Hez/5/4078, Washington to Jerusalem, May 18, 1967; Johnson, *Vantage Point*, p. 290.

75. Brown, *My Way*, p. 136; Higgins, "The June War," pp. 292–293; Wilson, *Personal Record*, p. 395.

76. PREM 13/1617, New York to FO, May 18, 1967; ISA, Hez/4/4078, Washington to Jerusalem, May 17, 1967.

77. ISA, Hez/4/4078; NA, RG59/1787, SD to Tel Aviv, May 17, 1967.

78. PREM 13/1617, New York to FO, May 17 and 19, 1967.

79. Haber, *War Will Break Out*, p. 153.

80. PREM 13/1617, Eshkol to Wilson, and Washington to FO, May 18, 1967; ISA, Hez/5/4080, Jerusalem to London, May 18, 1967.

81. Haber, *War Will Break Out*, p. 154; Dayan, *The Story of My Life*, p. 399; Rabin, *Service Notes*, pp. 148–149.

82. ISA, Hez/11/4088, Foreign Ministry Research Department, May 22, 1967. The only access to the Port of Eilat is through two passageways that run through the Straits of Tiran between the Island of Tiran and the Sinai Peninsula. The first passageway is

1.1 km long, the second 0.8 km. The distance between the Egyptian and Saudi Arabian coastlines, at the point closest to Island of Tiran, is 17 km, though at one point, slightly to the north, the distance is only 10 km. The land point closest to the passageway is Sharem el Sheikh in the Sinai Peninsula, which directly overlooks the Straits.

83. Eban, *Memoirs*, p. 322; Rafael, *Destination Peace*, p. 131; Brecher, *Decisions*, p. 372; Geist, "The Six Day War," p. 62.

84. Bar-On, "Rise and Fall," pp. 68, 89–90.

85. Haber, *War Will Break Out*, p. 153; NA, RG59/2230, Johnson to Eshkol, May 17, 1967.

86. ISA, Hez/30/5937, Washington to Jerusalem, May 20, 1967; Bar-Siman-Tov, *Israel*, pp. 95, 99.

87. Bar-Siman-Tov, p. 100; ISA, Hez/4/4078, Washington to Jerusalem, May 21, 1967.

88. Quandt, "Lyndon Johnson," p. 202; Johnson, *Vantage Point*, p. 290.

89. PREM 13/1617, Washington to FO, May 18, 1967; FCO 17/480, Minute by Morris, May 19, 1967.

90. PREM 13/1617, FO to Washington, May 21, 1967.

91. PREM 13/1617, FO to Tel, May 22, 1967.

92. Ibid.

93. ISA, Hez/4a/6444, Jerusalem to Washington, May 19, 1967; PREM 13/1617, Tel Aviv to FO, May 20, 1976.

94. PREM, 13/1617.

95. FCO 17/480, Eshkol to Wilson, May 18, 1967.

96. FCO 17/480, FO to Tel Aviv, May 21, 1967.

97. Ibid.; FCO 17/481, Record of Conversation, May 21, 1967; NA, RG 59/1788, SD to Tel Aviv, May 21, 1967.

98. FCO 17/582, Minute by Morris, May 21 and 22, 1967.

99. FCO 17/481, Minute by Morris, May 19, 1967 and a Record of Conversation, May 21, 1967.

100. PREM 13/1617, Wilson to Eshkol, May 21, 1967.

101. CAB 129/130, Memorandum by the Secretary of State, May 29, 1967.

102. *Knesset Debates*, 49, May 22, 1967; Eban, *Memoirs*, p. 325.

103. Gilbo'a, *Six Years*, p. 118; Bar-Siman-Tov, *Israel*, p. 101.

104. *Al Ahram*, May 24, 1967; Seguev, *Red Sheet*, p. 49; Parker, *Politics of Miscalculation*, pp. 47–48, 72–75; Ayalon, "Road to the Six Day War," p. 8.

105. Sadat, *In Search of Identity*, p. 172.

106. Geist, "The Six Day War," p. 62.

107. ISA, Hez/5b/644, Jerusalem to London, May 29, 1967.

108. See, for example, *Knesset Debates*, 22, March 4, 1967.

109. Haber, *War Will Break Out*, p. 164; Rabin, *Service Notes*, pp. 154–155.

110. Eban, *Memoirs*, pp. 329–330; Brecher, *Decisions*, pp. 378–379.

111. Rabin, *Service Notes*, pp. 154–155; *Ma'ariv*, Interview with Eshkol, October 4, 1967.

112. Haber, *War Will Break Out*, p. 169; Bar-Siman-Tov, *Israel*, p. 105.

113. Little, "Choosing Sides," p. 176; Haber, *War Will Break Out*, p. 165; Johnson, *Vantage Point*, p. 291.

114. ISA, Hez/3/5937, Washington to Jerusalem, May 23, 1967; NA RG59/1788, SD to Tel Aviv, May 23, 1967.

115. FCO 17/490, Note of a Meeting, 23 May 1967

116. FCO 17/490; NA RG59/1788, SD to London, May 23, 1967; Ziegler, *Wilson*, p. 341.

117. PREM 13/1617, Washington to FO, May 23, 1967.

118. Wilson, *Personal Record*, p. 395; CAB 128/42, Conclusion of a Meeting, May 23, 1967.

119. Morgan, *Callaghan*, p. 263; Ziegler, *Wilson*, p. 341.

120. Ziegler, *Wilson*, p. 341; Pearce, *Patrick Gordon Walker*, p. 314.

121. FCO 27/179, Healy to Wilson, May 24, 1967; PREM 13/1617, Note of a Meeting, May 23, 1967.

122. CAB 128/42, Conclusions of a Meeting, May 25, 1967.

123. CAB 128/42, Conclusions of a Meeting, May 23, 1967; Morgan, *Wilson*, p. 305; Johnson, *Vantage Point*, p. 292.

124. Wilson, *Personal Record*, p. 395.

125. ISA, Hez/5/4080, London to Jerusalem, May 24, 1967.

126. Eban, *Memoirs*, pp. 337–338; Wilson, *Chariot of Israel*, pp. 335–336; Gilbo'a, *Six Years*, p. 141.

127. ISA, Hez/5/4080, London to Jerusalem, May 24, 1967; PREM 13/1618, Record of Conversation, May 24, 1967.

128. PREM 13/1617, Note of a Meeting, May 23, 1967; Wilson, *Chariot of Israel*, p. 338.

129. Parker, *Politics of Miscalculation*, p. 54.

130. Ibid.; Quandt, "Lyndon Johnson," p. 207.

131. PREM 13/1618, Washington to FO, May 24, 1967.

132. CAB 130/323, Minute of Meeting, May 26, 1967.

133. Ibid.; NA, RG59/1791, Memorandum of Conversation, May 25, 1967; NA, RG59/1788, SD to London, May 26, 1967.

134. Rabin, *Service Notes*, pp. 161–165; Haber, *War Will Break Out*, pp. 187–188; Eban, *Memoirs*, pp. 345–346; NA, RG59/1788, SD to Cairo, May 25, 1967; Rafael, *Destination Peace*, pp. 133–134.

135. Spiegel, *Arab-Israeli Conflict*, p. 139. In a television debate, which took place on June 10, 1997, Israeli generals confirmed this appraisal. They pointed out that the delay was beneficial in that it helped turn the Israeli reserve force into a well-trained and professional army, ready for combat. Motti Hod, the head of the Israeli air force during the Six-Day War, felt that the delay was a boon, as almost a third of the Israeli air force did not have long-range capability. This meant that the larger the number of Egyptian soldiers entering Sinai the better, as the Israeli air force would be able to strike and destroy a greater part of Egypt's forces.

136. FCO 17/486, Record of Meeting, May 26, 1967; Cohen, "Balancing American Interests," p. 300; Johnson, *Vantage Point*, p. 293; Brecher, *Decisions*, p. 390.

137. Rabin, *Service Notes*, p. 165; NA, RG 59/1788, SD to Cairo, May 26, 1967.

138. Bar-Zohar, *Embassies*, p. 128; Eban, *Memoirs*, p. 363.

139. FCO 17/483, Washington to FO, May 27, 1967; ISA, Hez/30/5937, Note of a Meeting, May 26, 1967 and Washington to Jerusalem, May 27, 1967; NA, RG59/1789, Memorandum of Conversation, May 27, 1967.

140. ISA, Hez/5/4080, London to Paris, May 27, 1967.

141. *Al Ahram*, May 27, 1967; Parker, *Politics of Miscalculation*.

142. FCO 17/483, Moscow to FO, May 24, 1967.

143. FCO 17/490, Record of a Meeting, May 24–25, 1967.

144. FCO 17/492, Soviet Government's Statement, Translation from *Pravda*, May 24, 1967.

145. FCO 17/490, Record of Meeting, May 24, 1967; PREM 13/1617, Moscow to FO, May 24, 1967.

146. Parker, "June 1967 War," p. 182; Heikal, *Sphinx*, pp. 179–180.

147. FCO 17/482, Wilson to De Gaulle, May 24, 1967; FCO 17/485, FO to Paris, May 27, 1967; CAB 130/323, Minutes of Meeting, May 26, 1967.

148. PREM 13/1618, Paris to FO, May 24 and 25, 1967.

149. PREM 13/1618, Paris to FO, May 25, 1967.

150. FCO 17/484, Washington to FO, May 25, 1967.

151. PREM 13/1618, FO to Moscow, May 25, 1967; CAB 128/142, Conclusions of a Meeting, May 25, 1967.

152. FCO 17/484/ Wilson to Johnson, May 25, 1967; PREM 13/1618, Wilson to Brown, May 25, 1967.

153. NA, RG59/1789, Wilson to Johnson, May 28, 1967.

154. Baron, *Moshe Dayan*, p. 24; Haber, *War Will Break Out*, pp.192–195, 199–200; Rabin, *Service Notes*, pp. 171–172.

155. Interview with Eshkol, *Ma'ariv*, October 4, 1967.

156. PREM 13/1618, Record of a Meeting, May 24–25, 1967; NA, RG59/1789, Johnson to Eshkol, May 27, 1957; Eban, *Memoirs*, pp. 365–367; Quandt, *Decade of Decisions*, pp. 54–55.

157. Johnson, *Vantage Points*, p. 294. In this connection, Wilson wrote, "it was not Soviet warning but the American show of resolution which won the delay." Wilson, *Chariot of Israel*, p. 341. See also interview with Eshkol, *Ma'ariv*, October 4, 1967.

158. Eban, *Memoirs*, p. 369.

159. Haber, *War Will Break Out*, p. 192; Amit, "Six-Day War," p. 9.

160. FCO 17/510, Washington to FO, May 29, 1967.

161. CAB 128/42, Conclusions of a Meeting, May 30, 1967; Wilson, *Chariot of Israel*, p. 342.

162. PREM 13/1618, Wilson to Kosygin, May 28, 1967.

163. PREM 13/1618, FO to Paris and Paris to FO, May 29, 1967.

164. Gilbo'a, *Six Years*, p. 198.

165. Ibid., p. 192; Rabin, *Service Notes*, p. 169.

166. Parker, *Politics of Miscalculation*, p. 54.

167. FCO 39/250, Minute by Spears, May 30, 1967; Tibi, *Conflict and War*, p. 70.

168. Troen and Shalom, "Ben Gurion's Diary," pp. 196–197, 204–205; Nakdimon, *Approaching H-Hour*, pp. 152–202.

169. ISA, Hez/5b/6444, Jerusalem to London, May 29, 1967; PREM 13/1619, Tel Aviv to FO, May 20, 1967.

170. PREM 13/1618, Tel Aviv to FO, May 28, 1967.

171. PREM 13/1618, Cabinet Office to Ministry of Power, May 28, 1967; PREM 13/1619, Report by Officials and Cairo to FO, May 29, 1967.

172. FCO 17/490, Note of a Meeting, May 28, 1967.

173. DEFE5/174, Cos 58/67, Note by Secretary, May 29, 1967.

174. Howard, *Crossman Diaries*, pp. 350–351; Pearce, *Patrick Gordon Walker*, p. 316.

175. CAB 129/130, Memorandum by Secretary of State, May 29, 1967.

176. CAB 133/366, Brief by the FO, May 31, 1967; CAB 128/42, Conclusions of a Meeting, May 30, 1967.

177. CAB 128/42; CAB 129/130, Memorandum by Secretary of State, May 29, 1967; FCO 17/497, Minute by Morris, May 28, 1967.

178. NA, RG59/1789, SD to Tel Aviv, May 29, 1967.

179. ISA, Hez/30/5937, Washington to Jerusalem, May 31, 1967; NA, RG59/2230, Eshkol to Johnson, May 20, 1967 and Memorandum by Rostow, May 31, 1967; Quandt,

"Lyndon Johnson," p. 217. For a discussion of the issue, see Shalom, "Lyndon Johnson's Meeting," pp. 319–321.

180. Parker, *Retrospective*, pp. 124, 136–139; Amit, "Six-Day War," pp. 11–12.

181. Amit, "Head On," p. 239.

182. Ibid., pp. 12–13; Dayan, *Story of My Life*, p. 425; Haber, *War Will Break Out*, pp. 216–217; Parker, *Retrospective*, pp. 124, 136–139; Quandt, *Decade of Decisions*, p. 59. In this connection, see also the message sent by Secretary of State Rusk to the U.S. representatives in several Arab states and in Israel, NA, RG59/1790, Circular to Arab Capitals, June 3, 1967. Several scholars have examined the question of whether the United States gave Israel a green light. In his article "What Color Was the Light?" Quandt concludes that even though the Americans did not openly sanction an Israeli offensive or give Israel a green light to attack Egypt, they did award it a yellow light. General Amit admits that at no point did the Americans give Israel a green light. Nevertheless, upon his return from the United States, Amit was able to tell the Israeli government that the Americans favored an Israeli attack, having concluded from his conversations with American administration officials that the United States tacitly approved of an Israeli offensive as the only viable solution to the crisis. See Parker, *Politics of Miscalculation*, pp. 114–115, 118–119; Quandt, "Lyndon Johnson," pp. 222–223; Baron, *Moshe Dayan*, pp. 41–42. Zaki Shalom, from Ben Gurion University, argues that once Nasser closed the Straits, the Americans assumed that an Israeli military initiative was the sole solution to the crisis. It would, among other things, free the United States of the impossible bind it found itself in. See Shalom, "Lyndon Johnson's Meeting," p. 308. Nasser's Foreign Minister Mahmoud Riad believes that there was an American-Israeli conspiracy collusion to weaken or overthrow Nasser. He sees the 1967 crisis as a kind of repeat performance of 1956 with the Americans playing the role of the British. See Riad, *Struggle for Peace*, p. 37.

183. Quandt, "Lyndon Johnson," p. 227.

184. Mutawi, *Jordan in the 1967 War*, pp. 74, 101–103; Susser, "Jordan," p. 107; FCO 17/101, Record of Meeting, June 1, 1967; NA, RG59/1789, SD to all American Diplomatic Posts, May 30, 1967; Parker, *Retrospective*, pp. 100–101, 168.

185. Haber, *War Will Break Out*, p. 260.

186. Television Debate, June 10, 1997; Haber, *War Will Break Out*, pp. 260–261.

187. NA, RG59/1789, SD to Cairo, May 27, 1967.

188. NA, RG59/1790, Cairo to SD, June 2, 1967; NA, RG59/1792, Anderson to Johnson, June 2, 1967.

189. NA, RG59/1790, Cairo to SD, June 2, 1967.

190. NA, RG59/1790, Cairo to SD, June 4, 1967.

191. Ayalon, "Road to the Six Day War," p. 16; Geist, "The Six Day War," p. 65; Parker, *Politics of Miscalculation*, pp. 57–58; ISA, Hez/30/5937, Washington to Jerusalem, May 30, 1967.

192. FCO 17/490, Minute by Morris, June 1, 1967; PREM13/1618, Tel Aviv to FO, June 4, 1967.

193. FCO17/101, Record of a Meeting, June 1, 1967.

194. Ibid.

195. FCO 17/490, Wilson to Secretary of State, June 3, 1967; FCO 17/510, Note of a Meeting, June 2, 1967. Dean Rusk's memorandum to President Johnson offers a striking example of the sense of helplessness and impotence that pervaded the corridors of Washington at the time. In the memorandum, Dean suggested that the president "sound him

[Wilson] out as to the best means of breaking the impasse on [*sic*] Straits of Tiran." NA, RG 59/2562, Memorandum for the President, May 31, 1967.

196. FCO 17/510, Note of a Meeting, June 2, 1967; Wilson, *Chariot of Israel*, pp. 346–357; FCO 17/490, New York to FO, June 3, 1967.

197. FCO 17/490, Wilson to Brown, June 3, 1967.

198. Eiltes, "Six Day War," p. 95; PREM 13/1619, Tripoli to FO, June 4, 1967; FCO 17/489, Cairo to FO, June 3, 1967.

199. Haber, *War Will Break Out*, pp. 212–213.

200. Dayan, *Story of My Life*, p. 429; Eban, *Memoirs*, p. 393; NA RG59/1790, Johnson to Eshkol, June 3, 1967. ISA, Hez/30/5937, Paris to Jerusalem, June 3, 1967; Bar-Siman-Tov, *Israel*, p. 130.

201. Haber, *War Will Break Out*, p. 221; Dayan, *Story of My Life*, p. 424.

202. Eban, *Memoirs*, p. 397; FCO 17/495, Tel Aviv to FO, June 2, 1967; *Ma'ariv*, June 4, 1967.

203. PREM 13/1619, Tel Aviv to FO, June 4, 1967.

Conclusions

After the end of the Suez War, Britain began to withdraw from its Middle East strongholds. It was a lengthy and complicated process that demanded of Britain that it quit the majority of its bases in the region without endangering Western and British interests. Britain had, above all, to ensure the unimpeded supply of Middle East oil, the continued operation of its oil companies and the expansion of British trade with the region's oil-rich countries. It was in order to secure these interests that Britain maintained a large military presence in the Persian Gulf area, which included close to 100,000 soldiers and naval and air bases scattered throughout the region. Beyond securing the Western powers' material interests, Britain's armed forces also played a crucial role in preventing Soviet expansion in the Middle East.

The Soviet Union was the West's most powerful and dangerous adversary in the Middle East. Ever since the end of the Second World War, it had spared no effort to extend its influence into the region. The Arab-Israeli conflict afforded the Soviet Union, as it was soon to realize, with an excellent opportunity to achieve its ambitions by offering its support to the Arab states and thus currying favor with them. Accordingly, from the 1950s onward, the Soviets opened their weapons market to the Arab world. The Egyptian-Russian arms deal of September 1955, better known as the Czech arms deal and the first big arms deal between the Soviet Union and a key Arab state, marked a watershed in the Soviet Union's relationship with the Arab world. From that time on, the Soviet Union never looked back. In the early 1960s, it deepened its hold on the Arab world when it began to furnish Egypt with economic as well as military aid. Massive and ever-growing quantities of Soviet weapons now began to pour into Egypt and its fellow "progressive" states of Syria and Iraq.

Soviet penetration of the Middle East marked the arrival of the Cold War in the region. By 1960, Cold War rivalry, which, so far, had been more or less limited to Europe and Asia, had spilled over into the Middle East and Africa, with each superpower seeking to carve out and maintain as large a sphere of influence in the region as possible. The intense East-West competition led Britain to conclude that there was little hope of reaching any kind of agreement with the Soviet Union in the Middle East. Britain assumed correctly that tension and turmoil suited the Soviet Union well, with the result that it was hardly a partner in the search for peace and stability. In Britain's judgment, the Soviet Union would refuse to reduce its arms shipments to the Arab states, nor would it agree to curb its mischief making in the region. Unless, of course, the West, particularly Britain, offered it a quid pro quo in the form of voluntarily reducing their own influence and standing in the region. Under the circumstances, this was totally unacceptable.

Despite the obvious difficulties involved, Britain nonetheless assumed the onerous task of preserving a measure of stability in the Middle East. Not that Britain thought that it had much choice in the matter. Both Britain and the West's interests, whether oil, trade or containing the Soviet Union, depended on a stable Middle East. Hence, Prime Minister Macmillan's May 1963 statement that, echoing a similar declaration made by Kennedy a few days earlier, talked of the need to preserve the status quo in the Middle East and deter all forms of aggression. In Britain's view, Israel's military power, its ability to deter the Arab states, was one of the key factors that helped maintain regional stability. Accordingly, Britain religiously supplied Israel with weapons—submarines, tanks and other military equipment.

Until 1963, the Middle East enjoyed a reasonable measure of, albeit tenuous, stability. At the end of 1963, this always precarious stability came to an end. After five long years, Israel was finally on the verge of completing the National Water Carrier. The Arab world considered the Israeli water diversion a threat equal to that posed by the establishment of the state of Israel itself. The Arab states believed that, just as in 1948, the very existence of the Arab nation was now at stake. In January 1964, they convened a summit conference in Cairo attended by all the heads of the Arab states. At the summit conference, they decided to embark upon a counterdiversion scheme to stop Israel from exploiting the waters of Lake Tiberias. The plan was to divert the waters of the Jordan River at source, to divert the Hazbani River in Lebanon and the Banias River in Syria, link them to the Yarmuk and so prevent their waters from reaching Lake Tiberias.

Britain realized that the Cairo Summit Conference marked the beginning of a new chapter in the history of the Middle East. It ended the ephemeral stability that had characterized the region since the end of Suez War, replacing it with growing tension and turbulence. This turmoil would manifest itself primarily in the form of repeated border incidents between Israel and its Arab neighbors, border incidents that would, Britain assumed, eventually ignite a general military conflagration.

Having closely examined the Arab states' objections to Israel's water project, Britain pronounced them spurious and lacking in all foundation. The Israeli government was acting in accordance with international law. It was adhering to the water quota it had been allotted by the 1955 Johnston Plan. Nor would the National Water Carrier seriously effect the number of immigrants to Israel. Finally, as Israel intended to exploit the water mainly for urban and industrial use, very little water would actually reach the Negev. Accordingly, the Arab visions of a flourishing Negev, filled to the brim with Jewish settlements and settlers, were illusory, if not downright fallacious. In view of this, Britain concluded that what the Arabs were really after was to thwart Israel's water economy and the counterdiversion scheme was no more than a thinly disguised subterfuge to achieve this end.

Britain did not, however, make its conclusions public. Although it judged right to be on Israel's side, it believed that Britain's vital interests in the region were much too valuable and vulnerable to endanger by offering Israel overt and un-equivocal support. Britain's solution to the dilemma of having to choose between right and practical interest was to keep a low profile. Britain, or rather the For-eign Office, believed that, in the circumstances, the best policy Britain could adopt was not to take sides at all. It even refused to publicly endorse the John-ston Plan. The most the British government was willing to do, at this stage, was to declare, innocuously, that it supported the cause of peace, stability and eco-nomic development in the Middle East, which was true as far as it goes.

Not that the policy of keeping a low profile brought Britain much joy. The Arabs, naturally suspicious of Britain, instinctively interpreted its disinterested, even-handed stance as denoting support for Israel. Nor was this surprising. The memory of the British-Israeli collusion during the Suez crisis was still very much alive within the Arab world. As far as the Arab states were concerned, it was axiomatic that British policy was essentially pro-Israel and anti-Arab. After all, wasn't Britain still supplying Israel with weapons to be used against them?

As Britain predicted, the situation in the Middle East soon deteriorated. Con-stant Syrian provocations along Israel's northern border finally drew a furious, possibly excessive, Israeli response. On November 13, 1964, Israel launched a massive air strike against targets in Syria, taking the opportunity to destroy the Syrian diversion equipment, as well. Israel's decision to use its air force in order to retaliate against Syria was considered a minor revolution. It was a signal that Israel would not hesitate to use all the means at its disposal to thwart the coun-terdiversion scheme even at the price of a military confrontation with the Arab states. Thus, the November 13 incident heralded a further, significant escalation of the Arab-Israeli conflict.

In the early months of 1965, alarmed that a military confrontation was about to erupt, Britain did its best to persuade Israel that it had nothing to fear from the Arab counterdiversion scheme. It pointed out that the Arab states lacked the technical know-how and engineering skill to carry out the scheme. Nor did they have the vast sums of money needed to execute the project. Moreover, even if by some miracle they did manage to complete the scheme, it was highly doubt-ful whether the amount of water they could pump would exceed the Johnston Plan's quotas. Finally, Britain cunningly reminded Israel that if the Arab states did somehow manage to reduce its water supply, it could always retaliate in kind and block the Lower Jordan River, south of Lake Tiberias, cutting off Jordan's water supply.

Britain kept in close contact with Israel throughout the water dispute. Privately, it justified Israel's position, but, regrettably, owing to its extensive interests in the Arab world, its hands were tied. It was why Britain's contribution to resolving the water dispute took, in the main, the form of pressing Israel to moderate its policy of reprisals against the Arab world. Reprisals, Britain stressed, held the danger of war. It was, as Britain was well aware, a curiously contradictory policy. In March 1966, Michael Stewart, Britain's foreign minister admitted:

There is an apparent paradox in our existing policy and practise. Our declared policy is to be impartial, to avoid taking sides in the dispute; but no amount of assertion that we are being impartial can entirely disguise the fact that, because our policy favours the maintenance of the *status quo* its operation is more favourable to the Israelis than the Arabs. In spite of this, it appears that—especially in the higher level contacts—we find ourselves more often negative towards Israel, and critical of her actions and policies, than towards the Arab Governments.[1]

British exhortations fell of deaf ears. The Israeli government, impervious to Britain's arguments, was resolved to put an end to the counterdiversion scheme. Throughout the first half of 1965, it systematically and successfully destroyed Arab, specifically Syrian and Lebanese, engineering equipment. The Israeli air strikes against the counterdiversion sites and equipment finally persuaded the Arab states to postpone the scheme for an unlimited time, and by the second half of 1965, the water dispute no longer topped of the Middle East's agenda. Britain's fear of a conflagration was, it seemed, groundless. Or was it?

The water dispute may no longer have presented a threat, but it had left a dangerous legacy. It established a cyclical pattern of ever-escalating reaction and counterreaction, which set the dynamics of the Arab-Israeli dispute on a downward spiral. Moreover, in the beginning of 1965, the Palestinian organizations had stepped up their guerrilla activity against Israel. Once the water dispute had ended, Syria had taken the Palestinian organizations under its wing, believing them to be an ideal means of carrying on its struggle against Israel. As a result, by the second half of 1965, Palestinian terrorism had become a daily curse.

Throughout the water dispute and the ensuing border incidents, Arab policy, particularly Syrian policy, enjoyed the Soviet Union's unconditional support. The Soviet Union saw the water dispute and the subsequent escalation of Arab-Israeli tensions as a rare opportunity to increase its influence in the Middle East. As the tension rose, the Soviet Union increased and solidified its support of the Arab position. It gave the Arab states diplomatic support, supplied Egypt and Syrian with vast quantities of weapons and provided them with much needed and generous economic aid. Weapons, however, were the Soviet Union's principal means of penetrating the Middle East, which had the unfortunate effect of raising Egyptian and Syrian self-confidence. Although it has to be said that on the other side of the border, Israel's ever-growing stock of Western and American weapons also served to reinforce its self-confidence.

The Palestinian guerrilla attacks on Israeli lives and property prompted Israel to pursue a rigid policy of retaliatory action against countries that harbored, aided and abetted Palestinian organizations. The raid on the Jordanian village of Samua in November 1966 and the April 1967 air offensive over Syrian territory marked the acme of Israel's retaliation policy. Britain could see how its nightmare of an Arab-Israeli military confrontation, resulting from border incidents, was slowly becoming a reality.

Things took a turn for the worst, when Egypt, acting on Soviet misinformation that Israel was planning a wide-scale military strike against its Syrian ally, decided to return to the Sinai Peninsula. The first Egyptian troops set foot in Sinai on May 14, 1967. A week later, Nasser upped the ante and declared the Straits of Tiran closed to Israeli shipping. Israel held the closing of the Straits to be an act of aggression. To Israel's mind it constituted just and ample cause for war, and it began to prepare for the forthcoming campaign. War was just around the corner.

Fearful that a military confrontation between Israel and its Arab neighbors would have a detrimental effect on its interests, especially its economic interests, Britain began to make strenuous efforts to prevent war from erupting. Harold Wilson personally took over and managed Britain's foreign policy, abandoning in the process the Foreign Office's policy of keeping a low profile. Wilson's government hoped to organize an international naval task force to end the blockade. Unfortunately, only two countries—Canada and Holland—were willing to join the task force. The Soviet Union naturally refused to play ball, while France saw the crisis as an opportunity to improve its relations with the Arab world. Even the United States, terrified of another Vietnam-like entanglement, dawdled. Indeed, it seems that, ultimately, the Americans preferred an Israeli military solution to the crisis. The upshot was that Britain failed to end the blockade. Worse, its efforts to organize the naval task force convinced the Arabs that Britain was as pro-Israel as it ever had been.

War broke out on June 5, 1967. Britain, which had naturally considered the possibility that war would erupt, had always favored an Israeli over an Arab victory. Both would have an adverse effect on British interests, but the repercussions of an Arab victory would be ten times worse. An Arab victory would consolidate Nasser's hegemony over the Arab world and pave the way to the collapse of western pro-Arab regimes, such as Kuwait and Saudi Arabia, where most of Britain's interests were concentrated. An Arab victory would also allow the Soviet Union to tighten its grip on the Middle East.

The Six-Day War ended in a devastating Arab defeat. It had almost equally disastrous consequences for Britain. The closing of the Suez Canal hit Britain's balance of payments hard, as did the interruption of oil supplies from the Middle East. The result was that five months after the war ended, Britain was forced to do the unthinkable and devalue the pound.[2] Britain took some comfort in the thought that Israel's overwhelming victory was proof of its unrivaled power, of its ability to defend itself and successfully counter any Arab threat to its existence. Accordingly, Britain concluded that it could afford to disengage from the Arab-Israeli conflict and concentrate on rebuilding its relationship with the Arab world and preserving British regional interests. Britain's policy after the war, George Brown explained, would appear to be that of maximum practicable disengagement from this [Arab Israeli] dispute ... in our present military and economic situation ... we stand to lose more from activity which may be misunderstood ... than we gain from the wisdom and experience we may contribute to the problem. This may not sound a heroic stance, but it corresponds to the realities governing our economic interests in the area.[3]

Without saying it in so many words, the foreign minister was admitting that Britain no longer had a role to play in the Middle East. The Middle East had become the domain of and was, indeed, dominated by the two superpowers.

NOTES

1. FO 371/186426, Stewart to Hadow, March 29, 1966.
2. Wilson, *Chariot of Israel*, p. 399; Morgan, *Callaghan*, p. 264; Ziegler, *Wilson*, p. 342.
3. CAB 129/132, Memorandum by Secretary of State, July 7, 1967.

Bibliography

PRIMARY SOURCES

Public Record Office (PRO), London

Cab128	Cabinet Minutes
Cab129	Cabinet Memoranda
Cab130	Ad Hoc Committees
Cab131	Defense Committee
Cab133	Commonwealth and International Conferences
Cab134	Cabinet Committees
Cab148	Cabinet Office; Defense and Overseas Policy Committee
Defe4	Chiefs of Staff Committee; Minutes and Meetings
Defe5	Chiefs of Staff Committee; Memoranda
Defe6	Defense Planning Papers; Memoranda
Defe13	Private Office Papers
FCO	Foreign and Commonwealth Office, 7, 8, 17, 27, 39
FO371	Foreign Office General Correspondence
Prem 11, 13	Prime Minister's Office

Israel State Archive (ISA), Jerusalem

Abba Eban Correspondence
Department of Codes
Embassy in London
Foreign Office Correspondence
Foreign Minister's Bureau
National Water Carrier
Prime Minister's Bureau

National Archives, Washington D.C. (College Park, MD)

Record Group 59—General Records of Department of State (SD)

1964–1966: Pol. 1888, 2344–2358
DEF. 1644–1646

1967–1969: Pol. 1786–1795, 2224–2232, 2511, 2557, 2562
DEF. 1557

Published Documents

Foreign Relations of the U.S. Diplomatic Papers (FRUS)
1957   "Arab-Israeli Dispute," vol. xvii
1961–1962   "Near East," vol. xviii
1962–1963   "Near East," vol. xviii
1964–1968   "Arab-Israeli Dispute," vol. xviii
Moore, J.N. (ed.), *The Arab-Israeli Conflict*, vol. 3 (Princeton, N.J.: Princeton University Press, 1974).

Official Publications

Parliamentary Debates, House of Commons Official Report, 5th Series, vols. 677, 707, 709.
Knesset Debates (Israeli Parliamentary Debates), vols. 22, 38–47.

Newspapers

Arabic
Al Ahram
Ruz al Yusuf

Hebrew
Ha'aretz
Al Hamishmar
Davar
La-Merhav
Ma'ariv
Yediot Aharonot

English
The Times (London)
Jerusalem Post (Jerusalem)

French
Le Monde (Paris)

Media

Television Debates, June 10, 1992 (Israeli Television, Channel 1).

Memoirs

Amit, M. *Heud On ...* , Or Yehuda, 1999.
Brown, G. *In My Way: The Political Memoirs of Lord George Brown*. London, 1971.
Bull, O. *War and Peace in the Middle East*. New York, 1969.

Dayan, Moshe. *Story of My Life*. Jerusalem, 1976.

Eban, Abba. *Memoirs*. Tel-Aviv, 1978. Vol. 2.

Fahmi, I., *Negotiations for Peace in the Middle East*. Baltimore, 1983.

Haber, E., *"Today War Will Break Out"; The Reminiscences of Brig. Gen. Israel Lior, Aide-de-Camp to Prime Minister Levi Eshkol and Golda Meir*. Tel-Aviv, 1987.

Howard, A. (ed.), *The Crossman Diaries; Selections from the Diaries of a Cabinet Minister, 1964–1970 Richard Crossman*. London, 1979.

Johnson, L.B. *The Vantage Point: Perspective of the Presidency 1963–1969*. New York, 1971.

Katz, K., *Budapest, Warsaw, Moscow; Envoy to Lands Unfriendly*. Tel-Aviv, 1976.

Pearce, R. (ed.). *Patrick Gordon Walker; Political Diaries 1932–1971*. London, 1991.

Peres, S. *David's Sling*. Jerusalem, 1974.

Rabin, Yitzhak (with Yitzhak Goldshtein). *Service Notes*. Tel-Aviv, 1979.

Rafael, G. *Destination Peace; Three Decades of Israeli Foreign Policy*. Tel-Aviv, 1981.

Riad, Mahmoud. *The Struggle for Peace in the Middle East*. London, Melbourne, New York, 1981.

Rikhye, I.J. *The Sinai Blunder*. New York, 1978.

Sadat, A. el-. *In Search of Identity: An Autobiography*. New York, 1977.

Sharett, M. *Making of Policy; The Diaries of Moshe Sharett*. Tel-Aviv, 1979.

Von Horn, C. *Soldiering for Peace*. London, 1966.

Weizman, E. *On Eagles' Wings*. Tel-Aviv, 1975.

Wilson, H. *The Labour Government; A Personal Record, 1964–1970*. London, 1971.

SECONDARY SOURCES

Books

Abadi, J. *Britain's Withdrawal from the Middle East, 1947–1971: The Economic and Strategy Imperatives*. Princeton, 1982.

Abu-Lughod, I. (ed.). *The Arab-Israeli Confrontation of June 1967; An Arab Perspective*. Evanston, Ill., 1990.

Allan, J.A. and Mallat, C. (eds.). *Water in the Middle East: Legal, Political and Commercial Implications*. London, 1995.

Allen, H. and Volgyes, I. (eds.). *Israel, the Middle East and U.S. Interests*. New York, 1983.

Alteras, I., *Eisenhower and Israel: U.S.-Israeli Relations, 1953–1960*. Gainesville, Fla., 1993.

Bar-Siman-Tov, Y. *Israel, The Superpowers, and the War in the Middle East*. New York, 1987.

Bar-Yaacov, N. *The Israel-Syrian Armistice, Problems of Implementation 1949–1966*. Jerusalem, 1967.

Bark, D.L. and Gress, D.R. *Democracy and Its Discontents; 1963–1988*. Oxford, 1988.

Bar-Zohar, M. *Embassies in Crisis; Diplomats and Demagogues behind the Six-Day War*. Englewood Cliffs, N.J., 1970.

———. *Ben-Gurion; A Political Biography*. Tel-Aviv, 1977. Vol. 3.

Bhutani, S. *Israeli-Soviet Cold War*. Delhi, 1975.

Brecher, M., *Decisions in Israel's Foreign Policy*. London, 1974.

Bulloch, J. and Darwish, A. *Water War; Coming Conflict in the Middle East*. London, 1993.

Burns, W.J. *Economic Aid and American Policy toward Egypt, 1955–1981*. New York, 1985.

Cockburn, A. and Cockburn, L. *Dangerous Liaison*. Jerusalem, 1991.

Cohen, Aharon. *Israel and the Arab World*. London, 1970.

Cohen Avner. *Israel and the Bomb*. New York, 1998.

Cohen, W. *Dean Rusk*. Totawa, N.J., 1980.

Cohen, W.I. and Tucker, N.B. (eds.). *Lyndon Johnson Confronts the World; American Foreign Policy, 1963–1968*. Cambridge, 1994.

Cooley, J.K. *Green March, Black September; The Story of the Palestinian Arabs*. London, 1973.

Crosbie, S.K. *A Tacit Alliance: France and Israel from Suez to the Six Day War*. Princeton, 1974.

Cuau, Y. *Israel Attaque (5 Juin, 1967)*. Paris, 1968.

Dagan, A. *Moscow and Jerusalem*. London, 1970.

Darwin, J. *Britain and Decolinisation: The Retreat from Empire in the Post-War World*. London, 1988.

———. *The End of the British Empire: The Historical Debate*. Oxford, 1991.

Divine, R.A. (ed.). *The Johnson Year*. Lawrence, Ks., 1994. Vol. 3.

Draper, T. *Israel and World Politics: Roots of the Third Arab-Israeli War*. New York, 1967.

Druks, H. *The U.S. and Israel 1945–1973: A Diplomatic History*. New York, 1979.

Dupuy, T.N. *Elusive Victory: The Arab-Israeli Wars, 1947–1974*. London, 1968.

El Hussini, M.M. *Soviet-Egyptian Relations, 1945–1985*. London, 1987.

Evron, Y. *The Middle East: Nations, Super-Powers and Wars*. London, 1973.

Farid, A.M. and Sirriyeh, H. *Israel and Arab Water; An International Symposium, Amman 25–26 February, 1984*. London, 1985.

Garfinkle, A. *Israel and Jordan in the Shadow of War*. New York, 1992.

Gat, M. *Britain and Italy 1943–1949: The Decline of British Influence*. Brighton, England, 1996.

Gazit, M. *President Kennedy's Policy towards the Arab States and Israel*. Tel-Aviv, 1983.

Gee, J. *Mirage: Warplane for the World*. London, 1971.

Glassman, J.D. *Arms for the Arabs: The Soviet Union and War in the Middle East*. Baltimore, Md., 1975.

Golan, G. *Soviet Policies in the Middle East from World War II to Gorbachev*. Cambridge, England, 1990.

Gorst, A. and Johnman, L. *The Suez Crisis*. London, 1997.

Green, S. *Taking Sides: America's Secret Relations with a Militant Israel 1948–1967*. London, 1984.

Hammel, E. *Six Days in June; How Israel Won the 1967 Arab-Israeli War*. New York, 1992.

Heikal, M.H. *Nasser: The Cairo Documents*. London, 1970.

———. *Sphinx and Commissar: The Rise and Fall of Soviet Influence in the Arab World*. London, 1978.

Hersh, S.M. *The Samson Option: Israel's Nuclear Arsenal and American Foreign Policy*. New York, 1991.

Hillel, D. *Rivers of Eden; The Struggle for Water and the Quest for Peace in the Middle East*. New York, 1994.

Hirst, D. *The Gun and the Olive Branch: The Roots of Violence in the Middle East*. London, 1977.

Hurewitz, J.C. *Middle East Politics: The Military Dimension.* New York, Washington, London, 1969.

Inbar, E. *Rabin and Israel's National Security.* Washington, Baltimore, 1999.

Isaac, J. and Shuval, H. *Water and Peace in the Middle East.* Amsterdam, 1994.

Jackson, W. *Britain's Triumph and Decline in the Middle East.* London, 1996.

Kass, I. *Soviet Involvement in the Middle East; Policy Formulation, 1963–1973.* Boulder, Colo., 1978.

Kaufman, B.I. *The Arab Middle East and the United States; Inter-Arab Rivalry and Superpower Diplomacy.* London, 1996.

Kelly, J.B., *Arabia, the Gulf and the West.* London, 1980.

Kerr, Malcolm. *The Arab Cold War, 1958–1967.* London, 1967.

Khouri, F.J. *The Arab-Israeli Dilemma.* New York, 1985.

Kosut, H. (ed.). *Israel and the Arabs; The June 1967 War.* New York, 1968.

Kuniholm, B.R. *The Origins of the Cold War in the New East; Great Power Conflict and Diplomacy in Iran, Turkey, and Greece.* Princeton, 1980.

LaFeber, W. *America, Russia, and the Cold War 1945–1992,* 7th ed. New York, 1993.

Lederer, I.J. and Vucinich, W.S. (eds.). *The Soviet Union and the Middle East.* Stanford, 1974.

Lenczowski, G. *American Presidents and the Middle East.* London, 1990.

Louis, William R. (ed.). *The End of the Palestine Mandate.* London, 1986.

Lowi, M.R. *Water and Power; The Politics of a Scarce Resource in the Jordan River Basin.* Cambridge, England, 1993.

Lundestad, G. *East, West, North, South; Major Developments in International Politics 1945–1990.* Translated from Norwegian by Gail Adams Kvan. Oslo, 1991.

Mangold, P. *Superpower Intervention in the Middle East.* London, 1979.

Ma'oz, M. *Syria and Israel; From War to Peacemaking.* Oxford, 1995.

——— and Yaniv, A. (eds.). *Syria under Assad.* London, Sydney, 1986.

Moore, J.N. *The Arab-Israeli Conflict.* Vols. 1–2: Reading. Princeton, 1974.

Morgan, A. *Harold Wilson.* London, 1992.

Morgan, K.O. *Callaghan; A Life.* London, 1997.

———. *The People's Peace: British History 1945–1990.* Oxford, 1992.

Mutawi, S.A. *Jordan in the 1967 War.* Cambridge, England, 1987.

Neff, D. *Warriors for Jerusalem: The Six Days That Changed the Middle East.* New York, 1988.

Nogee, L.J. and Donaldson, R.H. *Soviet Foreign Policy since World War II.* New York, 1984.

O'Ballance, E. *Arab Guerilla Power, 1962–1972.* London, 1973.

Oron, I. (ed.). *Middle East Record.,* Vol. I. London, 1960.

Parker, R.B. *The Politics of Miscalculation in the Middle East.* Bloomington, Indianapolis, 1993.

——— (ed.). *The Six-Day War; A Retrospective.* Gainesville, Fla., 1996.

Paterson, P. *Tired and Emotional; The Life of Lord George Brown.* London, 1993.

Quandt, W.B. *Decade of Decisions: American Policy toward the Arab-Israeli Conflict, 1967–1976.* Berkeley, 1977.

———. *Peace Process; American Diplomacy and the Arab-Israeli Conflict since 1967.* Berkeley, Los Angeles, 1993.

Rabinovich, I. *Syria under the Ba'th 1963–66; The Army-Party Symbiosis.* Tel-Aviv, 1972.

Ramat, P. *The Soviet-Syrian Relationship since 1955; A Troubled Alliance.* Boulder, Colo., San Francisco, Oxford, 1990.

Reed, B. and Williams, G. *Denis Healey and the Policies of Power.* London, 1971.

Reich, B. (ed.). *The Powers in the Middle East: The Ultimate Strategic Arena.* New York, 1987.

Rogers, P. and Lydon, P. (eds.). *Water in the Arab World.* Cambridge, Mass., 1993.

Saliba, S.N. *The Jordan River Dispute.* The Hague, 1968.

Schoenbaum, D. *The United States and the State of Israel.* New York, 1993.

Sela, A. *The Decline of the Arab-Israeli Conflict; Middle East Politics and the Quest for Regional Order.* New York, 1998.

Shapland, G. *Rivers of Discord; International Water Dispute in the Middle East.* London, 1996.

Shemesh, M. *The Palestine Entity 1959–1974.* London, 1988.

Smith, D.C. *Palestine and the Arab-Israeli Conflict,* 2d ed. New York, 1992.

Spiegel, S.H. *The Other Arab-Israeli Conflict; Making America's Middle East Policy, from Truman to Reagan.* Chicago, 1985.

Spiegel, S.L. (ed.). *Conflict Management in the Middle East.* Boulder, Colo., 1992.

Stevens, G.G. *Jordan River Partition.* Stanford, 1965.

Tessler, M. *A History of the Israeli-Palestinian Conflict.* Bloomington, Indianapolis, 1994.

Tibi, B. *Conflict and War in the Middle East; From Interstate War to New Security,* 2d ed. New York, 1998.

Troen, S.I. and Shemesh, M. (eds.). *The Suez-Sinai Crisis 1956; Retrospective and Reappraisal.* London, 1990.

Vatikiotis, P.J. *Nasser and His Generation.* London, 1978.

Whetten, L.L. *The Canal War: Four-Power Conflicts in the Middle East.* Cambridge, Mass., 1974.

Wilson, H. *The Chariot of Israel: Britain, America and the State of Israel.* London, 1981.

Wolpert, S. *A New History of India,* 4th ed. Oxford, 1993.

Young, P. *The Israeli Campaign of 1967.* London, 1967.

Ziegler, P. *Wilson; The Authorised Life of Lord Wilson of Rievaulx.* London, 1993.

Books (Hebrew)

Aronson, S. *Nuclear Weapons in the Middle East.* Jerusalem, 1994.

Avidan, M. *Main Leading Aspects of Israel–U.S. Relations in the 50s.* Jerusalem, 1982.

Baron, A. *Moshe Dayan and the Six Day War.* Tel-Aviv, 1997.

Beeri, E., *The Officer Class in Politics and Society of the Arab East.* Merhavia, 1966.

Ben-Tzur, A. *Soviet Factors and the Six-Day War; The Influence of Power-Struggle in the Kremlin on the Middle East.* Tel-Aviv, 1975.

Churchill, S.R. *The Six Day War.* Ramat-Gan, 1967.

Gilbo'a, M., *Six Years—Six Days; Origins and History of the Six Day War.* Tel-Aviv, 1969.

Greenberg, Y. *Defence Budgets and Military Power; The Case of Israel 1957–1967.* Tel-Aviv, 1997.

Guvrin, Y. *Israel-Soviet Relations.* Jerusalem, 1990.

Kelee, E. *The Struggle for Water: History Structure and Functions of the National Water Project.* Kibbutz Beeri, 1965.

Nakdimon, S. *Approaching H-Hour: The Drama Leading to the Six-Day War.* Tel-Aviv, 1968.

Neuberger, B. (ed.). *Diplomacy and Confrontation: Selected Issues in Israel's Foreign Relations, 1948–1978.* Tel-Aviv, 1984.

Nimrod, Y. *Waters of Contradiction: The Dispute over the Jordan.* Givat Habiba, 1966.

Ohana, Y. and Yodfat, A. *The PLO; A Portrait of an Organization.* Tel-Aviv, 1985.

Reich, B. and Gutfeld, A. *U.S.A. and Israeli-Arab Conflict.* Tel-Aviv, 1977.

Safran, N. *Israel, The Embattled Ally.* Tel-Aviv, 1979.

Schelling, T.C. *Arms and Influence.* Tel-Aviv, 1976.

Seale, P. *Assad of Syria; The Struggle for the Middle East.* Tel-Aviv, 1993.

Seguev, S. *Red Sheet: The Six-Day War.* Tel-Aviv, 1967.

———. *Israel, the Arabs and the Great Powers.* Tel-Aviv, 1968.

Sela, A. *Unity within Conflict in the Inter-Arab System; The Arab Summit Conferences 1964–1982.* Jerusalem, 1983.

Shalev, A. *Co-operation under the Shadow of Conflict; The Israeli-Syrian Armistice Regime 1949–1955.* Tel-Aviv, 1989.

Shimoni, Y. *The Arab States, Their Contemporary History and Politics.* Tel-Aviv, 1994.

Shmueli, A., Sofer, A. and Kliot, N. (eds.). *The Lands of Galilee.* Haifa, 1983.

Susser, A. (ed.). *Six Days—Thirty Years; New Perspectives on the Six Day War.* Tel-Aviv, 1999.

Vered, Y. *Coup and War in Yemen.* Tel-Aviv, 1967.

Yaniv, A. *Politics and Strategy in Israel.* Tel-Aviv, 1994.

———. *Continuity and Change in French Policy towards Israel.* Haifa, 1977.

——— Ma'oz, M. and Kover, A. (eds.). *Syria and Israel Security.* Tel Aviv, 1991.

Yitzhaki, S. *In Arab Eyes: The Six Day War and After.* Tel-Aviv, 1969.

Yizhar, M. *The U.S. and the Middle East: American Policy towards the Middle East.* Tel-Aviv, 1974.

Yodfat, A. *The Soviet Union and the Middle East.* Tel-Aviv, 1973.

Zak, M. *Israel and the Soviet Union—A Forty Years' Dialogue.* Tel-Aviv, 1988.

Zeevy, R. and Doron, G. (eds.). *Elazar Papers 10; The Six Day War—Twenty Years Later.* Tel-Aviv, 1988.

Articles and Chapters

Bahgat, G. "'High Policy' and 'Low Policy': Fresh Water Resources in the Middle East." *Journal of South Asian and Middle Eastern Studies* 22:3 (Spring 1999).

Bar-Siman-Tov, Y. "The Limits of Economic Sanctions: The American-Israeli Case of 1953." *Journal of Contemporary History* 23 (1988).

Cohen, A. "Cairo, Dimona and the June 1967 War." *Middle East Journal* 50:2 (Spring 1996).

Cohen, W.I. "Balancing American Interests in the Middle East: Lyndon Baines Johnson vs. Gamal Abdel Nasser." In Cohen, I. and Tucker, N.B. (eds.), *Lyndon Johnson Confronts the World.* Cambridge, 1994.

Cooly, J.K. "The War over Water." *Foreign Policy* 54 (Spring 1984).

Curtis, M. "Causes of the 1967 Arab-Israel War." *Middle East Review* 9 (Summer 1977).

Dawn, C.E. "The Egyptian Remilitarization of Sinai, May 1967." *Journal of Contemporary History* 3 (July 1968).

Golan, G. "The Soviet Union and the Suez Crisis." In Toren, S.I. and Shemesh, M. (eds.), *The Suez-Sinai Crisis 1956, Retrospective and Reappraisal*. London, 1990.

Hareven, A. "The Six Day War in Retrospect: An Israeli View." *Middle East Review* 9 (Summer 1977).

Higgins, R. "The June War; The United Nations and Legal Background." *Journal of Contemporary History* 3 (July 1968).

Hisham, S. "Prelude to War." In Abu-Lughod, I. (ed.), *The Arab-Israeli Confrontation of June 1967; An Arab Perspective*. Evanston, 1990.

Holborn, L.W. "The Palestine Arab Refugee Problem." In Moore, J.N. (ed.), *The Arab-Israeli Conflict*. Vol. I. Princeton, 1974.

Hollis, R. "Great Britain." In Reich, B. (ed.), *The Powers in the Middle East: The Ultimate Strategic Arena*. New York, 1987.

Khouri, F.J. "The Jordan River Controversy." *Review of Politics* 27 (1965).

———. "The Policy of Retaliation in Arab-Israeli Relations." *Middle East Journal* 20:4 (1966).

Little, D. "'Choosing Sides': Lyndon Johnson and the Middle East." In Divine, R.A. (ed.), *The Johnson Years*. Lawrence, 1994. Vol. 3.

Mustafa, I. "The Arab-Israeli Conflict over Water Resources." In Isaac, Y. and Shuval, H.(eds.), *Water and Peace in the Middle East*. Amsterdam, 1992.

Nadelmann, E. "Setting the Stage: American Policy toward the Middle East, 1961–1966." *International Journal of Middle East Studies* 14 (1982).

Naff, T. "Conflict and Water Use in the Middle East." In Rogers, P. and Lydon, P. (eds.), *Water in the Arab World*. Cambridge, Mass., 1993.

Neff, D. "Israel-Syria Conflict at the Jordan River, 1949–1967." *Journal of Palestine Studies* 23:4 (Summer 1994).

Nimrod, Y. "Conflict over the Jordan—Last Stage." *New Outlook* 8:6 (September 1965).

Parker, R.B. "The June 1967 War: Some Mysteries Explored." *Middle East Journal* 46:2 (1992).

Quandt, W.B. "Lyndon Johnson and the June 1967 War: What Color Was the Light?" *Middle East Journal* 46:2 (1992).

Riyadh, M. "Israel and the Arab Water in Historical Perspective." In Farid, A.M. and Sirriyeh, H. (eds.), *Israel and Arab Water; An International Symposium, Amman 25–26 February, 1984*. London, 1985.

Shapland, G. "Policy Options for Downstream States in the Middle East." In Allan, J.A. and Mallat, C., *Water in the Middle East: Legal, Political and Commercial Implication*. London, 1995.

Sharabi, H. "Prelude to War: The Crisis of May-June 1967." In Abu-Lughod, I. (ed.), *The Arab-Israeli Confrontation of June 1967: An Arab Perspective*. Evanston, Ill., 1970.

Smolansky, O.M. "The Soviet Role in the Emergence of Israel." In Louis, William R. (ed.), *The End of the Palestine Mandate*. London, 1986.

Troen, S. and Z. Shalom, "Ben-Gurion's Diary for the Six-Day War: An Introduction." *Israel Studies* 4:2 (Fall 1999).

Vatikiotis, P.J. "The Soviet Union and Egypt: The Nasser Years." In Lederer, I.J. and Vucinich, W.S. (eds.), *The Soviet Union and the Middle East*. Stanford, 1974.

Wehling, F. "The Dilemma of Superpower: Soviet Decision-Making in the Six Day War, 1967." In Spiegel, S.L. (ed.), *Conflict Management in the Middle East*. Boulder, 1992.

Yaniv, A. "Syria and Israel." In Ma'oz, M. and Yaniv, A. (eds.), *Syria under Assad.* London and Sydney, 1986.

Yost, C.W. "The Arab-Israel War: How it Began." *Foreign Affairs* 46 (1968).

Articles and Chapters (Hebrew)

Amit, M. "The Six-Day War in Retrospect." *Ma'arakhot,* 325 (July 1992).

Ayalon, A. "The Road to the Six Day War." *Skira Hodshit* 5 (1986).

Bar-On, M. "The USSR and the Straits of Tiran, 1954–1967." *Iyunim Bitkumat Israel* 1 (1991).

Bar-On, Y. "The Rise and Fall of Friendship: French-Israeli Relations, 1956–1967." *State, Government and International Relations* 34–35 (1991).

Bar-Siman-Tov, Y. "The Power of Economic Sanctions: Benot Yaakov Bridge, 1953." *Ma'arakhot* 29 (January 1984).

Blechman, B.M. "The Impact of Israel's Reprisals on Behavior of the Bordering Arab Nations." In Neuberger, B. (ed.), *Diplomacy and Confrontation, Selected Issues in Israel's Foreign Relations, 1948–1978.* Tel-Aviv, 1984.

Cohen, A. "Kennedy, Ben-Gurion and the Battle over Dimona, April-June 1963." *Iyunim Bitkumat Israel* 6 (1996).

Eilts, H.F. "The Six Day War in the Eyes of Egypt." In Susser, A. (ed.), *Six Days—Thirty Years; New Perspectives on the Six Day War.* Tel-Aviv, 1999.

Geist, B. "The Six Day War: The Decision Making Process in Foreign Policy in Conditions of Crisis." *State, Government and International Relations* 8 (1975).

Golan, S. "The Conflict over the Jordan." In Shmueli, A., Sofer, A. and Kliot, N. (eds.), *The Lands of Galilee.* Haifa, 1983.

Greenberg, Y. "The 1963 Decision to Cut the Obligatory Military Service: Security Considerations and Social and Economic Aspects." *State, Government and International Relations* 40 (Summer 1995).

Harkabi, Y. "The Arab-Israeli Conflict from the Israeli Viewpoint." *Skira Hodshit* 1 (January 1960).

Harkabi, Y. "The Armistice Agreements in Retrospect." *Ma'arakhot,* 295–299 (July 1984).

Ma'oz, Y., and Inbar, M. "The Conflict over the Waters and the Development Projects of the Sources of the Jordan." *Ofakim Be-Geographia,* 45:9–10 (1984).

Peres, S. "The Dimension of Time." *Ma'arakhot* 146 (December 1962).

Rabin, Y. "From Battling over the Waters to the Six Day War." In Erez, Y. and Kfir, A. (eds.), *Zahal Be-Helo.* Vol. 4. Tel-Aviv, 1984.

Rabinovich, I. "The Conflict over the Jordan Waters as a Component in the Arab-Israeli Dispute." In Shmueli, A., Sofer, A. and Kliot, N. (eds.), *The Lands of Galilee.* Haifa, 1983.

Shalom, Z. "From a 'Low Profile' Policy to a 'Steamroller Strategy'—The Kennedy Administration and the Israeli Nuclear Build up 1962–1963." *Iyunim Bitkumat Israel* 5 (1995).

———. "Lyndon Johnson's Meeting with Abba Eban, 26 May 1967; An Introduction" *Yahadut Zmanen,* 11:12 (1998).

Shamir, S. "The Middle East Crisis on the Brink of War (14 May-4 June)." *Middle East Record, 1967* (1971).

———. "The Origin of May 1967 Escalation." In Susser, A. (ed.), *Six Days—Thirty Years: New Perspectives on the Six Day War.* Tel-Aviv, 1999.

Shemesh, M. "The Arab Struggle over Water against Israel, 1959–1967." *Iyunim Bitku-mat Isral* 7 (1997).

Susser, A. "Jordan and the Six Day War." In Susser, A. (ed.), *Six Days—Thirty Years: New Perspectives on the Six Day War.* Tel Aviv, 1999.

Troen, S. and Z. Shalom. "Ben-Gurion's Diary for the Six-Day War; An Introduction." *Israel Studies* 4:2 (Fall 1999).

Yaniv, A. "Brutal Dialogue." In Yaniv, A., Ma'oz, M. and Kover, A. (eds.), *Syria and Is-rael Security.* Tel-Aviv, 1991.

Yariv, A. "The Background to the War." In Zeevy, R. and Doron, G. (eds.), *Elazar Paper 10; The Six Day War—Twenty Years Later.* Tel Aviv, 1988.

Zisser, E. "Between Syria and Israel: The Six-Days War and Its Aftermath." *Iyunim Bitku-mat Israel* 8 (1998).

Index

About the Author

MOSHE GAT is Head of the Political Studies Department and Professor of Modern History in the General History Department at Bar-Ilan University, Israel.